English File

Intermediate Plus
Teacher's Guide

WITH TEACHER'S RESOURCE CENTRE

Christina Latham-Koenig
Clive Oxenden
Kate Chomacki

with Anna Lowy
Krysia Mabbott

OXFORD
UNIVERSITY PRESS

Great Clarendon Street, Oxford, OX2 6DP, United Kingdom

Oxford University Press is a department of the University of Oxford.
It furthers the University's objective of excellence in research, scholarship,
and education by publishing worldwide. Oxford is a registered trade
mark of Oxford University Press in the UK and in certain other countries

© Oxford University Press 2020

The moral rights of the author have been asserted

First published in 2020

2023
10 9 8 7

All rights reserved. No part of this publication may be reproduced, stored
in a retrieval system, or transmitted, in any form or by any means, without
the prior permission in writing of Oxford University Press, or as expressly
permitted by law, by licence or under terms agreed with the appropriate
reprographics rights organization. Enquiries concerning reproduction outside
the scope of the above should be sent to the ELT Rights Department, Oxford
University Press, at the address above

You must not circulate this work in any other form and you must impose
this same condition on any acquirer

Links to third party websites are provided by Oxford in good faith and for
information only. Oxford disclaims any responsibility for the materials
contained in any third party website referenced in this work

Photocopying

The Publisher grants permission for the photocopying of those pages marked
'photocopiable' according to the following conditions. Individual purchasers
may make copies for their own use or for use by classes that they teach.
School purchasers may make copies for use by staff and students, but this
permission does not extend to additional schools or branches

Under no circumstances may any part of this book be photocopied for resale

ISBN: 978 0 19 403914 7   Teacher's Guide

Printed in China

This book is printed on paper from certified and well-managed sources

ACKNOWLEDGEMENTS

Back cover photograph: Oxford University Press building/David Fisher

The authors would like to thank all the teachers and students round the world
whose feedback has helped us to shape English File.

The authors would also like to thank: all those at Oxford University Press (both
in Oxford and around the world) and the design team who have contributed
their skills and ideas to producing this course.

Finally very special thanks from Clive to Maria Angeles, Lucia, and Eric, and
from Christina to Cristina, for all their support and encouragement. Christina
would also like to thank her children Joaquin, Marco, and Krysia for their
constant inspiration.

*The publisher would like to thank the following for their permission to reproduce
photographs*: Getty Images pp.160 (drinks/Claire Cordier), 162 (visa/
PaulCowan), 165 (Adele/Kevin Winter), 165 (Croatia v England/Anadolu
Agency), 209 (safari/nicolamargaret); Oxford University Press pp.158 (Globe
theatre/Kamira), 188 (brunette woman/Yulia Durova), 188 (young woman/
Image Source), 195 (audience/Syda Productions), 196 (photographer/George
Dolgikh), 210 (batteries/Tatiana Popova), 216 (painting/Warren Goldswain);
Shutterstock pp.158 (ice cream/Diana Taliun), 158 (cold man/Andrey_Popov),
10 (using phone/siamionau pavel), 158 (beach/icemanphotos), 158 (pizza/
bestv), 160 (colleagues/Monkey Business Images), 160 (argument/SpeedKingz),
162 (house/Monkey Business Images), 162 (teapot/Alekseykolotvin),
162 (napkins/Madlen), 162 (laptop/Rawpixel.com), 162 (camera/Akugasahagy),
165 (theatre/Willy Barton), 165 (Scrabble/katerina_Minaeva), 167 (30 St Mary
Axe/Celso Diniz), 167 (The Chrysler Building/Songquan Deng), 170 (girl on
phone/Antonio Guillem), 170 (woman on phone/Asier Romero), 181 (washing
hair/JL-Pfeifer), 181 (woman with lugagge/mimagephotography), 181 (friends/
wavebreakmedia), 33 (wedding/Halfpoint), 186 (recycle bin/Mike Flippo),
186 (pollution/Mr.anaked), 187 (studying/ESB Professional), 187 (graduate/
michaeljung), 187 (office/Monkey Business Images), 187 (handshake/Shift
Drive), 188 (woman/goodluz), 188 (man/Tuzemka), 188 (girl/sweetOlli),
188 (young man/Nicholas Piccillo), 188 (tween/Lopolo), 188 (man at home/
stockfour), 195 (girl with burger/ViChizh), 195 (two friends/XiXinXing),
195 (playing violin/Martin Novak), 196 (photo session/Yuganov Konstantin),
201 (hiking/EB Adventure Photography), 201 (couple at beach/fokke baarssen),
209 (paparazzi/Andrea Raffin), 210 (bins/S M Wilkins), 210 (drinks can/
RTimages), 210 (grocery bag/sumire8), 210 (plastic bottles/Elnur), 210 (honey/
Alp Aksoy), 210 (biscuits/arrell Evans), 218 (businesswoman/WAYHOME
studio).

Illustrations by: Paul Boston/Meiklejohn Illustration pp.156, 214; Bess Harding
pp.154, 207, 215; John Haslam pp.153, 155, 159, 161, 180; Peter Hudspith
pp.163, 182; Anna Hymas/New Division pp.154, 169; Sophie Joyce p.215;
Joanna Kerr p.213; Adam Larkham/Illustration Ltd. pp.152, 168; Joe McClaren
p.194; Roger Penwill pp.157, 164; Gavin Reece pp.191, 192; Colin Shelbourn
p.166.

Grammar photocopiable activities written by: Amanda Begg

Contents

p.4	**Syllabus checklist**

p.8	**Course overview**

- **Introduction**
- **What do Intermediate Plus students need?**
- **For students**

| Student's Book |
| Online Practice |
| Workbook |

- **For teachers**

| Teacher's Guide |
| Teacher's Resource Centre |
| Classroom Presentation Tool |
| Class audio |
| Video |

p.12	**Lesson plans**	
p.12	File 1 A–B	Practical English Episode 1
p.27	File 2 A–B	1&2 Revise and Check
p.40	File 3 A–B	Practical English Episode 2
p.55	File 4 A–B	3&4 Revise and Check
p.69	File 5 A–B	Practical English Episode 3
p.83	File 6 A–B	5&6 Revise and Check
p.96	File 7 A–B	Practical English Episode 4
p.109	File 8 A–B	7&8 Revise and Check
p.123	File 9 A–B	Practical English Episode 5
p.137	File 10 A–B	9&10 Revise and Check

p.149	**Photocopiable activities**	
p.149	Introduction
p.150	Grammar activity answers
p.152	Grammar activity masters
p.172	Communicative activity instructions
p.179	Communicative activity masters
p.202	Vocabulary activity instructions
p.206	Vocabulary activity masters

Syllabus checklist

		GRAMMAR	VOCABULARY	PRONUNCIATION
1				
6	**A** Why did they call you that?	pronouns	names	vowel sounds
10	**B** Life in colour	adjectives	adjective suffixes	word stress
14	**Practical English Episode 1**	reporting lost luggage		
2				
16	**A** Get ready! Get set! Go!	present tenses	packing	/s/, /z/, and /ɪz/
20	**B** Go to checkout	possessive	shops and services	r and final -r
24	**Revise and Check 1&2**			
3				
26	**A** A Grow up!	past simple, past continuous, or *used to*?	stages of life	-*ed* endings, sentence rhythm
30	**B** Photo albums	prepositions	photography	word stress
34	**Practical English Episode 2**	renting a car		
4				
36	**A** Don't throw it away!	future forms: *will / shall* and *be going to*	rubbish and recycling	/aɪ/ and /eɪ/
40	**B** Put it on your CV	first and second conditionals	study and work	word stress
44	**Revise and Check 3&4**			
5				
46	**A** Screen time	present perfect simple	television	/w/, /v/, and /b/
50	**B** A quiet life?	present perfect continuous	the country	vowel sounds, sentence rhythm
54	**Practical English Episode 3**	making a police report		

SPEAKING	LISTENING	READING
talking about names, brand names, making suggestions	four people talking about their names, understanding proper names	checking hypotheses
talking about results, describing a room	listening for extra information	scanning for information
How good are you at preparing for a holiday?, expressing preferences	understanding advice	understanding linkers / cohesive devices
showing interest	recognizing positive / negative comments	predicting content from visual clues
What do you think is the best age for…?, events in your life	listening for detail	read and retell
taking photos, talking about an interesting photo	understanding advice	understanding the main point in a paragraph
zero waste, responding to plans and predictions	listening and taking notes	reading to check assumptions
agreeing / disagreeing and giving opinions, talking about work and studies	listening for factual information	focusing on key information
expressing enthusiasm	understanding answers	speculating based on visual clues
discussing problems and solutions	listening for point of view	understanding problems and solutions

			GRAMMAR	VOCABULARY	PRONUNCIATION
6					
	56	**A** What the waiter really thinks	obligation, necessity, prohibition, advice	at a restaurant	word pairs with *and*
	60	**B** Do it yourself	*can*, *could*, and *be able to*	DIY and repairs, paraphrasing	consonant clusters
	64	**Revise and Check 5&6**			
7					
	66	**A** Take your cash	phrasal verbs	cash machines, phrasal verbs	linking
	70	**B** Shall we go out or stay in?	verb patterns	live entertainment	homographs
	74	**Practical English Episode 4**	talking about house rules		
8					
	76	**A** Treat yourself	*have something done*	looking after yourself	sentence stress
	80	**B** Sites and sights	the passive, defining and non-defining relative clauses	historic buildings, wars and battles	silent consonants
	84	**Revise and Check 7&8**			
9					
	86	**A** Total recall	reported speech	word building	word stress
	90	**B** Here comes the bride	third conditional and other uses of the past perfect, adverbs	weddings	sentence stress
	94	**Practical English Episode 5**	giving directions in a building		
10					
	96	**A** The land of the free?	*be*, *do*, and *have*: auxiliary and main verbs	British and American English	stress on *be*, *do*, and *have*
	100	**B** Please turn over your papers	revision of verb forms	exams	revision of sounds
	104	**Revise and Check 9&10**			
	106	**Communication**	115 **Writing**	124 **Listening**	132 **Grammar Bank**

SPEAKING	LISTENING	READING
talking about bad service in restaurants, talking about tipping	listening for content words	understanding the main point in a paragraph
responding to other people's suggestions, paraphrasing, describing a process	understanding an anecdote	checking hypotheses
cash machines, raising money for charity	listening for news facts	understanding the conclusions of research
talking about entertainment and live events, What do you like doing with friends in your free time?	predicting the outcome of a story	understanding descriptions of games
looking after yourself, presenting a campaign	understanding interview questions	understanding whether people are being positive or negative
historical sites, role-play between a local and a tourist	understanding a guided tour – note-taking	understanding historical events
giving examples, stories and anecdotes	linking dates and events	understanding a theory
agreeing and disagreeing	understanding anecdotes	understanding a short story
Americanization	understanding examples – note-taking	working out vocabulary from context
exams, an exam task	exam skill – multiple-choice listening	exam skill – T / F reading

152 **Vocabulary Bank** 164 **Appendix** 165 **Irregular verbs** 166 **Sound Bank**

Course overview

Introduction

Our aim with *English File fourth edition* has been to make every lesson better and to make the package more student- and teacher-friendly. As well as the main A and B Student's Book lessons, there is a range of material that you can use according to your students' needs, and the time and resources you have available. Don't forget:

- videos that can be used in class in every File: Practical English, Video Listening, and Can you understand these people?
- Quick Tests and File tests for every File, as well as Progress Tests, an End-of-course Test, and an Entry Test, which you can use at the beginning of the course
- photocopiable Grammar and Communicative activities for every A and B lesson, and a Vocabulary activity for every Vocabulary Bank

Online Practice and the **Workbook** provide review, support, and practice for students outside the class.
The **Teacher's Guide** suggests different ways of exploiting the Student's Book depending on the level of your class. We very much hope you enjoy using *English File fourth edition*.

What do Intermediate Plus students need?

Intermediate Plus students need to practise their existing language skills in new and challenging contexts. They need motivating material and challenging tasks which will thoroughly revise the grammar and lexis they have learnt at Intermediate level, so that they can use these with confidence. To carry on expanding their vocabulary they also need a steady input of high frequency words and phrases and plenty of opportunities to speak and build oral fluency and accuracy.

Grammar

- Consolidation and extension of main grammatical structures
- Practice in using a range of tenses and forms accurately
- Practice in discriminating between different tenses and forms
- Encouragement to use the grammar they know with confidence

We have tried to provide contexts for new language that will engage students, using real-life stories and situations, humour, and suspense. The **Grammar Banks** give students a single, easy-to-access grammar reference section, with example sentences on audio, clear rules, and common errors. There are at least two practice exercises for each grammar point. Students can look again at the grammar presented in the lesson on **Online Practice**. The **Workbook** provides a variety of practice exercises and the opportunity for students to use the new grammar to express their own ideas.

Vocabulary

- Systematic expansion of topic-based lexical areas
- Work on collocations, phrasal verbs, and word building
- Opportunities to put new vocabulary into practice

Many lessons are linked to the **Vocabulary Banks** which help present and practise the vocabulary in class, give an audio model of each word, and provide a clear reference so students can revise and test themselves in their own time. Students can review the meaning and the pronunciation of new vocabulary on **Online Practice**, and find further practice in the **Workbook**.

Pronunciation

- Practice in pronouncing sounds, words, and connected speech clearly
- Continue to develop their instinct for rules and patterns
- Focus on word and sentence stress

Clear, *intelligible* pronunciation (not perfection) should be the goal of students at this level. There is a pronunciation focus in every lesson, which integrates clear pronunciation into grammar and vocabulary practice. There is an emphasis on the sounds most useful for communication, on word stress, and on sentence rhythm. **Online Practice** contains the Sound Bank videos which show students the mouth positions to make English vowels and consonants. They can also review the pronunciation from the lesson at their own speed. There is more practice of pronunciation in the **Workbook**, with audio, which can be found on **Online Practice**.

Speaking

- Motivating and accessible topics
- The key words and phrases necessary to discuss a topic
- Confidence that their language is clear and intelligible
- Practice in more extended speaking
- Increase in the range of language they can produce
- Improvement in accuracy as well as further development of their fluency

Lack of self-confidence can be a barrier to successful speaking at this level. Each speaking task is supported by the necessary Grammar, Vocabulary, and Pronunciation and

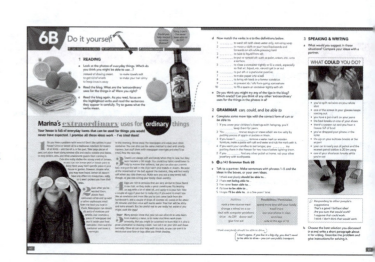

designed to help students to feel a sense of progress and to show that the number of situations in which they can communicate effectively is growing.

Listening

- Confidence-building, achievable tasks
- Practice in 'getting the gist' and listening for detail
- Practice in dealing with authentic spoken language
- Interesting, integrated, listening material

At Intermediate Plus level students need confidence-building tasks which are progressively more challenging in terms of speed, length, and language difficulty, but are always achievable. Longer listenings are broken into separate parts with different tasks, to avoid memory overload. Students are exposed to a wide variety of accents, including some non-native speakers of English. On **Online Practice**, for each File students can find further listening practice related to the topic. They can also access the listening activities from every lesson, to practise in their own time, and to read the script to check anything that they have found difficult.

Reading

- Engaging topics and stimulating material
- Exposure to a wide variety of authentic text types
- Challenging tasks which help them read more skillfully

Many students need to read in English for their work or studies, and reading is also important in helping to build vocabulary and to consolidate grammar. The key to encouraging students to read is to provide material where they feel there is a reason to read and tasks which help them to get the most out of a text. This level contains a variety of readings from real sources (the British press, magazines, websites, forums, infographics) and have been chosen for their intrinsic interest and potential to generate a reaction. The opinions expressed in these texts do not necessarily reflect the view of the *English File* authors or of Oxford University Press.

Writing

- Clear models for a variety of text types
- An awareness of register, structure, and fixed phrases
- A focus on 'micro' writing skills

It is often difficult to motivate students to write at this level. In *English File Intermediate Plus* each guided writing activity flows out of a main lesson to ensure that students have plenty of ideas to start with and focuses on key areas of language, style, and organization to help break the writing process down into a series of achievable tasks.

Students can use **Online Practice** to develop their writing skills further. The Discussion board also provides opportunities for informal written interaction.

Practical English

- Consolidation and extension of functional language
- Knowing what to say in typical social situations
- Getting used to listening to faster, more colloquial speech

The five *Practical English* lessons revise and extend common situations such as giving directions, and introduce and practise the language for new situations, like renting a car. The story line involving the two main characters, Jenny and Rob, continues from where it left off in *English File Intermediate* but it is self-standing, so it can be used equally with students who did not use the previous level. The lessons also highlight other key 'Social English' phrases, for example *I wish you were here* and *Thanks for letting me stay*. On **Online Practice**, students can use the interactive video to record themselves and hear their own voice in the complete conversation. They can also listen and record the Social English phrases. The **Workbook** provides practice of all the language from the Practical English lessons.

Revision

- Regular review
- Motivating reference and practice material
- A sense of progress

Students will usually only assimilate and remember new language if they have the chance to see it and use it several times. Grammar, Vocabulary, and Pronunciation are recycled throughout the course. After every two Files there is a two-page Revise & Check section. The left-hand page revises the grammar, vocabulary, and pronunciation of each File. The right-hand page provides a series of skills-based challenges, including street interviews, and helps students to measure their progress in terms of competence. These pages are designed to be used flexibly according to the needs of your students.

On **Online Practice**, for each File, there are three **Check your progress** activities. The first is a multiple choice activity for students to test themselves on the Grammar and Vocabulary from the File. The second is a dictation related to the topic and the language of the File for students to practise the new language in context. Finally, there is a **Challenge** activity, which involves a mini-research project based on a topic from the File. After every two Files, the **Workbook** contains a *Can you remember...?* page, which provides a cumulative review of language students have covered in the **Student's Book**.

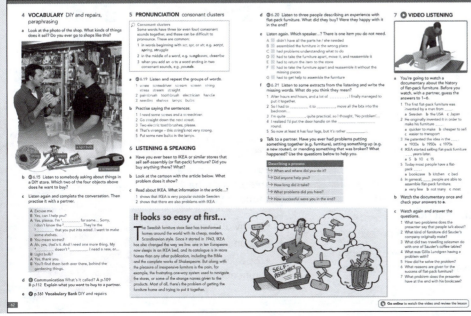

Course overview

For students

Student's Book

The Student's Book has 10 Files. Each File is organized like this:

A and B lessons

Each File contains two four-page lessons which present and practise **Grammar**, **Vocabulary**, and **Pronunciation** with a balance of reading and listening activities, and lots of opportunities for speaking. Every two Files (starting from File 2), the B lesson ends with a **Video Listening** section. All lessons have clear references to the **Grammar Bank**, **Vocabulary Bank**, and where relevant, to the **Sound Bank** at the back of the book.

Practical English

Every two Files (starting from File 1) there is a two-page lesson which teaches high-frequency, everyday English (e.g. language for asking for permission and making requests) and social English (useful phrases like *I'm sorry I can't take your call at the moment* and *It's all such a mess*). The video is in the form of a drama, featuring the two main characters, Rob and Jenny. The lessons have a storyline which runs through the level.

Revise & Check

Every two Files (starting from File 2) there is a two-page section revising the **Grammar**, **Vocabulary**, and **Pronunciation** of each File and providing **Reading**, **Listening**, and **Speaking**. The *'Can you…?'* section challenges students with engaging reading texts and street interview videos, which give students exposure to real-life English.

The back of the Student's Book

The lessons contain references to these sections: Communication, Writing, Listening, Grammar Bank, Vocabulary Bank, and Sound Bank.

The Student's Book is also available as an eBook.

Online Practice

For students to practise and develop their language and skills or catch up on a class they have missed.

- **Look again:** students can review the language from every lesson.
- **Practice:** students can develop their skills with extra Reading, Writing, Listening, and Speaking practice.
- **Check your progress:** students can test themselves on the main language from the lesson and get instant feedback, and try an extra challenge.
- **Interactive video** to practise the language from the Practical English lessons.
- **Sound Bank videos** to learn and practise pronunciation of English sounds.
- **Resources:** All Student's Book audio, video, scripts, wordlists, dyslexia-friendly texts, and CEFR Language Portfolio.

Workbook

For language practice after class.
- All the Grammar, Vocabulary, and Practical English
- Pronunciation exercises with audio. The audio can be accessed on **Online Practice**
    - *Can you remember…?* exercises for students to check their progress
- Available with or without key

Say It: English pronunciation app

For students to learn and practise the sounds of English

- Individual sounds
- Sounds in key words
- Speak and record functionality

For teachers

Teacher's Guide

Step-by-step procedural notes for all the lessons including:

- an optional 'books-closed' lead-in for every lesson.
- **Extra challenge** suggestions for ways of exploiting the Student's Book material in a more challenging way if you have a stronger class.
- **Extra support** suggestions for ways of adapting activities or exercises to make them work with weaker students.
- **Extra ideas** for optional activities.

All lesson plans include answer keys and audio scripts.
Over 50 pages of photocopiable activities.

Grammar
see pp. 150–171
- An activity for every Grammar Bank, which can be used in class or for self-study extra practice

Communicative
see pp.172–201
- Extra speaking practice for every A and B lesson

Vocabulary
see pp.202–217
- An activity for every Vocabulary Bank, which can be used in class or for self-study extra practice

There is more information on page 149 of this Teacher's Guide about the photocopiable worksheets and tips on how best to use them.

Teacher's Resource Centre

- All the Student's Book audio/video files and scripts
- Detailed lesson plans from the Teacher's Guide
- Answer keys
- All the photocopiable activities from the Teacher's Guide, including customisable versions
- All the Workbook audio files and scripts
- Tests and assessment material, including: an Entry Test; Progress Tests; an End-of-course Test; a Quick Test for every File; and complete test for every File. There are A and B versions of all the main tests and audio files for all the Listening tests
- CEFR documents

Classroom Presentation Tool

- The complete Student's Book
- Photocopiable activities from the Teacher's Guide
- All class audio and video, with interactive scripts
- Answer keys for exercises in the Student's Book and photocopiable activities
- Dyslexia-friendly texts

Class audio

All the listening materials for the Student's Book can be found on the **Teacher's Resource Centre**, **Classroom Presentation Tool**, **Online Practice**, **Student's eBook**, and the **Class Audio CDs**.

Video

Video listening
- Short documentary, interviews, or animation for students at the end of even-numbered B lessons (2B, 4B, 6B, etc.)

Practical English
- A unique series of videos that goes with the Practical English lessons in the Student's Book

Revise & Check video
- Street interviews filmed in London, New York, and Oxford to accompany the Revise & Check section

All the video materials for the Student's Book can be found on the **Teacher's Resource Centre**, **Classroom Presentation Tool**, **Online Practice**, **Student's eBook**, and the **Class DVD**.

1A Why did they call you that?

- **G** pronouns
- **V** names
- **P** vowel sounds

Lesson plan

In this first lesson, the topic of names provides a context for Sts to get to know each other, revise sounds, and practise basic reading and listening skills. The vocabulary focus is on working out meaning from context, and the grammar focus is on pronouns.

Sts begin by looking at some information about the names of famous people, and focus on words and phrases used when talking about names, e.g. *maiden name*, *pseudonym*, etc. Sts then use these terms to talk about someone they know. This is followed by a pronunciation focus on vowel sounds through common British names. The pronunciation focus can also be used to introduce the sound–picture system to Sts who have not previously used *English File*. Sts then read an article about naming customs around the world. The first part of the lesson ends with Listening & Speaking, where Sts listen to four speakers talking about their names, and Sts finally talk about their own names.

The second half of the lesson is about popular brand names. The grammar of pronouns is presented through a short text about the Amazon Kindle eBook reader. Sts then listen to a radio programme and find out the origin of some common brand names. The lesson ends with a speaking activity in which Sts read descriptions of new inventions and together come up with names for the products.

There is an Entry Test on the *Teacher's Resource Centre*, which you can give the Sts before starting the course.

More materials
For teachers
Photocopiables
Grammar pronouns *p.152*
Communicative Talk for a minute *p.179* (instructions *p.172*)
Teacher's Resource Centre
Entry Test
For students
Workbook 1A
Online Practice 1A

OPTIONAL LEAD-IN (BOOKS CLOSED)
Write your full name on the board, e.g. JOHN PHILIP SMITH, and elicit that this is your **full name**. Then elicit that:
- JOHN is your **first name**
- PHILIP is your **middle name**
- SMITH is your **surname** (or also **family name** or **last name**)

If you don't have a middle name, you could either invent one or use a celebrity's name.

1 VOCABULARY names

Vocabulary notes
Surname, *family name*, and *last name* are all synonyms, and Sts may see any of them on forms.
Pseudonym is normally used for a writer who writes under a different name. When an actor or singer uses a different name professionally, this is usually referred to as a *stage name*.

a Books open. Focus on the eight photos and ask Sts if they know any of the people. Don't worry if they don't recognize anyone.

Tell Sts to read about the people and then match them to their photo. Tell them to guess if they don't know. Point out that the first one (*1H*) has been done for them.

Get Sts to compare with a partner.

Then get Sts, in their pairs, to try to work out the meaning of the **bold** words and phrases.

b 🔊 **1.2** Play the audio for Sts to listen and check.

Check answers. Find out if any Sts got all the answers correct. You may want to tell them that J.K. (Rowling) stands for Joanne Kathleen and J.R.R. (Tolkien) stands for John Ronald Reuel.

2 C   3 A   4 F   5 E   6 B   7 D   8 G

🔊 **1.2**
See texts in Student's Book on *p.6*

Now elicit the meaning of the words and phrases in **bold** in 1–8, either explaining in English, translating into Sts' L1, or getting Sts to check in their dictionaries. Model and drill pronunciation. Point out the silent *p* in *pseudonym*. Model and drill its pronunciation.

1 **full name** /fʊl neɪm/ = the first name, any middle names, and last name of a person
   is short for /ɪz ʃɔːt fə/ = being a shorter form of a name
2 **initials** /ɪˈnɪʃlz/ = the first letters of all of a person's names
3 **maiden name** /ˈmeɪdn neɪm/ = a woman's family name before marriage
   married name /ˈmærɪd neɪm/ = when a person takes the last name of his / her spouse
4 **nickname** /ˈnɪkneɪm/ = an informal, often humorous, name for a person that is connected with their real name, their personality or appearance, or with sth they have done
   changed her name /tʃeɪndʒd hə neɪm/ = got a different name
5 **pseudonym** /ˈsuːdənɪm/ = a name used by sb, especially a writer, instead of their real name
6 **is named after** /ɪz neɪmd ˈɑːftə/ = to be given the name of a person or place
7 **first name** /ˈfɜːst neɪm/ = a name that was given to you when you were born, that comes before your family name
   middle name /ˈmɪdl neɪm/ = a name that comes between your first name and your family name
8 **'s called** /z kɔːld/ = having a particular name
   for short /fə ʃɔːt/ = being a shorter form of a name

c Focus on the instructions and put Sts in pairs.

Give Sts time to ask and answer the questions. Encourage them to ask for extra information.

Elicit some answers for each question.

2 PRONUNCIATION vowel sounds

Pronunciation notes

Many Sts find it difficult to pronounce common British names, often because of vowel sounds which don't exist in their L1.

This exercise will remind Sts who have used *English File* before of the sound–picture system. If your Sts are new to the series, you will need to explain that the sound pictures show the phonetic symbols, and give a clear example of a word with the target sound to help them remember the pronunciation of the symbol.

a 🔊 1.3 Focus on the eight sound pictures and elicit the words and sounds. Tell / Remind Sts that two dots in the phonetic symbol show a long sound, and two symbols together show a diphthong.

1 fish /ɪ/ 2 tree /iː/ 3 cat /æ/ 4 horse /ɔː/ 5 egg /e/
6 train /eɪ/ 7 phone /əʊ/ 8 bike /aɪ/

Now focus on the instructions and the first names. Point out that the sound that is being focused on is that of the pink letters in the names. Play the audio, pausing after each group to give Sts time to find the odd one out.

EXTRA CHALLENGE Give Sts time, in pairs, to find the odd one out in each set of four names. Remind them that this kind of exercise is easier if they say the words aloud to themselves. Then elicit answers and play the audio for Sts to listen and check.

Play the audio again if necessary, and then check answers.

1 Diana 2 Emily 3 Amy 4 Charlotte 5 Leo 6 Sam
7 Nicole 8 Mia

🔊 1.3
1 fish /ɪ/ Chris, Bill, Linda, Diana
2 tree /iː/ Peter, Steve, Emily, Eve
3 cat /æ/ Alex, Amy, Andrew, Anna
4 horse /ɔː/ George, Paula, Charlotte, Sean
5 egg /e/ Adele, Edward, Leo, Jessica
6 train /eɪ/ Sam, Grace, James, Kate
7 phone /əʊ/ Tony, Joe, Nicole, Sophie
8 bike /aɪ/ Caroline, Mia, Mike, Simon

EXTRA CHALLENGE In pairs, get Sts to decide the sound of the pink letter in the names they have circled. Then check answers.

1 Diana /aɪ/ 2 Emily /e/ 3 Amy /eɪ/ 4 Charlotte /ɑː/
5 Leo /iː/ 6 Sam /æ/ 7 Nicole /ɒ/ 8 Mia /iː/

EXTRA SUPPORT If these sounds are difficult for your Sts, it will help to show them the mouth position. You could model this yourself or use the Sound Bank videos on the *Teacher's Resource Centre*.

b Focus on the instructions. Give Sts a few minutes in pairs to decide which are men's names, women's names, or both.

Check answers, and each time ask Sts if the name is short for something. You may want to tell them that Toni with an *i* is short for Antonia, and Jo (without an *e*) is short for Joanna / Josephine.

1 Chris **B** (short for Christopher **M** or Christina / Christine **W**), Bill **M** (short for William), Linda **W**, Diana **W**
2 Peter **M**, Steve **M** (short for Stephen / Steven), Emily **W**, Eve **W**
3 Alex **B** (short for Alexander **M** or Alexandra **W**), Amy **W**, Andrew **M**, Anna **W**
4 George **M**, Paula **W**, Charlotte **W**, Sean **M**
5 Adele **W**, Edward **M**, Leo **M** (short for Leonard / Leonardo), Jessica **W**
6 Sam **B** (short for Samuel **M** or Samantha **W**), Grace **W**, James **M**, Kate **W** (short for Catherine / Katherine)
7 Tony **M** (short for Anthony), Joe **M** (short for Joseph), Nicole **W**, Sophie **W**
8 Caroline **W**, Mia **W**, Mike **M** (short for Michael), Simon **M**

c Tell Sts to go to **Communication Middle names quiz** on *p.106*.

Make sure Sts understand the task and give them time, in pairs, to do the quiz.

Check answers. You could elicit the names of films these actors have been in or whether Sts like them.

1 Ashton /ˈæʃtən/ 2 Reese /riːs/ 3 Brad /bræd/
4 Jude /dʒuːd/ 5 Dakota /dəkəʊtə/ 6 Bruce /bruːs/
7 Sean /ʃɔːn/ 8 Rihanna /riːænə/ 9 Hugh /hjuː/
10 Warren /ˈwɒrən/

Tell Sts to go back to the main lesson **1A**.

3 READING checking hypotheses

a Get Sts to cover the article and focus on the instructions. Put Sts in pairs to answer the questions.

Elicit some opinions, and encourage Sts to give reasons if they can, but don't tell them if they are correct.

b Tell Sts to uncover the article and focus on the title. Elicit / Explain the meaning of *customs* /ˈkʌstəmz/ (= an accepted way of behaving or of doing things in a society or a community). Model and drill its pronunciation.

Now tell Sts to read the article to check their answers to **a** and to make a note whether the first names in the list are male or female.

Get Sts to compare with a partner, and then check answers.

EXTRA SUPPORT Before Sts read the article the first time, check whether you need to pre-teach any vocabulary.

Yeon Seok: Korean male first name
Rakhmaninov: Russian (male) surname
López Ramírez: Spanish-speaking country surname
Aarushi: Indian female first name
Li: Chinese surname
Abdul Ahad: Afghan (Arabic) male first name
Jones: British surname

c Tell Sts to read the article again and answer questions 1–6. Check answers.

1 Korea and China 2 Afghanistan 3 Spanish-speaking countries 4 Russia 5 the UK 6 India

You may want to explain that in Spanish-speaking countries a child gets both their father's and their mother's first surname, so if Juan López Garcia and Ana Ramírez Soler have a daughter Maria José, her full name will be Maria José López Ramírez.

Deal with any other new vocabulary. Model and drill the pronunciation of any tricky words.

d Focus on the questions and make sure Sts understand them. If your Sts come from the same country, you could do this as a whole-class activity. If not, put Sts in pairs to discuss the questions, and then get some feedback from the class.

4 LISTENING & SPEAKING

a 🔊 **1.4** Focus on the instructions. Now play the audio for Sts to listen, write the name of each person, and add a tick if the people like their name.

Check answers by eliciting the names onto the board, getting Sts to spell them.

EXTRA SUPPORT Read through the script and decide if you need to pre-teach any new lexis before Sts listen.

1 Sean ✓   2 Deborah   3 Khari ✓   4 Anya ✓

🔊 **1.4**
(script in Student's Book on *p.124*)
I = interviewer, S = Sean, D = Deborah, K = Khari, A = Anya

1
I Excuse me. I'm doing a survey. Can I ask you some questions about your name?
S OK.
I So, what's your name?
S Sean Gibson.
I Is that S-E-A-N or S-H-A-U-N?
S S-E-A-N.
I Why did your parents call you that?
S I think I'm named after the actor Sean Connery, who played James Bond in the sixties. He was still very famous at the time when I was born.
I Do you have a nickname?
S Yes, at school they used to call me 'Gibbo' because of my surname, Gibson. I didn't really mind it because most people were called by some nickname or other.
I And are you happy with your first name?
S Mmm, I like it. I was usually the only Sean at school, which I think was quite a good thing. But people find it quite difficult to spell, especially as there are two possible spellings, and most foreign people find it really difficult to pronounce.
I Would you like to change it?
S No, no, I definitely wouldn't change it.

2
I So, what's your name?
D Deborah.
I Is that with an *h* at the end?
D Yes, D-E-B-O-R-A-H.
I Why did your parents call you that?
D Ah, I'm actually named after the hospital where I was born, Deborah Hospital in New Jersey – near New York. My dad thought of that.
I Do you have a nickname?
D No, but everyone calls me Debbie or Deb for short.
I Are you happy with your name?
D Not really.
I Would you like to change it?
D I don't know. When I was little, I started calling myself April, and then Caroline, but now I don't like those names, either.

3
I What's your name?
K Khari.
I How do you spell it?
K K-H-A-R-I.
I Sorry, K-A-H…?
K No, K-H-A-R-I.
I Why did your parents call you that?
K It was my mum's idea. When she was young, she went travelling in the Himalayas and she stayed at a monastery in Nepal called 'Khari' – I think she said it was also the name of the lama.
I Lama?
K Yeah, the head priest there. You know, like the Dalai Lama. Apparently, Khari means 'the precious one'.
I Oh, OK! Thanks – that's really interesting. Do you have a nickname?
K No, I don't.
I Are you happy with your name?
K Yeah.
I Would you like to change it?
K No, no way. My name's unique; I'm proud of it.

4
I What's your name?
A It's Anya, A-N-Y-A.
I Why did your parents call you that?
A Well, my dad's half Polish, and my parents wanted a Polish name. My mum originally wanted to call me Agnieszka, but my dad thought it would be too hard to spell, so they decided on Anya.
I Do you have a nickname?
A I do, but I don't want to tell you what it is – it's too embarrassing.
I Are you happy with your name?
A Yes, I am – it's quite an unusual name in the UK. I only know one other Anya. I think it's more common in Poland, but there it's spelt A-N-I-A.
I Would you like to change your name?
A No, I really like it. I often get compliments about it.

b Now tell Sts they are going to listen again and need to answer the three questions. Give Sts time to read them.

Play the audio again, pausing after each speaker to give Sts time to answer the questions.

Get Sts to compare with a partner, and then play the audio again if necessary.

Check answers.

EXTRA SUPPORT Play each speaker again, pausing to check the answers before playing the next speaker.

Speaker 1	1	He was named after Sean Connery.
	2	At school he was nicknamed 'Gibbo' because of his surname, Gibson.
	3	He wouldn't like to change it.
Speaker 2	1	She was named after a hospital in New Jersey.
	2	No, but people call her Debbie or Deb for short.
	3	She doesn't know.
Speaker 3	1	His mum called him after a place – a monastery in Nepal. It was also the name of the lama / head priest there.
	2	He doesn't have a nickname.
	3	He wouldn't like to change his name because it's unique and he's proud of it.
Speaker 4	1	Because her dad is half Polish and her parents wanted a Polish name.
	2	She has a nickname, but she doesn't want to say what it is.
	3	She wouldn't like to change it.

EXTRA SUPPORT If there's time, you could get Sts to listen again with the script on *p.124*, so they can see exactly what they understood / didn't understand. Translate / Explain any new words or phrases.

c Put Sts in small groups of three or four and get them to answer the questions about their names. You could demonstrate the activity by answering some of the questions yourself.

Get feedback from different pairs, and use this as an opportunity to learn Sts' names.

EXTRA IDEA Ask Sts if they know what their name is in English, and if they like it more or less than in their language.

5 GRAMMAR pronouns

a Focus on the instructions, making sure Sts know what a *brand name* is (= the name given to a product by the company that produces it). Now put Sts in pairs to discuss the questions.

Elicit some answers.

b Focus on the image and find out if any Sts have a Kindle or a Kindle app. Then ask if they know how the Kindle got its name. Don't tell Sts if they are correct.

Now focus on the instructions, and then give Sts time to read the text.

To check comprehension, ask Sts how the Kindle got its name.

> The designer Michael Cronan chose *kindle* because its meaning reminded him of the feeling people get when reading. Also, Victor Hugo, the French novelist, wrote 'to read is to light a fire'.

Now elicit Sts' opinions of the name. You may want to tell Sts that Jeff Bezos wanted a name for his company starting with *A* and chose *Amazon* because it's the biggest river in the world, and he wanted his company to be the biggest in the world.

c Put Sts in pairs and tell them to read the text again and decide what the highlighted pronouns refer to. You might want to remind Sts what a *pronoun* is (= a word that is used instead of a noun or noun phrase).

Check answers.

> them = Kindle eBook readers   it = Kindle eBook reader
> him = Michael Cronan   he = Jeff Bezos   it = the word *kindle*
> their = people

d Tell Sts to go to **Grammar Bank 1A** on *p.132*. If your Sts have not used the *English File* series before, explain that all the grammar rules and exercises are in this part of the book.

Grammar notes

The **Grammar notes** in this Teacher's Guide aim to add more information to the notes and rules on the **Grammar Bank** pages in the Intermediate Plus Student's Book where necessary. There is a direct link between the number of each rule in the Teacher's Guide and the Student's Book. If there is no extra information about a rule in the Teacher's Guide, this is either because we assume that Sts at this level should already know it, or because all the information needed is on the Student's Book page.

The **Grammar Bank** rules section usually begins with **Revise the basics**, showing what Sts should already know – in this case, the forms of all pronouns, and basic rules.

The examples on the audio and the rules are grammar which is either completely new (as in this case), or grammar which is complex in form or use and needs thorough recycling.

Pronouns

At this level, Sts will have met all of the pronoun forms, but may not have revised them since Elementary level.

It is also an area where many common errors persist, especially confusing the third person pronouns *he / she / they*, and mixing up subject and object pronouns or possessive adjectives and pronouns.

Remind Sts that pronouns are not usually stressed in sentences except for emphasis.

Direct / indirect object pronouns and word order

- **Rule 1:** Emphasize that when the direct object is a noun, we usually put the indirect object (without a pronoun) directly after the verb, and then the direct object, e.g. *I gave Jack / him my address* (*address* is the direct object and *Jack* or *him* is the indirect object) NOT *I gave to Jack / him my address*.

  However, we can also say *I gave my address to Jack / him* (= verb, direct object, *to* or *for* + indirect object), but highlight that the indirect object usually answers the question 'to whom?', e.g. *I gave it to **him***. The direct object answers 'what?', e.g. *I gave **my address** to him / I gave **it** to him*.

- **Rule 2:** Emphasize that when the direct object is a pronoun, the only possible order is verb + direct object + *to* or *for* + indirect object, e.g. *I gave it to Jack / him*.

  You may want to write a few more sentences on the board with indirect objects and elicit the different possibilities, e.g.
  They showed Jane the flat.
  They showed the flat to her.
  They showed it to her.

Focus on the first section, **Revise the basics**. Go through the examples and elicit the rules, e.g. *I* always being a capital letter in 1, the difference between a subject pronoun and an object pronoun in 2, etc. Then focus on the chart showing all the pronouns and possessive adjectives.

Now focus on the example sentences for **direct / indirect object pronouns and word order** and play audio 🔊 **1.5** for Sts to listen and repeat. Encourage them to copy the rhythm.

Then go through the rules with the class.

Now focus on the exercises and get Sts to do them individually or in pairs.

Check answers, getting Sts to read the full sentences.

> a
> 1 He, his   2 your, mine   3 their, hers   4 her, me
> 5 them, theirs   6 our, ours   7 your, mine   8 us, her
> 9 him, his   10 It's, its

1A

b
1 They sent it to me.
2 I gave them to her.
3 She found them for me.
4 My grandmother wrote them to me.
5 Will you lend it to him?
6 My son made it for me.
7 My parents offered it to us.
8 We didn't buy it for her.
9 I read it to them.
10 A friend sold them to me.

Tell Sts to go back to the main lesson **1A**.

EXTRA SUPPORT If you think Sts need more practice, you may want to give them the **Grammar** photocopiable activity at this point.

e 🔊 **1.6** Focus on the instructions and examples. Explain (or show on the board) that first Sts will hear a sentence, then they have to change it, by changing the direct object to a pronoun.

Play the first sentence and then elicit the new sentence from the class.

Play the rest of the audio, pausing after each sentence for Sts to listen and say the sentence.

EXTRA SUPPORT As Sts listen, pause the audio at the beep if they need more time.

🔊 **1.6**
1 Give me the book. (*pause*) Give it to me.
2 Give her the shoes. (*pause*) Give them to her.
3 We gave him the present. (*pause*) We gave it to him.
4 Show me the photo. (*pause*) Show it to me.
5 I'll give them the information. (*pause*) I'll give it to them.
6 Did you give her your number? (*pause*) Did you give it to her?
7 She didn't send me an email. (*pause*) She didn't send it to me.
8 He can't give us the details. (*pause*) He can't give them to us.

Then repeat the activity, eliciting responses from individual Sts.

f Focus on the task. Put Sts in pairs and tell them to take it in turns to talk about a couple they know, using the suggested topics and anything else they think is interesting. Focus on the example and remind Sts to use *he / his / him* when talking about a man, and *she / her / hers* when talking about a woman.

Monitor and help, encouraging Sts to use the appropriate pronouns.

Get some feedback from the class.

EXTRA SUPPORT Demonstrate the activity by telling Sts a little about a couple you know.

EXTRA CHALLENGE Get Sts to ask each other follow-up questions, e.g. *How did you meet them?*

6 LISTENING understanding proper names

a Focus on the photos of the brands and the task. Do the questions as a whole-class activity, or put Sts in pairs or small groups to discuss the questions and then get some feedback.

b 🔊 **1.7** Play the audio for Sts to listen to how each name is pronounced. Then elicit what kind of company they are and which ones are pronounced differently in your Sts' L1.

A Burberry /ˈbɜːbəri/ fashion items, e.g. raincoats, scarves, etc.
B Ferrari /feˈrɑːriː/ cars and related merchandising
C Vodafone /ˈvəʊdəfəʊn/ mobile phone networks
D Samsung /ˈsæmsʌŋ/ electronic products
E Nivea /nɪˈviːə/ cosmetics
F Nike /ˈnaɪkiː/ sportswear
G Starbucks /ˈstɑːbʌks/ coffee and coffee shops
H Bluetooth /ˈbluːtuːθ/ wi-fi technology

🔊 **1.7**
A Burberry
B Ferrari
C Vodafone
D Samsung
E Nivea
F Nike
G Starbucks
H Bluetooth

c Put Sts in pairs and give them time to think which brand name A–H has which meaning 1–7. You may want to point out that 7 has two answers. Tell them not to write their answers.

Elicit some answers from various pairs, but don't tell them if they are correct.

d 🔊 **1.8** Tell Sts they are going to listen to a radio programme about the brands they have just discussed and they should now match the brands (A–H) to their meanings in **c**.

Play the audio once the whole way through.

Get Sts to compare answers with their partner, and then play the audio again if necessary.

Check answers. Find out how many Sts had guessed correctly.

EXTRA SUPPORT Read through the script and decide if you need to pre-teach any new lexis before Sts listen.

1 D 2 E 3 C 4 G 5 H 6 F 7 A, B

🔊 **1.8**
(script in Student's Book on *p.124*)
I = interviewer, J = John
I Today we're talking to the Creative Director of a business that names companies and products. Welcome, John.
J Hello, Sarah.
I So, how do companies go about choosing their names?
J Oh, in all sorts of ways. Many, like Burberry clothes and accessories, and Ferrari cars, are named after the people who started them. Others are combination words, such as Vodafone, which is from letters in the words *voice, data,* and *telephone* – though actually, they changed the *P-H* in *telephone* to *F*. And Microsoft comes from the words *microcomputer* and *software*.
I Interesting…
J And other names come from phrases in the local language. A good example of that is Samsung, the big Korean electronics company. In Korean, Samsung means 'three stars'. The name was chosen back in the year nineteen thirty-eight, and at that time,

16 **1A**

three stars was the most impressive rating that people could imagine for hotels and things like that.
I So if they'd started the company today, they would probably have called it 'five stars' – whatever that is in Korean.
J Absolutely. Some names even come from Latin – the name of the cosmetics company Nivea comes from the Latin word *niveus*, which means 'snow white'. And talking of Latin, there's another famous brand name with a classical connection, which is Nike.
I I think I know this one. Nike is the Greek goddess of victory. Is that right?
J Yes, exactly. However, 'Nike' wasn't the company's original name. When it started in nineteen sixty-four, its original name was Blue Ribbon Sports. They changed their name to Nike a few years later, in nineteen seventy-one.
I I didn't know that.
J And a name ideally needs to have a strong sound. Take the coffee chain Starbucks, which was founded by two teachers and a writer, who decided to set up a business selling high-quality coffee beans and roasting equipment. Their advertising agency advised them that the letters *S-T* were powerful, and so they brainstormed words beginning with these letters and thought of a character called Starbuck from a nineteenth-century novel. The name didn't have anything to do with coffee, but they said that 'the sound seemed to make sense'.
I And do you have a favourite brand name?
J Well, one of my favourites is Bluetooth. This one comes from the name of a Viking king, Harald Blatand, so called because he had a dead tooth which had turned blue – *blatand* means 'blue tooth' in Danish. This king believed in good communication between people, which is an excellent model for developing new communication technologies. But also, the logo for Bluetooth on your phone screen, the *B* shape, is made up of the two Viking letters for the King's initials – the symbols for *H* – Harald – and *B* – Blatand. I love that.
I Thank you so much, John, for speaking with us this afternoon.
J You're very welcome.

e Focus on the instructions and make sure Sts understand all the lexis, e.g. *founders*, *Viking*.

Now play the audio again for Sts to listen and write their answers to each question. You could pause after each question is answered to give Sts time to make notes. Play again if necessary.

Get Sts to compare with a partner, and then check answers.

1 *Microcomputer* and *software*
2 1938
3 Blue Ribbon Sports
4 Because an advertising agency said they were powerful letters
5 *H* and *B*

Get feedback on what Sts found surprising about the brand names.

EXTRA SUPPORT If there's time, you could get Sts to listen again with the script on *p.124*, so they can see exactly what they understood / didn't understand. Translate / Explain any new words or phrases.

f If your Sts come from the same country, you could do this as a whole-class activity. If not, put Sts in pairs and then get some feedback from various pairs.

7 SPEAKING

a Focus on the instructions and make sure Sts understand the meaning of the phrase *raise money*.

Point out the **Glossary** and go through it with the class. Check that Sts understand *straw* /strɔː/, and *model* and drill its pronunciation.

Now give Sts time to read about one of the products on the website.

Elicit some opinions from the class. You could also tell the class what you think.

EXTRA IDEA Before focusing on the straws, ask *What brand and model of phone, car, and / or computer do you and your family have? Do you like the names?*

b Put Sts in pairs and tell them to discuss the two questions.

Elicit some opinions from various pairs. You could also have a class vote with a show of hands for each name.

Then tell Sts that the name that was chosen for the product was Lolistraw (a lollipop is a sweet on the end of a stick). The product raised $29,759 from 821 people.

c Focus on the task and on the **Making suggestions**, **Accepting suggestions**, **Rejecting suggestions** box and go through it with the class.

Set a time limit for Sts to read about the three products.

Then put them in small groups and get one person in each group to act as 'secretary', writing down all the possible ideas for names. Monitor and help, encouraging Sts to use expressions from the box.

d Now tell Sts to decide in their groups on the best names for each product.

Elicit ideas from each group for each product and write the names on the board.

Then have a class vote for the best name for each product.

Now tell the class the real names of the products and where the names come from. Ask Sts whether they think the real names are as good as the names they chose.

1 Quercus; the word is from the Latin name for the oak tree.
2 IQ bars; IQ means 'Intelligence Quotient'.
3 Pixl; the word is from a *pixel* which is a small individual coloured square on a computer screen – together these form the whole display.

Finally, ask *Which product do you think was the most popular?* (Pixl raised the most money from the most people on the website.)

1 Quercus raised £6,342 from 86 people.
2 IQ bars raised $73,664 from 1,500 people.
3 Pixl raised $225,017 from 4,018 people.

1B Life in colour

- **G** adjectives
- **V** adjective suffixes
- **P** word stress

Lesson plan

The topic of this lesson is colour. Sts start by taking a colour personality test and reading the results, which revises some adjectives of personality covered in *English File* Intermediate. They then focus on word-building with adjectives and suffixes, and this is followed by a pronunciation focus on word stress in adjectives. Next, Sts listen to a podcast about some facts about colours. The first half ends with a speaking activity in which Sts discuss various questions related to colours.

The second half of the lesson begins with the grammar focus, which is on adjectives, revising basic rules and extending Sts' knowledge of comparative and superlative adjectives, together with a focus on the use of *one / ones*. Next, Sts read and discuss an article about the psychology of colour – how the colour of a room can affect our mood. This lesson ends with Sts talking and then writing about their favourite room at home.

More materials
For teachers
Photocopiables
Grammar adjectives *p.153*
Communicative Good, better, best *p.180* (instructions *p.172*)
Vocabulary Adjective suffixes *p.206* (instructions *p.202*)
For students
Workbook 1B
Online Practice 1B

OPTIONAL LEAD-IN (BOOKS CLOSED)

Revise adjectives of personality by doing this quiz with the whole class, getting them to write the answers.

Ask: *What do you call someone who…?*
 1 *wants to be successful in life* (am<u>bi</u>tious)
 2 *isn't confident about himself / herself* (inse<u>cu</u>re)
 3 *refuses to change his / her opinion* (<u>stu</u>bborn)
 4 *is friendly and enjoys being with other people* (<u>so</u>ciable)
 5 *always thinks about himself or herself and not about other people* (<u>sel</u>fish)
 6 *has moods that change quickly and often* (<u>moo</u>dy)

Check answers and elicit the stressed syllable in each adjective.

1 VOCABULARY adjective suffixes

a Books open. Focus on the instructions and the eight colours on the page. Tell Sts to do *The colour test* individually. They should do this task quickly.

b Now tell Sts to go to **Communication The colour test** on *p.106* and read the results of the test.

Tell Sts to read about the colour they chose and to underline the points they agree with.

Tell Sts to go back to the main lesson **1B**.

! Don't ask Sts about their results yet, as they will be discussing these at the next stage. You might want to tell the class that this activity is based on the famous Max Lüscher colour test.

c Focus on the **Talking about results** box and go through it with the class.

Now put Sts in pairs to answer the two questions.

Monitor and encourage Sts to use the expressions in the box and to ask each other follow-up questions.

Elicit some feedback. You could also tell Sts which colour you chose and what you think of the results.

EXTRA IDEA Get Sts to vote with a show of hands for the most and least popular colours.

d Focus on the instructions and give Sts time to complete the adjectives with the correct suffixes.

Check answers, and elicit the meaning of the adjectives, especially if you didn't do the **Optional lead-in**.

ambitious   passionate   sensitive   sociable   successful

e Tell Sts to go to **Vocabulary Bank Adjective suffixes** on *p.152*.

Vocabulary notes
Describing people
Sts will have met several of these adjectives before. If they are new, encourage them to try out the words with the different endings to see which one sounds best.

Describing places and things
Some of the stems can be used with different suffixes, e.g. *useable* (= can be used) and *restive* (= unable to stay still). We have focused on the two more common adjectives, but you may also want to point out these two alternatives.

-ful and -less
Point out that *hopeless* can also mean 'not good', e.g. *I'm hopeless at maths*.

Look at **1 Describing people**. Focus on the **Word endings for adjectives** box and go through it with Sts.

Now get Sts to do **a** individually or in pairs.

EXTRA SUPPORT Let Sts use their dictionaries to help them with this section.

🔊 **1.9** Now do **b**. Play the audio for Sts to listen and check.

Check answers.

🔊 **1.9**
Adjective suffixes
1 Describing people
sociable, sensible, loveable, reliable, responsible
passionate, affectionate, compassionate, considerate
sensitive, assertive, attractive, creative, impulsive, possessive
ambitious, envious, glamorous, rebellious
successful, helpful, powerful, thoughtful

> Now either use the audio to drill the pronunciation of the adjectives, or model and drill them yourself. Give further practice of any words your Sts find difficult to pronounce.
>
> **EXTRA IDEA** If your Sts' L1 is a Latin-based language, some of these adjectives may be quite similar. Get Sts to highlight or circle the ones that are completely different.
>
> Now do **Activation** and tell Sts to cover the chart, look at the nouns and verbs in the list in **a**, and see if they can say the adjectives.
>
> Now focus on **2 Describing places and things** and get Sts to do **a** individually or in pairs.
>
> **EXTRA SUPPORT** Let Sts use their dictionaries to help them with this section.
>
> 🔊 **1.10** Now do **b**. Play the audio for Sts to listen and check.
>
> Check answers. Point out the difference in pronunciation between luxury /ˈlʌkʃəri/ and luxurious /lʌɡˈʒʊəriəs/.

🔊 **1.10**
2 Describing places and things
recognizable, affordable, comfortable, desirable, profitable, suitable
easy, dirty, healthy, messy, noisy, risky
addictive, expensive, impressive
dangerous, luxurious, spacious
useful, colourful, peaceful, restful, stressful

> Now either use the audio to drill the pronunciation of the adjectives, or model and drill them yourself. Give further practice of any words your Sts find difficult to pronounce.
>
> Now do **Activation** and tell Sts to cover the chart, look at the nouns and verbs in the list in **a**, and see if they can say the adjectives.
>
> Now look at **3 -ful and -less**. Focus on the **-ful and -less** box and go through it with the class.
>
> Focus on the instructions for **a** and make sure Sts understand what they have to do. Get them to do it individually or in pairs.
>
> 🔊 **1.11** Now do **b**. Play the audio for Sts to listen and check.
>
> Check answers.

🔊 **1.11**
3 -ful and -less
helpful, helpless
powerful, powerless
thoughtful, thoughtless
useful, useless
colourful, colourless
restful, restless

> Now either use the audio to drill the pronunciation of the adjectives, or model and drill them yourself. Give further practice of any words your Sts find difficult to pronounce.
>
> Tell Sts to go back to the main lesson **1B**.
>
> **EXTRA SUPPORT** If you think Sts need more practice, you may want to give them the **Vocabulary** photocopiable activity at this point.

2 PRONUNCIATION word stress

> **Pronunciation notes**
>
> Word stress can be difficult for Sts and needs lots of practice. The presence of prefixes and suffixes can add to the difficulty for Sts from L1 backgrounds where suffixes take the main word stress. The main thing for all Sts to learn is that suffixes and prefixes are not stressed in English. The only exception is the *a* in *-ation*, e.g. con<u>verse</u> – conver<u>sa</u>tion.

a Focus on the **Word stress on adjectives formed with suffixes** box and go through it with the class.

Then focus on the instructions and questions 1–10. Give Sts time to underline the stressed syllable in the **bold** adjectives.

EXTRA SUPPORT Remind Sts that the stress will never be on the prefix or suffix.

b 🔊 **1.12** Play the audio for Sts to listen and check. Check answers.

🔊 **1.12**
1 cr<u>ea</u>tive
2 pos<u>se</u>ssive
3 <u>en</u>vious
4 re<u>be</u>llious
5 <u>gla</u>morous
6 <u>com</u>fortable
7 un<u>hea</u>lthy
8 <u>sui</u>table
9 im<u>pre</u>ssive
10 lux<u>u</u>rious

> Now play the audio again, pausing after each adjective for Sts to listen and repeat.
>
> Finally, repeat the activity, eliciting responses from individual Sts.

EXTRA CHALLENGE Get Sts to match the stressed syllable in each adjective to its vowel sound (/e/, /iː/, etc.).

1 /eɪ/ 2 /e/ 3 /e/ 4 /e/ 5 /æ/ 6 /ʌ/ 7 /e/ 8 /uː/
9 /e/ 10 /ʊə/

c Focus on the instructions and put Sts in pairs, **A** and **B**. Tell Sts **A** to ask their partner questions 1–5 and Sts **B** to ask 6–10. Encourage them to ask for extra information where possible.

Monitor, making sure Sts stress the **bold** adjectives correctly.

Get feedback from the class.

EXTRA SUPPORT Get Sts to ask you a couple of the questions first. Encourage them to ask the follow-up questions for more information.

EXTRA IDEA Get Sts to reply to the questions with *What about you?*

1B

3 LISTENING listening for extra information

a You could do this as a whole-class activity, or put Sts in pairs and then get some feedback from various pairs.

You could elicit a few colours for each noun and write them on the board. Leave them up to help Sts when doing **e** later.

b Focus on the instructions and make sure Sts understand *fascinating* in the title. Model and drill its pronunciation.

Put Sts in pairs and tell them to read each fact and choose a colour from the list for each gap. Tell them <u>not</u> to write anything at this stage.

c 🔊 1.13 Focus on the instructions and make sure Sts know what a *podcast* is (= a digital audio file that can be taken from the internet).

Tell Sts that the podcast has a lot of information in it, more than just the text on the Student's Book page, and the first time they listen, they just have to check their answers to **b**.

Play the audio for Sts to listen and check.

Check answers. Find out how many Sts got all answers correct.

EXTRA SUPPORT Read through the script and decide if you need to pre-teach any new lexis before Sts listen.

| 1 red | 2 orange | 3 Pink | 4 purple | 5 blue | 6 green |
| 7 yellow | 8 white | 9 brown | 10 black | | |

🔊 **1.13**
(script in Student's Book on *pp.124–125*)
Look around you. Colour is everywhere in our lives. Did you know that, according to some experts, there are as many as ten million possible colours in our world, though many are too complex for the human eye? So how much do you really know about colour? Here are some fascinating facts.
Research shows that the world's most popular colour is blue, followed by purple, red, and green, while white, orange, and yellow are our least favourite colours.
Works of art using the colour red tend to be more expensive. This is because it's a powerful colour, which is considered lucky in many countries, such as China. The most expensive works by the artist Mark Rothko, for example, whose paintings are mainly just blocks of colour, are his two red paintings.
The word *orange* didn't describe a specific colour in English until the sixteenth century, when it was named after the fruit. Instead, people used the old English word *geoluhread*, which meant 'yellow-red'. This is why we have the word *redhead* for people with this colour of hair.
Pink has a calming effect and reduces anger and anxiety. Many prisons and hospitals paint their walls pink, to make prisoners and patients less anxious.
In Imperial Rome, the colour purple was produced with an extremely expensive dye made from thousands of seashells. The colour symbolized the power and wealth of the Roman Empire, and by the fourth century AD, only the emperor was allowed to wear it.
Mosquitoes are attracted to dark colours, especially blue. So, if you're planning to be outside in the evening in an area with a lot of mosquitoes, be careful what colour clothes you wear.
There is no such thing as a green mammal, even though it's a perfectly common colour for birds, reptiles, fish, and insects. One reason might be that most mammals can't see this colour, so it doesn't help with camouflage.
Van Gogh said that yellow was the colour of happiness, and it's the main colour of many of his paintings between eighteen eighty and eighteen ninety. The Dutch painter suffered from epilepsy, and doctors may have given him the drug *digitalis*, which can cause people to see this colour very strongly.
The safest colour for a car is white. Studies show that it is the most visible colour in all driving conditions except snow.
Most diamonds in their natural state are brown. These are used in industry as cutting tools, rather than in jewellery. The largest cut diamond in the world is this colour. It was found in nineteen eighty-five in South Africa and weighs one hundred and nine grams.
The name for the colour black hasn't always meant 'dark'. It comes from the root word *bhleg-*, which meant 'to burn, gleam, or shine'. This may explain why in languages like French and Spanish, *blanc* or *blanco* are actually the words for white.
These are just a few of the fascinating facts I discovered when I was researching colour. The next time you make a choice about colour, for example, for a new car, do some research first to find out exactly what it means.

d Now focus on the instructions and give Sts time to read questions 1–10. Make sure they understand them.

Play the audio again. You might want to pause it after each colour has been mentioned to give Sts time to answer the questions.

Get Sts to compare with a partner, and then play again if necessary.

Check answers.

| 1 white | 2 orange | 3 black | 4 yellow | 5 blue | 6 purple |
| 7 red | 8 pink | 9 brown | 10 green | | |

EXTRA SUPPORT If there's time, you could get Sts to listen again with the script on *pp.124–125*, so they can see exactly what they understood / didn't understand. Translate / Explain any new words or phrases.

e Do the question as a whole-class activity.

EXTRA IDEA You could ask Sts how many of their answers in **a** were the same as the information in the text. If you wrote Sts' ideas in **a** on the board, point to them.

4 SPEAKING

Focus on the questions, and go through them, making sure Sts can remember the meaning of *smart* and *dye*. You might also want to check they understand the question *What are they like?* They should answer this question after each person they have mentioned in the third section.

Monitor and help, encouraging Sts to use adjectives and to ask for extra information.

Get some feedback from the class.

5 GRAMMAR adjectives

a Focus on the task and then give Sts time to complete facts 1–8.

Get Sts to compare with a partner, and then check answers.

| 1 most | 2 than | 3 ones | 4 in | 5 more | 6 much |
| 7 as | 8 the | | | | |

b Tell Sts to go to **Grammar Bank 1B** on *p.133*.

Grammar notes
Adjectives
Revise the basics

Sts will have seen both these forms before, but may still be confusing comparative and superlative forms, e.g. ~~It's the more expensive watch in the shop.~~

Adjective + *one* / *ones*

In many languages, adjectives can be used as nouns, and Sts need to be encouraged to say, e.g. *the blue one* NOT *the blue*.

More rules for comparatives and superlatives
Rule 2: two-syllable adjectives
You may want to point out that:
- adjectives which end in *-ing*, *-ful*, and *-less* use *more* / *the most* for comparatives and superlatives, e.g. *boring, careful, painless*.
- two-syllable adjectives with a negative prefix which end in *-y*, e.g. *unhappy, untidy*, can make comparatives and superlatives with *-er* / *-est* or *more*, e.g. *unhappier* or *more unhappy*.
- although *the least* + adjective is very common, *less* + adjective is not as common – we tend to use *not as… as…*, e.g. *Today isn't as hot as yesterday* (rather than *today is less hot than yesterday*).

***a bit* and *much* + comparative adjective**

Highlight that *very* is not used with comparatives, e.g. ~~*very bigger*~~.
You could point out that we can also use *a little* instead of *a bit* with comparatives, and *far* or *a lot* instead of *much*.

Focus on **Revise the basics** and go through the examples, eliciting the rules for each one, e.g. that adjectives go before nouns in 1, that we never add an *s* to adjectives in 2, etc. Then focus on the chart for comparative and superlative adjectives and use it to revise the rules.

Now focus on the example sentences for **adjective + *one* / *ones*** and play audio 🔊 1.14 for Sts to listen and repeat. Encourage them to copy the rhythm. Then go through the rules with the class.

Repeat for **more rules for comparatives and superlatives** 🔊 1.15 and ***a bit* and *much* + comparative adjective** 🔊 1.16.

Now focus on the exercises and get Sts to do them individually or in pairs.

Check answers, getting Sts to read the full sentences.

a
1 ✗ the worst film   2 ✗ as sporty as   3 ✓   4 ✓, ✓
5 ✗ a cheap one   6 ✗ a better driver   7 ✗ the most comfortable ones   8 ✗ very successful   9 ✗ is easier than
10 ✓

b
1 Tom's brother is **luckier than** he is.
2 Our house is **much smaller than** theirs.
3 My old password was **more difficult / harder** to memorize than my new one.
4 This flat is **the nicest** of the three we've seen.
5 My children aren't **as helpful as** my sister's.
6 The weather was **worse than** we'd expected.
7 The book was **a bit more dramatic than** the film.
8 Red won't look **as good as** yellow for your kitchen walls.

Tell Sts to go back to the main lesson **1B**.

EXTRA SUPPORT   If you think Sts need more practice, you may want to give them the **Grammar** photocopiable activity at this point.

c Focus on the **Compare them!** section and the example answer.

Then get Sts to look at the **Extremes!** section and elicit the superlative of the adjectives in brackets. Tell Sts not to write them in the questions.

1 the saddest   2 the most positive   3 the most popular, the best   4 the furthest (or farthest)   5 the most generous
6 the most boring

Tell Sts to choose three topics or questions from each section to talk about.

Put Sts in pairs to discuss the topics and / or answer the questions, then swap roles.

Monitor and help, encouraging Sts to give reasons and explain their choices as fully as possible.

Get feedback from various pairs.

EXTRA IDEA   Tell Sts they have to try to talk for at least one minute on each topic they have chosen.

6 READING   scanning for information

a Focus on the instructions and make sure Sts understand the meaning of *colour scheme* (= the way in which colours are arranged, especially in the furniture and decoration of a room). Model and drill its pronunciation.

Put Sts in pairs to share their ideas.

Elicit some opinions from the class.

b Focus on the instructions, making sure Sts understand that they should read quickly to find which room in **a** generally follows the advice given in the article.

Check the answer.

EXTRA SUPPORT   Before Sts read the article the first time, check whether you need to pre-teach any vocabulary.

c the study

c Focus on the instructions and make sure Sts can remember the meaning of *suitable*.

Give Sts time to read the article again, complete the chart, and answer the question.

Get Sts to compare with a partner, and then check answers.

	Suitable colours
a bedroom	pink, blue, green, purple
a living room	green, brown
a dining room	red, orange
a kitchen	yellow
a study	purple, blue
a bathroom	blue

Not suitable for bedrooms: red, yellow, white

d Put Sts in pairs and tell them to answer questions 1–9.
Check answers.

1 Because, as it's a strong colour, it might be too much or give people headaches.
2 Pink can be a 'girlie' colour, so adding grey or black will make it attractive to more people.
3 Because it can make a room look smaller.

1B

> 4 It apparently discourages insects.
> 5 If it's all one shade of purple, it can make it difficult for people to relax.
> 6 Only green can make people feel lazy and fall asleep.
> 7 Brown on its own can be boring, so blue and green add extra mental stimulation.
> 8 People with white bedrooms work in bed a lot (and don't relax).
> 9 It's a dramatic colour and can work in any room in moderation.

e Do this as a whole-class activity.

> pale / light green 2   bright green 3   dark green 1

Now put Sts in pairs and get them to describe each colour using the adjectives in 1–3. You might want to do the first one as a class.
Check answers.

> beige = pale brown
> cream = pale yellow
> khaki = dark green
> maroon = dark brownish-red (brownish = quite brown)
> navy = dark blue
> scarlet = bright red
> turquoise = bright blue / green

Deal with any other new vocabulary. Model and drill the pronunciation of any tricky words.

f Do this as a whole-class activity, or put Sts in pairs and then get some feedback from the class. You could also tell Sts about the colours in the rooms in your house.

7 SPEAKING & WRITING describing a room

a Focus on the task and give Sts time to think of their answers. Make sure they understand all the lexis, e.g. *blinds*, etc.

Now put Sts in pairs and tell them to take turns to describe their favourite room. They can use the items in the list and anything else about their room that comes to mind. Encourage Sts to give as much information as possible and to ask their partner follow-up questions.
Get feedback from individual Sts.

EXTRA SUPPORT You could start by brainstorming vocabulary for furniture and accessories. You could also demonstrate the activity by describing your favourite room and getting Sts to ask you a few questions about it.

b This is the first time Sts go to the **Writing Bank** at the back of the Student's Book. In this section, Sts will find model texts with exercises and language notes, and a writing task. We suggest that you go through the model and do the exercises in class, but set the actual writing (the last activity) for homework.

Tell Sts to go to **Writing Describing a room** on *p.115*.
Focus on **a** and get Sts to look at the photo of Ana's room and describe what's in it.

Now give Sts time to read the description and answer the two questions. Tell them not to worry about the gaps.
Get some feedback.

Now focus on **b** and tell Sts to number the topics according to the paragraph in which they appear.

Get Sts to compare with a partner, and then check answers.

> 2 the size and colour of the room
> 3 what furniture there is
> 1 which room it is and where
> 4 why she likes it

Focus on **c** and tell Sts to read the description again and complete the gaps with prepositions in the list. They should use the photo of the room to help them. Remind Sts that some prepositions will be used more than once.
Get Sts to compare with a partner, and then check answers.

> 2 in   3 inside   4 from   5 in   6 on   7 above   8 on
> 9 in   10 with

Focus on **d** and tell Sts they are going to write a description of their favourite room. Remind them that they described it to their partner in the main lesson.
Tell Sts to plan their description by using 1–4 in **b** in the correct order. Encourage them to make brief notes on what they will write about.

! Emphasize to Sts that the planning stage of writing is usually the most important stage because it provides a structure for the piece of writing.

Now focus on the instructions in **e** and tell Sts they are going to write the description of their favourite room. They should write four paragraphs, as in the model, and use the language in the **Vocabulary Bank Adjective suffixes** on *p.152* to help.

You may like to get Sts to do the writing in class, or you could set it as homework. If you do it in class, set a time limit for Sts to write their description, e.g. 15–20 minutes.
In **f**, Sts should check their description for mistakes before giving it in.

EXTRA IDEA Ask Sts to take a photo of their room and add it to the description. Sts could also show each other the photos.

EPISODE 1

Practical English A bad start

Function reporting lost luggage, greeting someone you haven't seen for some time
Language *My suitcase hasn't arrived; It's medium size*, etc.

Lesson plan

This is the first in a series of five Practical English lessons (one every other File) which teach Sts basic functional language to help them 'survive' in an English-speaking environment. All the content for these lessons is on video. There is also an audio version if you are unable to show the video in class.

The storyline is based on two characters, Jenny Zielinski, an American journalist who works in the New York office of a magazine called *NewYork 24seven*, and her husband, Rob Walker, a British journalist who works for the same magazine. If your Sts did *English File* Intermediate, or any of the previous levels, they will already be familiar with the characters. If not, they will not be at a disadvantage because the story is stand-alone. In the audio-only version, a narrator has been added to tell the story, so that Sts will be aware of all the action even if they aren't watching the video. The storyline in this series of lessons is a mystery, which Jenny has to solve. Sts will enjoy the story much more if you build up the suspense and encourage them to speculate about what has happened, or is going to happen during and at the end of each episode. If any Sts have watched ahead in the *Online Practice*, ask them not to spoil the ending for those that haven't.

In the first scene, Jenny has just arrived in London for business, but she's planning to visit her father-in-law, Henry – Rob's father (Rob proposed to Jenny at the end of the Intermediate video) – for a few days first. She talks to fellow passenger Andrew Page in the airport while a mysterious man watches them. At Baggage Reclaim, Jenny discovers her suitcase is missing, and in the second scene she reports it to Lost Luggage. In the third scene, she and Henry then drive to his house in the countryside and Jenny later calls Rob, who is on assignment in Alaska, on Skype. Neither Jenny nor Henry realizes that the strange man, whose name is Grant, is watching them from outside the house.

These lessons can be used with *Class DVD*, *Classroom Presentation Tool*, or *Class Audio CDs* (audio only). Sts can find all the video content and activities in the *Online Practice*.

More materials
For teachers
Teacher's Resource Centre
Video Practical English Episode 1
Quick Test 1
File 1 Test
For students
Workbook Practical English 1
Can you remember? 1
Online Practice Practical English 1
Check your progress

OPTIONAL LEAD-IN (BOOKS CLOSED)
If your Sts did *English File* Intermediate, elicit anything they can remember about Jenny and Rob. Ask *Who's Jenny? Where does she work / live? Who's Rob?*, etc.

If your Sts didn't do *English File* Intermediate, tell Sts who Rob and Jenny are (see the **Lesson plan**) and explain that they are now married and living in New York.

1 ▶ JENNY IS BACK IN LONDON

a 🔊 **1.17** Books open. Focus on the photos and elicit that Jenny and Andrew, a man who was on her flight, are coming into the terminal at Arrivals, and that Jenny is carrying a lot of bags, which she then drops. Focus also on the photo of the man on the phone. Explain that he is called Grant, and is watching Andrew and Jenny. They will find out more about him as the story progresses.

Now focus on the instructions and the two questions. Play the video / audio once the whole way through for Sts to watch or listen.

Check answers.

EXTRA SUPPORT Before playing the video / audio, go through the listening scripts and decide if you need to pre-teach / check any lexis to help Sts when they listen.

> Andrew helps Jenny when she drops her bags, and carries one of them for her.
> Her suitcase hasn't arrived.

🔊 **1.17**
(The narrator's lines are on the audio, but not in the video.)
N = narrator, A = Andrew, J = Jenny, G = Grant
N Day one. Two p.m. Jenny Zielinski has just arrived in London. Her husband, Rob, is still in the States, but Jenny's going to visit his dad, Henry, before she starts work. She's carrying a lot of bags, and drops them. But a fellow passenger helps her.
A Are you all right? I'll carry that for you.
J Oh yeah, that'd be great. Thank you.
N They don't know it, but a man is watching them. He makes a phone call…
G We've just arrived on the flight from New York. He's talking to someone. I'll follow them.
N Jenny gets to the queue for Passport Control. She's chatting to Andrew, the man who helped her with her bags.
A …And have you been to the UK before?
J A few times, actually. I work for a magazine in the States – *NewYork 24seven* – and we have a sister company in London.
A I see. And are you here on business this time?
J Sort of. I'm here for a few meetings, but I have a couple of days off beforehand. I'm visiting my father-in-law in the countryside. How about you? How was your holiday in New York?
A It wasn't really a holiday. I was doing some research there.
J That sounds interesting.
A It was, but I didn't have much time for sightseeing! Is your husband coming, too?
J No, he's working.
A What does he do?
J He's a journalist. He's on assignment in Alaska at the moment.
A In Alaska? Wow!
J I know, right? I've never been, but he says it's incredible.
A I can imagine. A bit different from the English countryside!
J That's true.
A I'd better go. Oh, before I forget, here's your laptop.

PE1 23

J Oh yeah! Thanks a lot…Sorry, I didn't ask your name.
A Andrew Page. And yours?
J Jenny Zielinski. It was nice meeting you.
A You too.
J And thanks again for helping with my bags.
A No problem. Have a great time at your father-in-law's.
J I will…if I ever get through here!
A Bye, then.
J Yeah, bye. Take care.
N *Andrew leaves…but the man follows him. Jenny gets through Passport Control, but after waiting at Baggage Reclaim, she discovers that her luggage hasn't arrived. She goes to Lost Luggage and waits in another queue. While she's waiting, she calls Henry, her father-in-law.*
J Henry?…Hi, yeah, I'm here at last. The flight was late taking off…I'm so sorry you've had to wait for me…I know, I know. And you won't believe this – it looks like my suitcase didn't get here…I'm not sure, it's turning out to be a nightmare! I can't wait to just get back to your house and – oh, hang on, I have to go – it's my turn. Bye.

b Now focus on sentences 1–6 and go through them with Sts, making sure they know the meaning of *pleasure*.

Play the video / audio for Sts to watch or listen again and mark the sentences *T* (true) or *F* (false). Remind them to correct the false ones.

Get Sts to compare with a partner, and then check answers.

1 T
2 F (He was doing research.)
3 F (He's working in Alaska.)
4 T (Sts will later discover that, in fact, although Andrew gives Jenny back the laptop case, it is not her laptop. For the moment, they should believe that it is hers.)
5 F (His surname is Page.)
6 T

Now focus on the last two questions and get Sts to speculate about why the man (Grant) was watching them, and what he is going to do. Elicit ideas, but <u>don't</u> tell Sts if they are correct.

EXTRA SUPPORT If there's time and you are using the video, you could get Sts to watch again with subtitles, so they can see exactly what they understood / didn't understand. Translate / Explain any new words or phrases.

2 ▶ REPORTING LOST LUGGAGE

a 🔊 **1.18** Focus on the photo and elicit who Jenny is talking to (*an airline employee*).

Now tell Sts to focus on the four questions.

Play the video / audio once the whole way through for Sts to watch or listen and answer the questions.

Check answers. Sts may not know the word *toiletries*, so write it on the board and elicit that it means soap, shampoo, etc. Model and drill its pronunciation. Highlight also that *greyish* = with some grey in it / quite grey, and that the suffix *-ish* can be added to all colours and to some other adjectives.

1 Ten days
2 Greyish blue and hard plastic; medium size with wheels; it has a small lock, and a label with her name and phone number on it
3 Clothes, toiletries, and all her personal belongings
4 Up to 24 hours

🔊 **1.18**
A = attendant, J = Jenny
A Can I help you?
J Yeah, my suitcase hasn't arrived.
A Which flight were you on?
J Flight RT-one-six-three from JFK.
A I'll take your details and then I can issue you with a reference number. Can I have your name, please?
J My name's Jenny Zielinski. That's Z-I-E-L-I-N-S-K-I.
A And you're a visitor to the UK.
J That's right.
A How long are you staying for?
J Ten days.
A OK. How many bags are you missing?
J Just one – a suitcase.
A Can you describe it for me?
J Well, it's kind of greyish blue…and hard plastic, I think…
A And what size is it?
J Oh, it's medium size, like this. And it has wheels.
A Anything else?
J Yeah, there's a small lock and a label with my name and phone number on it.
A And what was in the suitcase?
J Just about everything! Clothes, toiletries, all my personal belongings, really.
A Can I have your address in the UK?
J Just a minute. It's The Grange, Marsh Lane, Long Crendon, Oxfordshire.
A And a contact number?
J Yes, it's oh-oh-one, two-oh-two, four-nine-four, oh-one-two.
A And finally, can you sign this?
J Of course. Do you have any idea where it is? I mean, do you think it's still in New York?
A It's possible. We're very sorry for the inconvenience. Here's your reference number. You can track the progress of your luggage online, or just give us a call. But we should be able to get it back to you within twenty-four hours.
J That'd be great. Thank you.

b Focus on the conversation in the chart. Elicit who says the **You hear** phrases (*the airline employee*) and the **You say** phrases (*the passenger*, here *Jenny*). These phrases will be useful for Sts if they ever lose their luggage after a flight.

Give Sts time to read through the conversation and to think about what the missing words might be. Now play the video / audio again and get Sts to complete the gaps. Play it again if necessary.

Get Sts to compare with a partner, and then check answers.

1 Which 2 details 3 visitor 4 long 5 bags 6 describe
7 size 8 in 9 address 10 contact 11 sign 12 sorry
13 online

Now go through the conversation and deal with any new vocabulary. Elicit / Explain that *your details* means information about you, and a *contact number* is a telephone number on which you can be contacted.

c 🔊 **1.19** Now focus on the **You say** phrases and tell Sts they're going to hear some of them again. Not all the phrases are given for Sts to repeat, as at this level, they should have no problem with, e.g. *ten days*. Get Sts to repeat these phrases, and encourage them to copy the rhythm and intonation.

Play the video / audio, pausing after the beep, if necessary, for Sts to repeat the phrases. Remind Sts that Jenny is American, so she says the letter *z* as 'zee' instead of 'zed' when she spells her name.

1.19

A = attendant, J = Jenny
- A Can I help you?
- J Yeah, my suitcase hasn't arrived. (*pause*)
- A OK. How many bags are you missing?
- J Just one – a suitcase. (*pause*)
- A Can you describe it for me?
- J Well, it's kind of greyish blue…and hard plastic, I think. (*pause*)
- A And what size is it?
- J Oh, it's medium size, like this. (*pause*)
  And it has wheels. (*pause*)
- A Anything else?
- J Yeah, there's a small lock and a label with my name and phone number on it. (*pause*)
- A And what was in the suitcase?
- J Just about everything! (*pause*)
  Clothes, toiletries, all my personal belongings, really. (*pause*)
- A And finally, can you sign this?
- J Of course. Do you have any idea where it is? (*pause*)
  I mean, do you think it's still in New York? (*pause*)
- A You can track the progress of your luggage online, or just give us a call. But we should be able to get it back to you within twenty-four hours.
- J That'd be great. Thank you. (*pause*)

d Put Sts in pairs, **A** and **B**. Sts **A** are the airline employee and Sts **B** the passenger. Get Sts to read the conversation in **b** aloud, and then swap roles.

Monitor and help, encouraging Sts to pay attention to rhythm and intonation.

e Focus on the **Useful language** box and go through it with the class.

Now focus on the instructions. Tell Sts they will both be playing the part of the passenger, so they should think about the suitcase or bag that they usually take when they're travelling and make sure they have all the language they need to describe it. Tell them also to decide how long they are staying, and to invent an address. You could elicit and write the names of a few hotel chains.

Put Sts in pairs, **A** and **B**. First, Sts **A** are the passenger and **B** the airline employee. Tell Sts **A** to close their books and Sts **B** to start with *Can I help you?* Then Sts practise the conversation with Sts **B** reading their role, and Sts **A** role-playing the passenger.

Monitor and help.

f When Sts have finished, they should swap roles.

You could get a few pairs to perform in front of the class.

3 AT HENRY'S HOUSE

a **1.20** Focus on the photos and ask Sts some questions, e.g. *Who do you think the man is? What is he doing? What is Jenny doing in the second photo?*

Now focus on the instructions and question. Play the video / audio once the whole way through for Sts to watch or listen.

Check the answer.

> Her laptop isn't working properly, possibly because of a virus.

1.20

N = narrator, J = Jenny, H = Henry, G = Grant, R = Rob, S = Selina
- N Day one. Four p.m. Jenny finally meets Henry and they walk to the car park where he's left his car.
- J …so then I had to go to Lost Luggage and report it missing.
- H You poor thing! What a journey!
- J Well, I'm here now.
- H And it's lovely to see you.
- J It's great to see you, too.
- H No, no, let me take that…
- J It's OK…
- H You've had a hard journey. Allow me.
- J Thanks, Henry.
- N Jenny and Henry drive off to Henry's house in the country, near Oxford. But the man from the airport has been following them. He makes another phone call.
- G We've got a problem.

***

- N Day one. Nine p.m. At Henry's house. Jenny calls Rob on Skype.
- R I can't believe I'm not there with you, Jenny.
- J Neither can I. It's weird, isn't it?
- R I really miss you.
- J Me too. How's Alaska?
- R Not great. It's been snowing all day! I haven't left the hotel.
- J Oh no! That's awful.
- R What are you drinking? Is that coffee?
- J No, it's tea.
- R Tea?
- J It's good. Really!
- R Where's Dad now?
- J Oh, I think he's getting me something. I'm not sure what.
- R So why are you using his computer?
- J Oh, it's crazy. You know my laptop?
- R Yeah?
- J This screen keeps popping up and asking me for a password. I've never seen it before. I'm worried I have a virus.
- R It's not your day, is it? First your suitcase, and then your laptop!
- J No, but your dad's being so nice. And he says your cousin Luke will be able to fix my computer for me. Apparently, he's kind of a computer geek.
- R Kind of? He's a genius. If he can't do it, nobody can.
- J Well, I'm going to go and see him tomorrow.
- H Here's a pair of my pyjamas you can use, Jenny.
- R Oh wow! You'll look great in those, Jenny!
- N Safe in the house, Jenny and Henry have no idea that the man, whose name is Grant, is outside in the dark…watching. He makes another phone call.
- S Selina Lavelle.
- G Selina? It's Grant. She's in the house, but she isn't alone. I could come back tomorrow with…
- S No. Stay there. All night if you have to.
- G Yes, boss.

b Focus on the instructions and give Sts time to read questions 1–6.

Play the video / audio again, pausing if necessary to give Sts time to answer the questions.

Get Sts to compare with a partner, and then check answers.

> 1 No, he isn't because it's been snowing all day and he hasn't left the hotel.
> 2 Tea
> 3 Henry's because she thinks her laptop has a virus
> 4 Rob's cousin
> 5 Tomorrow, so that he can fix her computer
> 6 A pair of his pyjamas

You could point out that *computer geek* is a slang expression for someone who's very good with computers.

Now focus on the last two questions and check the first answer. Then get Sts to speculate about the second.

Selina Lavelle is Grant's boss.

EXTRA SUPPORT If there's time and you are using the video, you could get Sts to watch again with subtitles, so they can see exactly what they understood / didn't understand. Translate / Explain any new words or phrases.

c Focus on the **Social English** phrases. In pairs, get Sts to see if they can remember any of the missing words.

EXTRA CHALLENGE In pairs, get Sts to complete the phrases before they listen.

d **1.21** Play the video / audio for Sts to watch or listen and complete the phrases.

Check answers. If you know your Sts' L1, you could get them to translate the phrases.

1 lovely   2 great   3 let   4 isn't   5 miss   6 awful
7 day   8 wow

1.21
1 (And) it's lovely to see you.
2 It's great to see you, too.
3 No, no, let me take that.
4 It's weird, isn't it?
5 I really miss you.
6 Oh no! That's awful.
7 It's not your day, is it?
8 Oh wow! You'll look great in those, Jenny!

Now play the video / audio again, pausing after each phrase for Sts to watch or listen and repeat.

e Focus on the instructions and make sure Sts understand what they have to do.

Get Sts to compare with a partner, and then check answers.

A 4   B 3   C 6   D 5   E 8   F 7   G 1,2

Now put Sts in pairs and get them to practise the conversations.

Finally, focus on the **CAN YOU…?** questions and ask Sts if they feel confident they can now do these things. If they feel that they need more practice, tell them to go to *Online Practice* to watch the episode again and practise the language.

Get ready! Get set! Go!

G present tenses
V packing
P /s/, /z/, and /ɪz/

Lesson plan
Preparing for holidays is the main topic for this lesson, which revises and extends Sts' understanding of the present simple and continuous. Packing for a holiday provides the context for learning vocabulary for items (including documents) that people often take with them. Then the pronunciation focus revises the sounds /s/, /z/, and /ɪz/, as used in the vocabulary just practised. In Listening, Sts first listen to a list of items British holidaymakers frequently forget to pack and then they listen to a journalist giving tips on how to pack. The first half of the lesson ends with a speaking activity in which Sts answer a questionnaire entitled *How good are you at preparing for a holiday?*

The second half of the lesson starts with a grammar focus on the present tenses. This is presented through holiday text messages, which helps Sts recognize the differences between the present simple and present continuous. After further grammar practice, Sts read an article from a website about things people only do when on holiday, e.g. buy useless souvenirs. Sts then talk about their own feelings about holidays and holiday preferences. The lesson finishes with a writing focus, where Sts write holiday messages to friends.

More materials
For teachers
Photocopiables
Grammar present tenses *p.154*
Communicative Ask me a question *p.181* (instructions *p.172*)
Vocabulary Packing *p.207* (instructions *p.202*)
For students
Workbook 2A
Online Practice 2A

OPTIONAL LEAD-IN (BOOKS CLOSED)
Write the following questions on the board:
WHEN WAS YOUR LAST HOLIDAY?
WHERE DID YOU GO?
WHAT LUGGAGE DID YOU TAKE WITH YOU?
DID YOU OVER-PACK OR UNDER-PACK?
First, answer the questions yourself. Then elicit answers from individual Sts.

1 VOCABULARY packing

a Books open. Focus on the first question and do it as a whole-class activity. Highlight that a break is specifically a <u>short</u> holiday.

> A *city break* is a short holiday spent in a city. People typically spend a few days sightseeing, going to museums or other local attractions, and eating out.

Now put Sts in pairs and tell them to answer the second question. Make sure they explain their choice. You could demonstrate the activity by answering the question yourself.
Elicit some ideas from the class.

b Focus on the instructions and make sure Sts know the verb *pack*.
In their pairs, Sts tell each other what items they would take.
Elicit some ideas.

c Tell Sts to go to **Vocabulary Bank Packing** on *p.153*.

> **Vocabulary notes**
> **Electronics**
> You could tell Sts that *earphones* and *headphones* are sometimes used interchangeably, although they are in fact different.
>
> **Toiletries**
> Highlight that a *washbag / sponge bag* is a small bag for holding toiletries such as soap, a toothbrush, etc. when you are travelling.
>
> You may also want to point out that while *brush* on its own usually refers to a hairbrush, it is used in compound nouns, e.g. *toothbrush*, *paintbrush*, etc.

Focus on **1 Things to take on holiday** and get Sts to do **a** individually or in pairs. Some of these words may already be familiar to them.

🔊 **2.1** Now do **b**. Play the audio for Sts to listen and check.
Check answers.

🔊 **2.1**
Packing
1 Things to take on holiday

Electronics		**Clothes and shoes**	
6	adaptor	27	bathrobe
5	batteries	21	flip-flops
7	charger	23	pyjamas
1	earphones	28	rain jacket
4	hairdryer	26	slippers
3	headphones	25	sun hat
2	travel iron	24	swimming trunks
Toiletries		20	swimsuit
16	brush	22	underwear
12	comb	**Others**	
15	deodorant	31	beach bag
11	insect repellent	29	first-aid kit
10	make-up	30	guidebook
17	razor	33	pack of cards
13	scissors	32	towel
18	shampoo		
9	sunscreen		
14	toothbrush		
19	toothpaste		
8	washbag		

Now either use the audio to drill the pronunciation of the words, or model and drill them yourself. Give further practice of any words your Sts find difficult to pronounce.

Focus on **Activation** and tell Sts to cover the words and look at the photos. Can they remember the words?

EXTRA IDEA Elicit any other things Sts often take on holiday, e.g. *hair straighteners*, etc.

Now focus on **2 Documents you may need** and get Sts to do **a** individually or in pairs.

🔊 **2.2** Now do **b**. Play the audio for Sts to listen and check.

Check answers.

1 d 2 a 3 c 4 b 5 e

🔊 **2.2**
2 Documents you may need
1 d You take your passport or ID card to allow you to leave and enter a country.
2 a You take a visa if you are travelling to a country which requires one, for example, the USA.
3 c You take travel insurance documents in case you have an accident or another problem.
4 b You take your driving licence if you want to rent a car.
5 e You take your booking confirmation to prove to a hotel or airline that you have paid for a room, flight, etc.

Now either use the audio to drill the pronunciation of the words for the documents, or model and drill them yourself. Give further practice of any words your Sts find difficult to pronounce.

Focus on **Activation** and either do the question as a whole-class activity, or put Sts in pairs and then get some feedback.

Now focus on **3 Packing verbs** and get Sts to do **a** individually or in pairs.

🔊 **2.3** Now do **b**. Play the audio for Sts to listen and check.

Check answers. Point out that the *o* in *fold* and *roll* is pronounced the same.

1 wrap 2 roll up 3 fold 4 pack 5 unpack

🔊 **2.3**
3 Packing verbs
3 fold
4 pack
2 roll up
5 unpack
1 wrap

Tell Sts to go back to the main lesson **2A**.

EXTRA SUPPORT If you think Sts need more practice, you may want to give them the **Vocabulary** photocopiable activity at this point.

d Focus on the instructions and give Sts time to write their list. Tell them to work individually.

Get Sts to compare lists with a partner and to find any differences.

Get some feedback from various pairs. You could tell the class what you would definitely take on a beach holiday (e.g. sunscreen, a beach towel, a book, etc.) and what you wouldn't take (e.g. any expensive items). You could ask Sts how their lists are different from the ones they made in **1b**.

2 PRONUNCIATION /s/, /z/, and /ɪz/

Pronunciation notes

Sts who have the sounds /s/ and /z/ in their L1 will not find them hard to pronounce, but what is confusing for most Sts is that the letter *s* in the middle or at the end of a word can be pronounced in different ways (usually /s/ or /z/). It is worth reminding Sts that the letter *z* in English (and *zz*) is always pronounced /z/. Point out that double *s* = /z/, as in *scissors*, is unusual.

a Focus on the instructions and the two sound pictures and elicit the words and sounds (*snake* /s/ and *zebra* /z/).

Put Sts in pairs and remind them that this kind of activity is easier if they say the words aloud to themselves.

b 🔊 **2.4** Play the audio for Sts to listen and check.

Check answers. Remind Sts that the *c* in *scissors* is silent.

EXTRA SUPPORT Do this as a whole-class activity. Write the two words on the board. Play the first word on the audio or say it yourself, and then elicit the sound for each pink letter. Do the same for the second word.

slippers: The first *s* = /s/; the final *s* = /z/.
scissors: The first *s* = /s/; the double *s* and final *s* = /z/.

🔊 **2.4**
See words in Student's Book on *p.16*

Give Sts time to practise saying the words and concentrate on the two sounds.

EXTRA SUPPORT If Sts are having problems noticing the difference between the two sounds, get them to place their finger and thumb on their throats and then say *scissors* slowly, feeling for the vibration in the /z/ sound. You could also use the Sound Bank videos on the *Teacher's Resource Centre*.

c Focus on the instructions and get Sts to write the words in the correct column.

EXTRA SUPPORT Say each word for Sts to listen and write the words in the columns.

EXTRA CHALLENGE Elicit the answers to **c** before playing the audio in **d**.

d 🔊 **2.5** Play the audio for Sts to listen and check. Check answers.

🔊 **2.5**
snake /s/ flip-flops, passport, swimsuit, sunscreen, toothpaste
zebra /z/ batteries, cards, pyjamas, razor, visa

Now play the audio again, pausing after each word or group of words for Sts to listen and repeat.

Then get Sts to practise saying the words.

Now ask Sts *In what position is the letter s never pronounced /z/?*

s is never pronounced /z/ at the beginning of a word.

e Focus on the instructions and the pronunciation of /ɪz/.

Give Sts time to circle the words ending in /ɪz/. Remind them that this kind of activity is easier if they say the words aloud to themselves.

28 **2A**

EXTRA CHALLENGE Elicit the answers to **e** before playing the audio in **f**.

f 🔊 **2.6** Play the audio for Sts to listen and check. Check answers.

> beaches, brushes, cases, sunglasses

🔊 **2.6**
See words in Student's Book on *p.16*

Get Sts to practise saying the words.

EXTRA SUPPORT Play the audio again, pausing after each word for Sts to listen and repeat.

Now ask Sts *When are the letters -es pronounced /ɪz/?*

> after *ch*, *sh*, *se*, *ss*, and *x* (also when a word ends in *ce*, as in *pieces*, or *ge*, as in *pages*)

3 LISTENING understanding advice

a Do this as a whole-class activity, or put Sts in pairs and then get some feedback. Tell Sts if you have ever forgotten to pack something really important, and what you did.

b Focus on the title of the article and ask Sts if they find it surprising. Ask why / why not.

Now focus on the instructions. Tell Sts to read the introduction, and, in pairs, guess the top three items. Elicit some ideas, but <u>don't</u> tell Sts if they're correct.

c 🔊 **2.7** Focus on the instructions and make sure Sts understand *in reverse order*.

Play the audio once the whole way through.

Elicit the top ten items in reverse order, and then ask the class if anyone got the top three correct.

> 10 passports 9 flip-flops 8 mobiles 7 toothbrushes
> 6 toothpaste 5 sunglasses 4 a good book
> The top three are:
> 3 sunscreen 2 phone chargers 1 comfortable shoes

🔊 **2.7**
(script in Student's Book on *p.125*)
In reverse order, here's the list of the things that the British most often leave behind when they go on holiday:
At number ten, we have…passports.
At number nine, flip-flops.
Number eight, mobile phones.
At number seven, toothbrushes, and at number six, toothpaste.
At number five, sunglasses, and at number four, a good book.
So, to the things people forget the most often:
At number three, sunscreen.
At number two, phone chargers.
And finally, the number one thing people forget to bring is…comfortable shoes!

EXTRA IDEA You could ask Sts if they think the list would be the same for people in their country. If not, why not? What about the top three?

d Focus on the instructions and give Sts time to read tips 1–8.
Now put Sts in pairs and give them time to guess what the missing words might be.

EXTRA CHALLENGE Elicit the answers to each tip in **d** before playing the audio in **e**.

e 🔊 **2.8** Play the audio for Sts to listen and check. Check answers. Find out if Sts predicted any correctly.

> 1 too much 2 shopping 3 order 4 clothes 5 chargers, adaptors 6 shoe 7 security 8 wallet

🔊 **2.8**
1 Don't pack too much.
2 Keep some space in your suitcase for shopping.
3 Pack in the right order.
4 Make sure your clothes arrive looking good.
5 Keep your chargers and adaptors together.
6 Use shoe bags.
7 Think about airport security.
8 Buy a travel wallet.

f 🔊 **2.9** Focus on questions 1–8 and make sure Sts understand all the lexis, e.g. *one third*, *hand luggage*, etc.

Now play the audio once the whole way through. You could pause after each tip to give Sts time to answer the question.

Get Sts to compare with a partner, and then play the audio again if necessary.

Check answers.

EXTRA SUPPORT Read through the script and decide if you need to pre-teach any new lexis before Sts listen.

> 1 Put them back in the cupboard.
> 2 Clothes, souvenirs, presents for the family
> 3 At the top of your suitcase
> 4 a) Roll T-shirts. b) Fold shirts.
> 5 All together in a separate bag, in your hand luggage
> 6 Socks and underwear
> 7 Your washbag, your laptop or tablet, and anything you might need to put on a separate tray at Security
> 8 You might lose your phone, or it may run out of battery when you need to show the documents.

🔊 **2.9**
(script in Student's Book on *p.125*)
The holiday season is here, and many of you will be about to travel, and that means that you need to start thinking about packing. Packing is often something we do at the last minute, and we frequently get it wrong – we take too much and then have to pay for extra luggage, or we forget some really important items. Often when we arrive and unpack, our clothes need ironing before we can wear them. So, to make things easier, here are my top eight tips for perfect packing.
My first tip is: 'Don't pack too much'.
Put all the clothes you think you want to take on your bed. Then put a third of them – yes, a third – back in the cupboard. And only pack things you really love, otherwise you probably won't wear them.
Now to my second tip: 'Keep some space in your suitcase for shopping'.
If you're planning to do some serious clothes shopping when you're away, or if you love buying souvenirs, or you want to buy presents for the family, make sure there's some empty space in your case. Think about what you might want to buy, and how much space you'll need.
My third tip is: 'Pack in the right order'.
Think about your itinerary, and put your first day's clothes at the top and your last day's clothes at the bottom. Then if you don't have space to unpack everything, you can just leave your suitcase under the bed, and every morning you'll easily find what you want to wear.
OK, tip number four: 'Make sure your clothes arrive looking good'.
Learn to pack your clothes like a professional. Roll your jeans, T-shirts, and pyjamas. The only things you really need to fold are

2A

shirts and jackets. Where possible, travel with clothes that don't need ironing.

My fifth tip is: 'Keep your chargers and adaptors together'.
We all need chargers for our gadgets these days. Pack them all together in a separate small bag, with adaptors if you're going to need them. It's also a good idea to put this bag in your hand luggage, and not in your checked-in luggage, to avoid losing it.

Tip number six: 'Use shoe bags'.
Never allow your shoes to have direct contact with your clothes – use shoe bags to keep them separate, and put socks and underwear inside your shoes.

Tip number seven: 'Think about airport security'.
If you're travelling with hand luggage only, put your washbag at the top or in an outside pocket of your case, so you can easily take it out at security. The same is true of laptops, tablets, and anything you might need to put on a separate tray.

And finally, my eighth tip: 'Buy a travel wallet'.
It's a good idea to print out all your important documents, like your itinerary or travel insurance, and keep them with your passport in a special wallet. It's true that nowadays you can keep a lot of documents on your phone, including boarding passes. But you might lose your phone, or it may run out of battery just when you need it.
So now you're ready to go. Have a great holiday!

EXTRA SUPPORT If there's time, you could get Sts to listen again with the script on *p.125*, so they can see exactly what they understood / didn't understand. Translate / Explain any new words or phrases.

g Do this as a whole-class activity, or put Sts in pairs and then get some feedback. You could have a class vote for the most useful tip. You could also ask Sts if they know any other packing tips.

4 SPEAKING

a Focus on the questionnaire and make sure Sts understand all the lexis, e.g. *How far in advance…*, *get your car serviced*, etc.

Give Sts time to think of their own answers.

b Focus on the instructions and the example.

Put Sts in pairs. Tell them to take turns to ask each other a question, and the same question can be returned using *What about you?*

Get some whole-class feedback by finding out, e.g. which websites Sts use, and asking individual Sts to talk about their preparation.

EXTRA SUPPORT You could model the activity first by getting Sts to ask you a couple of questions and eliciting follow-up questions if possible. Write WHAT ABOUT YOU? on the board to remind Sts to use it when they are taking turns.

5 GRAMMAR present tenses

a Focus on the instructions. Tell Sts to read Caroline's holiday messages quickly, then choose the correct form or tick both forms.

b Get Sts to compare their answers to **a** in pairs and discuss why they think each form is correct.

Check answers, getting Sts to explain why one form is correct and the other form is wrong, or why both forms are correct. (They can explain in their L1 if necessary.) You might want to tell Sts that timetable future sentences also work in the present continuous.

1 I'm wearing (It's happening now.)
2 I look like (*look like* is a non-action verb, not normally used in the continuous)
3 ✓ (The present simple can be used to talk about future events that are part of a timetable. The present continuous can be used for a future arrangement.)
4 I'm reading (It's happening now.)
5 I'm having (*have* is an action verb here, and is in the continuous to show the action is happening now.)

c Tell Sts to go to **Grammar Bank 2A** on *p.134*.

Grammar notes
Present tenses

You may need to remind Sts, especially if their L1 does not have continuous tenses, to use the present continuous to talk about actions in progress (*It's raining* NOT *It rains*).

Action and non-action verbs

Non-action verbs, not usually used with continuous forms, may refer to mental states (*believe*, *know*, *realize*), emotions (*admire*, *dislike*, *respect*), the senses (*feel*, *hear*, *smell*), and possession (*owe*, *own*, *possess*). Rather than simply memorize lists of such verbs, Sts should try to think about whether the verb is being used to indicate action, e.g. *read*, *play*, *drive*, or non-action.

Present continuous for future arrangements

The use of the present continuous to talk about personal arrangements in the future (*We're leaving next week*) is very similar to *going to*, but implies that something is an arrangement rather than a plan, i.e. it has been organized, tickets booked, etc.

Present simple for 'timetable' future

Highlight that the present simple is not usually used for the future, but when we refer to something that could be part of a timetable, e.g. a flight or a class time, we often use the present simple, e.g. *The next class starts in ten minutes*, because these things always happen at these times. We can also sometimes use the present continuous for timetabled activities when the emphasis is on that particular moment, e.g. *Hurry up! Our train is leaving / leaves in five minutes*.

Focus on **Revise the basics**. Go through the example sentences and use them to elicit the rules, e.g. in 1 that we add (*e*)s to third person, in 2 that we use *does* NOT *do* for third person, etc.

Now focus on the example sentences for **action and non-action verbs** and play audio 🔊 2.10 for Sts to listen and repeat. Encourage them to copy the rhythm. Then go through the rules with the class.

Repeat for **verbs which can have action and non-action meanings** 🔊 2.11, **present continuous for future arrangements** 🔊 2.12, and **present simple for 'timetable' future** 🔊 2.13.

Now focus on the exercises and get Sts to do them individually or in pairs. In **a** tell Sts to use the present simple (NOT continuous) for timetable future. Encourage them to use contracted forms rather than full forms in **b**.
Check answers, getting Sts to read the full sentences.

a
1 leaves 2 We need 3 we're going 4 we're staying
5 takes 6 we're breaking 7 gets in 8 are meeting
9 they're looking after 10 we're travelling 11 we're renting
12 We have

b
1 **Do** you **prefer** camping or staying in hotels?
2 We**'re thinking** of going on a safari next year.
3 **Do** we **need** to pack insect repellent?
4 She**'s flying** to Frankfurt for a business meeting next week.
5 Yes, I**'m looking for** a charger for my phone.
6 A This hotel **doesn't have** a restaurant.
   B It **doesn't matter**, we can eat in town.
7 A Hi. Can you hear me? What **are** you **doing**?
   B I**'m reading** by the pool and Tanya **is having** a spa treatment.
8 A What time **does** our flight **leave**?
   B It **leaves** at 9.50 and it **arrives** at 12.10.

Tell Sts to go back to the main lesson **2A**.

EXTRA SUPPORT If you think Sts need more practice, you may want to give them the **Grammar** photocopiable activity at this point.

d Put Sts in pairs, **A** and **B**, and tell them to go to **Communication** Caroline's holiday plans, **A** on *p.107*, **B** on *p.111*.

Go through the instructions, and focus on the holiday calendars, and the example questions and answers. Tell Sts to ask similar questions about all the incomplete entries and write the answers in the gaps. Elicit that most of the questions are in the present continuous, but the ones about her travel times, class, etc., are better in the present simple, as they refer to timetabled events.

When Sts have finished, get them to compare books to check their answers.

EXTRA SUPPORT Quickly revise telling the time before putting Sts in pairs.

EXTRA SUPPORT Elicit Sts **A**'s and **B**'s questions before they start:

Sts A
What time does she have her yoga class on Friday?
(*At half past seven in the morning*)
Where is she going sightseeing on Friday afternoon?
(*In Ibiza Town*)
What time is she having dinner at Bambuddha on Saturday?
(*At nine in the evening*)
What is she doing at six in the evening on Sunday?
(*She's having a massage at the hotel spa.*)
What time does she leave Ibiza on Monday?
(*At eight thirty-five in the morning*)

Sts B
Who is she going waterskiing with on Friday morning?
(*She's going waterskiing with Emma.*)
What is she doing at half past eight in the morning on Saturday?
(*She's going on a guided tour of the island.*)
What is she doing at eight in the morning on Sunday?
(*She's going on a boat trip to Formentera.*)
What time is she getting the bus to the airport on Monday?
(*At half past five in the morning*)
What time does she arrive at London Gatwick?
(*At ten o'clock in the morning*)

Tell Sts to go back to the main lesson **2A**.

e Focus on the instructions and the question prompts. Elicit that the ones that are habitual, show a 'timetable' future, or have a non-action meaning (e.g. *prefer*) use the present simple. The ones that are in progress at the moment or show future arrangements, use the present continuous if they have action verbs (e.g. *going*).

Elicit the questions from the class to check that they are forming the questions correctly, and that they are using the correct rhythm.

Holidays
Do you prefer summer holidays or winter holidays? Why?
Which places are you thinking about going to for your next holiday?
Why do you want to go there?
Weekends
What do you usually do at the weekend?
What are you doing this weekend?
Today
What time does this class finish? Where are you going after class today?
What are you doing this evening? Where are you having dinner?

Now get Sts to ask and answer the questions in pairs. Monitor and help, making sure Sts are using the present simple and present continuous correctly.

Make sure Sts swap roles.

Get some feedback from various pairs.

6 READING understanding linkers / cohesive devices

a Focus on the task, the words and phrases in the list, and the example. Then do this as a whole-class activity, or put Sts in pairs and then get some feedback.

EXTRA SUPPORT Demonstrate the activity by answering the question yourself.

b Tell Sts to read the article to see if any of the points they mentioned in **a** are there. Tell Sts not to worry about the gaps.

Elicit some feedback.

EXTRA SUPPORT Before Sts read the article the first time, check whether you need to pre-teach any vocabulary, but not the words in the highlighted phrases.

c Now set a time limit for Sts to read the article again and complete gaps 1–8 with phrases A–H. Check Sts understand the vocabulary in the phrases, e.g. *adventurous*, *super-sociable*, etc.

Get Sts to compare with a partner, and then check answers.

1 E 2 C 3 G 4 H 5 F 6 B 7 A 8 D

d Focus on the instructions and the highlighted phrases. Get Sts, in pairs, to try to work out what the phrases mean. Tell them to use the context to help them.

Check answers, either explaining in English, translating into Sts' L1, or getting Sts to check in their dictionaries. Model and drill pronunciation.

> 1 **whatever the reason** /wɒtˈevə ðə ˈriːzn/ = for lots of different reasons
> 2 **get your revenge on** /get jɔː rɪˈvendʒ ɒn/ = do sth to make sb suffer because they have made you suffer
> 3 **goes completely out the window** /gəʊz kəmˈpliːtlɪə aʊt ðə ˈwɪndəʊ/ = disappears completely
> 4 **have the urge** /hæv ðə ɜːdʒ/ = have a strong desire to do sth
> 5 **develop a magnetic pull** /dɪˈveləp ə mægˈnetɪk pʊl/ = have a powerful attraction

Deal with any other new vocabulary. Model and drill pronunciation of any tricky words.

e Put Sts in pairs and get them to discuss the question. Encourage them to answer with as much detail as possible.

Get some feedback from the class.

7 SPEAKING

a Focus on the task and the holiday options. Make sure Sts understand the question *Would you rather…?* (= Would you prefer to…?).

Now give Sts time to read each holiday option and, individually, choose the one they would prefer. Tell them to think of reasons as they will need to explain their choice in **b**. Tell them that in this activity, they are <u>not</u> allowed to reject both options – they must choose one of the options in each pair and say why it would be better than the other one.

b Focus on the **Expressing preferences** box and go through it with the class.

Put Sts in small groups and give them time to go through each holiday option in **a** and explain which they prefer and why. Encourage Sts to ask each other for more information.

Monitor and help, correcting any repeated mistakes.

Get some feedback from the class. Find out if any Sts in their groups liked the same kinds of holiday.

EXTRA SUPPORT Demonstrate the activity by choosing one of the options and telling Sts your own opinion.

8 WRITING holiday messages

Tell Sts to go to **Writing Holiday messages** on *p.116*.

a Focus on the task. Tell Sts to read the messages quickly and to answer the questions.

Check answers.

> Caroline, Mark, Michael, Sheila, and Sam are on holiday now.
> Haylee and Andrew are going to have a holiday soon.
> Danielle has just finished a holiday.

b Focus on the instructions. Get Sts to read the messages again and answer the questions individually or in pairs.

Check answers.

> **Suggested answers**
> Caroline feels great: *the most amazing experience, fantastic people*
> Mark feels relaxed: He uses *hard day* ironically; emoji of a winking smiley face, which can mean *I'm joking*
> Michael feels annoyed because of the noisy children on the plane: *Oh no!, the longest flight of my life*
> Haylee feels excited: *Can't wait!*

> Sheila feels happy and tired / relieved: *so beautiful, 13 hours, ready for a shower*
> Andrew feels stressed: *stressful, Not sure I want to go, stressed-face emoji*
> Danielle feels depressed: *Plants dead, no milk, Please send me back to the beach*
> Sam feels sad: *last…morning, work tomorrow,* emoji of sad face

c Focus on the **Writing messages** box and go through it with the class. You could point out that other possible changes to make full sentences include articles (*a / an, the*) and *some*.

Now get Sts to rewrite the last five messages (for Haylee, Sheila, Andrew, Danielle, and Sam) as complete sentences.

Get Sts to compare with a partner, and then check answers.

> **Haylee:** There are 48 hours until I'll be in Rio sipping a piña colada – or is it a caipirinha? I can't wait!
> **Sheila:** I've just got to Cuzco! It's so beautiful here! After 13 hours on a bus, I am ready for a shower!
> **Andrew:** I'm packing my bags. Holidays are really stressful! I'm not sure that I want to go!
> **Danielle:** I got back an hour ago. The plants are dead and there's no milk in the fridge. Please send me back to the beach.
> **Sam:** I'm making the most of the / my last glorious morning in the sun. I'm going home this evening and back to work tomorrow.

d Focus on the instructions. Now get Sts to imagine they're going to have a four-day holiday to any place they'd like to go to.

Go through the list of times and tell Sts to imagine themselves in the different situations.

e Focus on the instructions and make sure Sts understand what they have to do. Tell them to write one message for each day and time in **d**. Remind them to use the information in the **Writing messages** box.

You may like to get Sts to do the writing in class or you could set it as homework. If you do it in class, set a time limit for Sts to write their messages, e.g. 15–20 minutes, and if there is time, get Sts to compare their messages in pairs or small groups.

f Sts should check their work to make sure their messages are clear and as short as they can be.

2B Go to checkout

G possessives
V shops and services
P r and final -r

Lesson plan

The main topic in this lesson is shopping, with a focus on online shopping, whether people love it or hate it, and whether online shopping is putting other businesses at risk. In the first half, the grammar focus is on different ways of expressing possession. Sts revise the use of the possessive *'s* and learn to use other structures, e.g. *a friend of mine*, *my own business*, etc. Pronunciation follows with a focus on the letter *r*, paying special attention to when it is or isn't pronounced /r/ at the end of a word. Next, Sts listen to some people talking about how they feel about online shopping. Finally, Sts discuss their own experiences of online shopping.

The second half begins with a vocabulary focus on shops and services. This leads to questions prompting discussion about shops in Sts' own neighbourhoods. Next, Sts read about a bookshop chain that is fighting to survive against Amazon. The lesson ends with a video about Winchester farmers' market.

More materials
For teachers
Photocopiables
Grammar possessives *p.155*
Communicative Spot the difference *p.182-183* (instructions *p.173*)
Vocabulary Shops and services *p.208* (instructions *p.202*)
Teacher's Resource Centre
Video   A farmers' market
For students
Workbook   2B
Online Practice   2B

OPTIONAL LEAD-IN (BOOKS CLOSED)
Write on the board:

MARKET – SUPERMARKET – DEPARTMENT STORE

Elicit from Sts exactly what the difference is between the three (a *market* is usually an open area where people buy and sell things, often food but also clothes, antiques, etc.; a *supermarket* is a large shop usually on one level, which mostly sells food and drink; a *department store* is a very large building, usually on several floors, which sells a wide range of goods). Elicit examples of these stores that are near where Sts live.

Then ask Sts which ones they like / dislike shopping at and why.

1 GRAMMAR possessives

a Books open. Focus on the task and photos. Elicit what each photo represents (**A** *fruit and vegetables*, **B** *meat and fish*, **C** *clothes*, **D** *books*, **E** *electronic items*, **F** *shoes*, **G** *bread*).

Put Sts in pairs to answer the questions. You could demonstrate the activity by choosing a photo and answering the two questions about it.

Elicit some feedback from various pairs.

b Do this as a whole-class activity. You could also tell Sts if there is anything you would never buy online and why.

c Focus on the task and make sure Sts understand what they have to do. You could do the first one as a class. Before Sts start, tell them that there are some mistakes in punctuation in 1–6, but they shouldn't worry about it now as they will be focusing on it later.

Get Sts to compare with a partner, and then check answers.

> 1 in a shop   2 online   3 in a shop   4 online
> 5 online   6 in a shop

d Put Sts in pairs and get them to look at the highlighted words and phrases in sentences 1–6 in **c**, and insert apostrophes where necessary.

Check answers by eliciting the words and punctuation onto the board. If Sts ask why the apostrophe is in a particular place, elicit possible rules, but tell them they will be looking at this next in the **Grammar Bank**.

> 1 children's books   2 Carlos's / Carlos' present   3 Marta's
> 4 your husband's new car   5 my sister's sweater   6 My two daughters' friends

e Tell Sts to go to **Grammar Bank 2B** on *p.135*.

Grammar notes
Possessives

Most Sts will have met possessives at Elementary level and not revised them since, although Sts often continue making mistakes in this area. Here they also learn new rules, and other expressions to show possession.

More rules for possessive *'s*

- **Rule 3:** Apart from using the possessive *'s* for people's houses, many shops and businesses also use the possessive *'s*, as Sts will see when they do **Vocabulary Bank Shops and services**, e.g. *the hairdresser's*, *the dentist's*, *the chemist's* to mean *the hairdresser's salon*, etc. However, nowadays people sometimes drop the *'s*, e.g. *I'm going to the dentist*.

- **Rule 4:** Sts may find the following comparison useful:
We saw Tom and Mary's parents. = Tom and Mary are brother and sister. We saw their parents.
We saw Tom's and Mary's parents. = Tom and Mary are husband and wife. We saw Tom's parents and we saw Mary's parents.

More rules for *of* to show possession

In many languages, possession is expressed with *of*-phrases, so Sts tend to overuse *of*-phrases in English. Many languages also use an *of*-phrase, e.g. *the door of the car*, *the window of the shop*, where English uses a compound noun, e.g. *car door*, *shop window*, *summer holiday*.

Highlight that we use a pronoun, e.g. *mine*, in phrases like *a friend of mine*, not an adjective, e.g. *my*.

own

Remind Sts that *own* is also a verb (= possess).

Focus on **Revise the basics**. Go through the example sentences and use them to elicit the rules, e.g. that we use *'s* after a singular name or noun, etc.

Now focus on the example sentences for **more rules for possessive 's** and play audio 🔊 2.14 for Sts to listen and repeat. Encourage them to copy the rhythm and get the pronunciation of the *'s* correct. Then go through the rules with the class.

Repeat for **more rules for *of* to show possession** 🔊 2.15 and **own** 🔊 2.16.

Now focus on the exercises and get Sts to do them individually or in pairs.

Check answers, getting Sts to read the full sentences.

a
1 my friend's car   2 brothers'   3 the top of the building
4 travel agent's   5 Jim and Marie's   6 my husband's sister
7 my parents'   8 of mine   9 the centre of London
10 my own
b
1 ✗ women's clothes shops   2 ✓   3 ✗ their own flat
4 ✗ a colleague of hers   5 ✗ There's been a hairdresser's
6 ✗ Two of my friends' mothers   7 ✓   8 ✓   9 ✗ Keith and Brian's mother   10 ✓

Tell Sts to go back to the main lesson **2B**.

EXTRA SUPPORT If you think Sts need more practice, you may want to give them the **Grammar** photocopiable activity at this point.

2 PRONUNCIATION   *r* and final *-r*

Pronunciation notes

Here Sts are exploring the pronunciation of the letter *r*. At this level, Sts should be able to understand when and when not to pronounce *r*, depending on its position in a word (initial, middle, or final).

- *r* = /r/ at the beginning (e.g. *run*) and in the middle of a word (e.g. *umbrella*) when the *r* is followed by a vowel.
- *r* also = /r/ at the end of a word when the following word begins with a vowel (e.g. *her own*), in which case the words are linked.
- *r* is silent in British English when followed by a consonant either within the word (e.g. *car*, *work*), or if it comes at the end of a word and the following word begins with a consonant, e.g. *My brother works here*, or when it is the last word in a sentence, e.g. *That's my brother*.

You may want to point out that in American English *r* is always = /r/.

a 🔊 2.17 Focus on the sound picture and elicit the word and sound: *right* /r/.

Play the audio once the whole way through for Sts just to listen.

🔊 **2.17**
See words and sound in Student's Book on *p.20*

Then play the audio again for Sts to listen and repeat.

b 🔊 2.18 Focus on the instructions and the **Final -*r*** box.

Play the audio once the whole way through for Sts to listen and answer the question in the rule.

Check the answer.

vowel

🔊 **2.18**
See sentences in Student's Book on *p.20*

c Play the audio again, pausing after each sentence for Sts to listen and repeat.

Give Sts time to practise saying the sentences or questions.

d 🔊 2.19 Tell Sts they must listen and write the five sentences they hear.

Play the audio, pausing after each sentence to give Sts time to write.

Get Sts to compare with a partner.

Now play the audio again, pausing after each sentence to give Sts time to mark where the letter *r* is pronounced /r/.

Get Sts to compare with their partner.

Check answers. Elicit each sentence onto the board, and for each one, ask Sts which letter *r* is pronounced /r/ (see **bold** in script 2.19).

🔊 **2.19**
1 Chris and Pete**r** made thei**r** own website.
2 Ou**r** local shops don't delive**r** at weekends.
3 My French teache**r** lives nea**r** our house.
4 Is that all you**r** own work?
5 They're Sam and Andy's parents.

EXTRA SUPPORT Play the audio again, pausing after each sentence for Sts to listen and repeat.

EXTRA SUPPORT If this sound is difficult for your Sts, it will help to show them the mouth position. You could model this yourself or use the Sound Bank videos on the *Teacher's Resource Centre*.

3 LISTENING   recognizing positive / negative comments

a Focus on the task and the list, making sure Sts understand all the vocabulary, e.g. *push your way through crowds*, *interact*, *substitute*, etc. Tell Sts to put their tick(s) at the end of the sentences, and <u>not</u> in the boxes. Make sure they understand that they should only tick things they strongly agree with.

When Sts have finished, get them to compare in pairs.

Get some feedback from various pairs.

b 🔊 **2.20** Focus on the instructions and explain that first, Sts are only going to hear seven extracts from the main listening. They need to complete 1–7 and then decide if each extract is positive or negative. Encourage them to think about the reasons for their decisions.

Play the audio, pausing after each extract to give Sts time to write.

Get Sts to compare with a partner, and then play the audio again if necessary.

Check answers, first eliciting the missing words and then asking whether the extract is positive or negative. Then elicit / explain the meaning of each extract. Draw attention to the intonation of positive and negative expressions, i.e. that positive expressions usually have rising intonation at the end of the phrase, whilst negative expressions usually have falling intonation.

> 1 nightmare (negative)   2 convenient (positive)
> 3 bonus (positive)   4 pain (negative)
> 5 love (positive)   6 great (positive)   7 annoying (negative)

🔊 **2.20**
1 It's just a huge nightmare.
2 It's so convenient.
3 That's a real bonus.
4 It was a real pain.
5 I love the fact that…
6 It's great being able to…
7 That's so annoying.

c 🔊 **2.21** Tell Sts they are now going to listen to the five people talking about what they love or hate about online shopping. Sts need to listen to each speaker and write the speaker's number in the box he / she is speaking about in the lists in **a**.

Play the audio once the whole way through. You could pause the audio after each speaker to give Sts time to do the task. Then play again if necessary.

Check answers.

EXTRA SUPPORT Read through the script and decide if you need to pre-teach any new lexis before Sts listen.

> **Speaker 1**
> You can do your shopping in your pyjamas…
> If something isn't right, it can be a problem sending it back or getting it changed.
> **Speaker 2**
> Online shops are open 24/7.
> Clothes and shoes often don't fit…
> **Speaker 3**
> You don't have to carry heavy bags any more.
> Things are often bigger or smaller than you wanted because you didn't read the detailed description.
> **Speaker 4**
> You can buy things from shops that aren't near you.
> It's easy to send presents to people.
> You can't feel things or see exactly what they look like.
> **Speaker 5**
> You don't have to push your way through crowds of people.
> Your shopping is always delivered when you're out.

EXTRA SUPPORT Play each speaker again, pause, and elicit the answers.

🔊 **2.21**
(script in Student's Book on *p.125*)
1 Carol
I do a lot of shopping online. I love how convenient it is you know, I can be in my pyjamas and do the food shopping for the week, or clothes shopping. But one thing I hate about it, though, is how difficult it is to sort out any problems – because, you know, if you buy something in a shop, you go back to the shop and you sort it out, but if you've bought something online, returning it can be a pain, especially getting something replaced or changed if it's broken – it's just a huge nightmare.
2 Alex
I love online shopping. I guess because it's so convenient, because I can do it at any time of day or night, and I can do it from home. I don't particularly like going shopping, so that's a real bonus for me. But I hate having to send things back, particularly shoes. They never seem to fit when I buy them online.
3 David
I do quite a lot of shopping online. Mainly food – I usually do my supermarket shopping online. What I like best is that I don't have to take the shopping home. I live at the top of a hill, and I used to have to walk up the hill with a whole load of shopping bags. It was a real pain. The only thing I really don't like is that online, it's easy not to notice what size the packets are, so you can end up with a huge packet of things when you only want a tiny amount. For example, I ordered a box of tea bags and I wanted a small box of forty bags, but I didn't read the description properly and I ended up with a huge box with four hundred and sixty tea bags!
4 Anna
I do a lot of online browsing, looking for things I might buy. Not really for clothes, more shopping for, kind of, cooking things, or things on Amazon, presents for friends – that sort of thing. I love the fact that you have access to all kinds of shops, and access to brands that you can't necessarily find in shops that are near where you live. But I don't like not being able to feel things or know exactly what the colours are – they're often different from what you see online.
5 Chris
I do a lot of shopping online because I'm not very keen on going to places where there are crowds of people and it's really busy. It's great being able to avoid the big department stores and shopping streets especially at weekends, where you can hardly walk on the pavement because there are so many people there.
The only thing I hate is people delivering things when I'm not in. Some companies are really good and give you a one-hour delivery window, but with others, they say they'll deliver between eight in the morning and seven in the evening, so you stay in all day – but then just when you need to go out for an hour, that's when they come. That's so annoying.

d Focus on the questions and give Sts time to go through them.

Play the audio again, pausing after each speaker to give Sts time to answer the questions.

Get Sts to compare with a partner, and then check answers.

> **Speaker 5** likes knowing exactly when things he has bought are going to arrive.
> **Speaker 3** once bought a huge quantity of something by mistake.
> **Speaker 2** has one particular item she often has to return.
> **Speaker 4** enjoys looking on shopping websites.
> **Speaker 1** thinks it's easier to deal with problems in real shops.

EXTRA SUPPORT If there's time, you could get Sts to listen again with the script on *p.125*, so they can see exactly what they understood / didn't understand. Translate / Explain any new words or phrases.

e Do this as a whole-class activity. You could also tell the class your thoughts about online shopping.

4 SPEAKING

Focus on the instructions and go through the topics. Give Sts time to decide which three topics they are going to talk about.

Now focus on the **Showing interest** box and go through it with the class. Model interested intonation and get Sts to practise the phrases.

Put Sts in pairs (or small groups) and get them to discuss their topics. Encourage Sts to give and ask for as much detail as possible, and to use the phrases in the box to respond and get more information.

Monitor and help with any new vocabulary they need, but don't correct too much as the aim here is to encourage fluency.

EXTRA CHALLENGE Get fast finishers to talk about more topics.

5 VOCABULARY & SPEAKING shops and services

a Focus on the photos and do the questions as a whole-class activity.

A in a chemist's, sells medicines
B in a butcher's, sells meat
C in a car showroom, sells cars
D at a beauty counter (in a department store), sells make-up and beauty products

b Tell Sts to go to **Vocabulary Bank** Shops and services on *p.154*.

Vocabulary notes
Places

Some shops sometimes use another word, e.g. *bakery* instead of *baker's*, and *travel / estate agency* instead of *agent's*.

Point out that *deli* is short for *delicatessen* and that *hardware store* is another word for *DIY store*.

You may also want to point out that you can buy both medicines and things like cosmetics at a chemist's in the UK. In the USA, pharmacies just sell medicine, and drugstores sell medicines and other things.

You could also remind Sts that they can use 's for some other services, e.g. *the doctor's, the dentist's, the hairdresser's*, etc.

Remind Sts also, as pointed out in the **Grammar notes**, that nowadays people sometimes drop the 's at the end of these words, e.g. *I'm going to the hairdresser* (rather than *hairdresser's*).

Phrasal verbs related to shops and shopping

You may want to highlight the difference between *go shopping* (= go to look round several shops, e.g. in a mall or shopping street) and *go to the shops* (= go to buy something specific, e.g. food).

Focus on **1 Places** and get Sts to do **a** individually or in pairs. Point out or elicit that *DIY* stands for 'do-it-yourself', and this kind of shop sells tools and materials for doing jobs around the house or making things, e.g. furniture.

🔊 **2.22** Now do **b**. Play the audio for Sts to listen and check.

Check answers.

🔊 **2.22**
Shops and services
1 Places

13	baker's	21	florist's
15	barber's	4	garden centre
10	butcher's	6	greengrocer's
3	car showroom	20	hairdresser's
2	chain store	9	jeweller's
19	chemist's	18	launderette
8	deli	16	market stall
7	DIY store	22	newsagent's
5	dry-cleaner's	14	off-licence
17	estate agent's	1	stationer's
12	fishmonger's	11	travel agent's

Now either use the audio to drill the pronunciation of the words, or model and drill them yourself. Give further practice of any words your Sts find difficult to pronounce.

Do **Activation** and tell Sts to cover the words, look at the photos, and see if they can remember the places.

Go through the **Shop names with 's** box with the class.

Next, go through **Other places to buy things in the UK** with the class and ask Sts if these kinds of shops exist in their country.

Now focus on **2 Phrasal verbs related to shops and shopping** and get Sts to do **a** individually or in pairs. Some of these phrasal verbs will already be familiar to them. Encourage Sts to use the context of the sentence to help them with the meaning.

🔊 **2.23** Now do **b**. Play the audio for Sts to listen and check.

Check answers.

🔊 **2.23**
2 Phrasal verbs related to shops and shopping
1 d
A lot of local shops and businesses have closed down because of the recession.
2 f
A Do you need any help?
B No thanks, I just want to look round.
3 c
I wanted to get the coat in a large, but they'd sold out.
4 b
A Is there somewhere where I can try on this sweater?
B Yes, the changing rooms are over there.
5 e
Excuse me, can you help me? I'm looking for a butcher's. Someone told me there was one near here.
6 a
A Do you have these in a medium?
B I'm sorry, we're out of mediums at the moment, but we should be getting some in soon.

Focus on **Activation** and tell Sts to cover 1–6 and try to remember the phrasal verbs from the definitions, or vice versa.

Tell Sts to go back to the main lesson **2B**.

EXTRA IDEA Get Sts to close their books and revise the names for places by asking them either *Where would you go if you want to buy some meat?* or *What can you get at a butcher's?*

EXTRA SUPPORT If you think Sts need more practice, you may want to give them the **Vocabulary** photocopiable activity at this point.

c Put Sts in pairs and get them to discuss the difference between the pairs of words and phrases.
  Check answers.

1 **A stationer's** sells stationery (= paper, pens, envelopes, etc.).
  A newsagent's sells newspapers, magazines, sweets, cigarettes, etc.
2 **A dry cleaner's** cleans things that can't be put in a washing machine, e.g. coats, dresses, duvets, curtains, etc.
  A launderette is a place where you can pay to do your washing or sometimes have your washing done.
3 **An estate agent's** sells and rents out houses. **A travel agent's** sells holidays and plane / train tickets.
4 **The shop's closing** means it's time for people to stop shopping, as the shop will no longer be open. **The shop's closing down** means it's stopping trading or doing business.

d Focus on the *My local shops* questionnaire and go through the questions.
  Put Sts in pairs and get them to interview each other.
  Get some feedback from the class.

EXTRA SUPPORT Answer the first two questions yourself to demonstrate the activity.

6 READING predicting content from visual clues

a Focus on the instructions. In pairs or as a whole class, Sts use the headline and the clues in the photo to try to predict what the article is about. Elicit some ideas, but don't tell Sts if they are correct.

b Give Sts time to read the article to check their answer to **a**. Point out the **Glossary** and go through it with the class. You might want to point out how the name *Goliath* is pronounced /gəˈlaɪəθ/.
  Check the answer. Sts might be interested to know that James Daunt removed the apostrophe from the shop name *Waterstone's* when he took over the chain, presumably to indicate that it didn't belong to Tim Waterstone any more!

EXTRA SUPPORT Before Sts read the article the first time, check whether you need to pre-teach any vocabulary, but not the highlighted words in **d**.

The article is about how bookseller James Daunt managed to stop a chain of high street bookshops called Waterstones closing down in spite of huge competition from the online retailer Amazon.

c Focus on 1–5 and go through them with the class.
  Give Sts time to read the article again and choose the correct option a–c for each question.
  Get Sts to compare with a partner, and then check answers.

1 a 2 b 3 c 4 b 5 a

  Deal with any other new vocabulary. Model and drill the pronunciation of any tricky words.

d Focus on the instructions and make sure Sts understand what they have to do. Encourage them to use the context of each extract to work out the missing word before checking back with the article.
  Get Sts to compare with a partner, and then check answers.

1 branches 2 back 3 loyal 4 cut 5 stocks

EXTRA SUPPORT Get Sts to work in pairs.

e Do the question as a whole-class activity, or put Sts in pairs and get some feedback. You could have a class vote to see how many Sts agree with James Daunt.

EXTRA IDEA Ask Sts *How do you think other high street shops can attract back customers who are now shopping online?* and elicit ideas.

7 ▶ VIDEO LISTENING

This is the first of five **Video Listenings**, which are incorporated into the Student's Book. If you are unable to show the video in class, remind Sts that they can find the video on *Online Practice*, and ask them to watch the video and do the activities for homework.

a Do this as a whole-class activity. If you go to a local market, tell Sts about it.

! Don't elicit / explain what a farmers' market is yet as Sts will do this later.

b Tell Sts they are now going to watch a documentary about a farmers' market.
  Play the video once the whole way through for Sts to watch and answer the first question.
  Check the answer to the first question. Then ask Sts if they have similar markets in their country.

EXTRA SUPPORT Read through the script and decide if you need to pre-teach any new lexis before Sts watch the video.

Whereas a normal market sells a lot of products, a farmers' market sells locally produced food directly to the customers.

A farmers' market
Hi, I'm Louise. Today I'm at a farmers' market in Winchester, in the south of England.
There are now over seven hundred and fifty markets in Britain. Unlike normal shops, these markets move from place to place. They set up in each location at regular intervals. Some are weekly, some are fortnightly, and some are monthly.
At farmers' markets, producers can sell directly to customers. In an age of globalization and internet retailing, some people want to return to a simpler way of shopping. They like to touch and taste what they're buying. And, most importantly, they want to know where it comes from.
When you shop in the supermarket, it isn't always easy to find out who produces your meat, picks your fruit, or grows your vegetables. But at farmers' markets, customers buy directly from the producer, who can tell them all about the goods they sell.
Supermarkets also have a long supply chain. The food often has to travel from the producer to a distributor and a wholesaler before it reaches the supermarket shelf. This means food can often spend days in lorries and warehouses.
But at farmers' markets, there's no supply chain. It comes directly from the farm to the market. Producers sell it as soon as it's ready, so it's always fresh, organic, and tasty.

2B 37

Winchester Market is the largest regular farmers' market in the UK. It takes place twice a month, and it has around ninety stalls selling all kinds of food and drink. Bakers sell freshly baked bread and cakes; farmers sell meat, vegetables, and fruit; and beekeepers sell honey. There are lots of different stalls, and they sell everything from homemade meat pies to jams and sauces made from locally sourced ingredients.

The best part is that all this food comes from the local area. Winchester is in the county of Hampshire. All the businesses that have stalls at Hampshire farmers' markets must be based in the county or within fifteen kilometres of its borders. This is good news for customers. There's no middle-man, like a shop or a supermarket, so customers can find out anything they want to know about the product they're buying. It's also good for the local economy. The money stays in the area, and as these local businesses grow, they employ more local people.

This is Lyburn Farmhouse Cheesemakers. It's an excellent example of a local business which has benefited from these markets. They make all their produce in Salisbury, less than thirty miles away from here. Lyburn Farm is a family-run business. They milk their own cows and they use this milk to make their own cheese. Every morning the farm's cheesemakers collect the milk and separate it into curds and whey. When the curd is ready, they drain it, squeeze it, and put it into moulds. The next day they package the cheese and store it on the farm until it matures. At any one time, they have eight thousand cheeses maturing!

When the farm's cheese is ready, these employees bring it to markets like this, where they sell it directly to the customer. So this cheese comes straight from the farm. That's why it tastes so good! Everything about Lyburn Cheese is local. The employees work locally, the customers buy locally – even the cows are local!

This is why people come to farmers' markets. They want to support local producers and want to buy local produce. Here you know exactly what you're buying and where it's from. So more and more people are trying to use the supermarket less and buy fresh, locally produced food instead.

c Focus on the task and give Sts time to read sentences 1–10. Make sure they understand all the lexis, e.g. *fortnight*, *warehouse*, *to mature*, etc.

Put Sts in pairs to decide whether the missing information in each gap is a word or a number.

EXTRA SUPPORT Go through each sentence and elicit what Sts think is missing in each sentence before playing the video again.

d Now tell Sts they need to complete the gaps in **c** with the exact word or number. Play the video again the whole way through.

Get Sts to compare with a partner, and then check answers.

| 1 750 | 2 month | 3 producer | 4 lorries | 5 twice | 6 90 |
| 7 local | 8 family | 9 8,000 | 10 cows | | |

EXTRA SUPPORT You could get Sts to watch the video again with subtitles, so they can see exactly what they understood / didn't understand. Translate / Explain any new words or phrases.

e Do this as a whole-class activity.

1&2 Revise and Check

There are two pages of revision and consolidation after every two Files. These exercises can be done individually or in pairs, in class or at home, depending on the needs of your Sts and the class time available.

The first page revises the **grammar**, **vocabulary**, and **pronunciation** of the two Files. The exercises add up to 50 (grammar = 15, vocabulary = 25, pronunciation = 10), so you can use the first page as a mini-test on Files 1 and 2. The pronunciation section sends Sts to the Sound Bank on pp.166–167. Explain that this is a reference section of the book, where they can check the symbols and see common sound–spelling patterns for each of the sounds. Highlight the video showing the mouth position for each sound. If you don't want to use this in class, tell Sts to look at it at home and to practise making the sounds and saying the words.

The second page presents Sts with a series of skills-based challenges. First, there is a **reading** text which is of a slightly higher level than those in the File, but which revises grammar and vocabulary Sts have already learned. The **listening** is some unscripted street interviews, where people are asked questions related to the topics in the Files. Sts can either watch the interviews on video or listen to them on audio. You can find these on the *Teacher's Resource Centre*, *Classroom Presentation Tool*, *Class DVD*, and *Class Audio CDs* (audio only). Alternatively, you could set this section / activity as homework. Sts can find the video on *Online Practice*. Finally, there is a **speaking** challenge which assesses Sts' ability to use the language of the Files orally. You could get Sts to do these activities in pairs, or Sts can tick the boxes if they feel confident that they can do them.

More materials
For teachers
Teacher's Resource Centre
Video Can you understand these people? 1&2
Quick Test 2
File 2 Test
For students
Online Practice Check your progress

GRAMMAR

1 a 2 c 3 b 4 a 5 c 6 a 7 c 8 a 9 b 10 a
11 b 12 a 13 a 14 c 15 b

VOCABULARY

a 1 glamorous 2 considerate 3 reliable 4 sensible
   5 creative 6 suitable 7 luxurious 8 stressful 9 risky
   10 impressive
b 1 insect repellent 2 adaptor 3 toothpaste 4 pack
   5 swimsuit 6 driving licence 7 scissors 8 guidebook
c 1 butcher's 2 newsagent's 3 baker's 4 florist's
   5 chemist's 6 estate agent's 7 fishmonger's
   8 greengrocer's

PRONUNCIATION

c 1 ea**s**y /z/ 2 h**ea**dphones /e/ 3 sc**i**ssors /ɪ/
   4 **ch**emist's /k/ 5 st**a**ll /ɔː/
d 1 **i**nitials 2 **a**ffordable 3 l**u**xurious 4 **u**nderwear
   5 **fi**shmonger's

CAN YOU understand this text?

a Elephant & Castle and Piccadilly Circus
b 1 C 2 A 3 E 4 B 5 F

▶ CAN YOU understand these people?

1 a 2 c 3 b 4 b 5 c

🔊 **2.24**

1
I = interviewer, T = Tilly
I What's your name?
T My name's Tilly.
I Where does it come from?
T Um, it's actually short for Ottilie, which is spelled O-T-T-I-L-I-E, um, and I think it's Hungarian.
I Who chose your name?
T My dad.
I Would you like to change your name?
T I'm happy with my name, yeah, I quite like it.

2
I = interviewer, T = Tory
I What's the colour scheme of your bedroom?
T The colour scheme of my bedroom changes in dependence of my mood. Currently it's purple and white.
I Do you like it?
T Um, I stopped liking it once it was all sorted.
I Would you like to change it?
T All the time. But once I change it, then I'll want to change it again. It's a never-ending cycle.

3
I = interviewer, C = Claudia
I Are you good at packing when you go away?
C When I go away, I'm really good at packing because I don't pack a lot. I'm very efficient, I've moved a lot, I've travelled a lot, so I can pack lightly. It's always a very small carry…I like to travel with a carry-on, if I can.

4
I = interviewer, M = Maria
I Is there anything you only do when you're on holiday that you wouldn't do in everyday life?
C Um, when I'm on holiday, I usually go for more walks. So for example, after dinner, I would always go for a walk on holiday, but at home, I'd never do that. I'm always too tired, it's a bit cold in the UK, so, yeah, on holiday it's usually warmer and I'll go for walks after dinner.
I What's your favourite kind of holiday?
M My favourite kind of holiday, um, is somewhere warm, and somewhere that's, um, not too crowded and perhaps with some historical significance, a nice place to walk around. Um, I wouldn't like to go somewhere too, um, quiet.

5
I = interviewer, D = Diarmuid
I What sort of things do you buy online?
D I buy almost everything online these days, er, so clothes, um, all gadgets and equipment. Um, I don't buy food, but I know a lot of other people do.

3A Grow up!

- **G** past simple, past continuous, or *used to*?
- **V** stages of life
- **P** *-ed* endings, sentence rhythm

Lesson plan

The topic of this lesson is generational differences and stages of life.

In the first half, the focus is on adults and teenagers. Sts learn vocabulary to describe different stages of life. Then they read a newspaper article about when people feel that they are grown-ups. This is followed by a listening about the Mosquito Tone, a controversial sound which is used to keep teenagers away from certain areas. The first half of the lesson ends with Sts talking about at what age they did certain activities, such as learn to swim, and what age they think is the best for doing certain activities, e.g. having a baby.

The second half of the lesson begins with a grammar focus on three past forms: past simple, past continuous, and *used to*, which Sts revise and contrast through online posts about childhood. This leads into a pronunciation focus which revises the three different pronunciations of *-ed* endings. Sts then go on to practise sentence rhythm with the past forms presented in the grammar focus. The lesson ends with extended oral practice of the three past forms.

More materials
For teachers
Photocopiables
Grammar past simple, past continuous, or *used to*? p.156
Communicative When you were younger p.184 (instructions p.173)
For students
Workbook 3A
Online Practice 3A

OPTIONAL LEAD-IN (BOOKS CLOSED)
Write on the board MIDDLE-AGED and OLD.
Then do a class survey and ask Sts *How old is 'middle-aged'? How old is 'old'?* Have a class vote.

1 VOCABULARY stages of life

a Books open. Focus on the instructions and the photos. Give Sts time individually or in pairs to match the phrases to the photos.

b 🔊 **3.1** Play the audio for Sts to listen and check.

Check answers. Explain to Sts that a *toddler* is a child who has recently learned to walk (*toddle* = to walk in an unsteady way) and a *pre-teen* is someone who is not yet a teenager, e.g. a child of 11 or 12.

See script 3.1

🔊 **3.1**
6 He's a baby.
4 She's a toddler.
2 He's a child.
9 She's a pre-teen.
1 She's a teenager.
5 He's in his early twenties.
7 She's in her mid-thirties.
8 He's in his late forties.
3 She's retired.

Now play the audio again, pausing after each sentence for Sts to listen and repeat.

Next, focus on the **middle-aged, old, elderly** box and go through it with the class. You may want to tell Sts that the word *ancient* also exists, but it has a negative meaning (= very old and possibly incapacitated) when referring to a person, though it can also be used in a humorous sense.

EXTRA IDEA Give Sts more practice in using phrases like *in her early / mid- / late thirties*, e.g.:
T *a man, 48*   **Sts** *in his late forties*
T *a woman, 25*   **Sts** *in her mid-twenties*

c Focus on the task and go through the prompts, making sure Sts understand them. Model and drill any words your Sts find difficult to pronounce. Then focus on the example speech bubbles, and elicit the meaning of *any age* (= it doesn't matter what age).

Put Sts in pairs or small groups to discuss each item.

Get some feedback from the class. You could find out if Sts disagreed with each other about any of the items, or if they worked in small groups, all agreed on a stage of life for a particular prompt.

d Focus on the task and the example. Give Sts time to think of their three people.

Now put Sts in pairs and get them to tell each other about their three people. Monitor and help them with any new vocabulary they may need.

Get feedback from various pairs.

EXTRA SUPPORT Demonstrate the activity by telling Sts about three people you know.

2 READING read and retell

a Focus on the instructions and the cartoon. Now focus on the **grow up** box and go through it with the class. You could get Sts to look at the title of the lesson, *Grow up!*, and elicit / explain what it means (= used to tell somebody to stop behaving in a silly, juvenile way).

Do the question as a whole-class activity, and get Sts to explain their answers.

b Focus on the instructions and give Sts time to read the first paragraph.

Then get them to discuss the three questions with a partner.

Check answers.

EXTRA SUPPORT Before Sts read the article the first time, check whether you need to pre-teach any vocabulary.

1 11 years
2 You don't have children and live in your own house, and are not financially independent.
3 They both show that you're a grown-up.

Deal with any other new vocabulary. Model and drill the pronunciation of any tricky words.

c Tell Sts that they are now going to read two journalists' writing about feeling grown up. Put Sts in pairs, **A** and **B**. Tell them to go to **Communication A real grown-up?**, **A** on *p.107* and **B** on *p.111*.

Focus on the instructions. Sts **A** should read about Carol and complete the sentences in **a** whilst Sts **B** do the same for Hugo. Monitor and check how they are completing their sentences.

EXTRA SUPPORT Put two **A**s and **B**s together first to do **a**. Monitor and help if necessary. Then put Sts in pairs **A** and **B**.

Sts A (Carol)
1 does things that aren't very adult, for example **forgetting to charge her phone** and **being terrified of being in a bar or restaurant alone**.
2 thinks that the laws about being an adult are confusing because when you're 16, **you can work full-time, get married, and join the army,** but **you can't drive or buy an alcoholic drink**.
3 first felt like an adult when **she was driving alone in France in the middle of the night with a map and no phone**.
4 became a real grown-up when **her baby was in hospital**.

Sts B (Hugo)
1 thinks he must be an adult because he has **two kids, a mortgage, and a pension plan**.
2 thinks that it was clearer in the past when you became an adult because at 16 a boy **started wearing trousers instead of shorts, and left home to raise a family**.
3 says that adults now still do teenage things like **staying longer in the family home, finding it difficult to become financially independent, listening to pop music, and wearing T-shirts**.
4 says that having kids doesn't **make you feel like a grown-up**.
5 thinks that he will become a real grown-up when **he stops wanting a big night out once a month or four days a year at a music festival**.

When they are ready, Sts **A** should use their answers in **a** to tell Sts **B** about their texts. Then they swap roles.
Finally, Sts should decide who is more grown-up.
Elicit some opinions from the class.
Tell Sts to go back to the main lesson **3A**.

d Do this as a whole-class activity, or put Sts in pairs and then elicit ideas from various pairs. You could also tell the class if you have grown up yet.

3 LISTENING listening for detail

a Do this as a whole-class activity. Encourage Sts to explain their opinions and give examples.
b 🔊 **3.2** Tell Sts they are going to listen to **Part 1** of a local radio news report about teenagers.
Give Sts time to read questions 1–3.
Play the audio and pause just after the interviewer says, *Why don't we play the tone briefly now?*
Check the answer to question 1.

EXTRA SUPPORT Read through the scripts and decide if you need to pre-teach any new lexis before Sts listen.

1 It's a sound that only people under 25 can hear.

🔊 **3.2**
(script in Student's Book on *p.125*)
I = interviewer, M = Mark
Part 1
I Welcome back. Up next, age and the generation gap. We know how hard it can be to tell someone's age, but in fact it turns out there may be a way that's quite simple. It's called the 'Mosquito Tone Test', and Mark is here to tell us more.
M Thanks, Sue. The Mosquito Tone is a sound – a very high-pitched, very annoying sound, which is why it's named after the insect. What's interesting is that apparently as we age, we slowly lose our ability to hear this sound. According to scientists, almost everyone under the age of twenty-five can hear the Mosquito Tone, but almost no one over twenty-five can hear it!
I Really! Is that right?
M Yes. And to test this out, I actually played the tone for my family last night. My wife and I heard absolutely nothing at all, but our teenage daughters could hear it, and in fact they complained that it was an irritating sound that was quite painful to hear.
I Oh no! Well, at the risk of irritating some of our younger listeners' ears, why don't we play the tone briefly now?
M OK, here goes. I'm playing the tone in three, two, one…
I Have you played the tone yet?
M I just did. Or, at least, I think I did.
I Well, I suppose that just confirms that neither of us are under twenty-five!

Now play the rest of the audio and check the answers to questions 2 and 3. Find out which Sts could hear it. Ask those who said they could if they are under 25, and how the sound made them feel.

2 No, neither of them could hear it.

c 🔊 **3.3** Focus on the task and make sure Sts understand the expression *in favour of*.
Play the audio once the whole way through for Sts to listen to **Part 2** and answer the questions in pairs.
Check answers.

It's being used in shopping centres to keep teenage gangs away. Not everybody is in favour of it; some people are against it.

🔊 **3.3**
(script in Student's Book on *p.125*)
Part 2
I Now, Mark, apart from testing a person's age, what is the Mosquito Tone being used for?
M This has actually become an interesting controversy. Because the sound is so annoying, and because only the young can hear it, the Mosquito Tone is being used to keep teenagers away from certain places.
I What kinds of places?
M Well, for example, from shopping centres. As you know, in some towns you get large groups of young people hanging around shopping centres and causing trouble. And some shop owners say that these gangs can annoy other customers or frighten them away, which is obviously not good for business. So now these centres can play the Mosquito Tone over their audio system, and the groups of teenagers will feel uncomfortable and leave the area. But, of course, the sound won't annoy the other customers at all, as they don't hear it.
I Have you spoken to any of these shop owners?

3A 41

M Yes, I have, and they said that the Mosquito Tone has worked very well for them. And they also said that although it's true that the Mosquito Tone is certainly very annoying, it doesn't hurt the teenagers.
I It sounds like rather a good idea to me. But you said this was a controversy. Who's against it?
M Well, there are some groups of people who are trying to ban the Mosquito Tone. They've pointed out a number of problems with it. Firstly, they worry that the sound really is harmful, but more to the point, they say that the Mosquito Tone affects all young people, some of whom are well-behaved and just want to go shopping. And finally, they say that the Mosquito Tone doesn't actually stop the problem of teenage gangs; it just drives them from one place to another.
I Those do seem like good points.
M Yes, indeed. And there's also an interesting twist. Some teenagers have discovered an advantage to the Mosquito Tone.
I Oh yes?
M Well, the Mosquito Tone has also been released as a ringtone for your mobile. So in secondary schools that don't permit mobile phones, teens can use their phones in class. They can receive calls and messages during lessons and teachers don't have any idea what is happening.
I Because the teacher can't hear it! That must really annoy them.
M That's right. And if they can't hear it, they can't…

d Focus on the task and give Sts time to read items 1–5.
Play **Part 2** of the audio again for Sts to listen and answer the questions.
Get Sts to compare with a partner, and play the audio once more if necessary.
Check answers.

1 They cause trouble, annoy other customers, and frighten them away.
2 They say it has worked very well for them, and that it doesn't hurt the teenagers.
3 Because they worry that the sound might be harmful, and because it affects all teenagers, not just gangs.
4 It just makes teenagers go somewhere else.
5 They are using it as a ringtone for their phones at school.

EXTRA SUPPORT If there's time, you could get Sts to listen again with the scripts on *p.125*, so they can see exactly what they understood / didn't understand. Translate / Explain any new words or phrases.

e Do the question as a whole-class activity. Encourage Sts to give reasons to justify what they say.

4 SPEAKING

a Focus on the questions and make sure Sts know what a *nursery school* is. If Father Christmas is not traditional where you are teaching, replace it with a local example, e.g. in Spain *The Three Kings*.
Give Sts time to write the age at which they did each one. If Sts can't remember, tell them to guess the approximate age.
Now put Sts in small groups and get them to compare their answers.
Get some feedback from different groups.

b In their groups, Sts now discuss what they think is the best age to do certain activities.
Monitor and help if necessary.
Get some feedback from different groups. Find out if Sts disagreed strongly about any of the situations.

5 GRAMMAR past simple, past continuous, or *used to*?

a Focus on the task and list of adjectives. Make sure Sts understand them all, and model and drill pronunciation where necessary.
Give Sts time to choose two adjectives from the list in answer to the question and then think of another.
Now put Sts in pairs and get them to compare their answers. Tell them to explain their choices.
Get some feedback from various pairs, and tell them what you were like.

b Focus on the task and the title of the forum, *What kind of child were you…and have you changed?*
Tell Sts to read the four posts and answer the questions. Tell them not to worry about the options in the highlighted phrases.
Get Sts to compare with a partner, and then check answers.

1 Alex 2 David 3 Stephen 4 Magda

c Put Sts in pairs and tell them to circle the correct form of the highlighted verbs in the posts. They should tick the phrases if they are both correct.
Check answers.

1 used to like 2 ✓ 3 was holding 4 started
5 used to have 6 went 7 ✓ 8 always hated

EXTRA CHALLENGE Get Sts, in pairs, to discuss why one form is correct and the other not. Check answers.

1 You can't use the continuous form with a non-action verb (here *like*).
3 It was a long action that happened in the past.
4 It was a short action that happened and finished in the past. She started university on one occasion.
5 You can't use the continuous form with a non-action verb (here *have*).
6 The action isn't repeated. The mother only went into hospital once, not several times in the past.
8 You can't use the continuous form with a non-action verb (here *hate*).

d Tell Sts to go to **Grammar Bank 3A** on *p.136*.

Grammar notes
Past simple, past continuous, or *used to*?
Students at this level will have practised narrative tenses (past simple, past continuous, and past perfect) before, but here they contrast the past simple and continuous with *used to*. Sts often confuse these forms or use them incorrectly because they do not correspond exactly to equivalent forms in their L1. For instance, they use the past continuous to refer to a past habit or repeated past action, e.g. *I was living in Madrid when I was a child*.

Focus on **Revise the basics**. Go through the example sentences and use them to elicit the rules, e.g. in 1 that *was* is the past of *is*, and that we add (*e*)*d* to regular verbs to form the past tense.

Now focus on the example sentences for **past simple and past continuous** and play audio 🔊 **3.4** for Sts to listen and repeat. Encourage them to copy the rhythm. Then go through the rules with the class.

Repeat for **used to and past simple** 🔊 **3.5**. Remind Sts also how *used to* is linked and pronounced /ˈjuːst tə/.

Refer Sts to the **Irregular verbs** list on *p.165* and explain that this is their reference list. Get Sts to go through the list quickly in pairs, checking that they know what the verbs mean. Encourage them to highlight verbs they didn't know or whose past forms they had forgotten. Test the class or get Sts to test each other.

Tell Sts to go back to *p.136*.

Now focus on the exercises and get Sts to do them individually or in pairs.

Check answers, getting Sts to read the full sentences.

a
1 ✓ 2 ✗ did they get 3 ✗ I was working 4 ✓
5 ✗ I travelled 6 ✗ didn't use to get on 7 ✗ never studied
8 ✓ 9 ✗ I was watching 10 ✓

b
1 They **were already having** dinner when I **arrived**.
2 When we were young, our parents **used to take / took** us to the beach every weekend.
3 We **were still packing** when the taxi **came**.
4 **Did** your brother **teach** you to play the guitar when you were young?
5 When I was a child, I **didn't use to like / didn't like** vegetables.
6 He **used to have / had** a beard when he **was** at university.
7 We **used to spend / spent** all day playing together when we **were** children.
8 He **was talking** on his phone when the police **stopped** him.
9 I **went** to a boarding school for two years, from the age of 13 to 15.
10 They **didn't use to have / didn't have** a car when I first **knew** them.

Tell Sts to go back to the main lesson **3A**.

EXTRA SUPPORT If you think Sts need more practice, you may want to give them the **Grammar** photocopiable activity at this point.

e Focus on the instructions and then give Sts time to write their post.

Monitor and help with vocabulary if necessary. Correct any mistakes with the past simple, past continuous, or *used to*.

EXTRA IDEA Tell Sts not to write their names on their posts. Then collect all the posts and number them. Display them around the classroom. Sts should read each post and guess which classmate wrote it.

6 PRONUNCIATION -ed endings, sentence rhythm

Pronunciation notes

Sts at this level should be aware that the regular past simple ending *-ed* can be pronounced in three different ways, but they will probably still be making mistakes and will benefit from being reminded of the rules:

1 *-ed* is pronounced /t/ after verbs ending in these unvoiced sounds: /p/, /k/, /f/, /θ/, /s/, /ʃ/, and /tʃ/, e.g. *hoped, liked, laughed, washed,* etc.
2 *-ed* is pronounced /d/ after verbs ending in vowels or in voiced sounds, e.g. *enjoyed, played, tried, changed, showed, named, smiled,* etc. This group is the largest.
3 *-ed* is pronounced /ɪd/ after verbs ending in the sounds /t/ or /d/, e.g. *started, wanted, ended, decided,* etc.

a 🔊 **3.6** Focus on the sound pictures and remind Sts of the three different pronunciations of the *-ed* ending.

Play the audio once the whole way through for Sts just to listen.

🔊 **3.6**
See sentences in Student's Book on *p.28*

Now play the audio again, pausing after each pair of sentences for Sts to listen and repeat.

Finally, repeat the activity, eliciting responses from individual Sts.

EXTRA SUPPORT If these sounds are difficult for your Sts, it will help to show them the mouth position. You could model this yourself or use the Sound Bank videos on the *Teacher's Resource Centre*.

b 🔊 **3.7** Focus on the task. Give Sts time to read sentences 1–6 and decide if the *-ed* ending in the verbs is pronounced /t/, /d/, or /ɪd/.

Play the audio once the whole way through for Sts just to listen.

🔊 **3.7**
See sentences in Student's Book on *p.28*

Now play the audio again, pausing after each sentence to give Sts time to tick the correct box.

Get them to compare with a partner, and then check answers.

1 /ɪd/ 2 /t/ 3 /d/ 4 /d/ 5 /t/ 6 /ɪd/

EXTRA CHALLENGE Get Sts to tick the correct box in each sentence before they listen to the audio.

c Give Sts time to practise saying the sentences in **b**.

EXTRA SUPPORT Remind Sts that the most important rule is to not pronounce the *-ed* as /ɪd/, except after /t/ and /d/. Play the audio again, pausing after each sentence for Sts to listen and repeat.

3A

d **3.8** Go through the **Past or present?** box with Sts. Give examples of when the /t/ or /d/ pronunciation of the -ed ending can be hard to hear, i.e. when the next word begins with a consonant sound, e.g. *We liked them / We like them* or *They played badly / They play badly*.

Focus on the task and play the audio once the whole way through for Sts just to listen.

Now play the audio again, pausing after each sentence to give Sts time to write.

Get them to compare with a partner, and then check answers. Ask Sts to tell you which words helped them to understand if the sentences were past or present, e.g. *last summer*.

1 Past 2 Present 3 Past 4 Past 5 Present 6 Present

3.8
1 I worked as a waiter last summer.
2 We often play video games on Saturday evenings.
3 We lived in America for six months.
4 I watched too much TV last night.
5 I usually cook at weekends.
6 I look like my sister.

EXTRA SUPPORT First, elicit if each sentence is present or past. Then elicit the sentence onto the board.

e **3.9** Focus on the instructions.

Play the audio once the whole way through for Sts just to listen and to focus on the rhythm.

Ask Sts what kind of words are stressed and unstressed. Point out the **bold** words in the sentences.

Content words like verbs, nouns, and adjectives are usually stressed.
Prepositions, pronouns, and auxiliary verbs are usually unstressed.

3.9
See sentences in Student's Book on *p.28*

Now play the audio again, pausing after each line for Sts to listen and repeat.

Finally, put Sts in pairs and get them to practise the sentences.

7 SPEAKING

Focus on the three sections in the task and elicit / explain the meaning of *event* (= sth important that happens in your life) and *incident* (= sth unusual or unpleasant that happens).

Now focus on the *Events in your life* section. Tell Sts to think what the missing words might be, but not to write them in, as they should be able to produce them orally.

Check answers.

1 Where **were** you born?
  Where **did** you **live** when you **were** a child?
2 How old **were** you when you **started** primary school?
  Did you **enjoy** your first day?
  What **did** you **do**?
3 When **was** the first time you **travelled** abroad?
  Where **did** you **go**?

Now focus on the instructions and the example speech bubbles. Sts take it in turns to ask and answer the questions, using their own information. Tell them to answer with full sentences as much as possible.

Monitor to check they are pronouncing the past simple -ed endings correctly and using the correct sentence rhythm.

Next, focus on the instructions and example speech bubble for the *When you were younger* section. Go through the six statements and make sure Sts understand what they have to do. Stress that they should answer with full sentences and give as much information as they can. Encourage Sts to interact by asking each other questions.

Finally, focus on the instructions in *An incident in your childhood*. Give Sts time to choose one of the topics.

Focus on the example speech bubble. Then, in pairs, Sts take turns to describe the incident.

Monitor and help, encouraging Sts to get the sentence rhythm correct.

EXTRA IDEA You could get Sts to change partners for each section.

Get some feedback from the class for each section.

EXTRA SUPPORT Demonstrate the activity by answering some of the questions yourself in the first two sections, and then telling Sts about an incident in your childhood.

3B Photo albums

G prepositions
V photography
P word stress

Lesson plan

The topic of this lesson is photography. It begins with a vocabulary focus which includes useful phrases for describing photos and language related to taking photos. This leads into a pronunciation focus on word stress in words from the root word *photograph* and other multi-syllabic words. Next, Sts listen to an interview with a professional photographer who gives some tips on how to take good photos with a phone. In Speaking, Sts talk about their own preferences when taking photos and what they do with the results. Sts then write their own tips in an article on how to do something.

The second half of the lesson begins with a grammar focus on prepositions of place and movement, and dependent prepositions after verbs and adjectives. Sts then listen to people describing a holiday photo, before talking about a photo they took whilst on holiday. Finally, Sts read an article about storing digital photos safely, with some surprising revelations about why digital photos may not be as safe as we think they are. Before you get to this final stage, ask Sts to bring in a favourite holiday photo to the next class.

More materials
For teachers
Photocopiables
Grammar prepositions *p.157*
Communicative What's the preposition? *p.185* (instructions *p.173*)
Vocabulary Photography *p.209* (instructions *p.202*)
For students
Workbook 3B
Online Practice 3B

OPTIONAL LEAD-IN (BOOKS CLOSED)
Write on the board SELFIE and SELFIE STICK, and elicit / explain what they both are.
Then ask the class if they take a lot of selfies and why (not), and also if they ever use a selfie stick.
Finally, ask why they think people like taking selfies so much.

1 VOCABULARY photography

a Books open. Focus on the photo and elicit where it was taken. <u>Don't</u> tell Sts if they are correct.

b Focus on the title and, if you didn't do the **Optional lead-in**, elicit / explain what a *selfie* is (= a photo of yourself that you take).
Now tell Sts to read the article to quickly check their answer in **a**, and to answer the question. Tell them not to worry about the numbered highlighted options in the article.
Check answers.

a It was taken in Rio de Janeiro in Brazil.
b Because people are risking their lives to take the ultimate selfie.

c Tell Sts to read the article again and this time to circle the correct answer in the highlighted words or phrases.
Get Sts to compare with a partner, and then check answers.

1 taking   2 take   3 in the background   4 on top of

d Tell Sts to go to **Vocabulary Bank** Photography on *p.155*.

Vocabulary notes
Describing a photo
Check that Sts understand the difference between *opposite* and *in front of*, and between *foreground* and *background*.
You might want to highlight that *in the background* means behind the main objects, people, etc. in the photo, whereas *in the distance* means far away but still able to be seen.

Taking photos
Point out that the *subject* of a photo is the main person or thing you are photographing, and the *settings* are the positions for the controls on the camera.
You may want to explain that you can set a camera to a *landscape* position – one that's wider than it is high – or just hold the camera the other way round. Sts might have across the terms *landscape* and *portrait* when using computer software such as Word, so you might want to explain / elicit the difference:
portrait = printed so that the top of the page is one of the shorter sides
landscape = printed so that the top of the page is one of the longer sides
You may also want to point out that *zoom* can be used as a noun to describe the lens some photographers use for this function.

Focus on **1 Describing a photo** and go through the **on top of** or **at the top of** box with the class. Make sure Sts understand the difference in meaning.
Now tell Sts to do **a** individually or in pairs.
🔊 **3.10** Now do **b**. Play the audio for Sts to listen and check.
Check answers.

🔊 **3.10**
Photography
1 Describing a photo
Photo 1
1 **In the background**, there's a mountain and some low cloud.
2 **In the bottom right-hand corner**, there's a grandmother and three children.
3 The boy in an orange T-shirt is standing **in front of** his grandmother.
4 **In the centre** of the photo, there's a building with lots of steps.
5 There's a small building that looks like a temple **on top of** a small hill.

3B 45

Photo 2

6 **In the foreground**, there's a woman standing on a terrace looking at the view.
7 The woman is standing **behind** a low wall.
8 **Opposite** the woman, there's a building with a tower that looks like a church.
9 **In the distance**, on the right, you can just see the top of an old building which looks like a ruin.
10 **In the top left-hand corner**, there are some trees.

Now either use the audio to drill the pronunciation of the sentences, or model and drill them yourself. Give further practice of any words your Sts find difficult to pronounce.

Now do **Activation** and tell Sts to cover sentences 1–10, look at the photos, and describe them.

Now focus on **2 Taking photos** and get Sts to do **a** individually or in pairs.

🔊 **3.11** Now do **b**. Play the audio for Sts to listen and check.

Check answers.

🔊 **3.11**
2 Taking photos
1 e You use flash when you want to take a photo somewhere dark, for example indoors or at night.
2 a You zoom in when you're far away from something and you want to take a close-up of it.
3 g A photo can be out of focus if your camera isn't automatic and you haven't used the right settings.
4 d Many cameras have a portrait setting to use when you want to take a photo of a person.
5 c A photo can be overexposed if there's too much light on the subject when you're taking it.
6 b With good cameras, you can use different lenses, for example a wide-angle lens when you want to take a photo of a landscape, but you can't get all of it in.
7 f You edit a photo when you change the size, colour, or brightness.

Now do **Activation** and tell Sts to cover a–g, look at 1–7, and try to remember the rest of the sentences.

Tell Sts to go back to the main lesson **3B**.

EXTRA SUPPORT If you think Sts need more practice, you may want to give them the **Vocabulary** photocopiable activity at this point.

e Do this as a whole-class activity. You could demonstrate the activity by answering the two questions first.

2 PRONUNCIATION word stress

Pronunciation notes

Word stress can be difficult to perceive, especially if an English word is similar to the equivalent word in the Sts' L1 but is stressed differently. Remind Sts to underline the stressed syllable when they write down any new multi-syllable words.

a 🔊 **3.12** Focus on the words beginning with *photo*. Check that Sts know the meaning of *photogenic* (= sb who looks good in photographs) and *photoshop* (= change a photo using a computer). Get Sts to underline the stressed syllable in each word.

Play the audio for Sts to listen and check.

Check answers by writing the words on the board and underlining the stressed syllable.

🔊 **3.12**
1 <u>pho</u>to
2 <u>pho</u>tograph
3 pho<u>to</u>grapher
4 pho<u>to</u>graphy
5 photo<u>gra</u>phic
6 photo<u>ge</u>nic
7 <u>pho</u>toshop

EXTRA CHALLENGE Get Sts to tell you where each word is stressed before playing the audio.

Get Sts to practise saying the words, focusing on the stress.

EXTRA SUPPORT Play the audio again, pausing after each word for Sts to listen and repeat.

b Focus on the sentences and get Sts to underline the stressed syllable in each of the **bold** multi-syllable words.

c 🔊 **3.13** Play the audio for Sts to listen and check.

Check answers by writing the words on the board and underlining the stressed syllable.

1 <u>back</u>ground 2 <u>fore</u>ground 3 <u>dis</u>tance
4 be<u>hind</u> 5 <u>bot</u>tom, <u>cor</u>ner

🔊 **3.13**
See sentences in Student's Book on *p.30*

Give Sts time to practise saying the sentences.

EXTRA SUPPORT Play the audio again, pausing after each sentence for Sts to listen and repeat.

d Put Sts in pairs, **A** and **B**, and tell them to go to **Communication Spot the differences**, **A** on *p.107*, **B** on *p.112*.

Go through the instructions and the example with the class carefully.

Get Sts to sit face-to-face, and take turns to describe their pictures without looking at their partner's picture.

Monitor and help, correcting any mistakes with the vocabulary they have just learned.

When Sts have found all nine differences, tell them to compare pictures to see if they have correctly identified the differences.

Check answers.

1 A There's a hotel in the background.
  B There's a tower in the background.
2 A There's a man playing the guitar in the middle of the picture.
  B The man is taking a photo.
3 A There's a man riding a bike.
  B The man is walking with the bike.
4 A The woman is drinking a coffee.
  B She's eating something.
5 A The woman's bag is on the table.
  B Her bag is under the table.
6 A The waiter is walking away from the table.
  B The waiter is walking towards the table.
7 A There are some birds / pigeons on the fountain.
  B There aren't any birds on the fountain.
8 A The dog is standing on the steps, looking up at the fountain.
  B The dog is walking down the steps, away from the fountain.

9 **A** The man in the bottom right-hand corner is taking a photo.
  B The man in the bottom right-hand corner is playing the guitar.

Tell Sts to go back to the main lesson **3B**.

3 LISTENING understanding advice

a Put Sts in pairs to discuss the questions.
Get some feedback from various pairs.

EXTRA SUPPORT Demonstrate the activity by answering the questions first.

b Focus on the task. You could either get Sts to read about Darja Bilyk on their own or you could read it to the class, explaining / eliciting the meaning of *atmosphere* (= a feeling in a particular place or situation) and *mood* (= the way people feel at a particular time). Model and drill pronunciation.

Give Sts time to do the matching task and choose their favourite photo.

Check answers, eliciting what a *still life* is (= a photo of objects such as flowers, fruit, etc.).

1 A **2** E **3** C **4** D **5** B

Ask individual Sts which photo is their favourite and why. If you have a favourite, you could tell the class.

EXTRA IDEA Put Sts in pairs and get them to describe the photos, using language from **Vocabulary Bank Photography**.

c 🔊 **3.14** Focus on the instructions and give Sts time to read the ten tips, making sure they understand all the lexis, e.g. *to stick to* (= continue using the same style without changing), *unique*, etc.

❗ The term *grid* is explained in the audio.

Play the audio once the whole way through for Sts to listen and number the tips in the correct order.

Get Sts to compare with a partner, and then play the audio again if necessary.

Check answers.

EXTRA SUPPORT Read through the script and decide if you need to pre-teach any new lexis before Sts listen.

1 Be ready.
2 Don't think twice.
3 Learn about your phone camera.
4 Don't use zoom.
5 Light is important.
6 Use the grid.
7 Choose unique angles.
8 Don't stick to one style.
9 Select and edit.
10 Make your pictures come alive.

🔊 **3.14**
(script in Student's Book on *p.126*)
D = Darja, N = narrator
D You don't need expensive photographic equipment to take amazing photos. The camera on your phone can be just as good. Here are my top ten tips for taking great photos on your phone.
N Tip one.
D Be ready. It may be an obvious thing to say, but remember to charge your phone and to keep your lens clean. I carry a charger with me most of the time. Also, keep your phone in your hand, not in your bag. I always keep my phone in camera mode so that when I unlock it, it's ready to take pictures.
N Tip two.
D Don't think twice. Take photos whenever you want and of whatever you want! There's nothing to lose. Some moments will never be repeated. If you don't like your picture, you can always delete it, but you can't turn back time.
N Tip three.
D Learn about your phone camera. Read your phone manual, and make sure you're using your camera in the best way. Sometimes little tips can really help you to improve your photos. Learn how you can control the exposure or focus on the objects better. Know the strengths and weaknesses of your phone camera. My iPhone isn't good at night photography, so I try to only use it in the daytime.
N Tip four.
D Don't use zoom. Don't forget that this is just a phone. It does not work like a camera with a DSLR lens. If you want to take a close-up of something, use your legs and move nearer!
N Tip five.
D Light is important. Good photography is all about using light well. Even the most boring composition will be saved by good use of light, whether it's day or evening.
N Tip six.
D Use the grid. Imagine your picture is divided into nine equal squares. This is called 'the grid'. The important parts of your photo should be positioned where the lines cross. Learn to use the grid, and then, just as importantly, learn to do without it.
N Tip seven.
D Choose unique angles. Try looking at objects from a new perspective. Take a picture from the dog's view!
N Tip eight.
D Don't stick to one style. A lot of people nowadays try to take photos in the same style or colours. Don't do this! Show your creativity. Take any photos you like – landscapes, portraits, or unusual compositions. Your own unique style will develop.
N Tip nine.
D Select and edit. Be selective! Choose only your best pictures and then edit those. There are many apps that will help you to do this. But remember that sometimes a picture can be better without any filters.
N Tip ten.
D Make your pictures come alive. Print your pictures, send them as postcards, give them to your friends, and hang them on your walls. Holding your photos in your hands is such a lovely feeling – much nicer than looking at them on a screen.

d Tell Sts they are going to listen to the tips again and this time they must complete the advice in 1–10.

Give Sts time to read 1–10.

You could tell Sts that the pieces of advice follow the order of the tips on the audio. Play the audio again, pausing after each tip to give Sts time to write.

Get Sts to compare with a partner, and then check answers.

1 camera **2** delete **3** strengths, weaknesses
4 close-up **5** light **6** without **7** dog's
8 style **9** apps **10** screen

EXTRA SUPPORT If there's time, you could get Sts to listen again with the script on *p.126*, so they can see exactly what they understood / didn't understand. Translate / Explain any new words or phrases.

e Do this as a whole-class activity, or put Sts in pairs and then get some feedback from various pairs.

You could tell Sts that there are more of Darja's photos on her website if they are interested.

3B 47

4 SPEAKING & WRITING an article

a Focus on the task. Go through the questions, making sure Sts understand *panoramic* (= a view of a wide area), *slo-mo* (= slow motion), etc. You might want to tell Sts that *scenery* and *landscape* have the same meaning, but *scenery* is uncountable.

Put Sts in pairs and get them to discuss the questions.

Get some feedback from various pairs.

b Tell Sts to go to **Writing An article** on *p.117*.

Focus on the task in **a** and give Sts time to look at the three photos. Tell them not to read the text yet.

Elicit some opinions from the class.

Focus on the instructions in **b** and go through the headings, making sure Sts understand them.

Give Sts time to read the article and to match the headings to the paragraphs. Remind them there are two extra headings they don't need to use.

Get Sts to compare with a partner, and then check answers.

1 Don't look at me!
2 Don't make them pose
3 Try different angles

Focus on **c** and get Sts to answer the questions in pairs, small groups, or as a whole-class activity.

Get some feedback.

Focus on **d** and the **Useful language: tips and instructions** box and go through it with the class.

Put Sts in pairs and tell them to choose which topic they want to write three tips about.

Tell Sts to think of a heading for each tip and then to plan the content. Remind them to use the **Useful language**.

For **e**, you may like to get Sts to do the writing individually in class or you could set it as homework. If you do it in class, set a time limit for Sts to write their article, e.g. 15–20 minutes.

Finally, in **f**, Sts should check their article for mistakes before giving it in.

Tell Sts to go back to the main lesson **3B**.

5 GRAMMAR prepositions

a Focus on the photo with the text and tell Sts or elicit that it shows the Great Wall of China and that it was taken from a plane.

Now focus on the task and tell Sts to read the text quickly. Then in pairs, Sts complete the gaps with prepositions from the list.

b 🔊 **3.15** Play the audio for Sts to listen and check.

Check answers. Highlight the expression *It reminds me of…* (= it makes me remember) and tell Sts this is very common when you are talking about a favourite photo. You might also want to point out that the speaker uses the word *photograph*, not *photo*, as in American English the abbreviation is never used.

1 over 2 to 3 next to 4 at 5 of 6 in 7 at 8 of

🔊 **3.15**
I took this photograph when we were flying over the Great Wall of China – I was going back to the USA after a holiday in Beijing. I was sitting next to the window, so I had a great view. I'm not usually very good at taking photographs, but I'm quite proud of this one. It was a long flight, and by the time we finally arrived home in Washington, DC, I was exhausted. But when I look at this photograph, it reminds me of the fantastic trip I had to China.

EXTRA IDEA Ask Sts the following questions (elicit the answers in brackets) or write them on the board:

Which preposition shows where a person or thing is? (3 next to)
Which prepositions show where a person or thing is moving? (1 over, 2 to)
Which prepositions are examples of prepositions used after certain verbs? (6 in – after *arrived*, 7 at – after *look*, 8 of – after *remind*)
Which prepositions are examples of prepositions used after certain adjectives? (4 at – after *good*, 5 of – after *proud*)

c Tell Sts to go to **Grammar Bank 3B** on *p.137*.

Grammar notes
Prepositions

English prepositions are usually a problem area for Sts because they frequently do not correspond to prepositions in Sts' L1.

Prepositions of place and movement

This should be revision, but will be needed for many Sts, particularly in the case of prepositions of movement. This is because movement is expressed by a single verb in many languages, not a verb of movement plus a preposition.

Dependent prepositions after verbs and adjectives

These are often hard to remember. This is because in many cases the prepositions have no central meaning, which makes it all the more difficult for Sts to remember which ones to use. Remind Sts to record verbs and adjectives with dependent prepositions when they meet them, e.g. *depend on* or *proud of* rather than just *depend* or *proud*. There are also cases where verbs take a preposition in Sts' L1, but not in English, which can also lead to them inserting unnecessary prepositions, e.g. ~~I need to call to my friend~~.

Focus on the example sentences for **prepositions of place** and play audio 🔊 **3.16** for Sts to listen and repeat. Encourage them to copy the rhythm, reminding them that prepositions are not normally stressed unless they come at the end of a sentence or question. Then go through the rules with the class.

Repeat for **prepositions of movement** 🔊 **3.17** and **dependent prepositions after verbs and adjectives** 🔊 **3.18**.

Finally, focus on the information box and go through it with the class.

Refer Sts to the **Dependent prepositions** list on *p.164* and explain that this is their reference list of prepositions after verbs and of prepositions after adjectives. Get Sts to go through the list quickly, checking that they know what the expressions mean.

Tell Sts to go back to *p.137*.

Now focus on the exercises and get Sts to do them individually or in pairs.

Check answers, getting Sts to read the full sentences.

a
1 across 2 into 3 onto 4 between 5 round 6 on
7 off 8 under 9 into 10 next to 11 in 12 towards

b
1 I'm tired **of** all this work – I'm ready **for** a holiday!
2 I'm not looking forward **to** apologizing **for** what happened.
3 He's very proud **of** his new phone.
4 We need to discuss the problems with our IT department.
5 Mum! Josh won't share his sweets **with** me!
6 You can't always rely **on** the buses – they're often late.
7 I don't know what you're talking **about**.
8 The pilot told us not to worry **about** the turbulence.
9 Who's responsible **for** updating the website?
10 Let's not argue **about** it now – let's wait **for** the boss to get here.
11 Sarah married Anthony in July this year.
12 I'm interested **in** photography, but I'm not very good **at** taking photographs!

Tell Sts to go back to the main lesson **3B**.

EXTRA SUPPORT If you think Sts need more practice, you may want to give them the **Grammar** photocopiable activity at this point.

d Focus on the instructions and 1–10. Get Sts to complete the gaps individually.

Check answers.

1 of 2 to 3 to 4 for 5 with 6 over 7 on 8 on
9 for 10 up

Now tell Sts to choose four of the topics they want to tell their partner about.

Put Sts in pairs and tell them to give and ask for as much information as possible.

Monitor and help, correcting any mistakes with prepositions.

Get some feedback from various pairs.

EXTRA SUPPORT Write on the board: I'M GOING TO TELL YOU ABOUT…

Tell Sts to start each topic with this, and remind them to change *you* to *I*, *your* to *my*, etc.

6 LISTENING & SPEAKING

a 🔊 **3.19** Focus on the instructions and the three photos.

Play the audio once all the way through and get Sts to number the photos 1–3.

Get Sts to compare with a partner, and then check answers.

EXTRA SUPPORT Read through the script and decide if you need to pre-teach any new lexis before Sts listen.

A 3 B 2 C 1

Now ask Sts if all the photos were taken by the speakers.

No, Kate's photo (speaker 3) was not taken by her.

🔊 **3.19**
(script in Student's Book on *p.126*)
1 Chris
I took this photo last year when I was in Uganda. I was there working for three weeks with a charity, and before going back to London, the two friends I was working with and I decided to go and see the mountain gorillas which live in the rainforest on the border of Uganda. On the day of the trek, I was feeling very nervous because I wasn't sure whether I would manage it. I'm not very fit, and we basically had to walk up the mountain in the rainforest until we found the gorillas, which could take as long as five or six hours. Luckily, after two hours, just when I was wondering if I could carry on, we found them. The first gorilla we saw was this silverback, which is the large dominant male in the group. I couldn't believe my eyes – he was so close, only about a couple of metres away. I'll never forget that moment. We stayed with the gorillas for an hour, and then walked back down again. I love this photo because it reminds me of that moment, how proud and relieved I was to have got there, and probably the most amazing wildlife experience I've ever had. I keep it on my computer as my desktop background, and when I'm sitting working in rainy England, it reminds me of another world.

2 Tom
So, I took this photo in Australia, when I was visiting my girlfriend, Roz. She was studying out there for a year. It was taken in Byron Bay, which is the most easterly point of the Australian mainland. We were out walking along the beach, and in Byron, when the sun sets, it's a really special occasion. Lots of people go out onto the beach and watch the sun set over the bay, and so I took this photo just as the sun was setting. I really like the photo because I have some great memories of Byron Bay and Australia, because I'd been there before on my own, and I was really glad to go there with Roz. It was a really happy time of my life, and we were having a lovely holiday. And I like that you can see the silhouettes of people on the sand and in the water, and I love the way the light comes off the sea and sand. It's one of several photos, actually, from that trip, that we printed, and it's in a frame on a wall in our house.

3 Kate
This is a photo I really like. Me and my partner, David, were staying with friends who live on the edge of Dartmoor, a really wild and beautiful place in Devon, in the south-west of the UK. We had a big lunch, and then we all decided to walk up to the top of the hill behind their house. The weather wasn't very good on most of the walk – in fact, at one point it rained quite hard, but when we got to the top, the sun came out and there was a glorious blue sky, and we could see the most fantastic view of the countryside. We asked another walker up there to take the photo for us. That's me and David in the middle, in red and green, with our little black dog. I like this photo because it's so colourful and we all look really happy – it was just a lovely, memorable day. I have the photo on my phone and my iPad – at the moment, it's my Facebook profile photo.

---

b Focus on the task and give Sts time to read questions 1–5.

Play the audio again, pausing after each speaker to give Sts time to take notes.

Get Sts to compare with a partner, and then play the audio again if necessary.

Check answers.

Speaker 1 (Chris)
1 In Uganda. She took it.
2 With two friends
3 She was working for a charity there and they decided to go and see the mountain gorillas. After walking for two hours in the mountains, they had just found the gorillas.
4 It reminds her of the amazing experience.
5 She keeps it on her computer as her desktop background.

Speaker 2 (Tom)
1 Australia. He took it.
2 He was visiting his girlfriend Roz.
3 They were walking along a beach and the sun was setting.
4 Because he had great memories of that place, and he likes the silhouettes and light on the sea and sand.
5 He has it printed and framed on a wall in their house.

Speaker 3 (Kate)
1 In Devon in the UK. Another walker took it.
2 With her partner and friends
3 They had just walked to the top of a hill. The weather had been really bad, but when they got to the top, the sun came out.
4 Because it's colourful and they all look happy
5 She has it as her Facebook profile (homepage) photo and it's on her phone and iPad.

EXTRA SUPPORT If there's time, you could get Sts to listen again with the script on *p.126*, so they can see exactly what they understood / didn't understand. Translate / Explain any new words or phrases.

c Focus on the instructions and give Sts time to think of a photo and their answers to 1–5 in **b**.

Put Sts in pairs and tell them to first describe the photo. If they have the photo on their phone, tell them to show it to their partner. When they have finished describing the photo, they should answer the five questions. Encourage Sts to ask their partners follow-up questions.

Monitor and help, but don't correct too much as the aim here is to encourage fluency.

EXTRA SUPPORT Before putting Sts in pairs, demonstrate the activity by showing the class an interesting photo you took on your last holiday and describing it.

d Most Sts nowadays have photos on their phones. Get Sts to show some to each other, explaining where they were taken, who the people are, etc.

7 READING understanding the main point in a paragraph

a Focus on the question and go through the options.
Then get Sts to tell each other what they usually do with their photos.
Get some feedback.

EXTRA SUPPORT Do this as a whole-class activity.

b Focus on the article and headings A–F, and make sure Sts understand them. Elicit / Explain the meanings of *come and go* and *obsolete* (= no longer used because sth new has been invented).

Now focus on the **Glossary** and go through it with the class.

Tell Sts to read the article and match the headings to paragraphs 1–5. Remind them that there is one extra heading.

Get Sts to compare with a partner, and then check answers.

EXTRA SUPPORT Before Sts read the article the first time, check whether you need to pre-teach any vocabulary, but not the **bold** verbs and phrases in **d**.

1 C   2 F   3 E   4 A   5 D

c Focus on the instructions. Get Sts to read the article again, and give them time, individually or in pairs, to match the storage methods to the problems.
Check answers.

1 c   2 a   3 b   4 e   5 f   6 d

d Focus on the **bold** words and phrases in 1–5 and tell Sts to match them to their meaning a–e.
Check answers, either explaining in English, translating into Sts' L1, or getting Sts to check in their dictionaries.

1 e   2 d   3 a   4 b   5 c

Deal with any other new vocabulary and encourage Sts to write down any useful new lexis from the article.

EXTRA CHALLENGE Put Sts in pairs. Tell them to cover meanings a–e and see if they can guess the meaning of the **bold** words and phrases from their context.

e Do this as a whole-class activity and elicit opinions.

EPISODE 2

Practical English All kinds of problems

Function renting a car; recording a voicemail greeting and leaving a message

Language *Automatic or manual? Would it be possible to leave the car at the airport?*, etc.

Lesson plan

In this second Practical English lesson, the functional focus is language used to rent a car.

The mystery develops. In the first scene, Henry is about to take Jenny to see his nephew Luke when he realizes the two front tyres of his car have been punctured. Jenny decides to take the bus to Luke's house in Oxford, hoping that Luke can solve the problem with the laptop and that she will be able to hire a car. In the next scene, Jenny goes to the car rental company. In the final scene, she returns to Henry's house to find that her missing suitcase has been returned with the padlock broken. Henry is not at home, and Jenny, feeling the effects of jet lag, falls asleep. She wakes up four hours later to the sound of a TV news report saying that Andrew Page, the man she'd met at the airport, has been attacked and is now in a critical condition. Meanwhile, Henry is still not at home, and Jenny, starting to worry, phones Rob.

More materials
For teachers
Teacher's Resource Centre
Video Practical English Episode 2
Quick Test 3
File 3 Test
For students
Workbook Practical English 2
Can you remember? 1–3
Online Practice Practical English 2
Check your progress

OPTIONAL LEAD-IN (BOOKS CLOSED)

Before starting Episode 2, elicit everything Sts can remember about Episode 1. Ask *Who's Jenny? Why is she visiting the UK? What problems is she having? Who's Henry? Who is watching them?*, etc.

Alternatively, you could play the last scene of Episode 1.

1 ▶ HENRY'S CAR

a 🔊 **3.20** Books open. Focus on the photos at the top and bottom of the column, and elicit who Sts think the people are and what they think is happening. <u>Don't</u> tell them if they are correct.

Now focus on the instructions and the questions.

Play the video / audio once the whole way through for Sts to watch or listen and answer the questions.

Check answers. Sts should understand that there is a problem with Henry's car, even if they don't know the exact words. Write HIS TYRES ARE FLAT / ARE PUNCTURED on the board, and model and drill the pronunciation.

EXTRA SUPPORT Before playing the video / audio, go through the listening scripts and decide if you need to pre-teach / check any lexis to help Sts when they listen.

> He wants to take her to his nephew Luke's house in Oxford.
> He can't because two of the tyres are flat / punctured.
> She's going to take the bus.

🔊 **3.20**
N = narrator, J = Jenny, H = Henry, L = Luke
N *Day two. Nine a.m. Jenny has come to the UK for work and a bit of holiday. She's staying with her father-in-law, Henry, outside Oxford. She had some problems on her first day – her suitcase didn't arrive, and her laptop isn't working for some reason. Henry says that Luke, Rob's cousin, who lives in Oxford, will be able to fix her laptop. While they are walking to Henry's car to drive to Luke's house, Jenny's phone rings.*
J Hello?…Yes, it is…Oh that's great news. Thank you…Later today? Great. Now I won't have to buy new clothes. Yeah, that's the right address. Bye.
H Good news?
J Great news! They found my suitcase, and they're bringing it over later today.
H Excellent. Right, I'll take you to my nephew's house so he can fix your computer.
J I'm looking forward to meeting Luke.
H You'll like him. He's a bright boy. Not that I understand a word he says.
J I bet he doesn't know much about Greek mythology, either!
H You're probably right.
N *Henry looks at one of the front wheels of his car.*
H That's funny.
J What's wrong?
H The tyre's flat.
J Do you have a spare?
H Well, yes, but it shouldn't be flat; it's new and…
N *He walks round and looks at the other front wheel.*
H Oh, I don't believe it!
J What is it?
H They're both flat! They've been punctured!
J What? Somebody did that on purpose? In the English countryside?
H You get vandals everywhere these days. Well, I'll just have to stay here and see if I can get the AA to bring out another spare tyre. I'll call you a taxi.
J Isn't there a bus I could catch?
H Well, there's a bus stop on the main road. You could get the bus to Oxford from there, I suppose.
J How do I get to the bus stop?
H The quickest way is the footpath at the back of the house.
J I think I'll do that, then.
H Are you sure you want to get the bus? How will you find Luke's house?
J You gave me the address. I can look it up on my phone if I get lost.
H Ah, yes, of course. But this is really inconvenient for you. You were going to borrow my car, weren't you?
J No, don't worry, Henry. I'd actually decided to rent a car, anyway. I'll need it for work, and it'll probably be cheaper to rent here than in London. I can get one while Luke is working his magic.
H Well, if you're absolutely sure. Just go to the back door and you'll see the path. Follow that – it takes you to the bus stop.
J OK. Oh, I'd like to cook dinner this evening to thank you for having me.
H You don't need to do that!
J I want to.
H Well, if you're sure. What time?
J How about seven o'clock?
H Great! And I'll keep my phone on in case you need me.

PE2 51

J See you later, Henry.
H Bye!
N Jenny leaves to catch the bus and Henry phones the Automobile Association. Suddenly, a dark car draws up in front of the house. The driver is a strange man he's never seen before.
H Who's that?
N Day two. Eleven a.m. Jenny finally arrives at Luke's house in Oxford.
J Luke?
L You must be Jenny. Hi.
J Nice to meet you.
L You too. Come in. Would you like some coffee? I've just made some…
J I'd love to, but I'm running a bit late. We had trouble with the car, and then the bus took forever. And I really need to get to a car rental place. I'm really sorry, but could I just leave the computer with you?
L Yeah, no problem.
J That's great. I feel awful just leaving it here like this.
L Honestly, don't worry about it.
J Are you sure?
L Yeah, it's cool. I love doing this kind of thing. I'll send you a text and let you know how I'm getting on.
J That's nice of you, Luke. Thanks. See you later.
L See you later.

b Point out the **Glossary** and the **British and American English** box and go through them with the class.

Focus on the instructions and give Sts time to read 1–8.

Now play the video / audio again, so Sts can watch or listen a second time and circle the correct answers. Pause as needed.

Check that Sts understand the meaning of *vandals* and *vandalize*.

Get Sts to compare with a partner, and then check answers.

1 has been found   2 will like Luke   3 has two flat tyres
4 vandals   5 knows   6 rent a car   7 make dinner for Henry   8 doesn't wait

Finally, focus on the last two questions and get Sts to discuss them in pairs or as a whole-class activity.

EXTRA SUPPORT If there's time and you are using the video, you could get Sts to watch again with subtitles, so they can see exactly what they understood / didn't understand. Translate / Explain any new words or phrases.

2 ▶ RENTING A CAR

a 🔊 **3.21** Focus on the photo and elicit where Jenny is (*at a car rental company*). Ask Sts what they think she is doing (*She's showing the assistant her driving licence*). Focus also on the TV screen, and elicit that the man whose face they can see is Andrew Page, the man who helped her at the airport.

Now tell Sts to focus on questions 1–3.

Play the video / audio once the whole way through for Sts to watch or listen.

Get Sts to answer the questions with a partner, and then check answers.

1 Nine days   2 A Vauxhall Corsa (*Vauxhall* is what this brand of cars is called in the UK; in many other countries it is called *Opel*)   3 At the airport

🔊 **3.21**
N = narrator, Ne = newsreader, A = assistant, J = Jenny
N Inside a car rentals shop, the assistant is watching the news on TV on the counter. On the TV screen, there is a photograph of Heathrow Airport and the headline 'Airport Assault'.
Ne The man found unconscious at Heathrow Airport yesterday has been named as Andrew Page, a research scientist from Oxford. Police believe he was attacked…
A Hello. Can I help you?
J Oh, hi. I'd like to rent a car, please.
A Have you hired from us before?
J No.
A OK, could I see your driving licence, please? Great. So, what kind of car are you looking for?
J Oh, nothing too big. It's just for me.
A OK, so a compact. Three-door?
J Yeah, that'll be fine.
A For how long?
J Nine days.
A Automatic or manual?
J An automatic, please.
A Any additional drivers?
J No, just me.
A Great. Well, we have several models I can show you, but I'd recommend the Vauxhall Corsa. It's sixty-five pounds per day, and that includes insurance.
J That sounds promising. Can I take a look?
A Of course, but first I'd like to run through some of the basics. The petrol tank is full when you start, so if you return it with a full tank, there's no extra charge.
J Great.
A But if you get any parking tickets or speeding fines, you have to pay for them yourself.
J Fair enough! Would it be possible to leave the car at the airport?
A No problem, but that's a one-way rental, so there's an additional charge of £50.
J OK.
A And one last thing – have you driven in the UK before?
J Yes, I have. So driving on the left's not a problem.
A That's good. OK, let's go out and take a look at the car. We can go through the paperwork afterwards.
J Great.
N As Jenny and the assistant leave the office to see the car, the TV shows Andrew's photograph with the headline 'Airport Assault'.

Now focus on the last two questions and get Sts to discuss them in pairs or as a whole-class activity.

b Focus on the conversation on *p.35*. Elicit who says the **You hear** phrases (*the assistant at the rental company*) and who says the **You say** phrases (*the customer*, here *Jenny*). Highlight that these phrases will be useful for Sts if they ever rent a car.

Give Sts time to read through the conversation and to think about what the missing words might be. Then play the video / audio again and get Sts to complete the gaps. Play it again if necessary.

Get Sts to compare with a partner, and then check answers.

1 hired   2 see   3 kind   4 Three   5 manual
6 drivers   7 models   8 65   9 petrol   10 charge
11 parking   12 50   13 the UK

Now go through the conversation and deal with any new vocabulary. Elicit / Explain the meaning of *run through some of the basics* (= discuss the main points quickly), *fair enough* (= a colloquial expression meaning *that's OK*), and *assault* (= a physical attack on someone). You may also want to point out that *take a look* is an alternative to *have a look* and is more common in US English.

c ◉ **3.22** Now focus on the **You say** phrases and tell Sts they're going to hear some of them again, and should repeat them, copying the rhythm and intonation.

Play the video / audio, pausing after the beep for Sts to listen and repeat the phrases.

◉ **3.22**

A = assistant, J = Jenny
- A Hello. Can I help you?
- J Oh, hi. I'd like to rent a car, please. (*pause*)
- A Great. So, what kind of car are you looking for?
- J Oh, nothing too big. It's just for me. (*pause*)
- A OK, so a compact. Three-door?
- J Yeah, that'll be fine. (*pause*)
- A Automatic or manual?
- J An automatic, please. (*pause*)
- A Any additional drivers?
- J No, just me. (*pause*)
- A It's sixty-five pounds per day, and that includes insurance.
- J That sounds promising. (*pause*) Can I take a look? (*pause*)
- A But if you get any parking tickets or speeding fines, you have to pay for them yourself.
- J Fair enough! (*pause*) Would it be possible to leave the car at the airport? (*pause*)
- A And one last thing – have you driven in the UK before?
- J Yes I have. So driving on the left's not a problem. (*pause*)

d Put Sts in pairs, **A** and **B**. Sts **A** are the assistant and Sts **B** the customer. Get Sts to read the conversation in **b** aloud, and then swap roles.

Monitor and help, encouraging Sts to pay attention to rhythm and intonation.

e Focus on the **Useful language: describing cars** box and go through it with the class. You may also want to elicit the models of cars for the different categories.

Now focus on the instructions. Tell Sts that they will both be role-playing renting a car, so give them time to decide what kind of car they will want and for how long.

First, Sts **A** are the customer and Sts **B** the assistant. Tell Sts **A** to close their books. Sts **B** start with *Hello. Can I help you?* Then Sts practise the conversation, with Sts **B** reading their role and Sts **A** role-playing being a customer. Monitor and help.

f When Sts have finished, they should swap roles.

You could get a few pairs to perform in front of the class.

3 ▶ WHERE IS HENRY?

a ◉ **3.23** Focus on the photo and ask Sts where they think Jenny is and what is happening.

Now focus on the instructions and the questions.

Play the video / audio once the whole way through for Sts to watch or listen and answer the questions.

Check answers.

> a) Jenny's laptop is still with Luke, who needs more time to fix it.
> b) Her suitcase has arrived at Henry's house, but the lock is broken.
> She hears on the news that Andrew Page, the man she met at the airport, has been attacked and is now in hospital in a critical condition.

◉ **3.23**

N = narrator, J = Jenny, H = Henry, L = Luke, Ne = newsreader
- N *Day two. Five p.m. Jenny drives back to Henry's house. She's bought food to cook for dinner. She leaves the food on the table and looks for Henry.*
- J Henry? Henry? Henry?
- N *Henry doesn't seem to be there, so she phones him.*
- H This is Henry Walker. I'm afraid I can't take your call at the moment. Please leave your message after the tone.
- J Hi, Henry, it's Jenny here. I just wanted to let you know everything went fine. I got my car and I'm back home. Remember, I'm making dinner. See you soon.
- N *She notices some books on the floor and picks them up and puts them away. She then phones Luke.*
- J Hi, Luke. It's Jenny.
- L Hi, Jenny. What's up?
- J I just wanted to apologize for running off this morning.
- L You really don't need to! I should apologize, actually. It's going to take me longer than I thought to unlock your computer. It's like there's an extra security code or something.
- J That's really weird.
- L Don't worry, I'm sure I can crack it.
- J I just have no idea how it got there. Hang on.
- L What is it?
- J My suitcase has arrived!
- L Hey, that's great!
- J Oh, look at that. The lock's broken.
- L Must have been the baggage handlers!
- J Well, at least it's back.
- L So, how's Uncle Henry?
- J He isn't here. I called him, but he didn't answer.
- L He probably went for a walk. He often does that. He thinks about his research and stuff.
- J Well, I hope he's back in time for dinner!
- L He will be. He's always on time.
- J Yeah, Rob told me Henry's very punctual.
- L Unlike Rob!
- J Exactly.
- L Is that the jet lag catching up with you?
- J Yeah, I'm pretty tired.
- L You should have a nap. Don't worry, I'll get this computer working as soon as I can.
- J Thanks, Luke. See you later.
- L Bye!
- N *Jenny sits down on the sofa and turns on the TV, but soon she closes her eyes and falls asleep. The TV is still on. Jenny suddenly wakes up. She's been asleep for almost four hours.*
- J Oh no, dinner! Henry? Henry! That's strange.
- N *Jenny phones him again.*
- H This is Henry Walker. I'm afraid I can't take your call at the moment. Please leave your message after the tone.
- N *She then glances at the TV.*
- Ne The victim of last night's assault at Heathrow Airport has been named as Andrew Page. Mr Page is a research scientist from Oxford. Police believe he was attacked as he left the airport. He is now in hospital in a critical condition. Police are appealing to anyone who may have seen Mr Page to contact them immediately. Mr Page had just returned from New York, where he was conducting research on renewable energy.
- J Oh my gosh! Andrew!
- N *Jenny picks up her phone and dials.*
- R Hi, Jenny.
- J Rob, I need to talk to you.

b Focus on the instructions and give Sts time to read sentences 1–8. Elicit / Explain the meaning of *jet lag* (= the feeling of being tired and confused after a long plane journey, especially when there's a big difference in time).

PE2 53

Play the video / audio again, pausing if necessary to give Sts time to answer the questions. Tell them to mark the sentences *T* (true) or *F* (false). Remind them to correct the ones that are false.

Get Sts to compare with a partner, and then check answers.

1 F (Henry isn't at home.)
2 T
3 F (She thinks it's really weird.)
4 F (Luke thinks Henry has probably gone for a walk.)
5 F (He's very punctual.)
6 T
7 F (Henry still isn't home.)
8 F (She phones Rob because she needs to talk to him.)

Now focus on the last two questions, and elicit ideas from the class.

EXTRA SUPPORT If there's time and you are using the video, you could get Sts to watch again with subtitles, so they can see exactly what they understood / didn't understand. Translate / Explain any new words or phrases.

c Focus on the **Social English** phrases. In pairs, get Sts to see if they can remember any of the missing words.

EXTRA CHALLENGE In pairs, get Sts to complete the phrases before they listen.

d 🔊 **3.24** Play the video / audio for Sts to watch or listen and complete the phrases.

Check answers. If you know your Sts' L1, you could get them to translate the phrases.

1 afraid 2 tone 3 up 4 Hang 5 least 6 pretty 7 later

🔊 **3.24**
1 I'm afraid I can't take your call at the moment.
2 Please leave your message after the tone.
3 Hi, Jenny. What's up?
4 Hang on…my suitcase has arrived!
5 Well, at least it's back.
6 I'm pretty tired.
7 Thanks, Luke. See you later.

Now play the video / audio again, pausing after each phrase for Sts to watch or listen and repeat.

e Focus on the instructions and make sure Sts understand what they have to do.

Get Sts to compare with a partner, and then check answers.

A 3 B 6 C 4 D 1,2 E 7 F 5

Now put Sts in pairs and get them to practise the conversations.

Finally, focus on the **CAN YOU…?** questions and ask Sts if they feel confident they can now do these things. If they feel that they need more practice, tell them to go to *Online Practice* to watch the episode again and practise the language.

4A Don't throw it away!

G future forms: *will / shall* and *be going to*
V rubbish and recycling
P /aɪ/ and /eɪ/

Lesson plan
In this lesson, the topic is rubbish and recycling. Sts begin with a vocabulary focus on rubbish and recycling, followed by pronunciation practice contrasting the vowel sounds /aɪ/ and /eɪ/. This leads into a listening – an interview with a woman who invented an app to help reduce food waste by sharing any surplus you have. The first half of the lesson ends with Sts reading a questionnaire about their attitude to waste and recycling, and then discussing their responses in small groups.

In the second half, the grammar focus is on future forms: *will / shall* and *be going to*. These forms are revised and contrasted, and then the uses (e.g. predictions, offers, plans, etc.) are extended. Next, Sts read an article about what can and can't be recycled. Finally, they talk about their predictions for the future of recycling.

More materials
For teachers
Photocopiables
Grammar future forms: *will / shall* and *be going to p.158*
Communicative The Green Quiz *p.186* (instructions *p.173*)
Vocabulary Rubbish and recycling *p.210* (instructions *p.203*)
For students
Workbook 4A
Online Practice 4A

OPTIONAL LEAD-IN (BOOKS CLOSED)
Write the following list on the board:

BANANAS   BREAD
MILK   CAKES
BACON   CHICKEN
FIZZY DRINKS POTATOES

Ask Sts what they think these foods have in common. Elicit ideas, then tell them that these are the top eight foods that British households are guilty of throwing away every week, even though they're still OK to eat. Ask Sts if they think the top eight would be the same in their country.

1 VOCABULARY rubbish and recycling

a Books open. Do this as a whole-class activity, or put Sts in pairs and then elicit as much information as possible.
Try to elicit vocabulary for food, e.g. different kinds of fruit and vegetables, as this will help Sts later with the listening.

b Focus on the instructions and make sure Sts know what an *infographic* is (= information or data that is shown in a chart, diagram, etc., so that it is easy to understand).

Now tell Sts to read the information and match the highlighted words and phrases to definitions 1–5.
Check answers. Model and drill the pronunciation of any tricky words.

1 food waste 2 goes to waste 3 supply 4 supply chain
5 surplus

c Focus on the instructions and then put Sts in pairs to discuss their reaction to the facts.
Get some feedback from various pairs for each option, a, b, and c.

EXTRA SUPPORT Quickly revise / elicit how to say the numbers in the infographic, i.e. the fraction 1/3 and *per cent* for the symbol %.

d Tell Sts to go to **Vocabulary Bank Rubbish and recycling** on *p.156*.

Vocabulary notes
Rubbish: nouns and phrasal verbs
You may want to remind Sts that *waste* as a verb (e.g. *waste money*, *waste time*) means to use in a non-productive way, and that sometimes the noun *waste* also has this meaning as in the expressions *What a waste!* or *It's a waste of time*.
Point out that when *waste* refers to materials that are not needed it is uncountable, i.e. only used in the singular and not with *a*.
Highlight the pronunciation of *refuse* /ˈrefjuːs/ in *refuse collector*, so that Sts don't confuse it with the verb *refuse* /rɪˈfjuːz/.
You could also introduce the informal nouns *tip / dump*, which refer to a local centre where you can take household or garden rubbish or recyclable waste (verb **go to the tip / dump**).
Tell Sts that all four phrasal verbs are separable, i.e. they can have an object after the particle or between the verb and the particle. Remind Sts that if the object is a pronoun (e.g. *it*), then it <u>must</u> go between the verb and the particle, e.g. *Throw* **it** *away*.

Packaging
Explain / Elicit that:
- *polystyrene* is a lightweight, synthetic material, which is often used in packaging.
- *sell-by date* is the date after which a shop cannot legally sell a product. You could also mention the expression *best before…*, which is a date printed on a container or package advising you to use it before this date, as it will not be of such good quality after that.

Focus on **1 Rubbish: nouns and phrasal verbs** and get Sts to do **a** individually or in pairs.
🔊 4.1 Now do **b**. Play the audio for Sts to listen and check.
Check answers.

4.1
Rubbish and recycling
1 Rubbish: nouns and phrasal verbs
Nouns
1 rubbish
2 waste
3 bin
4 bin bag
5 waste-paper basket
6 refuse collector
7 landfill site

Now either use the audio to drill the pronunciation of the words, or model and drill them yourself. Give further practice of any words your Sts find difficult to pronounce.

Now get Sts to do **c** individually or in pairs.

4.2 Now do **d**. Play the audio for Sts to listen and check.

Check answers.

4.2
Phrasal verbs
1 If that pen doesn't work, just **throw** it **away**. I hate having pens around that don't work.
2 Please could you **take out** the rubbish? I did it last week.
3 I'm moving house in a few weeks, and I've decided to **give away** a lot of books and clothes to a charity shop.
4 In most countries, people throw away used glass, cardboard, etc. in special bins. Local councils then collect this waste and **take** it **away** to be recycled.

Now either use the audio to drill the pronunciation of the sentences, or model and drill them yourself. Give further practice of any words your Sts find difficult to pronounce.

Focus on **Activation** and get Sts to cover the nouns and phrasal verbs in **a** and **c**, and try to remember the definitions (1–7 in **a**) and sentences (1–4 in **c**).

Now focus on **2 Packaging**. Make sure Sts know the meaning of *packaging* /ˈpækɪdʒɪŋ/ (= materials used to wrap or protect goods that are sold in shops). Model and drill its pronunciation. Then get Sts to do **a** individually or in pairs.

4.3 Now do **b**. Play the audio for Sts to listen and check.

Check answers.

4.3
2 Packaging
5 bottle
6 can
14 cardboard box
3 carton
15 jar
9 lid
13 packet
12 plastic bag
4 pot
7 pouch
11 sell-by date
10 tin
8 tray
1 tub
2 wrapper

Now either use the audio to drill the pronunciation of the words, or model and drill them yourself. Give further practice of any words your Sts find difficult to pronounce.

Focus on **Activation**. Make sure that Sts know the meanings of the words in the list. Do this as a whole-class activity, or put Sts in pairs and then get some feedback.

biscuits – packet
cereal – cardboard box / plastic bag
chicken legs – polystyrene tray
ice cream – tub
milk – bottle / carton
olives – jar
pasta sauce – jar, pouch
sardines – tin
soft drinks – bottle, can / carton
yogurt – pot

EXTRA IDEA Get Sts to cover the words / phrases, look at the pictures, and remember the words.

Finally, look at **3 The prefix *re-*** and get Sts to do **a** individually or in pairs.

4.4 Now do **b**. Play the audio for Sts to listen and check. Check answers.

4.4
3 The prefix *re-*
1 There's a bottle bank at the local supermarket where you can recycle all your glass bottles and jars.
2 All supermarkets in the UK now charge extra for plastic bags. They prefer customers to have shopping bags which they can **reuse**.
3 If you're not sure about the project, you should **rethink** the whole thing.
4 You can **reheat** your dinner in the microwave.
5 They'll have to **replay** the match next Saturday.
6 You should **reapply** sunscreen every hour if you have fair skin.

Now either use the audio to drill the pronunciation of the sentences, or model and drill them yourself. Give further practice of any words your Sts find difficult to pronounce.

Elicit that the prefix *re-* = again, e.g. *reuse* = use again. You may want to point out that there is a secondary stress on *re-*.

EXTRA IDEA Get Sts to cover sentences 1–6 and try to remember the meaning of the verbs.

EXTRA CHALLENGE You could elicit other words which start with the prefix *re-*, e.g. *rewrite, remarry, restart*.

Tell Sts to go back to the main lesson **4A**.

EXTRA SUPPORT If you think Sts need more practice, you may want to give them the **Vocabulary** photocopiable activity at this point.

2 PRONUNCIATION /aɪ/ and /eɪ/

Pronunciation notes

Students may confuse the vowel sounds /aɪ/ and /eɪ/. They often make sounds influenced by their L1, e.g. pronouncing the letters *ay* as /aɪ/.

a Focus on the two sound pictures and elicit the words and sounds: *bike* /aɪ/ and *train* /eɪ/. Elicit / Remind Sts that these are both diphthongs.

Tell Sts to focus on the pink letters in the words in the list and write the words in the correct column. Remind Sts that this kind of activity is easier if they say the words aloud to themselves.

Get them to compare with a partner.

EXTRA SUPPORT Say the words in the list once for Sts just to listen before they write them in the correct column.

b ◆ **4.5** Play the audio for Sts to listen and check. Check answers.

◆ 4.5
bike /aɪ/ reapply, recycle, require, sell-by, site, supply
train /eɪ/ away, date, replay, tray, waste

Now play the audio again, pausing after each word or group of words for Sts to listen and repeat.

Give Sts time to practise saying the words.

c Tell Sts to look at the words in **a** and give them time to complete the rules in the /aɪ/ and /eɪ/ box.

Get Sts to compare with a partner, and then check answers.

ay is always pronounced /eɪ/.
a + consonant + *e* is usually pronounced /eɪ/.
i + consonant + *e* is usually pronounced /aɪ/.
Consonant + final -*y* in a stressed syllable is usually pronounced /aɪ/.

d Focus on the instructions and point out that the pink letters in the words in the list are either pronounced /aɪ/ or /eɪ/.

Give Sts time to decide which sound the pink letters are. Get them to compare with a partner.

EXTRA SUPPORT Play audio ◆ 4.6 once for Sts just to listen to the words before they decide how the pink letters are pronounced.

e ◆ **4.6** Play the audio for Sts to listen and check. Check answers and make sure that Sts know the meaning of all the words.

train /eɪ/ break, neighbour, straight, survey, weight
bike /aɪ/ buy, climate, eyes, flight, guy, height, wi-fi

◆ 4.6
See words in Student's Book on *p.36*

Now play the audio again, pausing after each word or group of words for Sts to listen and repeat.

Give Sts time to practise saying the words.

EXTRA SUPPORT If these sounds are difficult for your Sts, it will help to show them the mouth position. You could model this yourself or use the Sound Bank videos on the *Teacher's Resource Centre.*

3 LISTENING listening and taking notes

a Focus on the instructions and elicit / explain what *co-founder* means (= a person who starts an organization, institution, etc. with someone else).

Get Sts to read **Part 1** of the interview and then, with a partner, predict what the missing words might be. Encourage them to use the context for clues. Tell them <u>not</u> to write in the gaps, but on a piece of paper.

b ◆ **4.7** Play the audio for Sts to listen and check. Check answers.

EXTRA SUPPORT Read through the scripts and decide if you need to pre-teach any new lexis before Sts listen.

1 neighbours 2 businesses 3 sell-by date 4 baker's
5 fridge 6 share 7 photo 8 message

◆ 4.7
Part 1
I = interviewer, T = Tessa
I Tessa, can you explain what OLIO is, exactly?
T So, OLIO is a free app which connects neighbours with each other and with local businesses so that surplus food can be shared and not thrown away.
I What kinds of food?
T It could be food that's near its sell-by date in local shops, or home-grown vegetables that you're not going to eat, or bread from your baker's that hasn't been sold at the end of the day, or the food that's in your fridge when you're about to go away. Any food that people have that they're not going to use.
I And how does the app work?
T It's super easy! If you have some food that you want to share, you simply open the app, add a photo and a description, and say when and where the food can be collected from. And if you're looking for some food, you just put in your postcode and send a message to the person who's offering the food you want, and then you arrange a time to go and collect it.

❗ Don't ask Sts what they think of the app at this stage, as they will be discussing it later in the lesson.

c ◆ **4.8** Focus on the task and give Sts time to read the three questions.

Now play **Part 2** of the interview, pausing the audio when each question has been answered to give Sts time to write.

Get Sts to compare with a partner, and then play again if necessary.

Check answers.

1 Because she lived on a farm as a child, and learned how much hard work goes into producing food.
2 She was moving from Switzerland and packing up her flat, and she didn't want to throw away good food.
3 She was very excited. .

◆ 4.8
(script in Student's Book on *p.126*)
Part 2
I So how did you come up with the idea?
T Well, I've always been worried about food waste. My parents have a farm in the north of England, in North Yorkshire, and I learned as a child how much hard work goes into producing the food that we all eat. And so I grew up with the belief that food should be eaten; it ought not to be thrown away. But I got the idea for the app when I was living in Switzerland and I was packing up my flat because I was going to move back to the UK. When the removal people came to take all my things, I still had in my fridge some potatoes, a cabbage, and some pots of yogurt. The men told me to throw away the food, but it seemed such a terrible thing to do, to throw away good food. The removal men didn't want it, and my neighbours were out, and I thought to myself, 'This is absolutely crazy…This food is delicious. Why isn't there an app where I can share it with someone nearby who wants it?'
And so the idea for OLIO was born…When I told my friend Saasha about it…
I You co-founded OLIO with your friend Saasha, is that right?
T Yes. Saasha has always been passionate about recycling, and when I told her my idea, her eyes immediately lit up – she got very excited. In just an hour of talking, we'd come up with a name and made a plan.

4A

d 🔊 **4.9** Focus on the instructions and give Sts time to look at the phrases in the list. Make sure Sts know what *£700 worth of food* means.

Play **Part 3** of the interview once all the way through. Tell Sts just to listen and not write anything.

Now play the audio again for Sts to listen and take notes.

Get Sts to compare with a partner, and then if necessary, play the audio again, pausing after each answer is given. Check answers.

> In the UK, the average family throws away **£700 worth of food** each year.
> **One in three people** feel really terrible when they throw away good food.
> They invited **12 people** from the research survey, who said they hated throwing away good food, to join a closed WhatsApp group.
> They asked them to post photos of any surplus food they had into the group for **two weeks**, and see if anyone wanted it.
> The first item someone posted was **half a bag of onions**!
> They launched the OLIO app on **9th July 2015**.
> Now the app is being used in **41 countries**.
> A man messaged Tessa to say that someone had collected his vegetables **within an hour** after he posted on OLIO.

🔊 **4.9**
(script in Student's Book on *p.126*)
Part 3
I So what happened next?
T The first thing we did was some research, in order to understand how big the problem of food waste was, and what we discovered truly shocked us. For example, did you know that in the UK, the average family throws away seven hundred pounds' worth of food each year? That adds up to twelve point five billion…twelve point five billion pounds that's going straight in the bin! But our research also showed that one in three people feel really terrible when they throw away good food. But just because people hate throwing away food, that doesn't mean they'll take the next step, which is to share food. We needed a cheap and quick way to test whether our food sharing idea would work.
I How did you do that?
T We invited twelve people from our research survey, who said they hated throwing away good food, and we put them all in a closed WhatsApp group. We asked them to post photos of any surplus food they had into the group for two weeks, and see if anyone wanted it. Eventually, someone posted an item – half a bag of onions! And then more and more items of food were shared. Then, when the trial was over, we met face-to-face with everybody who took part, and asked for feedback. The conclusion was unanimous – 'it's an amazing idea'.
I So when did you actually launch the app?
T We launched it on the ninth of July, twenty fifteen. The very first version of the app could only be used in North London. But now it's being used in forty-one countries.
I So people love it and are using it?
T Absolutely. We get loads of messages on our website, and there was one the other day from this guy – I'm going to read it to you – he said, 'I had some vegetables I knew I wouldn't have time to eat and within an hour they'd been collected and I suddenly felt like a hero!' That's so great. People are helping each other, and helping the planet, and feeling good all at the same time.

EXTRA SUPPORT If there's time, you could get Sts to listen again with the script on *p.37* and the two scripts on *p.126*, so they can see exactly what they understood / didn't understand. Translate / Explain any new words or phrases.

e Do this as a whole-class activity. Encourage Sts to give reasons to justify what they say, and tell them what you think.

4 SPEAKING

a Focus on the *Zero waste* questionnaire and quickly go through the questions to make sure Sts understand all the vocabulary, e.g. *leftover food*.

Give Sts time to think about what they are going to say.

b Put Sts in small groups of three or four and tell them to take turns to ask each other the questions. Emphasize that they should give and ask for as much information as possible.

Monitor and help Sts with any vocabulary they need.

Get some feedback.

EXTRA SUPPORT Before putting Sts in groups, get them to ask you some or all of the questions.

5 GRAMMAR future forms: *will / shall* and *be going to*

a Focus on conversations 1–5 and tell Sts to complete the gaps with the correct form of *will*, *shall*, or *be going to* and the verb in brackets. Tell them to use the contracted form of *will* ('*ll*) and of *be* after pronouns.

Get Sts to compare with a partner.

b 🔊 **4.10** Play the audio for Sts to listen and check.

Pause after each conversation, check answers, and elicit why each form is correct.

> 1 We use *will / won't* for decisions made at the time of speaking.
> 2 We use *be going to* to talk about plans. Speaker A could also use the present continuous here. Speaker B made a decision at the time of speaking.
> 3 We use *will / won't* to make promises.
> 4 We use *shall* questions with *I* to make offers.
> 5 We use *will* to make predictions about what we think or believe will happen.

🔊 **4.10**
1 A Could you take the rubbish out? It's beginning to smell.
   B I**'ll do** it as soon as this programme finishes.
2 A **Are** you **going to finish** that pasta? You've hardly eaten any.
   B I can't, I'm just not hungry, but don't throw it away. I**'ll have** it for lunch tomorrow.
3 A Don't put bottles in the black bin. You need to put them in the recycling bin.
   B Sorry, I forgot. I **won't do** it again.
4 A This lasagne's been in the fridge for three days. **Shall** I **throw** it away?
   B No, don't waste it. Put it in the freezer.
5 A I'm a bit worried about this yogurt. The sell-by date was yesterday.
   B Don't worry, it**'ll be** fine.

Now get Sts to practise the conversations in pairs. Monitor and help, encouraging Sts to pay attention to rhythm and intonation.

Make sure Sts swap roles.

EXTRA IDEA Get pairs of Sts to perform the conversations in front of the class.

c Tell Sts to go to **Grammar Bank 4A** on *p.138*.

Grammar notes
Future forms: *will / shall* and *be going to*

Sts will have met these future forms several times in earlier levels of *English File*, but here their uses are combined and extended. The correct use of future forms in English is always complicated for Sts because it depends on the concept the speaker wants to convey (a plan, prediction, offer, etc.) and cannot be translated directly from Sts' L1.

Remind Sts not to use the present simple instead of *will* for offers or promises, e.g. NOT ~~I give you a lift to the airport.~~ Many Sts also tend to use *will* instead of the present continuous or *going to* for plans, e.g. ~~I'll go to see my grandmother at the weekend.~~ (This would imply that you have just made the decision.)

You may also want to highlight that:

- we can also use *won't* for 'refuse to', e.g. *The kids won't eat their vegetables*.
- *going to* is often pronounced /ɡənə/ and written informally as *gonna*, e.g. in song lyrics.

There is sometimes very little difference between a plan and an arrangement, and we can often use either *be going to* or the present continuous when there is an arrangement to do something – something has been organized, e.g.:
I'm going to the dentist tomorrow (= I have an appointment).
Liz and Nick are coming for dinner tonight (= we have invited them, and they have said they are going to come).

Point out that if we need to refer to the future from a time in the past, we use *was going to* (the past form of *be going to*). We often use this structure to talk about things we intended to do, but then didn't, e.g. *I was going to…, but* (something happened and I didn't do it).

Focus on the example sentences for **will / shall** and play audio 🔊 **4.11** for Sts to listen and repeat. Encourage them to copy the rhythm. Then go through the rules with the class.

Repeat for **be going to** 🔊 **4.12**.

Go through the **The future in the past** box with the class. Now focus on the exercises and get Sts to do them individually or in pairs. Encourage them to use contracted forms rather than full forms.

Check answers, getting Sts to read the full sentences.

a
1 ✓,✓   2 ✗ Shall I put, ✓   3 ✗ I'm going to get, ✗ Shall I help
4 ✓, ✗ I'll text her   5 ✓

b
1 **I'll turn on** the air conditioning.
2 Can I borrow £10? **I'll pay** you back tomorrow.
3 **I'm going to give** them to the charity shop.
4 A **Shall I buy** some more bread when I go out?
   B Yes, please. I've decided **I'm going to make** sandwiches for lunch.
5 Are you going home by bus? **I'll give** you a lift if you like.
6 OK. What film **shall** we **see**?
7 A What **are** you **going to do** with those old bottles and jars?
   B **I'm going to take** them to the bottle bank for recycling.
8 After 2040, diesel cars **won't be sold** in most European countries.

Tell Sts to go back to the main lesson **4A**.

EXTRA SUPPORT If you think Sts need more practice, you may want to give them the **Grammar** photocopiable activity at this point.

d In this speaking activity, Sts practise using future forms to talk about plans and predictions.

Focus on the **Responding to plans and predictions** box and go through it with the class. Model and drill the phrases and encourage Sts to use friendly intonation.

Put Sts in pairs and tell them to choose topics from both lists and make plans and predictions. If they don't actually have a plan, tell them to invent one.

Monitor and help, encouraging Sts to use the expressions in the box.

Get feedback from various pairs.

EXTRA SUPPORT Demonstrate one or two of the topics yourself, getting a strong student to respond.

6 READING & SPEAKING reading to check assumptions

a Do this as a whole-class activity. You could also answer the questions yourself.

b Focus on the instructions and the title of the article. Encourage Sts to work out all the lexis, e.g. *glittery*, from the photos.

Put Sts in pairs and get them to choose the correct answers based on what they do or what they have read / heard.

Elicit some answers from Sts, but don't tell them if they are correct.

c Now tell Sts to read the article and check their answers to **b**.

Check answers. You could tell Sts that more recently, some supermarkets have started to recycle black plastic trays.

EXTRA SUPPORT Before Sts read the article the first time, check whether you need to pre-teach any vocabulary, but not the compound nouns in **f**.

1 The bottles can be recycled, but the caps can't.
2 The white plastic tray can be recycled, but the black tray can't.
3 The glittery paper can't be recycled, but the one without glitter can.
4 The glass jar can be recycled, but the plastic pouch can't.
5 The pump-action bottle can be recycled, but the tube can't.
6 '4' means the packaging contains polyethylene, which can only be recycled in some centres.

Finally, find out if anyone got all answers correct.

d Focus on the instructions and make sure Sts know the meaning of *summary*.

Give Sts time to read the article again and match paragraphs 1–6 to summaries A–F.

Get Sts to compare with a partner, and then check answers.

1 C   2 E   3 D   4 F   5 B   6 A

Deal with any other new vocabulary. Model and drill the pronunciation of any tricky words.

4A 59

e Give Sts time to read a–c and then choose the one that conveys the main message of the article. Ask Sts to justify their answer, using information in the article.
Check the answer.

b

f Focus on the task and make sure Sts know what a *compound noun* is.
Give Sts time to complete the words. If Sts can't remember, they can check back with the article.
Check answers.

1 bottle 2 bin 3 tray 4 paper 5 food 6 sauce

g Do this as a whole-class activity.

h Focus on the instructions and four predictions. Remind Sts of the expressions for making predictions they saw in the **Responding to plans and predictions** box.
Put Sts in pairs and get them to discuss each prediction. Encourage them to justify their answers as much as possible.
Get some feedback from various pairs. You could find out if, on the whole, Sts feel positive about recycling in the future.

EXTRA SUPPORT Choose one of the predictions and tell the class what you think and why.

4B Put it on your CV

G first and second conditionals
V study and work
P word stress

Lesson plan

The main context for this lesson is study and work. In the first part of the lesson, Sts revise and extend vocabulary related to higher education and work. This includes a pronunciation focus on word stress, followed by extended oral practice. Sts then listen to a radio programme about internships, where two women talk about their experiences, i.e. working for a company in order to get experience for a very low (or sometimes no) salary. Next, the grammar focus revises and contrasts first and second conditionals, which are presented in the context of job interviews. The first half of the lesson finishes with oral grammar practice, where Sts talk about imagined situations.

In the second half, the topic of work is further developed with a newspaper article about part-time jobs once held by some well-known British people. This leads into a speaking activity in which Sts discuss their own experiences of part-time or holiday jobs, and their education or current job. Next, Sts watch a video about what happened to a music student who was working part-time. Finally, Sts learn to write a profile for LinkedIn or a similar career networking website.

More materials
For teachers
Photocopiables
Grammar first and second conditionals *p.159*
Communicative What if …? *p.187* (instructions *p.174*)
Vocabulary Study and work *p.211* (instructions *p.203*)
Teacher's Resource Centre
Video A part-time job that changed a student's life
For students
Workbook 4B
Online Practice 4B

OPTIONAL LEAD-IN (BOOKS CLOSED)
Write the following jobs on the board:

SECONDARY SCHOOL TEACHER   WAITER   NURSE
AIR TRAFFIC CONTROLLER   SHOP ASSISTANT

Put Sts in pairs and get them to brainstorm for each job: a) what qualifications or practical skills you need, and b) what personal qualities you need.

Elicit their ideas onto the board and see if they agree. Then ask Sts if they think they are qualified to do any of the jobs.

1 VOCABULARY & PRONUNCIATION study and work; word stress

a Books open. Focus on the three circles and the words in the list. Tell Sts to put four words or phrases in each circle, and point out that the first one (*A levels*) has been done for them. Elicit / Explain what *A levels* are (= a British exam taken in a particular subject, usually in the final year of school).

Get Sts to compare with a partner, and then check answers. Make sure Sts know the meaning of each word. Model and drill pronunciation, especially of the noun *graduate* /ˈɡrædʒuət/. You might want to point out that it can also be used as a verb, but with slightly different pronunciation /ˈɡrædʒueɪt/.

school: classroom, head teacher, pupil
university: campus, degree, graduate, professor
applying for a job: CV, experience, qualifications, reference

b Tell Sts to go to **Vocabulary Bank** Study and work on *p.157*.

Vocabulary notes
Higher education

In British higher education, a *tutor* is a university teacher who works regularly with one student or a small group of Sts.

PhD is short for 'Doctor of Philosophy', but this title is used for a doctorate qualification in any subject. If necessary, use Sts' L1 to clarify. Highlight that it is pronounced as three individual letters /piː eɪtʃ ˈdiː/.

Point out to Sts that the plural of *thesis* /ˈθiːsɪs/ is *theses* /ˈθiːsiːz/.

Applying for a job or course

Although *scholarship* and *grant* are often used synonymously, a grant tends to be awarded to Sts from lower income backgrounds, whereas a scholarship is often awarded on the basis of academic achievement.

Focus on **1 Higher education** and get Sts to do **a** individually or in pairs.

4.13 Now do **b**. Play the audio for Sts to listen and check.

Check answers.

4.13
Study and work
1 Higher education
1 campus
2 undergraduates
3 postgraduates
4 dissertation
5 thesis
6 professors
7 faculties
8 halls of residence
9 tutor
10 seminars
11 lectures
12 webinars

Now either use the audio to drill the pronunciation of the words, or model and drill them yourself. Give further practice of any words your Sts find difficult to pronounce.

Go through the text with Sts, checking that they understand all the phrases in **bold**. If necessary, use Sts' L1 to clarify. Find out if any words are similar in your Sts' language(s). If so, do they mean the same? Model and drill pronunciation as necessary.

Now get Sts to do **Activation** in pairs, and then get some feedback. Where there are differences, you could ask them which system they think they would prefer, and what the advantages / disadvantages are.

EXTRA SUPPORT Tell Sts to look only at the words in the list and try to remember their meaning or what they are associated with.

Focus on **2 Applying for a job or course** and get Sts to do **a** individually or in pairs.

🔊 **4.14** Now do **b**. Play the audio for Sts to listen and check.

Check answers.

🔊 **4.14**
2 Applying for a job or course
What you may need to have
1 **qualifications**
2 **experience**
3 **skills**
4 a **reference**

What you may need to do
5 look for a job **vacancy** or course
6 apply for a work **permit**, a place on a course, a grant or scholarship
7 write a **CV** and a covering letter
8 attend an **interview**
9 get a **job offer** or an offer for a place on a course
10 work as an **intern**

Now either use the audio to drill the pronunciation of the words, or model and drill them yourself. Give further practice of any words your Sts find difficult to pronounce.

Go through the bullets with Sts, making sure they understand all the words and phrases in **bold**.

Then focus on the information box and go through it with the class. Note that in some languages, *attend* and *assist* are false friends.

EXTRA SUPPORT Tell Sts to look only at the words in the list and try to remember their meaning or what they are associated with.

Tell Sts to go back to the main lesson **4B**.

EXTRA SUPPORT If you think Sts need more practice, you may want to give them the **Vocabulary** photocopiable activity at this point.

Pronunciation notes

Many of these words are similar in other languages, but are stressed on a different syllable. If necessary, remind Sts about word stress in English (see **Pronunciation notes** in **Lesson 3B** on *p.46*).

c Focus on the words in the list and get Sts to underline the stressed syllable in each one. Remind Sts that *PhD* is pronounced as the three individual letters.

EXTRA SUPPORT Play audio 🔊 4.15 once the whole way through for Sts just to listen before they underline the stressed syllables.

d 🔊 **4.15** Play the audio for Sts to listen and check. Check answers.

---

at**tend** disser**ta**tion PhD post**grad**uate pro**fes**sor quali**fi**cations **ref**erence **res**idence **schol**arship **sem**inar **tu**torial under**grad**uate **va**cancy

🔊 **4.15**
See words in Student's Book on *p.40*

Now give Sts a few minutes to practise saying the words, focusing on getting the stress correct.

EXTRA SUPPORT Play the audio again for Sts to listen and repeat.

e In pairs, Sts discuss the difference between the words and phrases in 1–8.

Check answers.

1 **An undergraduate** is somebody studying for a first degree at university. **A postgraduate** is somebody who is studying for a further degree.
2 **A Master's degree** is a one-year postgraduate qualification. **A PhD** is a three-year (or more) postgraduate qualification.
3 **A campus** is the buildings and land of a college or university. **A hall of residence** is a building where university students live while they are studying.
4 **A professor** is a highly ranked teacher at university. **A tutor** is a university teacher who pays special attention to the studies of a group of students.
5 **A seminar** is a university class where students discuss or study with their teacher. **A webinar** is a seminar conducted over the internet.
6 **A tutorial** is a class with a very small group of students. **A lecture** is a class where a large group of students listen to a talk, but do not participate.
7 **Qualifications** are exams that you have passed or a course of study that you have successfully completed. **Skills** are things that you can do well (e.g. speak a language).
8 **A CV** is a record of your education and work experience that you send when you apply for a job. **A covering letter / email** is a letter / email that you send with your CV when you apply for a job, usually explaining why you are applying.

2 SPEAKING

Focus on the task and make sure Sts understand all the points in the list, e.g. *an arts degree* (= the subjects you can study at university that are not scientific, such as languages, history, or literature).

Now focus on the **Agreeing / Disagreeing and giving opinions** box and go through it with the class.

Give Sts time to think about each statement and decide whether or not they agree and why.

Then put Sts in small groups of three or four. They should take turns to say what they think about a statement, and the rest of the group agree or disagree.

Monitor and help.

If your Sts are at university or have been to university, they could discuss each point both generally and personally. Encourage them to give as much information as possible and to give examples and reasons to justify what they say.

Get some feedback to see whether, generally speaking, Sts agree or disagree with the statements.

EXTRA IDEA If there's time, you could have a brief whole-class discussion on one or more of the topics.

3 LISTENING listening for factual information

a Do this as a whole-class activity. Ask Sts if they can think of any circumstances when working without pay could benefit them, e.g. to gain experience, to make contacts, or to help others.

EXTRA SUPPORT If you have had any experience of working without pay, tell the class about it.

b Focus on the instructions. Check Sts understand the title, *The ultimate guide to internships* (*ultimate* in this context means *best*, and they saw the term *internship* in the **Vocabulary Bank**).

Give Sts time to read the article and answer the questions. Check answers.

> Internships are paid if you're being trained, or producing work, but they are not paid if they are considered work experience.
> Internships are a good thing, according to the article.

EXTRA IDEA Ask Sts some comprehension questions to check they have understood the article, e.g. *What do you think 'shadowing other members of staff' means?* (Following other members of staff) *Which three groups of people is an internship good for?* (Students, graduates, and people who want a new career) *What are the benefits of doing an internship?* (You can try the job first, you can meet people, and you can include it on your CV), etc.

c 🔊 **4.16** Focus on the instructions. You could tell Sts that the website savethestudent.org was founded in 2007 and offers free, independent advice to university students on how to manage their money.

Explain that Sts are going to listen to a radio programme about being an intern and they must choose the correct option for the six statements. Give Sts time to read the statements and check they understand the meaning of the options. Point out the **Glossary** and go through it with the class.

Play the audio once the whole way through for Sts to listen and choose the correct options.

Get Sts to compare with a partner, and play the audio again if necessary.

Check answers.

EXTRA SUPPORT Read through the scripts and decide if you need to pre-teach any new lexis before Sts listen.

> 1 better   2 legal   3 have to   4 must   5 don't have to
> 6 choose his or her own hours

🔊 **4.16**
(script in Student's Book on *pp.126–127*)
I = interviewer, J = Jake Butler
Part 1
I Recently in the news, students and graduates have been complaining about how interns are treated, basically about the fact that many people doing internships are either very badly paid or not paid at all. We asked Jake Butler from the website save the student dot org to give us the facts. Hello, Jake. Nice to have you on the programme.
J Hi there.
I So what's the current situation with interns getting paid?
J Well, I'd like to make it clear that at Save the Student, we're strongly against unpaid internships. And thankfully, the situation is better than it used to be.
I But are unpaid internships actually legal?
J They can be. It all depends on your status as an intern: that is, whether you qualify as 'a worker' or not. And the law isn't completely clear about what being 'a worker' means.
I So how do you know if you should be getting paid?
J Well, if you're promised a contract for future work once the internship period is over, then you are an employee, so you're entitled to the National Minimum Wage – that's seven pounds seventy an hour – or the National Living Wage if you're over twenty-five, which is eight pounds twenty-one an hour.
I Are there any other situations in which you should definitely be paid?
J Yes. If you spend your day doing jobs that would usually be done by a paid employee, then you should also be paid the Minimum or Living Wage.
I So when is it legal for an employer not to pay an intern?
J You don't have to be paid if you're doing an internship as part of your university course, or if you're doing school work experience. And of course, if you're volunteering for a charity.
I Any other situations?
J Yes, you also don't have to be paid if the role you have is similar to work experience or shadowing – where you are in an office or another workplace just to observe and learn about what's going on, rather than actually working. But, and this is very important, if you're not getting paid for doing an internship, you shouldn't be given fixed working hours.
I So the important thing is to know your rights?
J Absolutely!
I Thank you very much, Jake.

---

d 🔊 **4.17** Focus on the instructions and the two photos. Play the audio, pausing at the end of each interview to check answers.

> Rosie was paid £15 a day for lunch and transport in one internship.
> Lauren was paid her travel expenses and her lunch in her last internship, but nothing in her previous ones.

🔊 **4.17**
(script in Student's Book on *p.127*)
I = interviewer, R = Rosie, L = Lauren
Part 2
I We're now asking people who either are interns or have just been interns to phone in and tell us about their experiences. Our first caller is Rosie. Hi Rosie, and thanks for calling. So, what's your experience?
R Well, I wanted to work in fashion – making hats, to be precise – and in the fashion industry, it's almost impossible to get a job unless you do an internship first, so I did several.
I And did you get paid?
R The most I got was about fifteen pounds a day for lunch and transport. Companies get so many applications for internships that they don't need to pay you.
I So it wasn't a good experience?
R Actually, it was. It was very hard work, but I learned loads about designing and making clothes. I sometimes worked later than eleven p.m., and that wasn't easy, but then I'd look in the newspapers and I'd see a model wearing a hat that I'd helped to make, and then I felt great.
I But it can't have been easy to survive, financially?
R No, it wasn't. My parents were able to help me a bit, but I had to earn money by working in a bar as well.
I Would you recommend doing an internship?
R Oh yes, overall, I think they're brilliant. I'd definitely advise someone to do one – despite the hard work and the debt, you learn so much that it's worth it.
I Thank you, Rosie. Our next caller is Lauren. Hi, Lauren.
L Hello.
I So what was your experience like?
L I've done four internships in Publicity. My last one was two months at a small Public Relations agency. They paid for my travel expenses and lunch, and I learned a lot. It really helped me when I applied for jobs because I knew what I was talking about.

4B

I So, a good experience.
L Absolutely. But in the other three, I worked ten-hour days, six days a week, and I got no money at all, so I also had to work in a pub to support myself. And each time they told me, 'Do well and there'll be a job at the end of it.' But then there were no jobs. It made me so angry.
I And were you working during these internships, or was it more observing others?
L I was working really hard. In fact, during one of those internships, the manager went on holiday for a month and I had to manage everything. And in another one, I worked from home, using my own phone, and I wasn't paid a penny, not even to cover the phone bill. I only met the boss once – it was all done by email. She promised me a job after three months, but it never happened.
I So you felt you were being exploited?
L Yes, totally.
I I'm really sorry to hear that, Lauren…

e Focus on the instructions and tell Sts that they are going to listen again and this time note down the key factual information both women give about their internship experiences: what work they did, what was good about it, and what was bad.

Play the audio again, pausing after each speaker for Sts to make notes.

Get Sts to compare with a partner, and play the audio again if necessary.

Check answers, eliciting as much information as possible about the two internships. Make sure Sts understand *publicity* (= a business which is all about attracting the attention of the public to sth, e.g. a product or event) and *public relations* / *PR* /pʌblɪk rɪˈleɪʃnz/ (= the business of giving the public information about an organization or person in order to create a good impression).

> **Rosie**
> **The kind of work:** fashion design / hat-making
> **The good side:** learned a lot about designing and making clothes; enjoyed seeing her hats in the newspaper
> **The bad side:** didn't get paid much; hard work; had to work late; had to work in a bar as well
>
> **Lauren**
> **The kind of work:** publicity / public relations
> **The good side:** paid travel expenses and lunch; learned a lot; experience helped when she applied for jobs
> **The bad side:** worked very long hours; earned no money; had to work in a pub; had to do the work of her manager; wasn't paid for using her own phone; was promised jobs at the end, but wasn't offered one

EXTRA SUPPORT If there's time, you could get Sts to listen again with the scripts on *pp.126–127*, so they can see exactly what they understood / didn't understand. Translate / Explain any new words or phrases.

f Focus on the questions and make sure Sts know the meaning of *fair* (= acceptable and appropriate in certain situations) and *industry* (= business) here.

Put Sts in pairs or small groups and tell them to discuss the questions.

Get some feedback from the class.

EXTRA SUPPORT Do some questions as a whole-class activity.

4 GRAMMAR first and second conditionals

a 🔊 4.18 Focus on the task and tell Sts they are going to hear the last few moments of two job interviews. Highlight that they will hear two different conditional forms in the interviews.

Play the audio, pausing after each interview for Sts to complete the gaps. Play the audio again as necessary.

Get Sts to compare with a partner, and then discuss the question.

Check answers. Elicit the difference between the two conditionals – the first refers to a real possibility, and the second to a hypothetical situation.

> 1 offer, will…be able
> 2 offered, would need

Now ask Sts who they think is going to get the job.

> The first person, Simon, has a real possibility of getting the job.

🔊 **4.18**
I = interviewer, S = Simon, A = Andrew
1
I Well, Simon, your qualifications are excellent and you've got a lot of great experience.
S Oh, thank you. I'm glad to hear it.
I If we offer you the job, when will you be able to start?
S How about tomorrow?
2
I OK, Andrew. You have some of the qualifications we're looking for, but not enough experience.
A I understand.
I If we offered you the job, you would need a lot of training. I'm afraid we don't have the budget for that at the moment.
A I see. Well, thanks very much for considering me.

b Tell Sts to go to **Grammar Bank 4B** on *p.139*.

> **Grammar notes**
>
> First and second conditionals have been presented in earlier levels of *English File*. They are revised and contrasted here.
>
> **First conditional**
>
> Emphasize that the *if*-clause uses a present tense, but has a future meaning, though we do not use a future tense here (NOT *If I'll see her, I'll give her your message.*)
>
> Remind Sts that the *if*-clause can come at the beginning or end of the sentence. When the *if*-clause starts the sentence, a comma separates it from the main clause. When the *if*-clause is at the end, there is no comma.
>
> **Second conditional**
>
> It may be confusing to Sts to use past tenses in the *if*-clause – emphasize that this is how we describe a hypothetical or imaginary situation. The meaning is usually present or future, not past.
>
> Remind Sts that *would* is often contracted to *'d*.
>
> Remind Sts also that we can use *unless* instead of *if…not* in both first and second conditionals, e.g. *I wouldn't go to the gym unless I really liked it* (= if I didn't really like it).

Focus on the example sentences for **first conditional** and play audio 🔊 **4.19** for Sts to listen and repeat. Encourage them to copy the rhythm. Then go through the rules with the class.

Focus on the *unless* box and go through it with the class.
Repeat for **second conditional** 🔊 4.20.
Finally, focus on the **First or second conditional** box and go through it with the class.
Focus on the exercises and get Sts to do them individually or in pairs.
Check answers, getting Sts to read the full sentences.

a
1 wouldn't 2 get 3 were 4 tell 5 think 6 You might
7 wouldn't 8 didn't 9 won't 10 earned

b
1 If I **decide** to stay at university, I'll probably do a PhD…
2 If you didn't spend so much on clothes, you **wouldn't have to** borrow money all the time.
3 I think my sister and her boyfriend **would get married** sooner if they could afford to pay for the wedding.
4 If I have time over the summer, **I'll apply** for an internship.
5 I think Andy might get a scholarship if he **keeps** on working hard.
6 If we **bought** a bigger house, we could rent a couple of rooms to students.
7 I might enjoy my job more if I **didn't have** such awful colleagues.
8 If I don't like the job after six months, I **won't stay**.
9 My tutor says I must attend all the seminars if I **don't want** to fail my exams.
10 I'd get more job offers if I **was / were** better qualified.

Tell Sts to go back to the main lesson **4B**.

EXTRA SUPPORT If you think Sts need more practice, you may want to give them the **Grammar** photocopiable activity at this point.

c 🔊 **4.21** This is an audio dictation to help Sts focus on the structure of first conditional sentences. Focus on the instructions and then play the audio once the whole way through for Sts just to listen.
Now play the audio again, pausing after each sentence to give Sts time to write.
Get Sts to compare with a partner, and then play the audio again if necessary.
Check answers by eliciting the sentences onto the board.

🔊 **4.21**
1 If you don't have any work experience, apply for an internship.
2 If you don't speak English, you won't be able to get a job abroad.
3 If you're asked to an interview, make sure you wear smart clothes.
4 If you make spelling mistakes on your CV, it'll give a bad impression.
5 If you use a social media site, you'll have more chance of finding work.

Finally, ask the whole class what they think of the advice.

d Focus on the instructions. Now focus on the example and show how the prompt for 1 has been transformed into a second conditional. Give Sts time to think about how to transform the other four sentences, and what they would do in each situation and why.
When Sts are ready, put them in pairs or small groups, and get them to compare what they would do and give their reasons.
Get feedback from different pairs or groups.

EXTRA SUPPORT Get Sts to write out their sentences before they tell them to each other.

5 READING focusing on key information

a Do this as a whole-class activity and elicit opinions. If you had any part-time jobs while you were studying, you could tell the class about them.

b Focus on the task and the illustrations. Point out the range of jobs they do now, and explain that these people are quite well known in the UK and successful in their respective fields.
Now focus on the **Glossary** and go through it with the class.
Give Sts time to read the article and complete the task.
Get Sts to compare with a partner, and then check answers.

EXTRA SUPPORT Before Sts read the article the first time, check whether you need to pre-teach any vocabulary, but not the words and phrases in **d**.

A (Sir Ranulph Fiennes) It's too long ago to know if I actually learned anything from the experience.
B (Russell Kane) I doubt that a Saturday job really teaches you anything.
C (Tony Ross) I learned the basics of working for money, like arriving on time and enjoying it no matter what.
D (Clive Stafford Smith) I've learned various important things from that job.
E (Adele Parks) I am good at talking and telling stories, and I think I learned it there…

Finally, ask who is the most positive about their part-time job.

C Tony Ross

c Focus on the instructions and tell Sts to read the article again and answer the questions. Set a time limit. You might like to suggest the following technique to help Sts focus on the key information in each paragraph. Use question 1 as the example. Tell Sts to look at the question, and underline the key words / phrases, e.g. in 1 <u>job</u> <u>badly paid</u>. Then scan through each paragraph quickly and try to look for words / phrases which link to the ones you underlined in the question, e.g. in paragraph D *paying a low wage*.
Get Sts to compare with a partner, and then check answers.

1 D 2 C 3 A 4 E 5 B

d Now tell Sts to read the definitions related to money and find the matching word or phrase in the article.
Get Sts to compare with a partner, and then check answers.

A cash B pocket money C earned D wage E checkout

EXTRA CHALLENGE Get Sts to try to remember the words and phrases before checking back with the article.

Deal with any other new vocabulary. Model and drill pronunciation of any tricky words.

e Do this as a whole-class activity.

6 SPEAKING

Focus on the instructions and the flow chart. Make clear that all Sts should answer the first question about part-time / holiday jobs. If they answer 'yes', they should continue with the following questions, and then follow whichever route is appropriate (studying or working). If they answer 'no' to the first question, they should go straight to whichever of the second section applies to them.

Put Sts in pairs. Monitor while Sts interview each other. Correct any pronunciation errors they make when they use the vocabulary they have practised in the lesson, and help them with any new vocabulary they need. Make a note of any common mistakes, and have a correction spot at the end of the activity.

Get some feedback from a few individual Sts.

EXTRA SUPPORT Get Sts to interview you first.

7 ▶ VIDEO LISTENING

a Tell Sts they are going to watch an interview with a young woman, Milly Forrest, whose part-time job changed her life. Give Sts time to read the two questions.

Play the video once the whole way through for Sts to watch and answer the questions.

Check answers. Make sure Sts know what an *usher* is (= a person who shows people where to sit in a church, public hall, etc.). Model and drill its pronunciation /ˈʌʃə/. You might want to tell Sts that the Wigmore Hall is a famous concert hall in central London. It was built in 1901 and has 552 seats. It specializes in small orchestral concerts (chamber music) and solo performances. it is also well known for encouraging talented young performers at the beginning of their careers.

EXTRA SUPPORT Read through the script and decide if you need to pre-teach any lexis before Sts watch the video.

> She wants to be a classical singer.
> While she was working part-time as an usher at the Wigmore Hall, Milly was asked to go on stage at short notice (in fact, because one of the performers was ill). The concert was a success and her story appeared in the press, which was good for her future career, and has inspired her to carry on.

A part-time job that changed a student's life

I = interviewer, M = Milly Forrest

I Since it was first established in eighteen eighty-two, the Royal College of Music in London has trained many of the world's most promising young musicians.
This is Milly Forrest, a twenty-four-year-old Masters student who is training to be a classical singer at the Royal College.
Today, Milly has a rehearsal and practice performance with her friend and accompanist, Joe. Many of the students here have already been playing and performing for years. And Milly is no different.

M So, I've been singing from about the age of seven. For as long as I can remember…I've always loved music. Um, I'm not from a very musical family, um, so I'm not really sure where my voice has come from but, yeah, from an early age I, I knew that I loved being on stage and loved performing.

I She knew that if she won a place at the Royal College of Music, it would be a real chance to turn her passion into a profession.

M I had decided to, to do a Masters at the Royal College of Music probably three years ago…and when I got in – because it's all audition-based – when I got in, er, I thought 'Oh, OK, well maybe I've got a good chance then'.
And, er, and it's been going well ever since. It's really fabulous. I'm improving all the time. Er, I have some lovely friends here. But it is tiring and the competition is really high. There are lots of singers out in London who, who are really talented.

I But while Milly is following her dream, isn't it difficult being a full-time student in London, one of Europe's most expensive cities?

M It is, absolutely, it's very expensive and so I've had to have a part-time job all the way through my studies. I've been working for six years alongside my training. At the moment, I'm an usher at the Wigmore Hall and I've been there for three years now.

I So what does a concert hall usher do?

M We mainly look after the audience when there are concerts and we do jobs such as checking tickets, and we're there in case there's a fire or emergency.

I In fact, many music students work as ushers and most of them dream of being on stage themselves one day. But for Milly, this opportunity came a little sooner than expected, in July twenty seventeen.

M Well, I had a call on the Wednesday evening and John Gilhooly, who's the director of the hall, told me that he'd like me to step in for a concert on the Saturday. So, I had a few days to prepare, but there was a rehearsal first thing on Thursday morning, so I stayed up until probably one in the morning that night desperately learning all the music. Um, I found the words particularly tricky actually – so, er, I mean a lot of the pieces were in French and German – so I got cracking straight away.

I And after just three days of preparation, Milly took to the stage. But did the audience know she was standing in for a singer who was ill?

M There was an announcement made at the beginning of the concert, which was lovely because I, I think the whole audience was on my side and everyone wanted me to do well.

I And it didn't take Milly long to impress with her voice.

M …there was a great applause everyone was smiling and clapping and I did have a feeling that I'd done well.

I And the audience weren't the only ones to take notice.

M So, after the concert everything went quiet for a couple of weeks, and life just went back to normal, um, and then just out of the blue, er, *The Times* asked whether they could do an article on me about what had happened and, um, it was a really nice story, so, um, I think it really warmed people's hearts and, er, and it was nice to make people smile. So, um, that day all of these different news channels got in touch…and I went to the BBC, and did an interview for them and then I met Sky as well and, um, it was really exciting. I must've done five or six interviews in the same day. And, er, and then I remember the next morning, um, the *Evening Standard* had, er, had bought out their, their newspaper and I saw my face on the front cover and when I got on to the Tube everyone was reading that paper, so I saw about a hundred Millies down the carriage – that, and that was, that was really surreal and I think that, that was when it had sunk in a little bit. Um, because the most exciting part for me was getting to sing in the Wigmore Hall along all these fabulous singers that I really admire and look up to, um, but then I, and I sort of hadn't focused on the media side as much so, er, yeah, it was, it was a lovely occasion.

I But has this opportunity helped Milly's career?

M I think it has. I think, um, it's given me a boost. It's made me really inspired and it's made me work harder over the last year, but actually life carries on and I still have a lot that I want to work on. My voice is nowhere near perfect and I'm my biggest critic but it's, it was nice to know that someone had me in mind and wanted to encourage me, so fingers crossed things will carry on that positively.

I And does she still work at the Wigmore Hall?

M I still work there as an usher. It's still really expensive living in London and, and every now and again someone comes in and asks 'Are you going to be performing here soon?' And I just have to, I just have to tell them that hopefully soon, hopefully soon because you never know what people are planning, um, but it was a lovely, it was a lovely story when it happened.

b Now focus on the instructions and on sentences 1–10. Go through them with Sts and make sure they understand them.

Play the video again the whole way through, and get Sts to mark the sentences *T* (true) or *F* (false). Remind them to correct the false ones.

Get Sts to compare with a partner, and then check answers.

1 F (She is studying at the Royal College of Music.)
2 F (She isn't from a very musical family and she doesn't know where her voice has come from.)
3 T
4 T
5 F (She looks after the audience, checks tickets, etc.)
6 F (She had three days to prepare.)
7 F (The audience smiled and clapped a lot.)
8 F (After the concert everything went back to normal.)
9 T
10 T

EXTRA SUPPORT You could get Sts to watch the video again with subtitles, so they can see exactly what they understood / didn't understand. Translate / Explain any new words or phrases.

c Do this as a whole-class activity, or put Sts in pairs and then get some feedback.

8 WRITING a LinkedIn profile

In this writing lesson, Sts practise writing a profile to post on LinkedIn or other career networking websites.

Tell Sts to go to **Writing A LinkedIn profile** on *p.118*.

a Ask Sts if they have ever used LinkedIn or similar websites. If they have, ask if they found the website(s) helpful. Why (not)?

Now go through the instructions with the class. Focus on the beginning of the profile and put Sts in pairs to discuss the questions.

Elicit some ideas, but <u>don't</u> tell Sts if they are correct.

b Give Sts time to read the rest of the profile to check their answers in **a**. Tell them not to worry about the mistakes in the profile at this stage.

Get Sts to compare with a partner, and then check answers.

Shopping Spy Ltd is a website that helps shoppers find good shops and sales in London.
She is studying for a degree in Communications and Marketing.

c Now tell Sts to look at the spelling mistakes underlined in Kate's profile and to correct them.

Check answers.

~~currantly~~ currently
~~Comunications~~ Communications
~~gradaute~~ graduate
~~profesion~~ profession
~~expierence~~ experience
~~collegues~~ colleagues
~~asisted~~ assisted
~~brouhgt~~ brought

d Focus on the **Useful language: writing a CV, covering letter, or LinkedIn profile** box and go through it with the class. You could tell Sts that if the company abbreviation ends with a full stop, e.g. *Apple Inc.*, then they should only use one full stop at the end of the sentence, e.g. *A few years ago I worked for Apple Inc.*

Tell Sts they are looking for a job, so they are going to write a profile for a website like LinkedIn. If they would like to do a real profile or update one they already have, they can go to the website and then print out their profile to give in.

Go through the plan with the class, highlighting that a summary should be brief and give a lot of information in just a few words. Sts should use Kate's profile as their model to help them. If Sts have not had any work experience, tell them to invent the details.

Remind Sts to use the **Useful language** and **Vocabulary Bank** Study and work on *p.157*.

e You may like to get Sts to do the writing in class or you could set it as homework. If you do it in class, set a time limit for Sts to write their profile, e.g. 15–20 minutes.

f Sts should check their profile for mistakes before giving it in.

3 & 4 Revise and Check

For instructions on how to use these pages, see p.39.

More materials

For teachers
Teacher's Resource Centre
Video Can you understand these people? 3&4
Quick Test 4
File 4 Test

For students
Online Practice   Check your progress

GRAMMAR

1 c 2 a 3 b 4 c 5 a 6 a 7 b 8 b 9 c 10 c
11 a 12 c 13 b 14 b 15 c

VOCABULARY

a 1 teenager   2 in his / her early twenties   3 toddler
   4 retired   5 in his / her late fifties   6 in his / her mid-forties
b 1 photographer   2 flash   3 in front of   4 bottom right-hand   5 background
c 1 refuse collector   2 cardboard   3 lid
   4 bin bag   5 wrapper   6 landfill site
d 1 covering   2 residence   3 qualifications   4 permit
   5 lectures   6 vacancies   7 attend   8 faculty

PRONUNCIATION

c 1 j**ar** /dʒ/   2 l**e**cture /tʃ/   3 w**o**rk p**e**rmit /ɜː/
   4 v**a**cancy /eɪ/   5 appl**y** /aɪ/
d 1 re**ti**red   2 **o**pposite   3 pho**to**grapher   4 re**cy**cle
   5 pro**fe**ssor

CAN YOU understand this text?

b
1 F (He sells food in boxes or jars and people bring their own containers.)
2 F (They haven't always been interested in environmental issues before.)
3 T
4 F (There's a plastic-free shop in London.)
5 F (The food industry is no longer saying that recycling will solve the problem.)
6 T
7 T
8 T

CAN YOU understand these people?

1 a   2 b   3 c   4 c   5 b

🔊 4.22

1
I = interviewer, E = Erica
I What kind of child were you?
E What kind of child was I? I was a very inquisitive child. I was the 'why' child, so anything you told me, I always responded with, 'Well, why?' and 'How come?' and 'Why is that?' And it was very annoying.
I Have you changed much?
E Um, I'm still very inquisitive, but I kind of ask more of why, like, I want to know more about your intentions as opposed to just why is something the way that it is.

2
I = interviewer, K = Keith
I Are you good at taking photos?
K I'm OK at taking photos. I have this technique now where instead of taking a photo with my camera, I'll take a video, um, and then I'll take screen, screenshots from the video stills. For example, if my son's playing football, whenever I try and take a photo, I'll always miss really what I was trying to capture, but by taking a video I can get various stills of the exact shot that I want, so, so yeah, I'm OK.
I What kind of photos do you take?
K Um, I take a lot of photos of my children, um, I like a lot of action shots, so I'll, I'll take photos of them doing things. Um, I like taking photos of nice places when I go anywhere, so scenic photos, that kind of thing.
I Do you have a camera, or do you use your phone?
K I always use my phone. Um, I do have a camera, but I've probably not used it in about five years. It was quite a good one as well, really expensive, but no, just the convenience of using my phone, and to be honest, it probably takes better photos.

3
I = interviewer, S = Shreeya
I How worried are you about plastic pollution?
S Um, yes, I would say I'm quite concerned about plastic pollution, um, the effect it has on sea life, the environment in general, um, and I think it's good that businesses are taking it more seriously, too.
I Are you doing anything to try to use fewer plastic products?
S I tend to not…while holding a plastic cup, um, can I put this down for that,…yes, if I'm shopping, I'll try to bring, um, a bag of my own, um, and if I have packed lunches for example, I'll reuse the same container and I have a water bottle as well, so I don't get plastic water, I, um, tend to refill it.

4
I = interviewer, E = Emma
I What did you study at university?
E Yeah, I'm studying at university now.
I What are you studying?
E Osteopathy.
I Why did you choose that subject?
E Um, because I used to be a competitive swimmer and, um, we, I used to get recurrent injuries and I was seeing a physiotherapist and I wasn't really getting anywhere, and then somebody suggested to me to see an osteopath. I went to see an osteopath and my injuries improved really quickly and it inspired me to be an osteopath.

5
I = interviewer, T = Thomas
I Have you ever had a part-time job?
T Yeah, I've, you know, when I was in graduate school I bartended, waited tables, um, you know, for, for part-time.
I Did you enjoy them?
T I loved them, I loved them, each, each one, um, had different things, but it's part of my personality I would say. I've never had a job where I said I didn't like it, you know, I always tried to find the good in it. And when you're bartending and waitering, you meet a lot of interesting people, you have a lot of good conversations, and you, you find, um, you meet a lot of people who, you know, I would say you'd see some of the bad of humanity and how they treat others, probably more so as a waiter than a bartender, you know.
I So people often complained, like about the bill?
T Yeah, and the service , and if their food's late, yeah. It's interesting. It was a lot of fun though. I had a good time.

5A Screen time

G present perfect simple
V television
P /w/, /v/, and /b/

Lesson plan

The topic of this lesson is television. Sts begin with a vocabulary focus on different kinds of TV programmes and common phrasal verbs used to talk about television. This is followed by a pronunciation focus contrasting three consonant sounds that Sts sometimes confuse or have problems producing: /w/, /v/, and /b/. The theme of television continues and Sts listen to seven speakers describing how they watch TV (i.e. on a device or a TV, binge-watch, etc.) and what they watch. Sts then revise and consolidate some important uses of the present perfect simple and expand their knowledge of different adverbs typically used with this form.

In the second half of the lesson, Sts read an article about the popularity of foreign-language drama series in the UK. The lesson ends with a speaking activity in which Sts consolidate the vocabulary, grammar, and pronunciation by talking about different TV series that they have just finished watching, have seen many times, etc.

More materials
For teachers
Photocopiables
Grammar present perfect simple *p.160*
Communicative Soap opera *p.188* (instructions *p.174*)
Vocabulary Television *p.212* (instructions *p.203*)
For students
Workbook 5A
Online Practice 5A

OPTIONAL LEAD-IN (BOOKS CLOSED)
Write on the board:
• DO YOU HAVE A TV IN YOUR LIVING ROOM? HOW BIG IS IT?
• DO YOU HAVE ANY OTHER TVS IN YOUR HOUSE? WHERE?
• WHO WATCHES THE MOST TV IN YOUR HOUSE?

Put Sts in pairs and give them a few minutes to answer the questions.
Get feedback from different Sts, and tell them about your TV(s).

1 VOCABULARY television

a 🔊 **5.1** Books open. Focus on the task and make sure Sts know what an *extract* is (= a short piece of writing, music, film, etc. taken from a longer whole). Model and drill its pronunciation /ˈekstrækt/.

Now focus on the types of TV programme and explain / elicit that a *sitcom* is a 'situation comedy' (= a TV comedy series in which a group of characters are involved in amusing situations, e.g. *Friends*, *The Office*, *The Big Bang Theory*, etc.). You might also want to point out the pronunciation of the adjective *live* /laɪv/ in *live sport*.

Play the audio once the whole way through, pausing after each extract.
Get Sts to compare with a partner, and then check answers.

a 5 **b** 4 **c** 3 **d** 2 **e** 6 **f** 1

🔊 **5.1**
1 This is *World Update*. I'm Katy Lee. Here are tonight's top stories. The Prime Minister has just announced that spending on education is to be increased…
2 A Johnson! Have you been sleeping on the job again?
  B No, Ms Lewis. I was just, er, resting my eyes.
  A But there's a pillow on your desk!
  B Uh-oh! I did it again!
3 A Yes…Yes…Where? OK, we're on our way.
  B What is it?
  A They've found a body. Next to the canal.
  B Do they think it's her?
  A They don't know yet. Come on, let's go.
4 Here, deep in the African forest, lives the green mamba, one of the world's most poisonous snakes. It spends much of its time in the trees, and adults can grow to a length of over two metres…
5 A Mark, welcome to the programme.
  B Thanks, Jake. It's a pleasure to be here.
  A Now I know you're over here promoting your latest film, and in a minute, I'm going to ask you about it, but first…
6 Now Parker on the ball…to Lennon…now to Dempsey, making a run. Lennon finds Dempsey; he's got room here…Dempsey! Oh my word! That changes everything!

b Tell Sts to go to **Vocabulary Bank Television** on *p.158*.

Vocabulary notes
Types of programme
There may be some programme types that Sts are not familiar with or that don't have a specific name in their L1, e.g. *sitcom*, so try to give as many examples as you can, from for example Netflix, that Sts might recognize.

Phrasal verbs
Highlight that phrasal verbs 1–4 are separable, i.e. you can also put the particle after the noun, e.g. *Please* **turn on** *the TV* **OR** *Please* **turn** *the TV* **on**, and if the object is a pronoun, it must go between the verb and the particle, e.g. *Please turn it on*.
Remind Sts that they can also use *switch on / off* or *switch over*, but not *switch up / down*.

Focus on **1 Types of programme** and get Sts to do **a** individually or in pairs.

🔊 **5.2** Now do **b**. Play the audio for Sts to listen and check.
Check answers.

🔊 **5.2**
Television
1 Types of programme
7 advert
6 cartoon
11 chat show
5 cookery programme
8 current affairs programme

5A 69

10 documentary
9 drama
4 live sport
13 period drama
2 quiz show
1 reality show
12 the news
3 the weather forecast

Now either use the audio to drill the pronunciation of the words and phrases, or model and drill them yourself. Give further practice of any words your Sts find difficult to pronounce.

Focus on the **series, soaps, and sitcoms** box and go through it with the class.

Finally, do **Activation** and put Sts in pairs to answer the question.

Then get some feedback from various pairs.

EXTRA SUPPORT Get Sts to cover the words and phrases and look at the photos. Can they remember all the types of programme?

EXTRA IDEA Draw a picture of a TV and remote control on the board and elicit what the different parts are, i.e. *the remote (control), the screen, the speakers, the stand*.

Now focus on **2 Phrasal verbs** and get Sts to do **a** individually or in pairs.

🔊 **5.3** Now do **b**. Play the audio for Sts to listen and check.

Check answers.

🔊 **5.3**
2 Phrasal verbs
1 **turn on** the TV
2 **turn off** the TV
3 **turn up** the TV
4 **turn down** the TV
5 the programme **is on** now
6 **turn over** to another channel

Now either use the audio to drill the pronunciation of the sentences, or model and drill them yourself. Give further practice of any words your Sts find difficult to pronounce.

EXTRA SUPPORT Get Sts to cover 1–6 and try to remember the meaning of the phrasal verbs in the list.

Finally, focus on **Activation** and get Sts to ask and answer the questions in pairs.

Get some feedback from various pairs.

EXTRA SUPPORT If you think Sts need more practice, you may want to give them the **Vocabulary** photocopiable activity at this point.

c Do this as a whole-class activity, or put Sts in pairs and then get some feedback. You could find out with a show of hands if there is a favourite type of TV programme in class.

2 PRONUNCIATION /w/, /v/, and /b/

Pronunciation notes

/w/, /v/, and /b/

These three sounds can be problematic for learners from a number of different first languages, for example in German and many Slavonic languages *w* is pronounced /v/ rather than /w/, and in other languages the /w/ sound doesn't really exist at all. Spanish speakers often have problems distinguishing between /v/ and /b/. It is important that all learners are able to perceive and produce all three sounds clearly. The first exercise reminds Sts of the three sounds using the sound pictures and the phonetic symbols. The next three exercises focus on learners distinguishing between and producing the different sounds.

a 🔊 **5.4** Focus on the sound pictures and elicit the words and sounds: *witch* /w/, *vase* /v/, and *bag* /b/.

Play the audio once the whole way through for Sts just to listen.

🔊 **5.4**
See words and sounds in Student's Book on *p.46*

Then play the audio again, pausing after each word or group of words and sound for Sts to listen and repeat.

EXTRA SUPPORT Ask Sts to watch your lips as you say *we, TV*, and *be*. As you say each word, point to your lips, and then ask Sts to tell you how the lips were used to make each sound. Elicit that:

1 for /w/ the lips make a 'kissing' shape
2 for /v/ the top teeth are in contact with the bottom lip
3 for /b/ the top and bottom lips are pressed together in a line

b 🔊 **5.5** Focus on the pairs of words and make sure Sts know what they mean.

Now play the audio once the whole way through for Sts just to listen.

Ask if they can hear the difference.

🔊 **5.5**
See words in Student's Book on *p.46*

Play the audio again, pausing after each pair for Sts to listen and repeat.

c 🔊 **5.6** Now tell Sts that this time, they will only hear one of the words in each pair and they must circle the one they hear.

Play the audio once the whole way through for Sts to complete the task.

Check answers.

1 **a** boat 2 **b** V 3 **b** berry 4 **b** win 5 **b** bull 6 **a** why
7 **a** vet 8 **a** wine

🔊 **5.6**
1 boat
2 V
3 berry
4 win
5 bull

6 why
7 vet
8 wine

EXTRA CHALLENGE Put Sts in pairs, **A** and **B**. Sts **A** say one of the options from the pairs of words in **b**, and Sts **B** have to indicate which word he / she heard.
Make sure Sts swap roles.
Throughout the activity, monitor, acting as the 'judge' when two Sts don't agree on what they said or heard.

EXTRA SUPPORT If these sounds are difficult for your Sts, it will help to show them the mouth position. You could model this yourself or use the Sound Bank videos on the *Teacher's Resource Centre*.

d Give Sts time to practise the sentences. Remind them to focus on the correct pronunciation of the sounds for the pink letters in the words.

EXTRA SUPPORT Model and drill each sentence first, before getting Sts to practise saying them.

3 LISTENING & SPEAKING understanding answers

a Focus on the instructions. Then put Sts in pairs, **A** and **B**. Sts **A** start by describing photo 1 and then Sts **B** describe photo 2.
Finally, they discuss how the photos illustrate the way in which watching TV has changed over time.
Get some feedback from various pairs.

EXTRA SUPPORT Tell Sts to quickly revise vocabulary for describing a photo in **Vocabulary Bank Photography** on *p.155*.

b Focus on the task and the questionnaire. Before Sts do the task, you might want to focus on the definitions on the right and explain / elicit the meaning of *slang* (= very informal words and expressions that are more common in spoken language) and an *idiom* (= a group of words whose meaning is different from the meanings of the individual words). Point out that the first one (*device*) has been done for them.

Now give Sts time to read the questionnaire and complete the definitions with the highlighted words and phrases.

Get Sts to compare with a partner, and then check answers. Model and drill pronunciation. You might want to point out that the plural of *device* is pronounced /dɪˈvaɪsɪz/.

2 watch a TV programme or series on one device while using another at the same time
3 a service that allows you to watch television programmes after the time when they were originally broadcast
4 watch several episodes of a TV series one after the other
5 a method of sending or receiving data over a computer network
6 a television station
7 a person who takes part in a game, quiz, or competition

EXTRA SUPPORT Get Sts to work in pairs.

c 🔊 **5.7** Focus on the photos and elicit what kinds of programmes Sts think they show.

Play the audio once, pausing after each speaker. Then elicit the programme or kind of programme they mention. You could ask Sts if they have seen any of the programmes mentioned. If Sts don't know, explain what the programmes are about: *MasterChef* is a TV cookery competition; *Mad Men* is a US drama series set in an advertising agency in Madison Avenue, New York; *Brideshead Revisited* is a UK period drama series; *Strictly Come Dancing* is a TV dance show where viewers vote for their favourite couple.

Get Sts to compare with a partner, and then check answers.

EXTRA SUPPORT Read through the script and decide if you need to pre-teach any new lexis before Sts listen. You may want to write the names of the four programmes on the board before Sts listen.

Speaker 1 D   Speaker 2 E   Speaker 3 C   Speaker 4 F
Speaker 5 B   Speaker 6 G   Speaker 7 A

🔊 **5.7**
(script in Student's Book on *p.127*)
I = interviewer, M = man, W = woman

1
I How do you watch TV programmes, on a television or on another device?
M I watch programmes on TV if I'm at home, or on my laptop, or on my iPad. I might watch something on my phone if I was…I don't know…I suppose when something has happened on the news, I might watch it live, or something like that.

2
I Do you 'two-screen' while watching TV? What kinds of things do you do?
W Yes, I can often be guilty of perhaps checking emails on my phone, or perhaps even doing a bit of online shopping while I'm watching TV. In fact, yesterday I was watching *MasterChef* – you know, the cookery competition – and I bought some small cake tins that you needed to make…to make a chocolate thing that one of the contestants was making.

3
I Do you normally watch live TV or catch-up?
M Both, though nowadays I watch more catch-up. But I watch the news live, and football or tennis – Wimbledon – things like that.

4
I Have you ever binge watched a TV series? How many episodes did you watch in one go?
W I haven't done it for a long time, but I did once watch eight episodes in one sitting of the American series *Mad Men*. But as I say, it was a long time ago.

5
I Do you use a streaming service like Netflix? What do you like about it?
M I have Netflix and I also buy things off Amazon Prime Video – is that a streaming service? I don't really use them for films, more for TV series, like old ones I missed when they first came out. For example, a few months ago, I watched all the episodes of *Brideshead Revisited*, the original series from the eighties, because I didn't see it then, but I'd heard that it was very good.

6
I How often do you watch YouTube, or online channels like Apple? What kinds of things do you watch?
W I sometimes watch YouTube – it's usually if I have a problem with my laptop or my phone and I want to find out how to fix it, and I sometimes…I sometimes use it for watching people cook recipes. In fact, I've just watched someone preparing a fish dish because I'm going to cook it this evening.

5A 71

7
I Do you ever interact with TV shows by voting for contestants?
W Not very often, but I do like *Strictly Come Dancing* and I have voted several times for contestants, when they've done a really good dance. And once, I was addicted to a TV show where the contestants were auditioning for a part in a West End musical, and I really liked one young singer, so I voted for him every week. And eventually, he won, and I remember shouting and jumping off the sofa when the results were announced!

d Focus on the instructions and make sure Sts understand that Speaker 1 answers question 1 in **b**, Speaker 2 question 2, etc.

Play the audio again for Sts to write how each speaker watches TV. You could pause the audio after each speaker.

Get Sts to compare with a partner and discuss how each speaker answered the question.

Check answers. You might want to point out how the last speaker uses the auxiliary *do* to add emphasis to her sentence '…, but I do like *Strictly Come Dancing*'.

Speaker 1
He watches TV programmes on a television, laptop, or iPad at home. And if he's out, maybe on his phone.

Speaker 2
She often checks emails or does online shopping while watching TV.

Speaker 3
He watches live TV and catch-up, but more catch-up.

Speaker 4
She doesn't binge-watch very often, but she once watched 8 episodes of a series (*Mad Men*).

Speaker 5
He uses a streaming service, like Netflix. He likes being able to watch old films and TV series that he didn't watch when they first came out.

Speaker 6
She watches YouTube if she has a problem and wants to find out how to fix it and for recipes.

Speaker 7
She has sometimes voted for contestants on *Strictly Come Dancing*, and once voted for a contestant who was auditioning for a TV show.

EXTRA SUPPORT If there's time, you could get Sts to listen again with the script on *p.127*, so they can see exactly what they understood / didn't understand. Translate / Explain any new words or phrases.

e Sts now take turns to interview each other and find out about their partner's television habits when watching a TV series. Put Sts in pairs and tell them to ask and answer the questions in **b**, giving as much information as possible.

Get some feedback from various pairs.

EXTRA IDEA If there's time, the class could interview you.

4 GRAMMAR present perfect simple

a Focus on the instructions and then give Sts time to see if they can remember any of the missing words.

Get Sts to compare with a partner, and to say why each tense was used.

b 🔊 5.8 Play the audio for Sts to listen and check.

Check answers and elicit why either the present perfect or the past simple is used in each one.

1 has (the present perfect for a period of time from the past until now)
2 bought (the past simple for finished past time)
3 for (the present perfect for a period of time from the past until now)
4 ago (the past simple for finished past time)
5 just (the present perfect with *just* for recent past time)
6 voted (the present perfect for past experiences without saying when)
7 was (the past simple for finished past time)

🔊 5.8
1 When something has happened on the news, I might watch it live.
2 Yesterday I was watching *MasterChef* and I bought some small cake tins.
3 I haven't done it for a long time.
4 For example, a few months ago, I watched all the episodes of *Brideshead Revisited*.
5 I've just watched someone preparing a fish dish.
6 I have voted several times for contestants, when they've done a really good dance.
7 Once, I was addicted to a TV show.

EXTRA SUPPORT Play the audio for Sts to listen and check what the missing words are. Put Sts in pairs and give them time to discuss why each tense is used. Finally, elicit answers.

c Tell Sts to go to **Grammar Bank 5A** on *p.140*.

Grammar notes
Present perfect simple

At Intermediate Plus level, Sts will have seen the present perfect simple several times, and will have contrasted it with the past simple, but, along with future forms, it is an area where they make a lot of mistakes and need frequent practice, mainly because some of its uses do not correspond exactly with similar tenses in other languages. The most problematic use for Sts of most nationalities is with *How long…?* and *for* and *since*, where their L1 may use a present form, and Sts have tended to say, e.g. ~~I work here for five years~~.

Focus on **Revise the basics** and use the chart to remind Sts of the form of the present perfect.

Then focus on the example sentences and play audio 🔊 5.9 for Sts to listen and repeat. Encourage them to copy the rhythm. Then go through the rules with the class.

Refer Sts to the irregular past participles in the **Irregular verbs** list on *p.165*.

Focus on the exercises and get Sts to do them individually or in pairs. Encourage them to use contracted forms rather than full forms in **b**.

Check answers, getting Sts to read the full sentences.

a
1 for   2 I've already had   3 I've never been   4 since we were at university   5 already   6 they've been married   7 have you been   8 all his life   9 we went   10 just

b
1 A **Did** you **see** that wildlife documentary last night?
   B No, I **missed** it.
2 A When **did** you **get** here?
   B I arrived at the weekend, so I**'ve only been** here for a few days.

3 A **Have** you **checked** the match results?
  B It **hasn't finished** yet. It **started** late.
4 A Bad news – Ben**'s had** a bike accident.
  B Oh no! When **did** that **happen**?
5 B I think she**'s just gone out** for lunch.
6 A **Have** you **ever beaten** him at tennis?
  B No, but I **won** a set last time.
7 A **Has** Marcus **already started** his new job?
  B Yes, his first day **was** last Monday.
8 A How long **have** you **had** a motorbike?
  B Not long! I **bought** it six months ago.

Tell Sts to go back to the main lesson **5A**.

EXTRA SUPPORT If you think Sts need more practice, you may want to give them the **Grammar** photocopiable activity at this point.

d Focus on the statements and the example. Tell Sts that they should only change the **bold** words in the statements to make them true for themselves.
  Give Sts a few minutes to think about their sentences.
  Put Sts in pairs and get them to discuss each one and ask each other follow-up questions.
  Highlight that Sts should use the present perfect simple at the beginning, but if they later refer to a specific time in the past, they need to use the past simple, e.g. *I've watched about four hours of TV, I think. I watched MasterChef and…*
  Get some feedback.

EXTRA SUPPORT You could model the activity first by choosing one of the statements and then eliciting follow-up questions.

5 READING speculating based on visual clues

a Do this as a whole-class activity, or put Sts in pairs and then get some feedback.

b Focus on the images and the instructions and get Sts to do the matching activity in pairs. Tell them to try to find clues, e.g. what languages the original titles look like or the actors, to help them.

❗ Don't ask Sts if they have seen any of the dramas as they will be discussing this later.

c Put Sts in pairs, **A** and **B**, and tell them to go to **Communication TV dramas**, **A** on *p.108*, **B** on *p.112*.
  Tell the class that Sts **A** will be reading about TV dramas A–D, and Sts **B** about TV dramas E–H.
  Focus on the instructions and make sure Sts understand what they have to do. You might want to explain / elicit the meaning of *where it's set* in **b**.
  When Sts have finished **a** and **b**, they should do **c** and take turns to tell each other about each series.
  Tell Sts to go back to the main lesson **5A**.
  Check answers to **b**.

| A Denmark | B Spain | C France | D Italy | E France |
| F Sweden / Denmark | | G Argentina | | H Brazil |

d Do this as a whole-class activity. If you have seen any of the series, you could tell the class.

e Focus on the instructions and three titles. Make sure Sts know the meaning of *foreign*. Model and drill its pronunciation.
  Give Sts time to read the first paragraph or read it aloud to the class.
  Check the answer.

Why is the UK in love with foreign TV series?

f Now focus on the **Glossary** and go through it with the class. Go through 1–5, making sure Sts understand all the lexis.
  Give Sts time to read the article and choose the correct options.
  Get Sts to compare with a partner, and then check answers.

EXTRA SUPPORT Before Sts read the article the first time, check whether you need to pre-teach any vocabulary.

1 b 2 a 3 a 4 c 5 b

Deal with any new vocabulary. Model and drill the pronunciation of any tricky words.

g Put Sts in pairs to discuss the question.
  Get some feedback from various pairs.

EXTRA SUPPORT Do this as a whole-class activity.

EXTRA IDEA Ask Sts if foreign TV series or films in their country are dubbed or subtitled. Then ask which they prefer and why.

6 SPEAKING

a Give Sts time to complete as many boxes as possible.

b Focus on the **Expressing enthusiasm** box and go through it with the class. Make sure Sts understand all the expressions, especially the informal phrase *to be hooked on sth* (= enjoying sth very much, so that you want to do it, see it, etc. as much as possible). Model and drill the intonation of the phrases, to show Sts how we use extra stress on the key words to demonstrate enthusiasm, e.g. *I think it's **absolutely brilliant**! I **adore** the main the character*, etc.
  Put Sts in small groups of three or four and give them time to discuss the questions in each box they completed.
  Monitor and help where necessary.
  Get some feedback from various groups.

EXTRA CHALLENGE Write the following statements on the board and get Sts to discuss them in groups.
1 YOU ENJOY A SERIES MORE IF YOU WATCH IT WEEKLY AND DON'T BINGE-WATCH.
2 CHILDREN UNDER THE AGE OF FIVE SHOULDN'T WATCH ANY TELEVISION AT ALL.
3 TV SCREENS SHOULD BE BANNED FROM BARS AND RESTAURANTS.
4 YOU ENJOY WATCHING LIVE SPORT ON TV MORE IF YOU WATCH IT WITH OTHER PEOPLE.
5 BOOK ADAPTATIONS WORK BETTER AS TV SERIES THAN AS FILMS.
6 THE NEWS ON TV IS NOT OBJECTIVE, AS MOST CHANNELS ARE CONTROLLED BY THE GOVERNMENT.

Get some feedback from various groups.

5B A quiet life?

G present perfect continuous
V the country
P vowel sounds, sentence rhythm

Lesson plan

The country, nature, and farming are the main topics of this lesson. In the first half of the lesson, Sts read an article about some Italian villages which are becoming ghost towns and what some local mayors are doing to prevent this from happening. Sts then discuss what they read and whether any of the solutions are good and come up with other ideas to help towns and villages survive. Next, Sts learn words and phrases related to the country. These are then recycled and practised in a pronunciation focus on vowels that can be pronounced in different ways.

In the second half, Sts listen to two British people who moved to the country and had very different experiences. This leads to Sts talking about someone they know who has moved from the city to the country or vice versa. They also imagine themselves moving and what they would enjoy and miss most. Next, they revise the form and uses of the present perfect continuous, and then practise it orally with the correct sentence stress in the pronunciation focus. Finally, Sts write an email in which they practise the grammar from the lesson.

More materials
For teachers
Photocopiables
Grammar present perfect continuous *p.161*
Communicative Why did you write…? *p.189-190* (instructions *p.174*)
Vocabulary The country *p.213* (instructions *p.203*)
For students
Workbook 5B
Online Practice 5B

OPTIONAL LEAD-IN (BOOKS CLOSED)

Write on the board:
VILLAGE TOWN CITY

Get Sts, in pairs, to try to write a definition for each word.

Check their definitions. You may want to tell them that in Britain a town has to have a cathedral in order to be called a city.

> a village = a small community in a rural area
> a town = a place with many shops, houses, etc. where people live and work. It is larger than a village, but smaller than a city.
> a city = a large, important town

Elicit names of towns, cities, and villages in the region where you are working, and if your Sts are from different places, do a class survey to find out whether they live in a village, town, or city. Also ask *Do you like living there? If not, where would you prefer to live?*

1 READING & SPEAKING understanding problems and solutions

a Books open. Focus on the instructions and the introduction to the article. Give Sts time to read it and answer questions 1–3.

Check the answer to the first question and elicit opinions for the other two.

> 1 Because people are leaving to go and work in the cities and birth rates are falling.

b Focus on the instructions and phrases A–D, making sure Sts understand all the lexis.

Give Sts time to read the first paragraph and complete the gaps.

Check answers.

EXTRA SUPPORT Get Sts, in pairs, to describe the photographs before they read the rest of the article.

EXTRA SUPPORT Before Sts read the article the first time, check whether you need to pre-teach any vocabulary.

> 1 B 2 D 3 C 4 A

c Now focus on the instructions and make sure Sts know what a *mayor* is (= the head of a town, usually elected). Model and drill its pronunciation /meə/.

Give Sts time to read the second paragraph and complete the tourist information.

Get them to compare with a partner, and then check answers.

> The mayor's idea was to charge people an entrance fee to visit the town.
> Entrance fee:
> Monday–Saturday €3
> Sunday and public holidays €5
> You can also book a private **tour** and you can buy refreshments.

d Now tell Sts to read the rest of the article and then answer questions 1–4.

Get them to compare with a partner, and then check answers. You could tell Sts that there are now more than 120 *Albergo Diffuso*.

> 1 It was in ruins, with only 70 inhabitants.
> 2 He was a Swedish-Italian millionaire who visited the village. His idea was to buy the houses and restore the buildings as hotel rooms.
> 3 He buys everything for the hotel rooms from local people, including food and room accessories, so he is keeping local crafts and the economy alive.
> 4 Now people are using the houses, and the economy has been revived; the village is alive again.

Deal with any other new vocabulary. Model and drill the pronunciation of any tricky words.

e Put Sts in pairs to discuss the three questions.

Monitor and help with any vocabulary.

Get some feedback from various pairs. You could find out with a show of hands which village most Sts would like to visit.

EXTRA SUPPORT Do all or some of the questions as a whole-class activity.

2 VOCABULARY the country

a Do this as a whole-class activity and elicit ideas and opinions. Encourage Sts to use *It could be* or *It might be* when they speculate.

b 🔊 **5.10** Tell Sts to listen to a woman talking about her life in the village in the photo. They must check their answer to **a**.

Play the audio once the whole way through.

Check the answer.

The photo shows a village in Turkey.

🔊 **5.10**
(script in Student's Book on *p.127*)
I used to live in a village in the province of Sakarya. It was an amazing place to live – just so beautiful. There's a large lake nearby and the hills are covered with pine trees – people go to picnic there. The coast is also not far away. When I lived there, it was as if time had stood still. People worked in the fields. Some things were annoying…there was no running water or electricity – we had our own well and generator – and there was only one shop. We had to wait for a minibus from the nearest town to bring fresh bread and the newspapers every morning! I worked in a school in a nearby town – in fact, the one that sent the bread and papers. I used to think, when I was living there, that there wasn't much choice of things to do, things to buy, but I made my own entertainment – I played tennis, went for walks, played the piano. In the end, I had to move for work, to Istanbul, which is the biggest and noisiest city in Turkey, and now I really miss the fresh food and fresh fish, the peace and quiet.

c Give Sts time to read the four questions.

EXTRA SUPPORT Put Sts in pairs before playing the audio again and give them time to see if they can remember any information from the first listening.

Now play the audio again. You could pause it after each question is answered to give Sts time to write.

Check answers.

1 It was very beautiful; the coast wasn't far away.
2 There was no running water or electricity, and only one shop. There wasn't much choice of things to do and buy.
3 In Istanbul
4 The fresh food, fresh fish, the peace and quiet

d 🔊 **5.11** Before playing the audio, get Sts to see if they can remember what the missing words are.

Play the audio, pausing after each extract to give Sts time to write.

Check answers, making sure Sts understand all the lexis.

1 lake   2 hills   3 fields   4 well

🔊 **5.11**
1 There's a large lake nearby…
2 …the hills are covered with pine trees…
3 People worked in the fields.
4 …we had our own well and generator…

e Tell Sts to go to **Vocabulary Bank** *The country* on *p.159*.

Vocabulary notes
Nature
Make sure Sts practise the pronunciation of the heading *Nature* /ˈneɪtʃə/ as many Sts have problems with this word.
Point out that a *wood* is a smaller area than a *forest*. *Wood* is also the material that comes from trees.
Elicit that the adjective from *mud* is *muddy*.

On a farm
Elicit that a male cow is a *bull* (Sts should know this word, as it is the example word in the Sound Chart for the /ʊ/ sound).
Highlight the silent *b* in *lambs*. You may want to point out that we often use *cock* instead of *cockerel*.

Focus on **1 Nature** and get Sts to do **a** individually or in pairs.

🔊 **5.12** Now do **b**. Play the audio for Sts to listen and check.

Check answers.

🔊 **5.12**
The country
1 Nature
19 branch
15 bush
9 cliff
14 fence
6 field
8 gate
17 grass
4 hedge
3 hill
11 lake
2 leaf
7 mud
1 path
10 rocks
16 sticks
13 stones
18 stream
20 valley
12 well
5 wood

Now either use the audio to drill the pronunciation of the words, or model and drill them yourself. Give further practice of any words your Sts find difficult to pronounce.

Get Sts to do **Activation** by covering the words, looking at the photos, and saying the words. They could do this individually or in pairs.

Focus on the ***the country* and *the countryside*** box and go through it with the class.

EXTRA IDEA Write the following pairs of words on the board and get Sts to say what the difference is.

A BUSH AND A TREE; A FENCE AND A HEDGE; A HILL AND A MOUNTAIN; A LAKE AND A STREAM; A GATE AND A DOOR; A PATH AND A ROAD; ROCKS AND STONES; A STICK AND A BRANCH; A FOREST AND A WOOD

Now focus on **2 On a farm** and get Sts to do **a** individually or in pairs.

🔊 **5.13** Now do **b**. Play the audio for Sts to listen and check.

5B

Check answers.

🔊 **5.13**
2 **On a farm**
5 barn
3 cockerel
9 cow
1 donkey
6 farmhouse
4 hens
7 lambs
2 sheep
8 tractor

Now either use the audio to drill the pronunciation of the words, or model and drill them yourself. Give further practice of any words your Sts find difficult to pronounce.

Get Sts to do **c** individually or in pairs.

🔊 **5.14** Now do **d**. Play the audio for Sts to listen and check.

Check answers.

1 grow   2 planted   3 harvested   4 pick

🔊 **5.14**
In the UK, especially in the east of England, a lot of farmers grow cereals – for example, wheat – vegetables, and fruit. Most crops are planted in the early spring and are harvested in the summer, for example, wheat in August, and most potatoes from June onwards. Soft fruits like strawberries are usually ripe in June and July, and many farms invite people to come and pick their own fruit.

Now either use the audio to drill the pronunciation of the sentences, or model and drill them yourself. Give further practice of any words your Sts find difficult to pronounce.

Go through the text with Sts, checking that they understand all the words in **bold**. If necessary, use Sts' L1 to clarify. Find out if any words are similar in your Sts' language(s)? If so, do they mean the same?

EXTRA IDEA Depending on where your Sts live and what kind of farming / countryside there is locally, you may want to teach some more words and phrases to help them to talk about their local situation.

For **Activation**, get Sts to cover the words in **a**, look at the photos, and say the words.

Tell Sts to go back to the main lesson **5B**.

EXTRA SUPPORT If you think Sts need more practice, you may want to give them the **Vocabulary** photocopiable activity at this point.

f Do the question as a whole-class activity.

3 PRONUNCIATION vowel sounds

Pronunciation notes
In this focus, Sts distinguish between a number of common vowel sounds which should be familiar to them from previous levels of *English File*. The main problem Sts have is when a vowel or a combination of letters can be pronounced in different ways, as in the examples in the exercise.

a Focus on the pairs of words. Give Sts two or three minutes to decide if the vowel sounds are the same or different in each pair of words.

EXTRA CHALLENGE Elicit answers to **a** before playing the audio.

b 🔊 **5.15** Play the audio for Sts to listen and check. Check answers and elicit the sound picture for each one.

(sound words shown in brackets)
1 S (tree /iː/)
2 D: bush (bull /ʊ/), mud (up /ʌ/)
3 S (car /ɑː/)
4 D: grow (phone /əʊ/), cow (owl /aʊ/)
5 S (fish /ɪ/)
6 D: rock (clock /ɒ/), stone (phone /əʊ/)
7 D: lamb (cat /æ/), grass (car /ɑː/)
8 S (tree /iː/)

🔊 **5.15**
See words in Student's Book on *p.51*

Finally, get Sts to practise saying the words.

EXTRA SUPPORT Before getting Sts to practise saying the words, play the audio again, pausing after each pair of words for Sts to listen and repeat.

EXTRA SUPPORT If these sounds are difficult for your Sts, it will help to show them the mouth position. You could model this yourself or use the Sound Bank videos on the *Teacher's Resource Centre*.

4 LISTENING & SPEAKING listening for point of view

a Focus on the title of the article, *From the city to the country and sometimes back again*, and the introduction. Read it as a class and then do the questions as a whole-class activity.

b Focus on the photos and tell Sts that Liz Jones and Bob Ayres moved to the country. Before Sts read each paragraph to find out why these people moved to the country, you might want to explain / elicit the meaning and pronunciation of *idyllic* /ɪˈdɪlɪk/ (= peaceful and beautiful) and *shooting* here (= a situation in which a person is shot with a gun).

Get Sts to compare with a partner, and then check answers.

Liz
She wanted somewhere quieter, simpler, more beautiful to live.
Bob
He and his wife had stressful jobs; they had often talked about moving to the country.

c 🔊 **5.16** Focus on the instructions and the extracts. You might want to explain / elicit the meaning of *shooting* in Liz's extract (= the sport of shooting animals and birds with guns). Point out the nesting herons in the photo.

Play the audio, pausing after each extract to give Sts time to complete the gaps.

Get Sts to compare with a partner, and then check answers.

Liz					
1 shop	**2** Mars	**3** hated	**4** view	**5** stars	
Bob					
6 donkey, horse	**7** sheep	**8** muddy	**9** hard	**10** farmers	

🔊 **5.16**

Liz
1 you have to drive miles to find a shop
2 they look at you as if you were from Mars
3 another thing I hated was the shooting
4 an amazing view and a pair of nesting herons
5 I sat outside underneath millions of stars

Bob
6 my wife always wanted to have a donkey or a horse
7 so we started with four sheep
8 it gets incredibly muddy
9 it can get physically very hard
10 there were some local farmers who didn't really like newcomers

Now play the audio again for Sts just to listen to the extracts and decide who stayed and who moved back to the city.

Either do the question as a whole-class activity, or get Sts to discuss it in pairs and get some feedback. Encourage Sts to give their reasons, but <u>don't</u> tell them if they are correct. You could get Sts to show their opinion with a show of hands.

d 🔊 **5.17** Focus on the **Glossary** and go through it with the class.

Now play the audio for Sts to listen to Liz and Bob talking about their experiences, and to check their answer to the question in **c**.

Check the answer.

EXTRA SUPPORT Read through the script and decide if you need to pre-teach any new lexis before Sts listen.

Bob stayed, and Liz moved back to London.

🔊 **5.17**
(script in Student's Book on *p.127*)

Liz
When I moved in, the house was cold and absolutely filthy, and the cooker didn't work. I discovered everything in the countryside is more expensive: you have to drive miles to find a shop, where everything costs twice as much as in my local supermarket in London. Local restaurants are really expensive, and if you tell the waiter that you're a vegetarian, they look at you as if you were from Mars. I never fitted in. I think that in the country, if you're a woman, you'll never be accepted unless you're a full-time mum. Another thing I hated was the shooting! I love animals – I had two horses and two dogs – and I just couldn't pass a group of men with guns, shooting rabbits and deer, without getting out of my car and saying, 'Do you really have nothing better to do on a Saturday morning?' That didn't make me very popular. I became so lonely I often used to sit in my car and listen to the kind voice of the satnav lady. After five years, I decided to go back to London. I'd learnt that an amazing view and a pair of nesting herons were not enough to make me happy. On my last night in the country, I sat outside underneath millions of stars and I thought to myself, 'I've come to the end of a five-year prison sentence.' I promised myself I would never, ever go back.

Bob
The first thing we had to do was find new jobs. Jean got part-time work with a local company that sells meat products, and I did work as a lawyer. Two years later, we had a barn built, and my wife always wanted to have a donkey or a horse, but in the end we thought sheep were less destructive to the land, so we kept with the sheep, better for the land. So we started with four sheep, which we kept in the garden at first, and then we bought a field, and then we bought ten more sheep and sold six for meat, and that was the start of our sheep business. Now we've got sixty-eight sheep and seven fields. At the moment, we've got twenty-five sheep that are expecting lambs, ready for the next season. In addition to that, we've got free-range hens which we rescued from battery farms. It hasn't all been easy. Um, it rains a lot where we live now, and um, it gets incredibly muddy, and of course the work with the animals – it can get physically very hard. At first, we had a little bit of resistance – there were some local farmers who didn't really like newcomers – but we've always employed local people and we buy food in the local shops, and we try and engage with the local community as much as we possibly can. We sell our meat and eggs to neighbours and friends, and we produce wool from the sheep as well now. We haven't really ever considered moving back, because we really enjoy it. We loved life in the city, but we would never think about going back now.

e Give Sts time to look at 1–8 and see if they can remember who each one refers to.

Now play the audio again for Sts to listen and mark each question with the person's initials or *Bo* for *both*.

Check answers.

1 L	**2** L	**3** B	**4** B	**5** L	**6** Bo	**7** B	**8** B

EXTRA SUPPORT If there's time, you could get Sts to listen again with the script on *p.127*, so they can see exactly what they understood / didn't understand. Translate / Explain any new words or phrases.

f Do the question as a whole-class activity.

g Put Sts in pairs and tell them to go to **Communication City or country?** on *p.106*.

Then tell Sts they should answer the top question *Do you know anyone who...* and then one set of questions if they live in a large town or city or the other set of questions if they live in a village or small town in the country. You could demonstrate the activity by answering one set of questions first.

EXTRA SUPPORT Do a quick revision of the form of the second conditional, which Sts revised in Lesson **4B**. Write on the board:
<u>IF I MOVED</u> TO THE COUNTRY, <u>I'D MISS</u> THE RESTAURANTS AND SHOPS.
<u>I WOULD ENJOY</u> THE PEACE AND QUIET.

Monitor and help with any vocabulary.

Get some feedback from various pairs.

Tell Sts to go back to the main lesson **5B**.

5 GRAMMAR present perfect continuous

a Focus on the photos and what the people are saying. Get Sts to circle the correct forms.

b Get Sts to compare with a partner and explain their choices.

Check answers.

1 I'm fixing (We use the present continuous for actions that are in progress now. The man is in the middle of fixing the tractor.)
2 I've been working (We use the present perfect continuous for continuous or repeated actions that started in the past and have either just finished or are still in progress. Here the man has been working in the fields all day and has just stopped.)

c Tell Sts to go to **Grammar Bank 5B** on *p.141*.

Grammar notes
Present perfect continuous

Sts should have met the present perfect continuous at Intermediate level. This form is difficult for many Sts, partly because a period of time up to now (*I've been learning English for three years*) is expressed with a present tense in many Sts' L1, and also because their L1 may not have continuous tenses. The present perfect continuous form and uses are revised here, with an emphasis on adverbs and expressions like *all day*, *recently*, etc.

It is important that Sts are really comfortable manipulating the present perfect continuous, and feeling confident with when to use it, before getting them to choose between the simple and continuous forms. This is focused on in *English File* Upper-intermediate.

- **Rule 1:** Remind Sts that we use the present perfect simple, not the present perfect continuous, with non-action verbs (e.g. *be*, *know*, *love*).
- **Rule 2:** Elicit some clear examples of actions with visible present results, e.g. *He's hot and sweaty; he's been working out at the gym. They're exhausted; they've been looking after their grandchildren all day*, etc. Remind Sts that if it is a short finished action that has a present result, it will be in the present perfect simple, e.g. *I've cut myself*. NOT *I've been cutting myself*.

Focus on **Revise the basics** and use the chart to revise the form of the present perfect continuous. Remind Sts that we normally contract *have* and *has* in spoken English.

Then focus on the example sentences and play audio 🔊 **5.18** for Sts to listen and repeat. Encourage them to copy the rhythm.

Then go through the rules with the class.

Focus on the **work** and **live** box and go through it with the class.

Now focus on the exercises and get Sts to do them individually or in pairs. Encourage them to use contracted forms rather than full forms.

Check answers, getting Sts to read the full sentences.

a
1 i I**'ve been sitting** in a traffic jam for two hours.
2 b No, thanks. I**'ve been drinking** too much caffeine lately.
3 f I hope so. We**'ve been looking for** a flat we can afford.
4 e No. They**'ve been eating** biscuits all afternoon.
5 g Yes, she**'s been learning** it for a long time.
6 h It's great – I**'ve been taking** pictures all day.
7 a She**'s been watching** a sad film on TV.
8 c I don't think so. It**'s been snowing** very heavily.
b
1 I've been living 2 she's been travelling 3 I haven't been doing 4 I'm staying 5 he's driving 6 I've been waiting 7 it's been raining 8 I'm trying 9 I've been seeing 10 It hasn't been working

Tell Sts to go back to the main lesson **5B**.

EXTRA SUPPORT If you think Sts need more practice, you may want to give them the **Grammar** photocopiable activity at this point.

6 PRONUNCIATION & SPEAKING sentence rhythm

Pronunciation notes

The rhythm of English, with its combination of stressed and unstressed syllables, can become especially difficult for learners when a verb tense requires the presence of auxiliary verbs, as is the case with the present perfect continuous. Some Sts may also have difficulty with the contracted form of *have*, and the weak form of *been* /bɪn/. If so, it is worth focusing specifically on these points to help with the overall rhythm.

These exercises give Sts the opportunity to practise getting the sentence rhythm correct and an opportunity to speak using the present perfect continuous.

a 🔊 **5.19** Focus on the task and then play the audio, pausing after each sentence to give Sts time to complete sentences 1–10. Remind them to use contractions when possible.

Get Sts to compare with a partner, and then play again if necessary.

Check answers.

1 've been working 2 haven't been sleeping
3 have been making 4 've been thinking 5 've been arguing
6 haven't been watching 7 've been feeling 8 've been doing 9 've been going out 10 've been spending

🔊 **5.19**
1 I've been working hard this week.
2 I haven't been sleeping well lately.
3 My neighbours have been making a lot of noise recently.
4 I've been thinking about getting a new phone.
5 I've been arguing with my family a lot recently.
6 I haven't been watching much TV lately.
7 I've been feeling very stressed for the last few weeks.
8 I've been doing a lot of exercise this month.
9 I've been going out a lot recently.
10 I've been spending a lot of time on social media.

b Play the audio again, pausing after each sentence for Sts to listen and repeat, copying the rhythm.

c Focus on the task and the example. Tell Sts that if the sentence is not true for them, they should make it negative, e.g. *1 isn't true for me. I haven't been working hard this week because…*

Give Sts a few minutes to decide what is true or not for them and to think of reasons.

Put Sts in pairs and get them to do the task.

Monitor and help with the rhythm of the present perfect continuous verbs.

Get feedback by asking a few Sts about some of the sentences.

EXTRA SUPPORT You could demonstrate the activity yourself to show Sts exactly what they have to do.

d Focus on the task and give Sts time to think about what they are going to say.

Focus on the example, highlighting that the student listening must show interest.

Now put Sts in pairs, **A** and **B**, and tell Sts **A** to start. Then make sure they swap roles.

Get feedback from various pairs.

EXTRA SUPPORT You could demonstrate the activity yourself to show Sts exactly what they have to do.

7 WRITING an informal email

Tell Sts to go to **Writing An informal email** on *p.119*.

a Focus on the task and give Sts time to read Bob's email and answer the two questions. Tell them not to worry about the gaps in the email.

Check answers.

> The weather
> He says it's a problem because they can't get to the supermarket.

b Focus on the instructions and get Sts to read the email again before completing the gaps with verbs from the list in the present perfect continuous. Remind them to use contractions, which are common in informal emails.

Get Sts to compare with a partner, and then check answers.

> 1 haven't been studying   2 's been snowing
> 3 've been trying   4 've been listening   5 's been working
> 6 've been moving   7 've been waiting   8 have…been doing

c Focus on the instructions and make sure Sts understand what they have to do.

Check answers.

> 1 Glad you're well.   2 Hope you haven't been studying too hard.   3 Miss you lots

Now focus on the **Useful language: informal emails** box and go through it with the class. You could point out that in the sentences without the pronoun *I*, e.g. *Glad you're well*, it can be inserted and have the same meaning (i.e. *I'm glad you're well*). Likewise, in the sentences with the pronoun *I*, e.g. *I'm sorry to hear that…*, it can be omitted (i.e. *Sorry to hear that…*).

d Focus on the instructions and tell Sts to think of a friend or family member they would like to send an email to.

Then focus on the plan and go through it with Sts. Encourage them to make brief notes on what they will write.

e Now get Sts to write the email, following the plan they made in **d**. Remind them to use the **Useful language** to help them. Sts could write an actual email to send to a real person if they would like to.

You may like to get Sts to do the writing in class or you could set it as homework. If you do it in class, set a time limit for Sts to write their email, e.g. 15–20 minutes.

f Remind Sts to check their email for mistakes before giving it in.

EXTRA IDEA Get Sts to write and send emails to each other.

5B

EPISODE 3 Practical English Time to tell the police

Function making a police report; describing someone's appearance and routine

Language *He's average height and build*; *He has grey hair and glasses*, etc.

Lesson plan

In this third Practical English lesson, the functional focus is on key expressions used in reporting a missing person to the police.

In the first scene, Jenny phones Rob to tell him about the worrying events – first, the news reports about the attack on the man she met at the airport, and then the fact that Henry still hasn't come back. Rob advises her to go and stay at Luke's flat and to go with him to the police to report both incidents. In the next scene, Jenny and Luke go to the police station to make the report. The suspense builds in the third scene when Luke finally manages to get into Jenny's laptop, only to find that the username is not *Jenny*, but *A. Page*, the name of the man Jenny met at the airport and who was attacked shortly afterwards. Then Jenny receives a video message from Henry, who has been kidnapped by people who want the laptop. Jenny is also warned not to go to the police again.

More materials

For teachers

Teacher's Resource Centre
Video   Practical English Episode 3
Quick Test 5
File 5 Test
Progress Test Files 1–5

For students
Workbook   Practical English 3
           Can you remember? 1–5
Online Practice   Practical English 3
                  Check your progress

OPTIONAL LEAD-IN (BOOKS CLOSED)
Before starting Episode 3, elicit what Sts can remember about Episode 2. Ask *What's wrong with Henry's car? What other strange things have happened? Who is Andrew Page and why is he in the news? Where is Henry at the end of the episode?*, etc.

Alternatively, you could play the last scene of Episode 2.

1 ▶ A WORRIED PHONE CALL

a 🔊 **5.20** Books open. Focus on the photos and ask *Where is Jenny? Who's she talking to? How does she look?*

Now focus on the instructions and the question.

Play the video / audio once the whole way through for Sts to watch or listen.

Check the answer.

EXTRA SUPPORT   Before playing the video / audio, go through the listening scripts and decide if you need to pre-teach / check any lexis to help Sts when they listen.

Rob tells Jenny she should go to the police. He also tells her to go and stay at Luke's flat and to go to the police with him.

🔊 **5.20**
N = narrator, R = Rob, J = Jenny
N   Day two. Five past nine in the evening. Jenny's at Henry's house. She has just heard on the news that Andrew Page – the man she met at the airport – was attacked soon after she left him. She immediately phones Rob, who is still in Alaska, to tell him about it, and also to tell him that Henry still hasn't come home.
R   He was attacked?
J   That's right. The police found him at the airport.
R   You're sure it's the same person?
J   Definitely. I saw his picture. His name's Andrew Page and he's a scientist.
R   And you spoke to him?
J   He helped carry my bags! I mean, I could have been the last person to see him before it happened.
R   I think you should go to the police.
J   I know. And Rob, there's something else.
R   What is it?
J   Well, I don't want to worry you, but your dad hasn't come home. We were supposed to have dinner at seven.
R   What time is it now?
J   It's a little after nine.
R   What? That is worrying. Dad's usually really punctual.
J   Should I call the police?
R   I think you should. It's really not like him.
J   OK, and Rob?
R   Yeah?
J   Oh, it's nothing.
R   What is it?
J   I know this seems odd, but the house feels strange.
R   What do you mean?
J   I don't know, but I don't like being alone here.
R   Well, it's late and you're tired.
J   That's true. But I don't think I'll be able to sleep here.
R   Why don't you ring Luke? You could stay with him, and you could go to the police together and tell them about Dad.
J   OK, I think I'll do that.
R   I'll ring you later.
J   OK. Rob, I'll be fine. Don't worry. Bye.

b   Give Sts time to read questions 1–5.

Play the video / audio again, pausing as necessary to give Sts time to answer the questions. Play it again if necessary.

Get Sts to compare with a partner, and then check answers.

1   Yes, she is because she saw his picture on the news and he told her his name.
2   At seven
3   It's a little after nine. Rob is worried because Henry is usually really punctual.
4   She says it feels strange.
5   She doesn't think she'll be able to sleep in Henry's house.

EXTRA SUPPORT   If there's time and you are using the video, you could get Sts to watch again with subtitles, so they can see exactly what they understood / didn't understand. Translate / Explain any new words or phrases.

Now focus on the last question and, with a show of hands, find out how many Sts answer *yes* or *no*. Then encourage them to give reasons why (not).

2 ▶ MAKING A POLICE REPORT

a 🔊 **5.21** Focus on the photos and ask Sts some questions, e.g. *Where are Jenny and Luke? Who do you think the woman is? What is Luke showing her? Why?*

Now tell Sts to focus on the questions.

Play the video / audio once the whole way through.

Get Sts to answer the questions with a partner.

Play the video / audio again if necessary, and then check answers.

> The police officer asks how long Henry's been missing; for his description; the time when Jenny last saw him; what he was wearing; what his plans were for the day; about his normal routine.
> They describe Henry as 62, average height and build, grey hair, glasses, brown eyes; last seen wearing a brown jacket, dark green shirt, and jeans.

🔊 **5.21**

N = narrator, La = Laing, J = Jenny, L = Luke

N *Day two. Ten p.m. Jenny and Luke are at Oxford Police Station, in the police interview room. Jenny has told the inspector, DCI Laing, about her meeting with Andrew Page. Now she is going to tell her about Henry.*
La And that was the last time you saw Mr Page?
J Yes. Is he going to be OK?
La We don't know yet, I'm afraid. You also said that your father-in-law – Henry Walker – hasn't returned home yet. How long has he been missing?
J He was supposed to be home three hours ago.
La OK. It's a bit early to report him missing, but I'll take a statement. So, your name's Jenny Zielinski.
J That's right.
La And you're staying at The Grange, Marsh Lane, Long Crendon.
J Yes.
La OK. Can you describe Mr Walker?
J He's sixty-two, I think.
L Yeah.
J He's average height and build. He has grey hair and glasses. I don't know what colour his eyes are.
L They're brown. Here is a photo of him.
La When did you last see him?
J This morning. Around ten.
La Where were you?
J At his house in Long Crendon.
La And do you remember what he was wearing?
J Oh, just a brown jacket, a dark green shirt, and jeans.
La Do you remember anything unusual about the last time you saw him?
J Yes, actually. We were going to go to Oxford, but Henry's two front tyres had been punctured.
La Really? So you left for Oxford and he stayed to fix the car?
J Yes.
La Do you know what his plans were for the rest of the day?
J No.
La Can you give me some idea of his normal routine?
J Not really…
L Well, he's an academic. He teaches at the university a few days a week, but he often works from home. He goes on a lot of long walks, but never this late.
La And Jenny, do you remember seeing anything unusual when you got back to the house this afternoon?
J Well, there was my suitcase. The airport had returned my lost luggage and the lock was broken.
La Is there anything else?
J There were some books on the floor.
L Really? That's weird. Henry's normally really tidy.
La OK. Try not to worry – we'll look into this. In the meantime, perhaps you should stay with Luke, and if you think of anything else, or he turns up, give me a call.

b Focus on the conversation on *pp.54–55*. Elicit who says the **You hear** phrases (the police officer) and who says the **You say** phrases (Jenny and Luke). You could tell Sts that the sentences in italics are the ones Luke says.

Give Sts time to read through the conversation and to think about what the missing words might be. Then play the video / audio again and get Sts to complete the gaps. Play it again if necessary.

Get Sts to compare with a partner, and then check answers.

> 1 missing 2 take 3 describe 4 last 5 wearing
> 6 unusual 7 plans 8 routine 9 remember
> 10 else 11 worry

Now go through the conversation and deal with any new vocabulary. Check that Sts know the meaning of *turns up* here (= arrives).

c 🔊 **5.22** Now focus on the **You say** phrases and tell Sts they're going to hear some of them again and repeat them. Encourage them to copy the rhythm and intonation.

Play the video / audio, pausing if necessary, for Sts to listen and repeat the phrases.

🔊 **5.22**

La You also said that your father-in-law – Henry Walker – hasn't returned home yet. How long has he been missing?
J He was supposed to be home three hours ago. *(pause)*
***
La OK. Can you describe Mr Walker?
J He's sixty-two, I think. *(pause)* He's average height and build. *(pause)* He has grey hair and glasses. *(pause)* I don't know what colour his eyes are. *(pause)*
La When did you last see him?
J This morning. Around ten. *(pause)*
La Where were you?
J At his house in Long Crendon. *(pause)*
La And do you remember what he was wearing?
J Oh, just a brown jacket, a dark green shirt, and jeans. *(pause)*
La Do you remember anything unusual about the last time you saw him?
J Yes, actually. *(pause)* We were going to go to Oxford…but Henry's two front tyres had been punctured. *(pause)*
***
La And Jenny, do you remember seeing anything unusual when you got back to the house this afternoon?
J Well, there was my suitcase. *(pause)* The airport had returned my lost luggage and the lock was broken. *(pause)*

> **EXTRA SUPPORT** If there's time and you are using the video, you could get Sts to watch again with subtitles, so they can see exactly what they understood / didn't understand. Translate / Explain any new words or phrases.

d Put Sts in groups of three, **A**, **B**, and **C**. **A** is the police officer, and **B** and **C** are reporting the missing person. Get Sts to read the conversation on *pp.54–55* aloud, and then take it in turns to swap roles so that everyone has a chance to be the police officer.

Monitor and help, encouraging Sts to pay attention to rhythm and intonation.

e Put Sts in pairs, **A** and **B**, and tell them to go to **Communication Reporting a missing person**, **A** on *p.108*, **B** on *p.113*.

PE3

Go through the instructions with Sts carefully. Give them time to read the situation and prepare what they are going to say / ask. When they are ready, tell Sts **B** that they are the police officers and that they should start. Tell them to use the form to ask Sts **A** questions about the missing person.

Monitor and help.

Sts then swap roles in **c**. Give them time again to prepare. When they have finished, get feedback. Ask Sts if they thought the police officer was helpful.

EXTRA SUPPORT You could elicit (some of) the questions that the police officers will need to ask and write these on the board. You could also allow Sts to make notes next to their role cards.

Tell Sts to go back to the main lesson **Practical English 3**.

3 ▶ A THREATENING MESSAGE

a 🔊 **5.23** Focus on the photos and ask Sts some questions, e.g. *What are Luke and Jenny looking at? What is on Jenny's phone?*

Now focus on the questions. Play the video / audio once the whole way through for Sts to watch or listen and answer the questions.

Check answers. Elicit / Explain the meaning of *username* (= the name you use in order to use a computer program or system), *cracked* (= solved) here, and *encrypted* (= information put into a special code, usually to prevent others from looking at it).

> The good news is that Luke has managed to get into the laptop. The bad news is that Henry has been kidnapped by people who want the laptop.

🔊 **5.23**
N = narrator, J = Jenny, L = Luke, H = Henry
N *Day three. Eight a.m. They are at Luke's house. Luke is awake and working on Jenny's laptop. He's still trying to get into it. Jenny, who was sleeping in the spare room, has just got up.*
J Good morning.
L Hi.
J Thanks for letting me stay. I feel a lot safer here.
L What? Oh, no problem.
J I tried Henry again. Still no answer. I wonder if…
L Yes! I've done it! I'm in.
J What?
L I've cracked the security code on your computer.
J That's great, Luke, but Henry…
L Wait a minute, that's not right. The username says *A Page*…and all the files are encrypted.
J *A Page*? Are you sure?
L Let me just see if I can open the files. What the…? Jenny, take a look at this. It's a formula or something.
J What does it mean?
L I have no idea.
J It's a message from Henry!
L What?! What does it say?
J It's a video. Hang on.
H Hello, Jenny. As you can see, I'm all right. I can't tell you where I am. But listen carefully. These people want some documents on your computer. They want you to leave it at the house. To prove that I'm OK, here's a copy of this morning's paper.
N *On the video screen Henry looks very tense and worried. He seems to be in a darkish room. He holds up a newspaper. On the front, there's a large picture of Andrew Page and the headline reads:* Oxford scientist attacked at airport.

H There's one last thing that they want me to tell you. Don't go to the police again. If you go to the police, you know what'll happen. Now Jenny, please don't worry. Tell Rob his old man will be in his study again soon.
N *Jenny and Luke look at each other in shock.*
J We need to call Rob.

b Focus on the instructions and give Sts time to read sentences 1–8.

Play the video / audio again, pausing if necessary, to give Sts time to circle the correct answers.

Get Sts to compare with a partner, and then check answers.

> 1 safer 2 isn't 3 a formula 4 a video message 5 laptop
> 6 today's 7 not to go 8 to give Rob a message

Elicit / Explain that *his old man* is an informal way of saying *his father*.

Now focus on the final questions and get Sts to speculate about the answers.

EXTRA SUPPORT If there's time and you are using the video, you could get Sts to watch again with subtitles, so they can see exactly what they understood / didn't understand. Translate / Explain any new words or phrases.

c Focus on the **Social English** phrases. In pairs, get Sts to see if they can remember any of the missing words.

EXTRA CHALLENGE In pairs, get Sts to complete the phrases before they listen.

d 🔊 **5.24** Play the video / audio for Sts to watch or listen and complete the phrases.

Check answers. If you know your Sts' L1, you could get them to translate the phrases.

> 1 letting 2 mean 3 no 4 message 5 all right
> 6 carefully

🔊 **5.24**
1 Thanks for letting me stay.
2 What does it mean?
3 I have no idea.
4 It's a message from Henry!
5 As you can see, I'm all right.
6 Listen carefully.

Now play the video / audio again, pausing after each phrase for Sts to watch or listen and repeat.

e Focus on the instructions and make sure Sts understand what they have to do.

Get Sts to compare with a partner, and then check answers.

> A 5 B 1 C 6 D 4 E 3 F 2

Now put Sts in pairs and get them to practise the conversations.

Finally, focus on the **CAN YOU…?** questions and ask Sts if they feel confident they can now do these things. If they feel that they need more practice, tell them to go to *Online Practice* to watch the episode again and practise the language.

6A What the waiter really thinks

G obligation, necessity, prohibition, advice
V at a restaurant
P word pairs with *and*

Lesson plan

The topic of this lesson is how to behave in restaurants, with a focus on complaining and tipping – the latter is first related to restaurants, but then extended to all services where people sometimes tip. The lesson begins with a vocabulary focus on restaurant language and common verb phrases. This is followed by a pronunciation spot on food and restaurant-related word pairs with *and*, such as *oil and vinegar*. Next, Sts read an article about how to complain successfully in restaurants. The first half ends with Sts listening to three people talking about bad experiences in restaurants, and Sts then discuss their own experiences of bad service.

The second half of the lesson starts with the grammar. A text about tipping in restaurants in different countries revises and consolidates modals and other phrases used to express obligation, necessity, prohibition, and advice. This is followed by an interview with an American woman talking about the very different rules for tipping in the USA. Sts then discuss tipping in general – who and when to tip, how much, etc. The lesson ends with a writing focus where Sts write a restaurant review.

More materials
For teachers
Photocopiables
Grammar obligation, necessity, prohibition, advice *p.162*
Communicative What's the problem? *p.191–192* (instructions *p.175*)
Vocabulary At a restaurant *p.214* (instructions *p.204*)
For students
Workbook 6A
Online Practice 6A

OPTIONAL LEAD-IN (BOOKS CLOSED)
Ask Sts how often they eat out and do a class survey, e.g. more than once a week, about once a week, only on special occasions.

Then ask them to think of a restaurant where they have enjoyed eating out for a special occasion, like a birthday or anniversary. Elicit the names and descriptions of a couple of places and ask Sts to say why they liked going there (the food, the atmosphere, etc.).

If you think your Sts eat out quite often, you could get them to discuss their places in pairs, and then get feedback.

1 VOCABULARY at a restaurant

a Books open. Focus on the phrases and give Sts time to decide who says each one.

Check answers, making sure Sts understand each one.

1 W 2 W 3 C 4 W 5 C 6 W 7 W 8 C 9 C 10 C

EXTRA SUPPORT Get Sts to work in pairs before checking answers.

b Tell Sts to go to **Vocabulary Bank At a restaurant** on *p.160*.

Vocabulary notes
Things on the table
Highlight the difficult consonant cluster in *corkscrew*, which has four consonant sounds together, and give extra practice of this word.

You may want to explain the difference between a *cup* and a *mug* (a cup is smaller and usually comes with a saucer). You could also teach the word *cutlery* /ˈkʌtləri/ (= the collective noun for knives, forks, and spoons).

Things people do in restaurants
You may want to teach *set the table* as a synonym for *lay the table*, and as the US English expression.

Focus on **1 Things on the table** and get Sts to do **a** individually or in pairs.

🔊 6.1 Now do **b**. Play the audio for Sts to listen and check.

Check answers.

🔊 6.1
At a restaurant
1 Things on the table
11 bowl
 2 candle
 5 corkscrew
19 cup
14 fork
 6 glass
18 jug
12 knife
16 mug
13 napkin
 3 oil and vinegar
10 plate
 7 salt and pepper
21 saucer
 4 serving dish
 9 spoon
 8 tablecloth
15 teapot
20 teaspoon
17 tray
 1 wine glass

Now either use the audio to drill the pronunciation of the words, or model and drill them yourself. Give further practice of any words your Sts find difficult to pronounce.

Do **Activation** and elicit answers from the class, encouraging Sts to use vocabulary from **a**.

6A 83

Finally, focus on the **food, plate, dish, meal,** and **course** box and go through it with the class.

Now focus on **2 Things people do in restaurants** and get Sts to do **a** individually or in pairs.

🔊 **6.2** Now do **b**. Play the audio for Sts to listen and check.

Check answers.

🔊 **6.2**
2 Things people do in restaurants

waiters	customers
4 lay the table	9 book a table
1 take an order	8 order food
5 recommend a dish	7 try the wine
6 carry a tray	11 send something back
2 serve customers	12 ask for the bill
3 pour the wine	10 leave a tip

Now either use the audio to drill the pronunciation of the phrases, or model and drill them yourself. Give further practice of any words your Sts find difficult to pronounce.

Focus on **Activation** and tell Sts to cover the verb phrases and look at the photos. Can they remember the verb phrases?

Tell Sts to go back to the main lesson **6A**.

EXTRA SUPPORT If you think Sts need more practice, you may want to give them the **Vocabulary** photocopiable activity at this point.

c Put Sts in pairs. Tell them to discuss the differences between each pair of words or phrases.

Check answers.

1 **A cup** is a small container shaped like a bowl, usually with a handle, used for hot drinks like tea and coffee, whereas **a glass** is a container made of glass, usually used for cold drinks.
2 **A plate** is a round, flat dish that you eat food off, whereas **a saucer** is a small, shallow round dish that a cup stands on.
3 **A jug** is a container with a handle and a lip, for holding and pouring liquids, whereas **a mug** is a tall cup for drinking from, usually with straight sides and a handle, used without a saucer.
4 **A tablecloth** is a piece of material used to cover a table, whereas **a napkin** is a piece of material or paper used at meals to protect your clothes, and clean your lips and fingers.
5 **A plate** is a round, flat dish that you eat food off, whereas **a dish** is a flat, shallow container for serving from.
6 **A meal** is an occasion when people sit down to eat food, whereas **a course** is any of the separate parts of a meal.
7 **Lay the table** is to arrange knives, forks, plates, etc. on a table, ready for a meal, whereas **clear the table** is to take away the dirty plates, etc. after a meal.
8 **Take an order** is when the waiter writes down what the customer wants, whereas **order food** is when the customer asks the waiter for food.

EXTRA CHALLENGE You could ask Sts to ask and answer about a few more pairs, e.g. *spoon* and *teaspoon*, *pour the wine* and *try the wine*.

2 PRONUNCIATION word pairs with *and*

Pronunciation notes

At this stage, Sts will be well aware that what is written and what is pronounced in English are often not the same thing. These exercises focus on the word *and*, which is typically pronounced in its weak form, and can be heard as /ən/, as in the photograph in **a**.

The exercises aim to get Sts to correctly recognize the different weak form pronunciations of *and* in natural speech. If they can comfortably pronounce /ən/ where appropriate, this will help them to be more fluent when speaking in English.

a Focus Sts' attention on the photo. Get them to suggest what the *n* stands for and why it is written like that.

It stands for *and*.
It is written like that to reflect the pronunciation of *and* when it is unstressed (/ən/).

b 🔊 **6.3** Focus on the phrases and play the audio once the whole way through for Sts just to listen.

🔊 **6.3**
See phrases in Student's Book on *p.56*

Now play the audio again, pausing after each phrase for Sts to listen and repeat.

Then repeat the activity, eliciting responses from individual Sts.

EXTRA SUPPORT If Sts are having problems with /ən/, get them to write out the phrases as a single word, but with no letter *d* in *and*, e.g. *fishanchips*, *oilanvinegar*, etc. They can then try to pronounce what they have written as one word.

c Focus on the **Word pair order** box and go through it with the class.

Put Sts in pairs and get them to tell each other what they can see in each photo.

EXTRA CHALLENGE Elicit the answers before playing the audio in **d**.

d 🔊 **6.4** Play the audio for Sts to listen and check.
Check answers.

🔊 **6.4**
1 bacon and eggs
2 bread and butter
3 strawberries and cream
4 ice and lemon
5 tea and biscuits
6 milk and sugar

EXTRA SUPPORT Play the audio again, pausing after each phrase for Sts to listen and repeat.

3 READING understanding the main point in a paragraph

a Focus on the title of the article, *How to complain in restaurants…without losing your cool*, and make sure Sts know the meaning of *losing your cool* (= becoming angry).

Do the questions as a whole-class activity, or put Sts in pairs and then get some feedback. You could also tell Sts if you have ever 'lost your cool' and what happened.

b Focus on the question and make sure Sts know the meaning of *sympathize* (= feel sorry for). Model and drill its pronunciation /ˈsɪmpəθaɪz/. Tell Sts that if they can answer this question correctly, they have understood the overall message and tone of the whole article.

Give Sts time to read the article and answer the question. Check the answer. Elicit some examples from the article to support their answer.

EXTRA SUPPORT Before Sts read the article the first time, check whether you need to pre-teach any vocabulary, but not the highlighted words.

> He sympathizes with restaurant staff – the article says 'the waiters are often innocent victims' of bad management; they are often overworked.

c Focus on headings A–H and make sure Sts understand the idiom *put yourself in their shoes* (= imagine yourself in their situation) and the noun *expertise* /ˌekspɜːˈtiːz/. Also check Sts understand *wholemeal* (para 6).

Now get Sts to read the article again and complete it with the headings.

Get Sts to compare with a partner, and then check answers.

> **1** C **2** F **3** A **4** E **5** B **6** H **7** D **8** G

d Now tell Sts to focus on the highlighted words and work out the meaning of *over-* and *under-* from the context.

Get Sts to compare with a partner, and then check answers.

> *over-* = more than necessary
> *under-* = less than necessary

EXTRA CHALLENGE You could teach a few more words with *over-* and *under-* prefixes, e.g. *overcharge / undercharge, overpaid / underpaid, overrated / underrated*. Point out that not all words with the prefix *over-* have an *under-* equivalent, e.g. *overcrowded, overpriced, overworked*.

Deal with any other new vocabulary. Model and drill the pronunciation of any tricky words.

e Do this as a whole-class activity and elicit opinions.

4 LISTENING & SPEAKING

a 🔊 **6.5** Focus on the task and make sure Sts understand that they are only going to hear extracts this time.

Play the audio once the whole way through for Sts to listen and write the food words they hear. You may want to pre-teach *coeliac* /ˈsiːliæk/ (= a person who cannot eat food containing gluten). Model and drill its pronunciation.

Get Sts to compare with a partner, and then check answers.

> **Speaker 1:** grilled sardines, fried sardines
> **Speaker 2:** lasagne
> **Speaker 3:** wheat, onions, a plain omelette

🔊 **6.5**
1
We ordered some grilled sardines to share, and after a few minutes, the waiter came with a big plate of fried sardines and put them down on our table.
2
We ordered very simple things like lasagne, which is easy to just heat up.
3
…and there was a vegan and a coeliac – you know, someone who can't eat wheat…
…there was even a woman who said she didn't like onions…
There was also a little boy and I got the kitchen to make a plain omelette for him.

---

b 🔊 **6.6** Tell Sts they are going to hear the full stories this time. First, give Sts time to read the questions in the chart. They will need to copy the chart onto a piece of paper.

Now play the audio again, pausing after each speaker to give Sts time to write.

Get Sts to compare with a partner, and then play the audio again if necessary.

Check answers.

EXTRA SUPPORT Read through the script and decide if you need to pre-teach any new lexis before Sts listen, e.g. *brasserie*.

> **Speaker 1**
> A customer.
> At a restaurant in Portugal.
> That they were charged for food they hadn't ordered but the waiter gave them by mistake.
> He took the fried sardines off the bill after a long argument.
> **Speaker 2**
> A customer.
> At a famous brasserie in Paris.
> That they had to wait for their food for ages and then the waiters were aggressive when they asked about the food.
> They got their food, ate it, and left.
> **Speaker 3**
> A waiter.
> At a restaurant in London.
> The very small tip a woman left even though he had gone to a lot of trouble with the complicated food orders.
> He left the tip on the table.

🔊 **6.6**
(script in Student's Book on *pp.127–128*)
1
I remember we once went to a restaurant in Portugal – beautiful location, upstairs overlooking the River Douro. We ordered some grilled sardines to share, and after a few minutes, the waiter came with a big plate of fried sardines and put them down on our table. And we thought, well, we'd ordered grilled sardines, but hey, they're really busy and these look really nice. So we each took a fried sardine and ate it, at which point the waiter came back and said, 'These aren't yours' and took them away, and in a few minutes came back with a plate of grilled sardines. So this was all fine, and we had a nice meal, but when we got the bill we saw that we'd been charged for both the fried sardines and the grilled sardines. So we complained to the waiter and then to the manager and said, you know, 'This was your mistake.' But the manager said, basically, 'You ate them, so you have to pay for them' and we had quite a long argument. Eventually, when we said that we wanted to make a formal, written complaint, very reluctantly he agreed to take them off the bill. We didn't leave a tip.

6A

2
We went to lunch one Sunday in a place, a Parisian brasserie called Delaville. It's a beautiful place – it's from about nineteen hundred, with wonderful old furniture, mirrors, and all that – really nice. We ordered very simple things like lasagne, which is easy to just heat up, but we waited and waited, and it didn't come. The place was crowded, but not completely full, and there were quite a few waiters, but when we realized that we had been waiting for two hours, we went to speak to them, and we asked them, 'What about our food? Have you forgotten us?' And instead of apologizing, they were really aggressive with us, so we became more and more angry with them. And finally, we got our dishes and ate them and left. We should have left earlier, but we kept thinking that the food would come, and also it was too late to find somewhere else. But it was a terrible experience because it was a very famous place – very – with a good reputation, where all the famous people go. But that's the type of service they offer. First, I thought maybe they were treating us like that because we're not famous, but in fact, I heard lots of other people complaining.

3
I had a table recently at the restaurant I'm working at in London, and I went to all sorts of trouble with them. It was a group of six and there was a vegan and a coeliac – you know, someone who can't eat wheat – and anyway, I went through the menu with them and explained what they could have – there was even a woman who said she didn't like onions, so I had to check all the dishes to make sure they didn't have any. There was also a little boy and I got the kitchen to make a plain omelette for him. Anyway, one of them, an elderly woman, asked for the bill, and she paid in cash, and when I came back with the change, she said, 'Don't worry about that; you've been great. Keep it.' It was sixteen p. I mean, I know service was included, but in that case, much better not to tip at all. I left the sixteen p on the table.

EXTRA SUPPORT If there's time, you could get Sts to listen again with the script on *pp.127–128*, so they can see exactly what they understood / didn't understand. Translate / Explain any new words or phrases.

c Get Sts to answer questions 1–3 in pairs. Encourage them to think about their experiences in informal places like cafés and takeaways as well as restaurants.

Get some feedback from various pairs. You could do question 3 as a whole-class activity.

5 GRAMMAR obligation, necessity, prohibition, advice

a Do the questions as a whole-class activity.

❗ Make sure Sts only talk about what *they* do and <u>not</u> the situation regarding tipping in their country, as they will be doing this next.

b Focus on the instructions and then give Sts time to read the article and answer the questions.

Get Sts to discuss their answers in pairs.

Get some feedback from various pairs. If your country isn't mentioned in the article, you could tell Sts how much people usually tip.

c Focus on the instructions and remind Sts to use the context to help them. Sts could do this individually or in pairs.

Check answers.

1 you have to   2 you don't have to, you needn't
3 You mustn't   4 you should   5 you shouldn't
Other verbs are: 1) must, 4 and 5) ought to / ought not to

d Tell Sts to go to **Grammar Bank 6A** on *p.142*.

Grammar notes
Sts will have seen most of these modals and other expressions in earlier levels of *English File* and should be fairly comfortable with their forms and basic uses. Here the emphasis is on contrasting their uses and expressing them in a range of tenses.

You may want to remind Sts that *should*, *ought to*, and *must* are modal verbs. They don't add -s in the third person and don't have any other forms (e.g. past, infinitive). They can be used to talk about the present and the future.

Obligation and necessity
Rule 2: Remind Sts not to use *to* after *must*, e.g. NOT ~~You must to be careful~~.

No obligation / No necessity
Here Sts learn to use *needn't*, which has some grammatical characteristics of a modal. *Needn't* and *don't need to* have the same meaning, but *don't need to* is a full verb.
Highlight that unlike *don't need*, *needn't* must be followed by a verb, e.g. *We don't need any more eggs*, but NOT ~~We needn't any more eggs~~.

Prohibition
You could point out that *mustn't* and *can't* mean the same thing (= something is not allowed), though the prohibition is usually stronger with *mustn't*.
Highlight that the first *t* in *mustn't* /ˈmʌsnt/ is silent. Model and drill the pronunciation.
A typical mistake is confusing *mustn't* (prohibition) and *don't have to* (not necessary / not obligatory), e.g. ~~Today is a public holiday, so we mustn't go to work. You don't have to text while you're driving~~.

Advice
Remind Sts that the letter *l* in *should* /ʃʊd/ and *shouldn't* /ˈʃʊdnt/ is silent.

Focus on the example sentences for **obligation and necessity** and play audio 🔊 **6.7** for Sts to listen and repeat. Encourage them to copy the rhythm. You might want to point out the weak form of *must* in *You must pay him back as soon as possible*. Then go through the rules with the class.

Repeat for **no obligation / no necessity** 🔊 **6.8**, **prohibition** 🔊 **6.9**, and **advice** 🔊 **6.10**.

Now focus on the exercises and get Sts to do them individually or in pairs.

Check answers, getting Sts to read the full sentences.

a
1 don't have to   2 ✓   3 shouldn't   4 ✓   5 ✓
6 don't need to   7 mustn't   8 ✓   9 ✓   10 oughtn't to
b
1 You **mustn't** turn your phone on until the plane has landed.
2 Here's the form. You **have / need** to sign it at the bottom.
3 I think perhaps you **ought** to buy a new table,…
4 We **don't** have to leave until 2.30…
5 She **needn't** come if she doesn't want to. Nobody will mind.
6 Our journey back was a nightmare. We **had** to wait hours for the bus.
7 You **must / should** read his new book! You'll love it.
8 You **oughtn't** to drink so many fizzy drinks. They're really not good for you.
9 Do I **have / need** to write a thank-you letter or can I just…?

6A

Tell Sts to go back to the main lesson **6A**.

EXTRA SUPPORT If you think Sts need more practice, you may want to give them the **Grammar** photocopiable activity at this point.

e Put Sts in pairs and give them time to circle the correct options in sentences 1–7. You might want to check that they know the meaning of *mediocre* (= not very good, of only average standard). Model and drill its pronunciation /miːdiˈəʊkə/.

Check answers.

1 You shouldn't	2 You mustn't	3 You oughtn't to
4 You have to	5 You shouldn't	6 You don't have to
7 You needn't		

EXTRA IDEA You could ask Sts if there are any statements in 1–7 that they disagree with.

6 LISTENING understanding prices and percentages

a 🔊 6.11 Focus on the instructions. You could ask Sts what they know about tipping in the USA and what they remember from the article they read in **5b** (i.e. that in the US 'there's no upper limit' when tipping).

Focus on the British words in the list and tell Sts to listen to the two extracts.

Play the audio once the whole way through for Sts to hear what American words the woman uses in the extracts for the British equivalent in the list.

Check answers. Point out that Americans do in fact sometimes use the words *tip* and *waiter*, but often use the US alternatives.

tip = gratuity
bill = check
waiter or waitress = server
note = bill

🔊 6.11
1
Presenter And how much should you tip?
Sally A normal gratuity is around fifteen to twenty per cent of the check. But it can be as much as twenty-five per cent for amazing service, or in very expensive reataurants. It sounds a lot, but servers work really hard and I think generally they deserve it!
2
Presenter And what should you do in bars?
Sally Well, take lots of dollar bills with you because the normal gratuity in bars is one dollar a drink.

b 🔊 6.12 Focus on the question and tell Sts they are now going to listen to the whole interview.

Play the audio once the whole way through for Sts to listen and answer the question.

Get Sts to compare with a partner, and then play the audio again if necessary.

Check answers.

EXTRA SUPPORT Read through the script and decide if you need to pre-teach any new lexis before Sts listen.

You don't have to tip if the service is absolutely terrible, if the bill says 'gratuity included', or for fast food / takeaway coffee.

🔊 6.12
(script in Student's Book on *p.128*)
P = presenter, S = Sally
P In many countries, tipping is an optional extra. But in the USA, it's a serious business! There are no actual laws on tipping, but the unwritten rule is that you should always leave a tip in a restaurant unless you want to deal with some very unhappy waiters. But how much is reasonable, and who exactly do you have to tip? Sally from the US is here to help us. Hello, Sally.
S Hi.
P So first of all, why is it so important to leave a tip?
S I absolutely get that in countries where servers are paid well, you shouldn't have to tip at all, unless you want to because the service was great. But in the US, many servers earn just two to three dollars per hour for their services because it's assumed that the tips will make it up to the minimum wage, which varies between the different states, but is generally around eight dollars per hour. Now, I know you may think this is wrong, and many Americans, myself included, would agree, but that is the situation right now, until the law changes.
P And how much should you tip?
S A normal gratuity is around fifteen to twenty per cent of the check. But it can be as much as twenty-five per cent for amazing service, or in very expensive reataurants. It sounds a lot, but servers work really hard and I think generally they deserve it!
P OK, so it doesn't happen often, but what about if the service is bad? Do you still have to tip?
S I'd say you do, but if it really was bad maybe just ten per cent – that will give the message. And if you feel you don't want to leave even that, then you should probably call the manager and complain, and explain why you're not leaving a tip.
P Do you need to tip even if the restaurant has already added a service charge to your bill?
S There's no automatic service charge added in the US, but some restaurants will add a gratuity to your check if you're in a big group of eight people or more, if it's a public holiday, or sometimes if you're in a busy tourist area. You don't have to leave any more money if the check already includes the service charge.
P Do you have to tip for fast food or takeaway coffee?
S No, no. If you buy food or drinks over the counter, people don't usually leave any gratuity, but there's always a tip jar close by if you'd really like to!
P And what should you do in bars?
S Well, take lots of dollar bills with you because the normal gratuity in bars is one dollar a drink. Order and pay for your drink at the bar, and leave the dollar bill on the bar. Don't worry about putting it in the bartender's hand.

c Focus on the instructions and give Sts time to read 1–6.

Now play the audio again for Sts to listen and complete the missing numbers.

Get Sts to compare with a partner, and then play the audio again if necessary.

Check answers.

1 2 (to) 3 **2** 7.25 **3** 15 (to) 20 **4** 25 **5** 10 **6** 1

EXTRA SUPPORT If there's time, you could get Sts to listen again with the script on *p.128*, so they can see exactly what they understood / didn't understand. Translate / Explain any new words or phrases.

d Focus on the questions and make sure Sts can remember the meaning of *fair* (they saw it in Lesson **4B**).

Do the questions as a whole-class activity.

7 SPEAKING

a Focus on the instructions and photos, and either put Sts in pairs to answer the two questions, or do them as a whole-class activity.

If Sts worked in pairs, check answers.

> A hairdresser, cuts people's hair
> B taxi driver, drives people to their destination
> C porter, carries luggage
> D masseur, gives massages
> E bar tender, makes drinks
> F tour guide, takes people on tours
> G delivery person / courier, delivers parcels
> H chambermaid / cleaner, cleans hotel rooms, other people's homes or offices

b Focus on the task and put Sts in pairs to answer the questions. You could demonstrate the activity by answering one or two of the questions yourself.

Get some feedback.

8 WRITING a restaurant review

Tell Sts to go to **Writing A restaurant review** on *p.120*.

a Focus on the task and give Sts time to read the two restaurant reviews for Bistro Giacomo. Remind them to try to guess new words from context as they read.

Get Sts to compare with a partner, and then check answers.

> They agree that the service and the food were good.
> Rafael thinks the atmosphere was lively and the prices were reasonable, but Zoe thinks the music was too loud, the tables were cramped, and the prices were too expensive.

b Focus on the instructions and questions 1–4. Get Sts to read the reviews again and then answer the questions individually or in pairs.

If Sts worked alone, get them to compare with a partner.

Check answers to 1–4 and then elicit opinions for the final question in **bold**.

> 1 Zoe 2 Rafael 3 Rafael 4 Zoe

c Focus on the **Useful language: describing restaurants** box and go through it with the class, making sure Sts understand all the lexis, e.g. *dreadful*.

Now tell Sts to read the reviews again and work out the meaning of the highlighted words and then put them in the correct gaps in the **Useful language** box. Tell them to read the whole sentence as the context will help them.

Get Sts to compare with a partner.

Check answers, either explaining in English, translating into Sts' L1, or getting Sts to check in their dictionaries.

> 2 cramped 3 delicious 4 fresh 5 tasty 6 reasonable
> 7 pricey

EXTRA CHALLENGE Get Sts to add more words and expressions to the chart, both positive and negative. Elicit their ideas and write them on the board.

d Tell Sts they are going to write a review for a website about a café, bar, or restaurant. If they haven't been to one recently, tell them to invent the details.

Now focus on the two possible plans and go through them with Sts. Encourage them to make brief notes on what they will write about.

e Sts write their review, following the plan they've made. Remind them to use the **Useful language** and **Vocabulary Bank At a restaurant** on *p.160* to help them.

You may like to get Sts to do the writing in class or you could set it as homework. If you do it in class, set a time limit for Sts to write their review, e.g. 15–20 minutes.

f Sts should check their review for mistakes before giving it in.

EXTRA IDEA You could get Sts to post their corrected reviews on a website like TripAdvisor.

6B Do it yourself

- **G** *can*, *could*, and *be able to*
- **V** DIY and repairs, paraphrasing
- **P** consonant clusters

Lesson plan

The topic of this lesson is DIY (do-it-yourself) and things that people do around the house, e.g. repairing things that are broken and assembling flat-pack furniture. The lesson begins with an article about everyday items that we have in our homes and which have more uses than we expect. Sts revise and extend the uses of *can*, *could*, and *be able to* for ability, possibility, permission, and deduction. This leads into an extended speaking and writing activity in which Sts think of solutions to problems.

The second half begins with a vocabulary focus on words and phrases used to talk about DIY and repairs around the home. This is followed by a pronunciation focus on consonant clusters. The new vocabulary is consolidated through a listening and speaking activity about IKEA, the well-known Swedish store which sells flat-pack furniture, and some people's (bad) experiences of trying to assemble furniture. Finally, Sts watch a documentary about the history of flat-pack furniture.

More materials
For teachers
Photocopiables
Grammar *can*, *could*, and *be able to* p.163
Communicative What can I do? *p.193* (instructions *p.175*)
Vocabulary DIY and repairs *p.215* (instructions *p.204*)
Teacher's Resource Centre
Video The history of flat-pack furniture
For students
Workbook 6B
Online Practice 6B

OPTIONAL LEAD-IN (BOOKS CLOSED)
Write the following jobs on the board:

CLEANING THE OVEN   PAINTING   CHANGING A LIGHT BULB
CHANGING THE SHEETS   PUTTING A PICTURE ON THE WALL   IRONING

Mime any verb phrases that Sts are not sure about. Tell Sts that these are among the most hated household jobs in the UK.
Put Sts in pairs and tell them to find out who does these household jobs in their partner's home.
Ask them if there are any jobs in the list that they have never done themselves.

1 READING checking hypotheses

a Books open. Focus on the question and make sure Sts understand all the lexis.
Then put Sts in pairs and tell them to discuss possible uses for the items in the photos.
Elicit some ideas for which item could work for each use, but don't tell Sts yet if they are correct.

EXTRA SUPPORT You could do this as a whole-class activity.

b Tell Sts to read the blog to check their ideas in **a**.
Check answers. Find out if any Sts got all the answers correct. You could also find out if any Sts had heard of any of the ideas in the blog, or already done some of the things suggested.

EXTRA SUPPORT Before Sts read the blog the first time, check whether you need to pre-teach any vocabulary, but not the highlighted verbs.

A to keep insects away
B to make your hair shiny
C to get rid of smells
D to make towels soft
E instead of shaving cream

c Give Sts time to read the blog again and try to guess the meaning of the highlighted verbs. Encourage them to use the context to work out meaning.
Get Sts to compare with a partner.

EXTRA SUPPORT Sts could work in pairs.

d Individually or in pairs, Sts now match the highlighted verbs in the blog to definitions 1–10.
Check answers, and model and drill pronunciation.

1 rinse   2 rub   3 absorb   4 apply   5 seal   6 place
7 crumple   8 restore   9 keep away   10 stuff

Deal with any other new vocabulary. Model and drill the pronunciation of any tricky words.

EXTRA SUPPORT Get Sts to cover the words on the left, read the definitions, and see if they can remember the verbs.

e You could do this as a whole-class activity, or put Sts in pairs or small groups and then get some feedback.

2 GRAMMAR *can*, *could*, and *be able to*

a Focus on the task and then get Sts to complete the five tips from Marina's blog with the correct form of *can* or *be able to*.
Check answers.

1 be able to   2 can   3 been able to   4 can   5 can't

Finally, ask Sts if they had heard of any of these tips before. If not, do they believe them? If so, which might they try?

b Tell Sts to go to **Grammar Bank 6B** on *p.143*.

Grammar notes

Sts will have met these forms before, so this grammar focus should be mainly revision and consolidation, although **Rule 5** will probably be new. The emphasis here is on the use of these forms in various functions.

You may want to remind Sts that *can* and *could* don't add *-s* in the third person and don't have any other forms (e.g. infinitive). They can be used to talk about the present and the future.

Ability, possibility, and permission

Rule 1:
- Emphasize that *can* is the natural and most common form to use when the meaning is *know how to*, e.g. *I can swim*. Remind Sts not to use *to* after *can*.
- The conditional form *could* is often used as an alternative to *would*, for instance in 2nd or 3rd conditional sentences, e.g. *If I had more experience, I could get a good job. If you hadn't tried to book so late, you could have got a table.*

Rules 3–5:
- Sts will focus on when to use *be able to* rather than *can / could*.
- Highlight that we often use *can* when we're talking about decisions and future arrangements, e.g. *I can meet you for coffee after class. The doctor can see you next Monday*. In most other cases we use *will be able to* for the future, for instance when we talk about a skill or ability that we don't have now, but will have in future, e.g. *I'll be able to speak basic Spanish when the course is over* (NOT *I can speak basic Spanish…*).

Focus on the example sentences for **ability, possibility, and permission** and play audio 🔊 **6.13** for Sts to listen and repeat. Encourage them to copy the rhythm. Then go through the rules with the class.

Repeat for **deduction** 🔊 **6.14**.

Now focus on the exercises and get Sts to do them individually or in pairs.

Check answers, getting Sts to read the full sentences.

a
1 ✗ He can sew 2 ✗ you can phone / you'll be able to phone
3 ✓ 4 ✗ You can't be 5 ✓ 6 ✗ she might be able to help
7 ✓ 8 ✗ Will I be able to use 9 ✗ I was able to get 10 ✓

b
1 This screw is much too short – it **can't** be the right one.
2 I hate not **being able to** try things on.
3 If we **could** afford it, we'd eat out every week.
4 **Could / Can** you see if they have these jeans in my size?
5 If it doesn't fit you, you should **be able to** change it.
6 They **couldn't / weren't able to** find the book anywhere in the UK, so they ordered it from a US website.
7 I've never **been able to** pronounce her name correctly.
8 Fifty pounds for two pairs of socks? They **can't** cost that much!
9 I spent ages looking for the right paint, and in the end I **was able to** find the perfect colour.
10 She's got a beautiful voice. I'd love **to be able to** sing like that.

Tell Sts to go back to the main lesson **6B**.

EXTRA SUPPORT   If you think Sts need more practice, you may want to give them the **Grammar** photocopiable activity at this point.

c Focus on the task and point out the two different groups of verb prompts and the examples. Tell Sts that they should make sentences beginning with the phrases 1–5 and use the prompts, e.g. *I think everybody should be able to give first aid*.

Give Sts time to think about their sentences.

EXTRA SUPPORT   You could give Sts enough time to write their five sentences.

Now put Sts in pairs and get them to tell each other their sentences. Encourage them to react and to ask for more information where possible.

Finally, get some feedback from various pairs. Find out whether Sts mostly agreed or disagreed with their partner.

EXTRA SUPPORT   Demonstrate the activity by completing one or two statements yourself.

EXTRA CHALLENGE   Get Sts to complete the sentence stems with their own ideas.

3 SPEAKING & WRITING

a Focus on the instructions and go through the list of problems, making sure Sts understand phrases like *power cut*, etc.

Now focus on the **Responding to other people's suggestions** box and go through it with the class. Model the responses with natural intonation.

Put Sts in pairs and get them to discuss their ideas for solving the problems.

Monitor and help, encouraging Sts to use expressions from the box.

Get some feedback from the class.

Possible ideas
- red wine – put salt or white wine on it
- screw in glasses – put nail varnish over the end of the screw
- pen mark on your jeans – rub it with hairspray
- the heel breaks – break off the other heel, so both shoes are the same / find a quick-repair heel bar
- freezer power cut – don't open the door; cover it with towels to keep the temperature the same
- phone in toilet – put it in a bowl of rice to soak up the liquid
- zip breaks on suitcase – have your case wrapped in plastic film / buy some luggage straps or string to tie round them
- car nearly out of petrol – drive very slowly, and take your car out of gear when you're going down a hill
- shoelace breaks – use string, or the wire from your earphones, or cut the remaining one in half

EXTRA SUPPORT   Demonstrate the activity by choosing one of the problems and telling the class your own solution.

EXTRA IDEA   Ask Sts if they know any other practical solutions for household problems.

b Focus on the task. Tell Sts to choose their best solution to a problem from **a** and write a paragraph about it.

Tell Sts to start by describing the problem and then offering a solution. They could refer back to the blog in **1b**. Encourage them to use the expressions they practised in the grammar focus.

Sts should check their paragraphs for mistakes and then swap them with another student to read.

EXTRA IDEA If there's time, put Sts in small groups of three or four and get them to read each other's work. Each group votes for the best one. The winners from each group read their paragraphs to the class, and the class votes for a winner.

4 VOCABULARY DIY and repairs, paraphrasing

a Do this as a whole-class activity. Focus on the photo and the questions. Elicit that the shop is a DIY store and sells tools and materials for DIY. Find out how many Sts go to DIY stores from time to time.

b 🔊 **6.15** Focus on the instructions and the four objects at the bottom of the photo. Model and drill their pronunciation. Tell Sts that the man wants to buy two of these things.

Tell Sts to cover the conversation in **c**. Alternatively, you could write the four objects on the board and get Sts to close their books.

Play the audio once the whole way through for Sts to listen and choose the two items.

Check answers.

> He wants to buy some screws and a light bulb.

🔊 **6.15**
A Excuse me.
B Yes, can I help you?
A Yes, please. I'm looking for some…Sorry, I don't know the word. They're the things that you put into wood. I want to make some shelves.
B You mean screws?
A Ah, yes, that's it. And I need one more thing. My lamp doesn't work. I need a new, er…
B Light bulb?
A Yes, thank you.
B You'll find them both over there, behind the gardening things.

c Tell Sts to uncover the conversation. Focus on the instructions and give Sts time to read the conversation. Tell them to complete each gap with one word as they listen.

Play the audio again, pausing as necessary to give Sts time to write.

Check answers.

> 1 looking   2 word   3 things   4 lamp   5 work

EXTRA CHALLENGE Get Sts to try to complete the missing words first and then play the audio for them to listen and check.

EXTRA SUPPORT Get Sts to practise the conversation with a partner.

d Refer Sts back to A's expression *They're the things that you put into wood* from the conversation in **c**. Tell Sts that it's very common, even in your own language, to forget the exact word for something, e.g. a tool, and when this happens, people explain what they want using other words. They are now going to practise doing this.

Put Sts in pairs, **A** and **B**, preferably face-to-face. Tell them to go to **Communication What's it called?**, **A** on *p.109*, **B** on *p.112*.

Go through the instructions with Sts carefully and make sure they understand what they have to do.

Point out the **Paraphrasing** box and go through it with the class.

Remind Sts that in the first part, **A** is the customer and **B** is the shop assistant. Tell Sts **B** to start by saying *Can I help you?*

To demonstrate, you could role-play the first exchange with a strong student in front of the class.

The customers should write the names below the three items after hearing them from the shop assistant, who should spell the words if necessary.

Sts then swap roles, and **A** is the shop assistant, **B** the customer.

Get feedback from various pairs to see how well they communicated what they wanted to buy. Model and drill the pronunciation of all the objects that both **A** and **B** were given.

EXTRA CHALLENGE Get some Sts to role-play their exchange in front of the class after they have done this in pairs.

Tell Sts to go back to the main lesson **6B**.

e Tell Sts to go to **Vocabulary Bank DIY and repairs** on *p.161*.

> **Vocabulary notes**
> **In a shed: tools and other things for repairs**
> Sts might have come across the term *cable*, e.g. a computer cable, so you might want to explain the difference between *cable* (= set of wires, covered in plastic or rubber, that carries electricity, telephone signals, etc.) and *wire* (= metal in the form of thin thread).
> **Verb phrases**
> Highlight the unusual sound-spelling of *sew* /səʊ/.

Focus on **1 In a shed: tools and other things for repairs**. Point out that a *shed* is a small building used for storing tools, gardening equipment, bicycles, etc. Get Sts to do **a** individually or in pairs.

🔊 **6.16** Now do **b**. Play the audio for Sts to listen and check.

Check answers.

🔊 **6.16**
DIY and repairs
1 In a shed: tools and other things for repairs
15 brick
11 bucket
9 drill
5 hammer
2 ladder
14 nail
10 padlock
6 paintbrush
12 piece of wood
8 rope
7 screwdriver
13 screw
4 spanner
3 tap
1 tile
16 wire

Now either use the audio to drill the pronunciation of the words, or model and drill them yourself. Give further practice of any words your Sts find difficult to pronounce.

EXTRA SUPPORT Get Sts to cover the words and look at the photos to see if they can remember what they are.

Now focus on **2 In a drawer: useful things around the house** and make sure Sts know how to pronounce *drawer* /drɔː/. Model and drill its pronunciation.

Get Sts to do **a** individually or in pairs.

🔊 **6.17** Now do **b**. Play the audio for Sts to listen and check.

Check answers.

🔊 **6.17**
2 In a drawer: useful things around the house
2 box of matches
7 drawing pin
8 fuse
6 glue
11 handle
4 light bulb
5 needle and thread
9 penknife
10 Sellotape
1 string
12 tape measure
3 torch

Now either use the audio to drill the pronunciation of the words and phrases, or model and drill them yourself. Give further practice of any words your Sts find difficult to pronounce.

EXTRA SUPPORT Get Sts to cover the words and look at the photos to see if they can remember what they are.

EXTRA CHALLENGE You may want to teach other things for the shed / drawer, e.g. *a saw*, *elastic bands*, etc.

Now focus on **3 Verb phrases** and get Sts to do **a** individually or in pairs.

🔊 **6.18** Now do **b**. Play the audio for Sts to listen and check.

Check answers. Point out that you can also *mend* sth made of material or paper that's torn, such as clothes or a page of a book.

🔊 **6.18**
3 Verb phrases
1 c change a light bulb or a wheel
2 g drill a hole in a wall or in a piece of wood
3 h mend something that's broken
4 i put together flat-pack furniture
5 f put up shelves or curtains
6 e set up a new wi-fi network or a home cinema system
7 b sew a button on a shirt
8 a stick something together with glue or Sellotape
9 d tie two things together, for example, your shoelaces or two pieces of string

---

Now either use the audio to drill the pronunciation of the verb phrases, or model and drill them yourself. Give further practice of any words your Sts find difficult to pronounce.

EXTRA SUPPORT Get Sts to cover verbs 1–9, look at the phrases, and say the verbs.

Finally, focus on the **Synonyms** box and go through it with the class.

Tell Sts to go back to the main lesson **6B**.

EXTRA SUPPORT If you think Sts need more practice, you may want to give them the **Vocabulary** photocopiable activity at this point.

5 PRONUNCIATION consonant clusters

Pronunciation notes

Consonant clusters are two or more consonant sounds that come together in a word, either at the beginning of the word (*script*, *spring*, *struggle*), in the middle (*sunglasses*, *describe*), or at the end of the word (*pounds*). They can also occur if a word that ends in two consonant sounds is followed by a word beginning with one or more consonant sounds. Clusters are common in languages like Polish or Russian and will not be difficult for learners of English from such language backgrounds.

In contrast, for learners whose first language does not have so many clusters, including Arabic, Spanish, Turkish, or Portuguese, this area of pronunciation will be difficult. Faced with a problematic cluster, learners usually apply one of two strategies:

- they insert a short vowel (usually /ɪ/ or /ə/), so that *screw* sounds like /ɪskruː/ or /sɪkruː/, and *paintbrush* sounds like /ˈpeɪntəbrʌʃ/.
- they delete one of the consonant sounds, so that *screw* sounds like *crew*, for example, and *paintbrush* sounds like /ˈpeɪnbrʌʃ/ or /ˈpeɪnrʌʃ/.

If learners can pronounce a cluster without adding small vowels or deleting consonant sounds, this is ideal. If they need to add a small vowel, this is usually comprehensible. If they delete any of the consonants, this is not generally comprehensible.

a 🔊 **6.19** Focus on the **Consonant clusters** box and go through it with the class. Use the examples in the box to demonstrate the concept of consonant clusters.

Point out that words like *card* or *walk* do not contain clusters. Although both end in two consonant letters, *r* and *l* are silent in these words; a cluster refers to two or more consonant <u>sounds</u> that come together.

Play the audio once the whole way through for Sts just to listen. Focus their attention on the clusters shown with the pink letters.

🔊 **6.19**
See words in Student's Book on *p.62*

Now play the audio again, pausing after each word or group of words for Sts to listen and repeat.

Then repeat the activity, eliciting responses from individual Sts.

b Focus on the sentences and point out that sometimes clusters are created when a word ends in a consonant sound and the next word begins in one or more consonant sounds.

Individually or in pairs, Sts practise saying the sentences.

Finally, get individual Sts to say the sentences.

EXTRA SUPPORT Model each sentence first for Sts to listen and repeat. Then put Sts in pairs to practise saying the sentences.

6 LISTENING & SPEAKING understanding an anecdote

a Focus on the first question. You could tell Sts that the company is called IKEA because *I* and *K* are the initials of Ingvar Kamprad, the company's founder; *E* is for Elmtaryd, the farm where Ingvar Kamprad grew up; and *A* is for Agunnaryd, the name of a village near his hometown.

Then do the questions as a whole-class activity, or get Sts to answer in pairs and then get some feedback.

b Focus on the cartoon and elicit answers from the class.

Possible answer
Self-assembly (or flat-pack) furniture isn't as easy to put together as some people think.

c Tell Sts they are going to read the beginning of an article about IKEA. Tell them to look at the title, *It looks so easy at first…*, and speculate about what the article will say (i.e. it probably won't be so easy).

Give Sts time to read the beginning of the article once all the way through. They should find the answers to the two questions and either underline them in the text or make notes.

Get Sts to compare with a partner, and then check answers.

1 one in ten Europeans now sleeps in an IKEA bed, and its catalogue is in more homes than any other publication, including the Bible and the complete works of Shakespeare.
2 the frustrating one-way system used to navigate the stores; the strange names given to the products; the problem of getting the furniture home and trying to put it together

d 🔊 **6.20** Tell Sts they are going to listen to three people tell a short anecdote about an experience with flat-pack furniture. Focus on the two questions.

Now play the audio, pausing after each speaker to give Sts time to write.

Get Sts to compare with a partner, and then check answers.

EXTRA SUPPORT Read through the script and decide if you need to pre-teach any new lexis before Sts listen.

Speaker 1: a wardrobe; yes
Speaker 2: kitchen cupboards; yes
Speaker 3: a table; not really (it's wobbly)

🔊 **6.20**
(script in Student's Book on *p.128*)
1
I love IKEA. Especially the bookshelves. We have several. And I'm usually pretty good at putting their stuff together. But I have had a few problems over the years. I remember I once had some trouble with a wardrobe. After hours and hours, and a lot of swearing, I finally managed to put it together. But I'd assembled it in my study, next to the bedroom, which was where the wardrobe was going, because I had more space there. And when my husband and I tried to move it into the bedroom, we couldn't get it to fit through the door. So I had to take it to pieces, move all the bits into the bedroom, and start all over again. I suppose it was my fault, though, not IKEA's. And the wardrobe looked very nice and has lasted for ages.
2
About three years ago, my girlfriend and I went to IKEA to buy a kitchen. The units were cheap and cheerful, but they also looked quite well-designed, and we were very excited by how good it was all going to look. The guy in the store said they were easy to put up, that it wouldn't take long, etc., etc., and I'm quite handy – quite practical – so I thought, 'No problem' – though I admit my girlfriend was a bit sceptical. Anyway, when we got home, I thought I'd assemble one cupboard, just to see how easy it was going to be. It was a nightmare. The instructions were incomprehensible – it took me the whole afternoon just to do this one cupboard, and when it was finished, I realized I'd put the door handle on the wrong way round. In the end, we had to pay someone to come and do it all for us. But at least they looked good.
3
I have lots of things from IKEA – it's great for students because, generally speaking, it's pretty cheap. Anyway, I bought a table there with my boyfriend not long ago. We started putting the table together, and at one point we had three legs screwed in. Then we reached for the screws to attach the fourth leg – and realized there were no more screws. We had to take off the other three legs, take one screw off every one of them and reassemble the table. So now at least it has four legs, but it's rather wobbly, and I'm not very happy with it. It does annoy me when they don't give you the right number of nails or screws or whatever, and it's not the first time it's happened to me. Now I always check before I bring stuff home.

e Give Sts time to go through questions A–G and to compare with a partner to see what they remember. Remind them that there is one item they do not need.

Then play the audio again, pausing after each speaker. Play the audio again if necessary.

Check answers.

A 3 B 1 C 2 D 1 F 3 G 2

f 🔊 **6.21** Focus on the instructions and give Sts time to read the five extracts. Elicit who said each one (*Speaker 1 said extracts 1 and 2, Speaker 2 said extracts 3 and 4, and Speaker 3 said extract 5*).

Then play the audio, pausing after each sentence for Sts to complete the gaps.

Get Sts to compare with a partner, and then play the audio again if necessary.

Check answers, getting Sts to say how they think the words are spelled and then writing them on the board. Model and drill pronunciation.

1 swearing 2 take, pieces 3 handy 4 wrong way
5 wobbly

🔊 **6.21**
1 After hours and hours, and a lot of swearing, I finally managed to put it together.
2 So I had to take it to pieces, move all the bits into the bedroom…
3 I'm quite handy – quite practical – so I thought, 'No problem'…
4 I realized I'd put the door handle on the wrong way round.
5 So now at least it has four legs, but it's rather wobbly…

Now get Sts, in pairs, to guess what the words mean. Tell them to read the whole sentence as the context will help them guess.

Check answers, either explaining in English, translating into Sts' L1, or getting Sts to check in their dictionaries.

EXTRA SUPPORT If there's time, you could get Sts to listen again with script 6.20 on *p.128*, so they can see exactly what they understood / didn't understand. Translate / Explain any new words or phrases.

g Focus on the instructions and go through the questions, making sure Sts understand the different meanings.

Then focus on the **Describing a process** box and go through it with the class.

Put Sts in pairs and tell them to use the questions in the box to guide them. If your Sts haven't done any of these things themselves, tell them to talk about a time somebody they know did them, e.g. a family member.

Monitor and help.

Get some feedback from various pairs.

EXTRA SUPPORT Model the activity first by talking about one of the topics yourself. You could pick up on some of the natural language typical of telling anecdotes in **f**.

7 ▶ VIDEO LISTENING

a Tell Sts they are going to watch a documentary about the history of flat-pack furniture. Go through questions 1–6, making sure Sts understand all the lexis, e.g. *patented*, etc.

Give Sts time, in pairs, to try to guess the answers.

b Play the video once the whole way through for Sts to watch and check their answers in **a**.

Get Sts to compare with a partner, and then check answers. Find out if any Sts got all the answers correct.

EXTRA SUPPORT Read through the script and decide if you need to pre-teach any new lexis before Sts watch the video.

1 b 2 c 3 b 4 a 5 a 6 c

The history of flat-pack furniture

Hi there, I'm Daniel. I've just bought a new bookcase. All I need to do is put it together. It shouldn't be difficult. After all, all I need to do is follow the instructions.

OK…this might not be as easy as I thought. I don't know why I'm surprised. People have warned me about flat-pack furniture!

Almost everybody has a story about complicated instructions and missing parts. But it's incredibly popular, and today most people own at least one piece of flat-pack furniture. So, how has this concept come to dominate the entire furniture industry? Well, the story begins with a man called Erie J. Sauder.

Sauder owned a furniture business in Ohio in the nineteen thirties. He made benches, but with the spare wood he made small coffee tables. Because Sauder used leftover wood, the tables were cheap but high quality. In nineteen forty, two travelling salesmen noticed these tables. They really liked them. So they took one and displayed it at a furniture show in Chicago. A few days later they returned with an order for twenty-five thousand tables!

Sauder had to transport all of these new tables to Chicago, so he invented furniture that he could take apart and put into boxes. This made it easy to transport, and people could put it together at home. He patented the idea in nineteen fifty-one, and the ready-to-assemble furniture industry was born.

***

But the idea didn't become popular immediately. Five years later, a Swedish man named Gillis Lundgren was moving some furniture. He had never heard of ready-to-assemble furniture, and he was finding it very difficult to fit a table into his car. But then he realized that if he took the legs off, he would be able to put it in the car and put it together again at home. He discussed the idea with his employers, a small, local firm…called IKEA. They loved it and decided to focus their entire business on it.

IKEA launched their first flat-pack product in nineteen fifty-six. Today, it's the largest furniture retailer in the world, generating sales of over twenty-seven billion euros a year. So it's safe to say that the flat-pack concept has been a huge success.

Today almost everybody has a flat-pack wardrobe, table, or bookcase. But did you know there are entire flat-pack rooms? You can have a flat-pack bedroom, bathroom, or kitchen. You can even build an entire house out of flat-pack!

There are many reasons why this type of furniture has been successful. Manufacturers are able to produce it quickly and transport it easily, so it's cheaper and more convenient than other furniture. And while it might look complicated at first, it is generally very well designed, so it's very, very easy to put together. In fact, anyone can do it!

I'm nearly finished, and I've only been working on it for a few minutes! I haven't used these bits, but they're probably not important. So, what do you think?

c Now tell Sts they are going to watch the documentary again and this time they must answer questions 1–7. Give Sts time to read the questions and see if they can remember any of the answers. They could do this individually or in pairs.

Play the video again the whole way through. You could pause the video after Sts have heard about Sauder and the birth of flat-pack furniture (see *** in the script), and elicit answers to questions 1–3.

Get Sts to compare with a partner, and then check answers.

1 Complicated instructions and missing parts
2 Benches and coffee tables
3 They displayed it at a furniture show in Chicago.
4 He was finding it very difficult to fit a table into his car.
5 He took the legs off, put it in the car, and put it together again at home.
6 Manufacturers are able to produce it quickly and transport it easily; it's cheaper and more convenient; it's generally very well designed and easy to put together.
7 There are some bits he hasn't used.

EXTRA SUPPORT You could get Sts to watch the video again with subtitles, so they can see exactly what they understood / didn't understand. Translate / Explain any new words or phrases.

5&6 Revise and Check

For instructions on how to use these pages, see *p.39*.

More materials
For teachers
Teacher's Resource Centre
Video Can you understand these people? 5&6
Quick Test 6
File 6 Test
For students
Online Practice Check your progress

GRAMMAR

1 b 2 a 3 c 4 a 5 b 6 c 7 c 8 b 9 a
10 a 11 c 12 b 13 b 14 a 15 c

VOCABULARY

a
1 barn (the others are farm animals)
2 episode (the others are types of TV programmes)
3 rope (the others are tools)
4 tray (the others are cutlery)
5 saucer (the others are things you drink out of)
b
1 turn 2 soap 3 forecast 4 current 5 box
c
1 leaves 2 stream 3 valley 4 pick 5 lamb
d
1 ladder 2 torch 3 thread 4 screws 5 set up
e
1 ask 2 leave 3 take 4 sew 5 change

PRONUNCIATION

c
1 dram**a** /ə/ 2 v**a**lley /l/ 3 w**oo**d /ʊ/ 4 **kn**ife /n/
5 b**u**cket /ʌ/
d
1 **p**rogramme 2 documentary 3 vinegar 4 recommend
5 screwdriver

CAN YOU understand this text?

a
2 watch a video
b
1 wasn't able 2 recipes 3 alone 4 themselves 5 so
6 filmed 7 how

▶ CAN YOU understand these people?

1 a 2 c 3 b 4 b 5 a

🔊 **6.22**

1
I = interviewer, R = Rafael
I How much TV do you watch?
R I watch a fair amount of television, maybe at least one, maybe two, three hours a day.
I Do you think you watch too much TV?
R Maybe, since I fall asleep in front of it.
I What kind of shows do you watch most?
R Some news, um, some entertainment, late night talk shows and then some French TV or some drama.

2
I = interviewer, M = Melanie
I Would you like to live in a city or in the country?
M I live in Brooklyn, New York, so I live in a different borough.
I Would you like to move to the country?
M I lived in a place that was more country than here, and while I found it really peaceful, I didn't find it that stimulating, so I definitely would prefer to live in a city, at least, at least right now, you know, I'm twenty-five, I kind of want lots of things going on. You know.

3
I = interviewer, R = Royce
I What is more important to you when you eat out, the food or the service?
R The food is much more important when I go out to eat. If the service is bad, I can forgive that.
I Is there anything that waiters do that really annoys you?
R Um, mostly just when they're, um, when you can't get their attention and when they ask you how things are when you've just taken a big bite of food.

4
I = interviewer, J = Julia
I Do you usually tip in restaurants and taxis?
C Um yes, I usually tip in restaurants and taxis.
I How much?
C Um, I usually just do the standard, like the twenty per cent, yeah.
I Are there any situations where you feel embarrassed to tip?
C Um, sometimes I'm embarrassed to tip at hair salons, or if I'm getting my nails done, which I almost never do, but just cos I'm not sure how much.

5
I = interviewer, L = Lynn
I Are you good at DIY?
L Yes, I'm really good and I love renovating and refurbishing, and doing everything myself, and I mean really by myself because I don't invite friends or anyone, I just do it alone and I love it.
I What was the last thing you did?
L The last thing was my bedroom. I renovated my bedroom. It was waiting for three years to be renovated. Yes, that's the last thing I did.

Revise and Check 95

7A Take your cash

- **G** phrasal verbs
- **V** cash machines, phrasal verbs
- **P** linking

Lesson plan

The topic of this lesson is money. The lesson starts with a vocabulary focus on cash machines, where Sts learn the history of its invention and some useful lexis for using cash machines in English. This is followed by a listening about two news stories about ATMs. Sts finally talk about their own use of cash machines.

In the second half, Sts go to the Vocabulary Bank to learn more new phrasal verbs, and revise the ones from Files 1–6. This leads into the grammar focus on phrasal verbs. The three types of phrasal verbs (separable, no object, and inseparable) are revised and practised. In Pronunciation, Sts practise linking in phrasal verbs. Then they consolidate what they have learned in a speaking activity. Finally, Sts read a short article about the relationship between money and happiness, and then true stories about people giving money away to help others.

More materials

For teachers

Photocopiables
Grammar phrasal verbs *p.164*
Communicative Talking of money… *p.194* (instructions *p.175*)
Vocabulary Phrasal verbs *p.216* (instructions *p.204*)

For students
Workbook 7A
Online Practice 7A

OPTIONAL LEAD-IN (BOOKS CLOSED)
Write on the board:

- GO TO THE BANK
- USE ONLINE BANKING
- USE A CASH MACHINE

Ask Sts *How often do you…?*, using the prompts on the board.
Now write on the board:

- _____ POINT
- HOLE IN THE _____
- AT_____

Ask Sts to try to complete the three other terms for *cash machine*.
Check answers and ask Sts to guess why it's also called a *hole in the wall* (a hole in the wall was originally a cash machine installed in a hole in the wall outside a bank, but it is now sometimes used to refer to any cash machine). You could tell Sts that ATM stands for Automated Teller Machine – a teller is a person whose job is to receive and pay out money in a bank.

cash point   hole in the **wall**   AT**M**

1 VOCABULARY cash machines

Vocabulary notes
Cash machine instructions
These vary slightly from machine to machine, depending on which bank they belong to, but the ones on *p.67* are fairly standard.

a Books open. Get Sts to look at the image and if you didn't do the **Optional lead-in**, elicit / explain what a *cash machine* is (= a machine in or outside a bank, etc., from which you can get money from your bank account by using a special plastic card).

Now focus on the task and give Sts time, in pairs, to work out what the missing words are.

Check answers to the first question. You could also check Sts know the meaning of *temporarily* (= to last a short time).

1 cash machine   2 out   3 order

Now get Sts, in their pairs, to discuss the other two questions.
Get some feedback.

b Tell Sts they are going to read a text about the history of the cash machine. Go through questions 1–4, making sure Sts understand all the lexis. The text explains the meaning of *ATM* and *PIN*. You might want to check Sts know the meaning of *digit* (= any of the numbers from 0 to 9).
Give Sts time to read the text and answer the questions.
Get Sts to compare with a partner, and then check answers. Highlight that *PIN* is always pronounced /pɪn/, not P-I-N. Elicit more ideas for question 4 (e.g. check your balance, deposit money, pay in cheques, etc.).

1 Because his bank was closed when he needed some cash.
2 Because Barron's wife said that she could only remember four digits.
3 £10 in £1 notes
4 Print a bank statement, top up your phone, print photos

c Focus on the instructions and the cash machine instructions A–I. The formal terms used on the cash machine screens are focused on in **e**.
Give Sts time to match the instructions to the screens.

EXTRA SUPPORT Get Sts to work in pairs.

d ◆) **7.1** Play the audio for Sts to listen and check.
Check answers. For 4A you might want to make it clear to Sts that other transactions, such as checking your balance, can be chosen.

1 F 2 C 3 G 4 A 5 H 6 E 7 D 8 I 9 B

◆) **7.1**
How to use an ATM to withdraw cash
1   F   A Insert your card.
         B Put your card into the machine.
2   C   A Select your language.
         B Choose the language you want.

96 7A

3 G A Enter your PIN.
     B Key in your four-digit PIN. Then press ENTER.
4 A A Select a transaction.
     B Choose 'Withdraw cash' from the main menu.
5 H A Select the account type.
     B Choose the bank account you want to use.
6 E A Select or enter the amount.
     B Choose or key in the amount of money you want to take out. Then press ENTER.
7 D A Remove your card.
     B Take your card out of the machine.
8 I A Take your cash.
     B Take your money out of the machine within thirty seconds.
9 B A Do you want a receipt?
     B Decide if you want a receipt, and press YES or NO.

e Focus on the instructions and point out that 1–5 are formal words that appear on the cash machine screen. Sts must match them to phrasal verbs a–e. Tell Sts to look at the screens in **c** to help them.
Check answers.

1 c 2 a 3 b 4 e 5 d

2 LISTENING & SPEAKING listening for news facts

a 🔊 **7.2** Tell Sts they are going to listen to two different news stories about cash machines.

Focus on the pictures and the questions.

Play the audio once the whole way through for Sts to listen and answer the two questions.

Get Sts to compare with a partner, and then play the audio again if necessary.

Check answers.

EXTRA SUPPORT Read through the script and decide if you need to pre-teach any new lexis before Sts listen.

Story 1: The cash machine gave double the amount of cash people had keyed in.
Story 2: The cash machine gave their money and notes asking for help.
Both stories have a happy ending because in Story 1 the people were allowed to keep the cash, and in Story 2 the man who was sending the notes was able to get out.

🔊 **7.2**
(script in Student's Book on *p.128*)
Story 1
Tonight we're going to start with a good news story – well, good news for some people! Yesterday, bank customers in a village in Hampshire were thousands of pounds richer after an ATM started giving out double the money people had asked for.
When people heard the news, they rushed to take money out of the faulty machine, and long queues formed. For two hours, around two hundred residents continued to withdraw money. It was mostly middle-aged people, but a few children arrived on their bikes with their parents' bank cards. One villager, who asked not to be named, said that some people had used five or six bank cards and had got three hundred pounds free with each card. At first, people thought it was funny, but then some people became a bit aggressive when other people started pushing into the queue.
Finally, after two hours, the police arrived and switched off the ATM. They even posted a message on Twitter to stop more people arriving. They warned that receiving too much money from a cash machine might be a crime, and that the bank would ask people to pay back the money. However, later the bank said that it wasn't the customers' fault and that no one would have to return the money.

Story 2
And finally on *Texas News* this Wednesday evening, the man who got trapped inside an ATM. Customers who were using an ATM in Corpus Christi earlier today got a big surprise. While they were withdrawing money from the machine, several people received handwritten notes, asking for help.
A man, who asked not to be named, had locked himself in while he was changing the lock to the ATM room at the bank. Unfortunately, he'd left his cell phone and the swipe card he needed to get out of the room outside, in his van. When he realized that he couldn't get out and couldn't phone for help, he started passing notes through the ATM receipt slot to customers who were taking out cash. One of them read, 'Please help. I'm stuck in here and I don't have my phone. Please call my boss!'
At first, the customers thought the notes were a trick. But eventually, one of them called the police. When the police arrived, they heard a very quiet voice coming from inside the ATM. An officer went into the bank, broke down the door to the room behind the cash machine, and found the man. Senior Officer Richard Olden said, 'We thought it was a joke. It was just crazy that somebody was stuck in the ATM. Luckily, the man is OK.'

b Give Sts time to read the questions. You could put Sts in pairs and see if they can remember any of the answers.

Play the audio, pausing after the first story to give Sts time to answer the questions.

Get Sts to compare with a partner, and then play the audio again if necessary. Repeat the process for Story 2.
Check answers.

Story 1
1 They rushed to take money out of the machine.
2 200 residents for 2 hours
3 Middle aged, and a few children
4 Because people started pushing into the queue
5 Switched off the ATM, and posted a message on Twitter to stop people from coming
6 It wasn't the customers' fault and they didn't have to pay the money back.

Story 2
1 He was changing the lock to the ATM room.
2 His phone and his swipe card
3 Because he couldn't get out of the room and he couldn't call for help.
4 By passing notes through the machine to people who were taking money out
5 That it was a trick
6 They broke down the door and found the man.

EXTRA SUPPORT If there's time, you could get Sts to listen again with the script on *p.128*, so they can see exactly what they understood / didn't understand. Translate / Explain any new words or phrases.

c Focus on the two extracts and answer the question as a whole-class activity.

Possible answers
The villager probably didn't want other villagers to know that he / she had spoken to the press.
The man who was stuck in the ATM was probably very embarrassed.

d Put Sts in pairs and get them to discuss the questions, giving as much information as possible.

Monitor and help with vocabulary if necessary. You will probably need to pre-teach the expression *It swallowed my card*, as this is one of the most common problems that people have with cash machines.

Don't over-correct, but encourage Sts to communicate. Get some feedback from the class.

EXTRA SUPPORT Choose one of the questions and answer it yourself, giving as much information as possible.

3 VOCABULARY & GRAMMAR phrasal verbs

a Focus on the task and get Sts to choose the odd one out.

Get them to compare with a partner, and then check answers. You could elicit / explain the meaning of the two phrasal verbs that can be used with the **bold** noun.

1 settle down 2 close down 3 look round
4 set up 5 grow up

b Tell Sts to go to **Vocabulary Bank** Phrasal verbs on *p.162*.

Vocabulary notes

Many Sts worry that there are so many phrasal verbs, some even with more than one meaning, that they will never manage to learn them all. It is important to encourage Sts to learn them bit by bit, ideally in a context, and to just treat them like any other vocabulary item.

Common phrasal verbs with two meanings that Sts should know are *take off* (clothes and a plane) and *give up* (stop doing sth or surrender).

Here they have been grouped in three different ways, according to the topic, according to the particle, and according to the verb, as different Sts find some ways easier to remember. Some of these phrasal verbs have come up before, so Sts shouldn't feel too overwhelmed.

Focus on the **Phrasal verbs revision** box and check that Sts remember the meaning of the different verbs.

Remind Sts of the difference between the three types, but don't spend too long on this, as Sts will be practising the grammar of phrasal verbs in **d**. Tell Sts that a good dictionary will tell them if a phrasal verb that takes an object is Type 2 or 3. Point out to Sts that the green, red, and blue text in sections 1–3 corresponds to the Type 1, 2, 3 colour-coding in the information box.

Now focus on **1 Phrasal verbs to do with money** and get Sts to do **a** individually or in pairs.

🔊 **7.3** Now do **b**. Play the audio for Sts to listen and check.

Check answers.

🔊 **7.3**
Phrasal verbs
1 Phrasal verbs to do with money
1 e If I lend you the money, can you pay me back next week?
2 f I need to take out some money. Where's the nearest cash machine?
3 b I won't be able to pay off my student loan until I'm forty-five.
4 c He's so generous. When he won the lottery, he gave nearly all the money away.
5 d Nowadays it's difficult for couples to live on only one salary.
6 a I had to live off my parents while I was at university.

EXTRA SUPPORT Get Sts to cover definitions a–f, read the sentences, and see if they can remember the meaning of the coloured phrasal verbs. Or Sts can cover sentences 1–6 and try to remember the phrasal verbs from the meanings a–f. They could do this individually or in pairs.

Now focus on **2 Phrasal verbs with *away* and *back*** and go through the box **The meaning of the particle** with the class.

Get Sts to do **a** individually or in pairs.

🔊 **7.4** Now do **b**. Play the audio for Sts to listen and check.

Check answers.

🔊 **7.4**
2 Phrasal verbs with *away* and *back*
away
1 Don't **run** away! I won't hurt you.
2 The boss will **be** away until the end of next week. He's at a conference in Mexico.
3 Please **put** your toys away. They're all over the floor.
4 If you take a paracetamol, it'll **take** the pain away!
back
5 I'm sorry, but I'm confiscating your phone. You'll **get** it back at the end of day.
6 He's out, I'm afraid. Could you **call** back in about half an hour?
7 A Where are you going?
   B Just to the shops. I'll **be** back in ten minutes.
8 That's my book! **Give** it back.

EXTRA SUPPORT Get Sts to cover the sentences and try to remember the phrasal verbs from the list.

Finally, focus on **3 More phrasal verbs with *take*** and get Sts to do **a** individually or in pairs.

🔊 **7.5** Now do **b**. Play the audio for Sts to listen and check.

Check answers.

🔊 **7.5**
3 More phrasal verbs with *take*
1 Sorry, I can't come tonight. I'm taking my girlfriend **out** for dinner.
2 They're taking **on** ten new interns at Radio London. Why don't we apply?
3 I take **after** my mother. We're both very outgoing.
4 The plane took **off** twenty minutes late.
5 Unfortunately, my company was taken **over** by a multinational firm, and I lost my job.
6 Take **off** your shoes, please. I've just cleaned the floor.
7 You need to take the keyboard **apart** to clean it properly.
8 I need to do more exercise. I think I'll take **up** cycling.

EXTRA SUPPORT Get Sts to cover the sentences and try to remember the phrasal verbs from the list.

Tell Sts to go back to the main lesson **7A**.

EXTRA SUPPORT If you think Sts need more practice, you may want to give them the **Vocabulary** photocopiable activity at this point.

c Focus on the instructions and point out that in 1–4 each sentence is repeated three or four times, but with a different word order. Tell Sts to decide which sentences have the correct word order.

Check answers.

1 He gave away his money. He gave his money away. He gave it away.
2 We asked for the bill. We asked for it.
3 She got up early.
4 I'm looking forward to my holiday. I'm looking forward to it.

EXTRA SUPPORT Get Sts to work in pairs.

d Tell Sts to go to **Grammar Bank 7A** on *p.144*.

Grammar notes

Phrasal verbs are always difficult for Sts, mainly because there are so many, and because even when Sts think they know the meaning of a phrasal verb, they then discover that it may have several more meanings. However, the grammar of phrasal verbs is not difficult, and Sts should have seen the rules before.

Type 1: Highlight that as in Type 3, the verb and particle in these phrasal verbs are never separated, e.g. by a time adverbial (NOT *He came three days later back*).

The phrasal verbs used in the exercises have all been taught before and should be known.

Focus on the example sentences for **Type 1 phrasal verbs with no object** and play audio 🔊 **7.6** for Sts to listen and repeat. Encourage them to copy the rhythm. Then go through the rules with the class.

Repeat for **Type 2 phrasal verbs with an object – separable** 🔊 **7.7** and **Type 3 phrasal verbs with an object – inseparable** 🔊 **7.8**.

Focus on the exercises and get Sts to do them individually or in pairs.

Check answers, getting Sts to read the full sentences.

a
1 ✓   2 sent it back   3 ✓   4 live off their parents
5 took it back   6 ✓   7 paid her back   8 ✓   9 grew up in Wales   10 out of these trousers

b
1 Could you **pick them up** at the airport?
2 I'm really **looking forward to it**.
3 No, they **closed it down** a month ago.
4 Please **take it away**.
5 No, and I've been **looking for them** for half an hour!
6 I **gave it away**.
7 I'm going to **throw it away**.
8 She was with her husband for 20 years, and she **looked after him** during his final illness.
9 No, but I've **asked for it**.
10 Could you **turn it up** a bit?

EXTRA SUPPORT If you think Sts need more practice, you may want to give them the **Grammar** photocopiable activity at this point.

Tell Sts to go back to the main lesson **7A**.

4 PRONUNCIATION linking

Pronunciation notes

This exercise gives more practice of linking, especially the linking between a word that finishes in a consonant sound and a word beginning with a vowel, which is very common with phrasal verbs.

a Focus on the **Linking** box and go through it with the class. Highlight that with words ending in -w, the w is not normally pronounced (*new*, *throw*, etc.), but if the word is followed by a word beginning with a vowel, as in *throw away*, the w is pronounced. You could write some more phrases on the board for Sts to practise saying, e.g. NEW AGE, I SAW IT, and CAN I BORROW A PEN?, etc.

Focus on the instructions and get Sts to match 1–6 to a–f.

EXTRA SUPPORT Get Sts to work in pairs.

b 🔊 **7.9** Play the audio for Sts to listen and check. Check answers.

🔊 **7.9**
1 c The machine says 'Insert your card'. Put it in.
2 f Your shoes are really dirty. Take them off.
3 d Waiter, I can't finish this steak. Take it away.
4 b This chicken's past its sell-by date. Throw it away.
5 a The rubbish is beginning to smell. Take it out.
6 e It's probably on Wikipedia. Look it up.

c 🔊 **7.10** Tell Sts they must listen and repeat a–f, paying attention to the linkers. Elicit / Explain that the preposition in a phrasal verb is unstressed unless it comes at the end of a sentence or phrase, e.g. *When did you set off?*

Play the audio, pausing after each sentence for Sts to listen and repeat.

🔊 **7.10**
See a–f in **a** in Student's Book on *p.68*.

Then repeat the activity, eliciting responses from individual Sts.

EXTRA SUPPORT Put Sts in pairs and get them to practise saying sentences a–f. This will help them for the next activity.

EXTRA IDEA Ask Sts to look for linking in sentences 1–6 in **a**, e.g. *says⌒insert*, *shoes⌒are⌒really*, etc.

d Focus on the instructions and put Sts in pairs, **A** and **B**.

Sts **B** (books open) should start by reading a sentence from 1–6, and Sts **A** (books closed) should answer using one of the sentences in a–f from memory.

Monitor the linking in a–f as Sts are doing the task. Make sure they swap roles.

e 🔊 **7.11** Focus on the instructions and the example.

Play the audio, pausing at the first beep, and elicit the response from the class.

Now play the rest of the audio, pausing at the beep in each sentence.

🔊 **7.11**
1 You owe me money. (*pause*) Pay me back.
2 The music's too loud. (*pause*) Turn it down.
3 There's a towel on the floor. (*pause*) Pick it up.
4 No one's watching the TV. (*pause*) Switch it off.
5 Your clothes are everywhere. (*pause*) Put them away.
6 Here's the form. (*pause*) Fill it in.
7 I can't hear the TV. (*pause*) Turn it up.
8 Those shoes would look great on you. (*pause*) Try them on.

Then repeat the activity, eliciting responses from individual Sts.

EXTRA SUPPORT If Sts find it difficult to say the second sentence after hearing the sentence on the audio, give them more time and tell them to write the answer. After they have heard the last sentence on the audio, get them to compare their answers with their partner. Play the audio for Sts to listen and check. Finally, play the audio again, and ask Sts to try to say the correct response without looking at their written answers.

5 SPEAKING

Focus on the questions and make sure Sts understand the lexis, e.g. *a missed call*.

Put Sts in pairs to answer the questions, giving as much information as possible. Monitor to check that Sts are using the phrasal verbs correctly.

Get feedback by eliciting answers to the different questions from individual Sts.

EXTRA SUPPORT Demonstrate the activity by answering one or two of the questions yourself.

6 READING understanding the conclusions of research

a Focus on the six ways of spending money and make sure Sts know what they all mean.

Give Sts time to choose the three that would make them the happiest.

Get Sts to compare with a partner. Tell them to explain their choices if possible.

Get some feedback from various pairs.

EXTRA IDEA Ask Sts *Can money buy you happiness?* and elicit opinions from the class. Have a vote with a show of hands to see what the majority thinks. You could also tell the class what you think.

b Tell Sts they are now going to read a short article that looked at some research into the relationship between money and happiness. Point out the **Glossary** and go through it with the class.

Give Sts time to read the article and answer the question. Check the answer.

EXTRA SUPPORT Before Sts read the article the first time, check whether you need to pre-teach any vocabulary.

> - buying a birthday present for a friend
> - giving a donation to charity
> - giving a few coins to a homeless person
>
> Because spending money on others makes you happier than spending it on yourself or paying bills.

Deal with any other new vocabulary. Model and drill the pronunciation of any tricky words.

c Focus on the instructions. You could elicit some ideas from Sts why someone would choose not to work for a charity.

Set a time limit for Sts to read the article to find the answer. Tell them not to worry about the gaps.

Get Sts to compare with a partner, and then check the answer. Then elicit Sts' opinions.

EXTRA SUPPORT Before Sts read the article the first time, check whether you need to pre-teach any vocabulary.

> He decided not to work for a charity because he thought that if he donated a large part of his salary, he would make a bigger difference.

d Set a time limit for Sts to read the article again and complete the gaps with verb phrases A–H.

Get Sts to compare with a partner, and then check answers.

> 1 C 2 B 3 D 4 A 5 H 6 E 7 G 8 F

Deal with any other new vocabulary. Model and drill the pronunciation of any tricky words.

EXTRA IDEA Focus Sts' attention on the money expressions in the article, e.g. *a six-figure salary*, *handed over* (*money*), *donate regularly*, *frugal*, etc.

e Put Sts in pairs, **A** and **B**, and tell them to go to **Communication** Giving it away, **A** on *p.110*, **B** on *p.113*.

Give Sts time to read their articles and answer the five questions.

When they are ready, tell Sts **A** to share their story with their partner by using the answers to the questions. Then they should swap roles.

Finally, get Sts to answer the question in **d**.

You could elicit the two stories from the class as well as have a vote of hands for the question in **d**.

Tell Sts to go back to the main lesson **7A**.

f Focus on the questions and make sure Sts know the meaning of the adjective *inspiring* (= exciting and encouraging you to do or feel sth). Model and drill its pronunciation.

In pairs or small groups, get Sts to ask and answer the questions.

Elicit some feedback from the class.

7B Shall we go out or stay in?

G verb patterns
V live entertainment
P homographs

Lesson plan

The topic of this lesson is entertainment, both going out to see something and staying at home. The first half of the lesson focuses on going out, specifically on live entertainment. Sts begin with a vocabulary focus which provides the lexis to talk about live entertainment. Next, the pronunciation focus looks at homographs – words with the same spelling but different pronunciations, e.g. *live* and *row*, or spelled and pronounced the same way, e.g. *stalls*. Sts then listen to three people talking about a live event they went to, but didn't enjoy. The first half of the lesson finishes with Sts talking about their own experiences of going to live events, and then writing about it.

In the second half, Sts begin with the grammar focus, which revises and extends their knowledge of verb patterns with gerunds and infinitives. This is followed by an article about a café in Oxford where people have something to eat and drink, and play board games. The lesson ends with Sts talking about what they like to do with friends in their free time if they go out or stay in.

More materials

For teachers

Photocopiables
Grammar verb patterns *p.165*
Communicative Talk for 30 seconds *p.195* (instructions *p.176*)

For students
Workbook 7B
Online Practice 7B

OPTIONAL LEAD-IN (BOOKS CLOSED)
Write on the board:
SATURDAY NIGHT WITH FRIENDS: GO OUT OR STAY IN?
Elicit that *stay in* = *stay at home*.
Now ask for a show of hands to answer the question. Elicit the advantages and disadvantages of the two options and write them on the board.

1 VOCABULARY live entertainment

Vocabulary notes

Although *crowd* is usually used in the context of a sport like football, where there is a large number of people watching, it can also be used for a huge concert given, e.g. in a sports arena.

The final whistle = the end of any sports match where the referee has a whistle, e.g. football, basketball, etc.

a Books open. Focus on the questions. Make sure Sts understand the meaning and pronunciation of a *live event*. You could remind them of the term *live sport*, which they saw in Lesson **5A**.

Put Sts in pairs and give them time to discuss the questions.
Elicit some feedback.

EXTRA SUPPORT With a small class, or if you think your Sts don't go out much, you may want to do this as a whole-class activity.

b 🔊 7.12 Focus on the instructions. Play the audio once the whole way through for Sts just to listen.
Play it again, pausing after each conversation for Sts to match it to an event and to answer the question.
Check answers. You could write the answers on the board to help Sts with the next activity.

1 a sporting event (during)   2 a concert (after)
3 a play (before)

🔊 7.12
(script in Student's Book on *p.128*)
1
Hi. Yeah, not bad… Yeah, it's half-time… One–all. Yeah, there's a really good crowd. The stadium's packed… No, no trouble. The Liverpool fans are making a bit of a noise, but nothing major… OK, I'll call you when it's over. With a bit of luck, we'll be in the semi-final in an hour's time.
2
A So, tell me all about it!
B It was absolutely brilliant. We were in the second row, just near the stage, and when he was singing – I swear – a few times he looked right at me!
A Did he sing *Baby Baby*?
B Of course! All the best songs. It was just an amazing performance.
A Were Sandy and Annette there?
B Yeah, we met for a drink in the interval.
A Gosh, you're so lucky you got tickets!
3
A OK, I'm looking for tickets now…There's a matinee at three o'clock and then it's on again in the evening at eight.
B Let's go at eight if we can get seats.
A Well, there aren't any in the stalls, but there are two upstairs in the circle, in the second row.
B OK. Go for it. It's a small theatre anyway, so we should have a good view wherever we sit.
A OK. Right, we've got them. We can pick them up at the box office.

c Focus on the instructions. If you didn't write the answers on the board for **b**, elicit from the class which event each speaker was talking about (*speaker 1: a sporting event*, *speaker 2: a concert*, *speaker 3: a play*).
Give Sts time, in pairs or individually, to number some of the words if possible.
Play the audio, pausing after each conversation for Sts to write *1*, *2*, or *3* in the boxes.
Check answers, and elicit the meaning where necessary.

❗ Don't drill the pronunciation yet as this will be done in **e**.

box office 3   crowd 1   half-time 1   interval 2   matinee 3
performance 2   stadium 1   stage 2   stalls / circle 3

d Focus on the chart headings and elicit / explain what a *musical* is.

7B 101

Get Sts to first put the words from **c** in the correct columns, and then add the words in the list in **d**.

EXTRA SUPPORT Get Sts to only write the words from **c** in the correct columns, and check answers.

> **Sporting event:** crowd, half-time, stadium
> **Play, musical, or concert:** interval, matinee, performance, stage, stalls / circle
> **Both:** box office

Then get Sts to add the words in the list to the chart.

EXTRA SUPPORT Get Sts to work in pairs.

e 🔊 **7.13** Play the audio for Sts to listen and check.

Check answers and elicit the meaning of any of the words in **d** that you think Sts may be unsure about. You could tell Sts that *box office* can be used for both categories, but *ticket office* is more common in sport. Also, stadiums are sometimes used for other purposes, e.g. a concert.

🔊 **7.13**
Sporting event crowd, half-time, stadium, extra time, final whistle, opponent, score, spectators
Play, musical, or concert interval, matinee, performance, stage, stalls / circle, audience, curtain, plot, scene
Both box office, arena, fans, programme, row, tickets

Now play the audio again, pausing after each word for Sts to listen and repeat.

EXTRA SUPPORT Give Sts time, in pairs, to practise saying the words.

2 PRONUNCIATION homographs

> **Pronunciation notes**
> **Homographs**
> There are many homographs of type 1 – many of which Sts will have met before as words with more than one meaning, e.g. *book* (verb and noun), *well* (adverb and noun), etc.
> Type 2, where the pronunciation changes, is more unusual, but it is important when Sts come across these words to point out the different meanings and pronunciation.

a 🔊 **7.14** Focus on sentences 1–4. Play the audio once the whole way through for Sts just to listen.

🔊 **7.14**
See sentences in Student's Book on *p.70*

Now play the audio again, pausing after 1 for Sts to listen and repeat both sentences.

Ask Sts what the highlighted words mean in each sentence and whether they are pronounced the same or differently.

> differently: in **a** it's the adjective /laɪv/ and in **b** it's the verb /lɪv/

Then repeat the same process for 2–4.

> 2 same: **a** *fan* = a person who admires sb / sth or enjoys watching or listening to sb / sth very much; **b** *fan* = a machine with blades that go round to create a current of air

> 3 differently: **a** *row* /rəʊ/ = a number of people standing or sitting next to each other in a line; **b** *row* /raʊ/ = a serious disagreement
> 4 same: **a** *stage* = a raised area, usually in a theatre, etc., where actors, dancers, etc. perform; **b** *stage* = a period or state that sb passes through while developing

EXTRA CHALLENGE Put Sts in pairs and get them to do the activity without the audio. Then play the audio to check answers. Finally, play it again for Sts to listen and repeat.

b Focus on the **Homographs** box and go through it with the class. Make sure the two types are clear.

Put Sts in pairs and get them to identify the type of homograph in sentences 1–4 in **a**.
Check answers.

> Sentences 1 and 3 are type 2. Sentences 2 and 4 are type 1.

c Focus on the six words in the list and definitions 1–6. Point out that 1–6 have two definitions each and Sts have to match them to words in the list.
Get Sts to compare with a partner.

d 🔊 **7.15** Play the audio for Sts to listen and check.

Check answers and elicit in which three pairs of words the pronunciation is different.

> **bear** 5   **close** 1   **lie** 6   **minute** 4   **second** 2   **wind** 3
> Pronunciation is different in 1, 3, and 4.

🔊 **7.15**
1 close [= /kləʊz/], close [= /kləʊs/]
2 second, second
3 wind [= /wɪnd/], wind [= /waɪnd/]
4 minute [= /maɪˈnjuːt/], minute [= /ˈmɪnɪt/]
5 bear, bear
6 lie, lie

---

3 LISTENING predicting the outcome of a story

a Focus on the questions and the words in the list. Do this as a whole-class activity, or put Sts in pairs and then get some feedback. You could tell the class your preference.

b 🔊 **7.16** Focus on the task and then play the audio, pausing after each speaker to give Sts time to answer the questions.

Get Sts to compare with a partner, and then check answers.

EXTRA SUPPORT Read through the script and decide if you need to pre-teach any new lexis before Sts listen.

> 1 (The men's quarter final) tennis matches at the Wimbledon tennis championships in London
> 2 A play (*The Woman in Black*) in Oxford
> 3 A (Leonard Cohen) concert in (the velodrome) in Valencia

🔊 **7.16**
1 Andy
A few years ago, I went to Wimbledon, the tennis championships which take place in June in south-west London. And it's quite difficult to get tickets, but I was very lucky and got two tickets for the men's quarter-final matches on Centre Court, which are usually fantastically exciting, with lots of big names. The tickets were very expensive, but I was really pleased because they were right in the front row.

2 Cathy
Once, when my daughter was about fourteen, our local theatre, the Playhouse in Oxford, put on a play called *The Woman in Black*. It's a classic ghost story, full of suspense and quite scary – it's been made into a film starring Daniel Radcliffe, you know, who played Harry Potter. Anyway, I decided to take my daughter, and I got quite good seats in the stalls, so she could see well.

3 Clive
I'd been a fan of Leonard Cohen since I was a teenager, but I'd never, ever heard him sing live. But then, in – I think – about two thousand and nine, I read that he was going to do a world tour and that he was coming to Valencia in Spain, where I lived. I was really excited, and I thought, 'Even though he's in his mid-seventies, I'm finally going to get to hear him!' The concert was in September in the velodrome in Valencia, so in the open air.

c 🔊 **7.17** Focus on the instructions and give Sts time, in pairs, to think of different reasons why each speaker in **b** didn't enjoy the event they went to.

Elicit some ideas, but <u>don't</u> tell Sts if they are correct.

Now play the audio for Sts to listen to the rest of each story and find out if any of their predictions were correct.

Get Sts to compare with a partner, and then play the audio again if necessary.

Check answers. Find out if any Sts predicted correctly.

EXTRA SUPPORT Read through the script and decide if you need to pre-teach any new lexis before Sts listen.

1 It rained, so the matches were cancelled.
2 Some schoolchildren spoilt the atmosphere by screaming.
3 Leonard Cohen collapsed during the fourth song and was taken to hospital.

🔊 **7.17**
1 Andy
And on the day, my partner and I, we got up and drove to Wimbledon – it took about two hours. And as we were driving, it started to rain – the weather forecast was for showers, and at that time, there was no roof on Centre Court, and the players couldn't play if it was raining. But we got there, parked the car, and went in and found our seats and sat under our umbrella. Play was supposed to start at two o'clock, and at half past one the rain stopped. Then at two o'clock, the players came on and the atmosphere was brilliant. And then at two fifteen…the rain started again! The match was stopped and the court was covered over, and that was all the tennis we saw all day. We just sat there for four hours, hoping to see some more, but in the end, we just went home, very cold and very disappointed. It was a very expensive fifteen minutes.

2 Cathy
When we got there, we found our seats and sat down. The theatre wasn't full, but then just before the play was going to start, the rows of seats in front of us suddenly filled up with a group of about thirty teenagers. They were obviously a school group, and they were a bit noisy, but I thought they'd settle down when the play started. So the curtain went up and the audience went very quiet, and there was spooky music, and the tension started to grow. But then, every time anything happened onstage, the teenage girls in front of us screamed, even though nothing was really happening yet, so then we couldn't hear what the actors were saying for a few minutes until they quietened down again. In fact, they carried on doing this all the way through the first half, and it totally ruined the atmosphere for absolutely everyone. Their teachers obviously said something to them during the interval, or maybe someone had complained, but they weren't much better during the second half. It basically ruined the whole evening.

3 Clive
I went with a group of friends, and when he came on stage and started singing, I was amazed at how great his voice still was. We were having a wonderful evening, but then when he was on his fourth song, one of his old classics called *Bird on the Wire*, he suddenly collapsed on the stage! The other musicians all rushed up to help him and carried him off. We waited there, hoping that he was OK and that the concert would continue, but after almost an hour, there was no announcement – nothing – and we thought maybe he'd died. Finally, someone came on and said that he'd been taken to hospital and so the concert wouldn't continue. We went home terribly disappointed. I'd waited all my life to hear him sing live, and we just got three and a half songs. Luckily, he recovered, and went on with his tour, but he never came back to Valencia, and then he died in twenty sixteen, so I never got to hear him live again.

d 🔊 **7.18** Tell Sts they are now going to listen to the three stories again. Focus on the chart and give Sts time to see if they can remember any of the information.

Play the audio again, pausing after each speaker to give Sts time to tick the relevant boxes.

Check answers. Some Sts might not tick *went with a family member* for Andy as they might not consider a partner as part of their family.

Who…?	Andy	Cathy	Clive
1 went in the evening		✓	✓
2 had very good seats	✓	✓	
3 went to an outdoor event	✓		✓
4 went with a family member	✓	✓	
5 waited for a long time for something to happen	✓		✓

🔊 **7.18**
(script in Student's Book on *pp.128–129*)
See scripts 7.16 and 7.17

EXTRA SUPPORT If there's time, you could get Sts to listen again with the script on *pp.128–129*, so they can see exactly what they understood / didn't understand. Translate / Explain any new words or phrases.

e Focus on the question and make sure Sts understand *frustrating* (= causing you to feel annoyed and impatient). Do this as a whole-class activity.

4 SPEAKING & WRITING

a Focus on the instructions and the prompts, and give Sts time to make some notes or think about what they are going to say.

b Focus on the instructions. Put Sts in pairs and give them time to tell each other about their live event, using their answers to the prompts in **a**. Encourage Sts to ask each other for more information and to give as much detail as possible.

For the question *Would you like to have gone to your partner's event?*, get Sts to answer *yes* or *no* and then explain why (not). Make sure Sts understand the question, but don't focus specifically on its structure at this time, as the aim here is to encourage fluency.

EXTRA SUPPORT To help Sts to express their answer correctly, write on the board:
I'D LIKE / I WOULDN'T LIKE TO HAVE GONE TO…BECAUSE…

Monitor and help with vocabulary if necessary.
Get some feedback from various pairs.

c Focus on the instructions and give Sts time to write about their event.
Monitor and help if necessary. You could set this for homework if you don't want Sts to spend too much class time writing.

5 GRAMMAR verb patterns

a Focus on the instructions and get Sts to complete the sentences with the correct form of the verbs in brackets. Get Sts to compare with a partner.

b 🔊 **7.19** Play the audio for Sts to listen and check. Check answers.

> 1 to go, say 2 watching 3 stay, to spend, studying
> 4 going, being 5 going, staying (*to stay* would also be acceptable here as it refers to a specific event, but it is not worth bringing up unless Sts mention it)

🔊 **7.19**
1 If a friend asked me to go to a classical music concert, I think I'd say no.
2 I love watching films in 3D – they're much better than ordinary ones.
3 My parents didn't use to let me stay out late during the week when I was young. They wanted me to spend my evenings studying.
4 I hate going to clubs. I don't like being in places where there are lots of people and noise.
5 I never feel like going out on New Year's Eve. I prefer staying in.

Finally, put Sts in pairs and get them to discuss whether the sentences in **a** are true for them. Tell them to give as much information as possible.
Get some feedback.

c Tell Sts to go to **Grammar Bank 7B** on *p.145*.

Grammar notes

Verb patterns with gerunds and infinitives (both with or without *to*) will already be familiar to Sts. However, because there are no real rules to know whether a verb is followed by a gerund or infinitive, it is a grammar area where Sts always need a lot of practice.

You may want to remind Sts that certain verbs, e.g. *start*, *begin*, and *continue* can be followed either by an infinitive (with *to*) or a gerund, with no difference in meaning.

Remind Sts that the verbs *like*, *love*, *hate*, and *prefer* are usually followed by a gerund, although the infinitive (with *to*) is also possible. After *would like*, *would love*, *would hate*, and *would prefer*, we always use the infinitive (with *to*), e.g. *I would love to go to Australia*.

Some verbs, e.g. *stop*, *remember*, and *forget*, may be followed either by an infinitive (with *to*) or a gerund, but with a difference in meaning. This point will be dealt with at Upper-intermediate.

Focus on **Revise the basics** and use the example sentences to elicit the basic rules for using infinitives with or without *to*, and gerunds. Refer Sts to the list of **Verb patterns** on *p.164*. Get Sts to go through the list quickly in pairs, checking that they know what the verbs and other phrases mean. Encourage them to get a feel for which verb forms go with each pattern, rather than attempting to memorize the list all at once.
Tell Sts to go back to *p.145*.

Now focus on the example sentences for **verbs + infinitive (with or without *to*)** and play audio 🔊 **7.20** for Sts to listen and repeat. Encourage them to copy the rhythm. Then go through the rules with the class.

Repeat for **verbs + gerund (verb + -*ing*)** 🔊 **7.21** and **verbs + object + infinitive (with or without *to*)** 🔊 **7.22**.

Now focus on the exercises and get Sts to do them individually or in pairs.
Check answers, getting Sts to read the full sentences.

> a
> 1 We went to the box office **to pick up** the tickets.
> 2 **Going** to a live sporting event is much more exciting than **watching** it on TV.
> 3 I hate **not being able** to visit my family more often, but they live so far away.
> 4 I tried **to buy** tickets for the concert, but I didn't manage **to get** any.
> 5 Nowadays, it's cheaper **to go** to the theatre than to a football match.
> 6 She moved from London to a small village and she really misses **going** to plays and exhibitions.
> 7 They told me **not to sit** in the front row.
> 8 We needn't **hurry**. Amy's always late.
> 9 I can't afford **to live** in the city centre.
> 10 Now it's difficult **to imagine not having** a mobile phone.
>
> b
> 1 They persuaded **me to go to the cinema**.
> 2 He refused **to help** her.
> 3 Karen's teacher let **her leave** school early.
> 4 My husband wants **me to go** to the dentist's.
> 5 The police made **him move** his car.
> 6 I spend 20 minutes a day **practising** the piano.
> 7 They invited **us to have dinner** with them.
> 8 We've given up **going to** concerts.

Tell Sts to go back to the main lesson **7B**.

EXTRA SUPPORT If you think Sts need more practice, you may want to give them the **Grammar** photocopiable activity at this point.

d Focus on the instructions and go through 1–8 with the class. Stress that Sts must complete the sentences with verb phrases, not with nouns. Set a time limit for Sts to complete the sentences. You may want to get them to write their sentences on a piece of paper.

EXTRA SUPPORT Choose one of the sentences and show Sts what they should and shouldn't do, e.g. *I'd like to be able to afford to go on a luxury holiday*. NOT ~~I'd like to be able to afford a luxury holiday.~~

e Put Sts in pairs and get them to read their sentences to their partner.
Get feedback from various pairs to find out how many were the same.

EXTRA CHALLENGE Sts now tell each other their sentences.

6 READING understanding descriptions of games

a Focus on the five games and the types of game. Find out if any Sts have played any of the games.

   Give Sts time to match them.

b 🔊 **7.23** Play the audio for Sts to listen and check.

   Check answers.

> **Candy Crush** is a video game.
> **Dungeons and Dragons** is a role-playing game.
> **Poker** is a card game.
> **Scrabble** is a board game.
> **Sudoku** is a brain-training game.

🔊 **7.23**

> *Candy Crush* is a video game where you have to move pieces to make a row or column of at least three matching pieces.
>
> *Dungeons and Dragons* is a role-playing game in which you control a single character and have adventures by interacting with other players' characters.
>
> *Poker* is a card game where you bet on the values of the cards people hold in their hand.
>
> *Scrabble* is a board game in which you have to score points by putting letters onto a board to make words.
>
> *Sudoku* is a brain-training game where you have to complete a grid of eighty-one squares with the numbers one to nine.

c Focus on the article and the photo of the café, and give Sts time to read the first part of the article and answer the two questions.

   Get Sts to compare with a partner, and then check answers.

   EXTRA SUPPORT Before Sts read the article, check whether you need to pre-teach any vocabulary, but <u>not</u> the phrases in **f**.

> It's a café where people play board games.
> The café's name comes from wanting a drink (*thirsty*) and the pieces gamers play with (*meeples*, a word invented by combining *my* + *people* to describe wooden people used as counters in some games).

d Focus on the task, photos A–E of games, and questions 1–5.

   Give Sts time to read the article again and answer the questions.

   Check answers.

> 1 C 2 D 3 B 4 E 5 A

e Tell Sts they are now going to read the rest of the article and they need to find three reasons why, according to the article, board games have become popular again.

   EXTRA CHALLENGE Before Sts read the second part of the article, get them to speculate on why board games have become popular. They then read the article to see if their ideas are mentioned.

   Get Sts to compare with a partner, and then check answers.

> 1 Games and customers are very different today (customers are young professional people).
> 2 More women are playing games.
> 3 The growth of video games has made playing games a normal thing for adults to do.

f Focus on phrases 1–7 and tell Sts to read the second part of the article again and work out what they mean.

   Put Sts in pairs and give them time to discuss each phrase.

   Check answers, either explaining in English, translating into Sts' L1, or getting Sts to check in their dictionaries.

> 1 it is thriving = it's doing well
> 2 young professional couples = couples where both people work and have a profession, e.g. doctors, lawyers, etc.
> 3 rather than going out to the pub = instead of going to the pub
> 4 much wider appeal = more different kinds of people like them
> 5 one of the biggest factors = one of the most important reasons
> 6 not just staring at screens = not just looking at phones, tablets, etc.
> 7 in the real world = not in the virtual world

   Deal with any other new vocabulary. Model and drill the pronunciation of any tricky words.

g Focus on the questions. Do this as a whole-class activity, or put Sts in pairs and then get some feedback.

7 SPEAKING

a Focus on the task and the two lists, *If you go out* and *If you stay in*. Make sure Sts understand all the activities.

   Get Sts to mark the activities they like or don't like doing with friends. Highlight that they should add one of their own to each list.

b Put Sts in small groups of three or four and get them to compare their lists. Monitor and help while Sts are talking, encouraging them to give reasons to justify what they say.

   Get some feedback from the class.

c Focus on the question. Tell Sts what you did last time you spent an evening with friends. Then get Sts to do the same with a partner. Encourage them to give as much detail as possible.

   Get some feedback from various pairs.

EPISODE 4

Practical English Is it a clue?

Function asking about and explaining house rules, suggesting and agreeing on a plan of action
Language *Do you mind if I…?; You can't…; You mustn't…,* etc.

Lesson plan

In this fourth Practical English lesson, the functional focus is on explaining house rules when people share a flat or house.

In the first scene, Jenny and Luke tell Rob the bad news about his father's kidnapping. After hearing Henry's video message, Rob tells them <u>not</u> to go to the police. Meanwhile Luke invites Jenny to stay on at his house as it isn't safe for her to be at Henry's. In the next scene, Luke explains the house rules as agreed by Luke and his flatmate Simon, and Jenny agrees to them. In the final scene, Luke and Jenny are discussing a plan of action when Rob rings on Jenny's phone. Rob thinks the clue *old man* may be connected to something in Henry's study and urges them to return to Henry's house to search. Jenny and Luke form a plan to go back to the house after dark.

More materials
For teachers
Teacher's Resource Centre
Video Practical English Episode 4
Quick Test 7
File 7 Test
For students
Workbook Practical English 4
Can you remember? 1–7
Online Practice Practical English 4
Check your progress

OPTIONAL LEAD-IN (BOOKS CLOSED)
Before starting Episode 4, elicit what Sts can remember about Episode 3. Ask *What did Jenny and Luke tell the police inspector? What did Luke find on Jenny's computer? What's happened to Henry?*, etc.

Alternatively, you could play the last scene of Episode 3.

1 ▶ ROB GETS INVOLVED

a 🔊 **7.24** Books open. Focus on the photo and ask Sts what they think is happening.

Now focus on the instructions and the question. Elicit / Explain the meaning of *clue* (= a piece of evidence or some information that helps solve a mystery).

Play the video / audio once the whole way through for Sts to watch or listen and answer the question.

Check the answer.

EXTRA SUPPORT Before playing the video / audio, go through the listening scripts and decide if you need to pre-teach / check any lexis to help Sts when they listen.

The two clues are Henry's sentence 'his old man will be in his study again soon', and the sound of a church bell ringing.

🔊 **7.24**
N = narrator, J = Jenny, R = Rob, L = Luke, H = Henry
N Day three. Eight fifteen a.m. Jenny and Luke have just discovered that Henry has been kidnapped. They Skype Rob immediately.
J Rob, are you OK?
R Yes…no…I don't know.
J What are you going to do?
R I need to get to England as soon as possible. I wish I was there with you now.
J Me too. I just don't know what to do. Should we go back to the police?
R I don't think so. You heard what they said. They're obviously watching you and I don't want them to hurt Dad!
L And we can't just give them the laptop. We know what they're capable of.
R You're right. You know, there's something bothering me about Dad's message. It's the words he used.
J What do you mean?
R I'm not sure. Can you play the end of the message again for me?
H Please don't worry. Tell Rob his old man will be in his study again soon.
R That sounds strange.
L What sounds strange?
R *His old man.*
L Why is that strange? He is your dad!
R But he'd never call himself my *old man*. It's just not like him.
J So what are you saying? That he said it deliberately?
R I think it could be a clue.
J But *old man*? What on Earth can that mean?
R I don't know. But I'm sure it means something.
J You know, there was something else. I could hear something in the background.
L Like a generator or something?
J Not just that. At the beginning of the video. It sounded like a church bell ringing.
L That could be anywhere.
J You're right.
R Anyway, I need to try and get a flight to London.
J OK. Good luck. We'll call you later.
R Bye, guys.
J Bye.
L Well, you definitely can't go back to Henry's house now.
J You're right. I'll need to find a room in a hotel or a B&B.
L Don't be silly. You can stay here as long as you like.
J Won't Simon mind?
L Simon? No, he'll understand. And we've got the spare room.
J Are you sure?
L Of course I'm sure.
J Thanks, Luke. That's very nice of you.
L No worries. I'll tell you about the house.

b Now focus on 1–7 and go through them with the class.

Play the video / audio again for Sts to watch or listen again and mark the sentences *T* (true) or *F* (false). Remind them to correct the ones that are false.

Get Sts to compare with a partner, and then check answers.

1 F (Rob doesn't think they should ask the police for help because the kidnappers are watching them and he doesn't want them to hurt Henry.)
2 T
3 F (Rob noticed something strange about what his father said.)
4 F (The phrase that really surprises Rob is *his old man*.)
5 T
6 F (He hasn't booked a flight, but he's going to try.)
7 F (She's going to continue to stay at Luke's.)

106 PE4

Now focus on the last two questions and get Sts to speculate about the answers.

EXTRA SUPPORT If there's time and you are using the video, you could get Sts to watch again with subtitles, so they can see exactly what they understood / didn't understand. Translate / Explain any new words or phrases.

2 ▶ TALKING ABOUT HOUSE RULES

a 🔊 **7.25** Focus on the task and *Rules for guests*. Give Sts time to read sentences 1–6, making sure they understand them.

Get Sts to cover the conversation in **b** on *pp.74–75*. Play the video / audio once the whole way through for Sts to watch or listen and complete the rules.

Get Sts to compare with a partner, and then play again if necessary.

Check answers. Elicit / Explain the meaning of *eco-friendly* (= not harmful to the environment) and *dryer* (= a machine for drying clothes).

> 1 smoking   2 meat, meat   3 password   4 eco-friendly
> 5 hot   6 dryer, washing line
> Luke asks Jenny to move her car because the kidnappers might see it and recognize them.

🔊 **7.25**
N = narrator, L = Luke, J = Jenny
N Luke and Jenny are in the kitchen.
L It's a great location, and the rent is cheap, but Simon can be a bit difficult.
J Oh, right.
L He's got a few rules. After all, it is his house.
J That's fine.
L To start with, it's a no-smoking house.
J Great.
L And he's a strict vegetarian, so you can't cook meat or leave meat products in the fridge.
J Uh-huh.
L He just feels really strongly about not eating meat.
J That's not a problem.
L What about you? Is there anything you need?
J There is one thing – could I connect my phone to your wi-fi?
L Sure. The password is *lukeandsimonrule*, all lower case, all one word.
J Got it.
L Anything else?
J Yeah. I have some clothes I need to wash. Is it OK if I use your washing machine?
L Of course you can. But Simon prefers us to use the eco-friendly detergents. There's some in the cupboard.
J Cool.
L Oh, and you mustn't use a hot water programme. He's very keen on saving energy.
J OK, and do you mind if I use your dryer, too?
L Sorry, we don't have one, but you can hang it out on the washing line.
J Great. Is there anything else I should know?
L No, I don't think so – oh! You should probably move your car.
J I guess Simon doesn't like cars, either.
L Well, no, but it's not that. We know the kidnappers have been watching us, right? They might see it and recognize us.
J You're right. I'll move it right away.
L Look, I'll come with you and we can get a coffee. There's a nice café around the corner.
J Thanks, Luke.

b Tell Sts to uncover the conversation, and give them time to read it and to think about what the missing words might be.

Play the video / audio again and get Sts to complete the gaps. Play it again, pausing if necessary, after the gapped words.

Get Sts to compare with a partner, and then check answers.

> 1 you can't   2 meat   3 problem   4 anything   5 connect
> 6 Sure   7 password   8 else   9 OK   10 course   11 mustn't
> 12 do, mind   13 Sorry   14 anything   15 should   16 so

Now go through the conversation and deal with any new vocabulary.

c 🔊 **7.26** Tell Sts to focus on the highlighted phrases in the conversation in **b**. They should listen and repeat the phrases, copying the rhythm and intonation.

Play the video / audio, pausing after the beep for Sts to listen and repeat.

🔊 **7.26**
See highlighted phrases in Student's Book on *pp.74–75*

d Put Sts in pairs and tell them to practise the conversation in **b**.

Monitor and help, encouraging Sts to pay attention to rhythm and intonation.

Make sure Sts swap roles.

e Put Sts in pairs, **A** and **B**, and tell them to go to **Communication** Renting a room, **A** on *p.109*, **B** on *p.114*.

Go through instructions **a–c** with the class and make sure Sts understand the situation. Give enough time for Sts **A** to decide what other rule they might have and Sts **B** to decide what else they want to ask about. When they are ready, tell Sts **A** to start. Monitor and help.

When they have finished, focus on instructions **d–f** and give Sts time to prepare before they do the role-play.

Get feedback after the role-play. Find out how many Sts managed to rent a room.

EXTRA IDEA Ask Sts if they have ever rented a room or lived in a hall of residence (e.g. at university). If so, what rules did they have to follow?

Tell Sts to go back to the main lesson **Practical English 4**.

3 ▶ TAKING A RISK

a 🔊 **7.27** Focus on the photo and ask Sts some questions, e.g. *Where are Jenny and Luke? How do they look?*

Now focus on the instructions. Play the video / audio once the whole way through for Sts to watch or listen.

Check answers.

> They're going to go back to Henry's house to try to find something in the study that Rob thinks might explain the 'old man' clue.

PE4 107

🔊 7.27

N = narrator, J = Jenny, L = Luke, R = Rob
N Day three. Eleven a.m. Jenny and Luke are in a café.
J Oh, I hope we're doing the right thing.
L What do you mean?
J Maybe we should just go to the police.
L We can't. You heard what the kidnappers said.
J I know, I know…but it's all such a mess. What will we do if we can't find him?
L We will!
J I hope so. I just don't know.
L Is that Rob?
J Yes. Rob, hi!
R Hi, Jenny.
J Any news?
R It's snowing really heavily and there aren't any flights to London. I don't know when I'm going to get back.
J Oh, Rob, that's terrible!
R I know, but I'll keep trying.
J Is there anything we can do?
R Yes, actually. I've been thinking about Dad's message. That *old man* business.
J What about it?
R He must be telling us where he is. It's the only explanation.
J But what can we do about it? We don't know what it means.
R Well, Dad also mentioned something about his study, didn't he?
J Yeah, but…
R I'm sure I remember something about an old man – it's the name of a book or a painting or something – and I think it's in the study.
J Henry's study?
R Yeah. Listen, Jenny, I think you'll have to go back there.
J Back to Henry's house? But we know they're watching.
R I know, and I'm really sorry, but it's our only chance.
J You're right. Luke and I will figure something out.
R Thanks, Jenny. I wish I was there to help.
J Don't worry, we'll be OK. Talk to you soon.
R Bye, Jenny. And be really careful!
J Did you get that?
L Yes, but we can't go to the house now. If they're there, they'll see us immediately.
J We'll have to go when it's dark.
L But they still might see us.
J We can sneak in the back way. There's a footpath.
L Good idea. I know that way really well. I used to play around there when I was a kid.
J We'll need flashlights, though.
L I've got some.
J OK. We'll have to be careful, but we just might be able to do this!

b Focus on the instructions and give Sts time to read questions 1–6.

Go through the **British and American English** box with the class.

Play the video / audio again, pausing if necessary, to give Sts time to answer the questions.

Get Sts to compare with a partner, and then check answers. Point out that when Rob says *that old man business*, he means the topic or situation. People often use the word *business* in this way. Elicit / Explain the meaning of *sneak in* (= go in secretly, to avoid being seen).

1 Luke is more optimistic at the beginning.
2 No, he hasn't. There are no flights to London because of the snow.
3 He thinks they might refer to the name of a book or painting, or something else in Henry's study.
4 He thinks they need to go back to Henry's house.
5 They're going to use a footpath at the back of the house.
6 He used to play there when he was a child.

Now focus on the last question and get Sts to speculate about what will happen at the house.

EXTRA SUPPORT If there's time and you are using the video, you could get Sts to watch again with subtitles, so they can see exactly what they understood / didn't understand. Translate / Explain any new words or phrases.

c Focus on the **Social English** phrases. In pairs, get Sts to see if they can remember any of the missing words.

EXTRA CHALLENGE In pairs, get Sts to complete the phrases before they listen.

d 🔊 7.28 Play the video / audio for Sts to watch or listen and complete the phrases.

Check answers. If you know your Sts' L1, you could get them to translate the phrases.

1 such   2 so   3 news   4 keep   5 business   6 get

🔊 7.28
1 It's all such a mess.
2 I hope so. I just don't know.
3 Any news?
4 I know, but I'll keep trying.
5 I've been thinking about Dad's message. That 'old man' business.
6 Did you get that?

Now play the video / audio again, pausing after each phrase for Sts to watch or listen and repeat.

e Focus on the instructions and make sure Sts understand what they have to do.

Get Sts to compare with a partner, and then check answers.

A 5   B 3   C 6   D 1   E 4   F 2

Now put Sts in pairs and get them to practise the conversations.

Finally, focus on the **CAN YOU…?** questions and ask Sts if they feel confident they can now do these things. If they feel that they need more practice, tell them to go to *Online Practice* to watch the episode again and practise the language.

8A Treat yourself

G have something done
V looking after yourself
P sentence stress

Lesson plan

The main topic of this lesson is looking after yourself, both in terms of physical fitness and appearance. In the first half of the lesson, the structure *have something done* is presented and then practised in a pronunciation focus on sentence stress. Sts then talk in pairs about various services they have done. The theme of looking after yourself continues with the topic of hair. Sts go to the Vocabulary Bank and learn specific vocabulary related to hairdressing and hairstyles. After that, Sts listen to an interview with a London hairdresser. Finally, Sts talk about their own experience of haircuts and hairstyles.

In the second half, Sts return to the Vocabulary Bank and focus on words and phrases related to fitness and beauty treatments. This leads into Reading & Listening, where Sts read the introduction to an article about two journalists who spend a day at a health spa, trying different spa treatments. Sts read about one of the treatments, and then listen to the journalists' thoughts on two more. The lesson ends with Sts talking about ways of looking after yourself. Then, in small groups, they have to create and present a campaign to help young people eat healthily.

More materials

For teachers

Photocopiables
Grammar have something done *p.166*
Communicative Do it yourself? or Have it done? *p.196*
(instructions *p.176*)
Vocabulary Looking after yourself *p.217*
(instructions *p.204*)

For students
Workbook 8A
Online Practice 8A

OPTIONAL LEAD-IN (BOOKS CLOSED)
Write the following sentences on the board:
1 SOME DOCTORS RECOMMEND A HOT LEMON AND HONEY DRINK TO TREAT A SORE THROAT.
2 DON'T TREAT ME LIKE A CHILD! I'M 17 YEARS OLD!
3 ON MY BIRTHDAY, MY BOYFRIEND TREATED ME TO DINNER AT MY FAVOURITE RESTAURANT.
4 MY COLLEAGUES INVITED ME TO A SPA TO CELEBRATE MY ENGAGEMENT. IT WAS A REAL TREAT.

Focus on 1 and elicit the meaning of *treat* (= give medical attention). Repeat for 2 (= behave in a particular way towards sb). Ask what the noun would be for these uses of *treat* and elicit *treatment*.

Now focus on 3 and elicit what *treat* means here (= do sth nice for sb, and where it costs money, paying for it).

Finally, focus on 4 and elicit that with the meaning in 3, the noun is *a treat*. Explain that anything can be a treat, from a holiday to a cake.

1 GRAMMAR have something done

a Books open. If you didn't do the **Optional lead-in**, start by focusing on the title and explaining what it means. Focus on the photos and the questions. Do this as a whole-class activity, or put Sts in pairs and then check answers.

1 B 2 A 3 C 4 D 5 E 6 F 7 H 8 G

EXTRA SUPPORT Elicit the difference between the photos in each pair, i.e. in one of the photos, the person is doing something him- / herself; in the other photo, someone else is performing the task or service for the person.

b Tell Sts to go to **Grammar Bank 8A** on *p.146*.

Grammar notes

Have something done will be a new grammar point for many Sts. This structure is a type of passive.

Highlight that we normally use this form without *by* (i.e. *by somebody*), although we occasionally say who 'the doer' is, e.g. *I had my hair cut by the new stylist at the salon*. Encourage Sts not to overuse *by*.

Tell Sts that we can also say *get something done*, e.g. *I'm getting my car repaired tomorrow*. The meaning is the same as *have something done*.

Focus on the example sentences for **have something done** and play audio 🔊 8.1 for Sts to listen and repeat. Encourage them to copy the rhythm. Then go through the rules with the class.

Focus on the **Using *get* instead of *have*** box and go through it with the class.

Now focus on the exercises and get Sts to do them individually or in pairs.

Check answers, getting Sts to read the full sentences.

a
1 Have you had your eyes tested recently?
2 We don't need to have the roof repaired.
3 I would never have my teeth whitened.
4 My sister told me not to have my hair cut short.
5 It's too expensive to have the carpets replaced.
6 He's going to have his photo taken.
7 My children had their faces painted at the festival.
8 We ought to have the air conditioning fixed.
9 I had my car cleaned at the shopping centre.
10 I have to have my passport renewed before I go on holiday.
b
1 She needs to have her car serviced.
2 He's having his front door replaced.
3 I'm having the lock changed.
4 They should have their windows cleaned.
5 She ought to have her shopping delivered.
6 He doesn't want to have his photo taken.
7 She's having her portrait painted.
8 He wants to have his suit dry-cleaned.

8A 109

Tell Sts to go back to the main lesson **8A**.

EXTRA SUPPORT If you think Sts need more practice, you may want to give them the **Grammar** photocopiable activity at this point.

c Tell Sts to cover sentences 1–8 in **a**, look at the photos, and say what is happening. They could do this individually or in pairs.

EXTRA SUPPORT Put Sts in pairs, **A** and **B**. Sts **A** (sentences 1–8 covered) describe photos A–D whilst Sts **B** (sentences 1–8 uncovered) help with vocabulary if necessary. They then swap roles for photos E–H.

2 PRONUNCIATION & SPEAKING sentence stress

Pronunciation notes

Remind Sts or elicit that the words which are stressed more strongly in sentences are those that carry key information, like nouns, verbs, adjectives, and adverbs. In this structure, *have* is a main verb, not an auxiliary, so it is stressed, e.g. *I'm having my hair cut tomorrow*.

a ▶ 8.2 Focus on the sentences and give Sts time to read them.

Play the audio, pausing after each sentence for Sts to listen and repeat, copying the rhythm.

▶ 8.2
See sentences in Student's Book on *p.76*

Then repeat the activity, eliciting responses from individual Sts.

Finally, put Sts in pairs, and get them to say whether any of the sentences are true for them.

Get some feedback from various pairs. You could tell the class if any of the sentences are true for you.

b Focus on the two groups of questions, making sure Sts understand all the lexis in the prompts, e.g. *dyed, fortune,* etc. Then tell Sts that the first group is in the present simple and the second group in the present perfect, although when they describe an experience for the second group, they will be using the past simple. Give an example if necessary.

Put Sts in pairs. Get them to ask and answer the questions. Encourage them to give as much detail as possible and to ask follow-up questions. Monitor the sentence stress and the correct use of the structure. Sts could answer about people in their family as well (or instead).

EXTRA SUPPORT Get Sts to ask you one question from each group to demonstrate the activity.

Get some feedback from individual Sts. Get them to tell you about their partner, e.g. *Juan had his photo taken by a professional photographer when he…*

3 VOCABULARY & LISTENING looking after yourself; understanding interview questions

a Focus on the photos and the questions. Elicit / Teach the name of any specific styles, e.g. 1 *a comb-over*, 3 *dreadlocks*, 6 *a perm*. Do this as a whole-class activity, or put Sts in pairs and then get some feedback.

b Tell Sts to go to **Vocabulary Bank** Looking after yourself, Part 1 on *p.163*.

Vocabulary notes

At the hairdresser's or barber's

You may want to tell Sts that you can also say *pigtails* instead of *bunches* and *crew cut* is an alternative phrase for *buzz cut*.

Point out that a *barber's* is only for men, whereas a *hairdresser's* caters for both genders.

Explain that a *treatment* involves putting a product on your hair to make it soft or shiny; *highlights* are when small strands of hair are dyed lighter than the rest, and *lowlights* are when they are dyed darker.

Focus on **1 At the hairdresser's or barber's** and get Sts to do **a** individually or in pairs.

▶ 8.3 Now do **b**. Play the audio for Sts to listen and check.

Check answers.

▶ 8.3
Looking after yourself
1 At the hairdresser's or barber's
4 bunches
5 a buzz cut
3 a fringe
1 a parting
6 a ponytail
2 plaits
11 have your hair bleached
7 have your hair curled
10 have your hair dyed
8 have your hair put up
9 have your hair straightened
13 have a blow dry
12 have a perm
14 have a shave
16 have a treatment
17 have a trim
15 have highlights

Now either use the audio to drill the pronunciation of the words and phrases, or model and drill them yourself. Give further practice of any words your Sts find difficult to pronounce.

EXTRA SUPPORT Get Sts to cover the words / phrases, look at the photos, and test themselves.

Focus on **Activation** and either get Sts to answer the questions in pairs, or do it as a whole-class activity.

Tell Sts to go back to the main lesson **8A**.

Tell them they will be doing the sections **Keeping fit** and **Beauty treatments** in the second half of the lesson.

c Focus on the instructions and the photo of Dino Karveli, a hairdresser who has a salon in London.

Give Sts time to read the information about Dino Karveli.

Put Sts in pairs and focus on the questions that the interviewer is going to ask Dino Karveli. Get Sts to read each question and try to guess what the missing words might be.

d 🔊 **8.4** Play the audio for Sts to listen and check. Check answers.

> 1 choose 2 training 3 love 4 hate 5 qualities
> 6 women 7 men 8 results 9 experience 10 cut
> 11 disagreed 12 tips

🔊 **8.4**
- I Dino, what made you choose hairdressing?
- I What sort of training did you do?
- I What sort of things do you love or hate doing in hairdressing?
- I What do you think are important qualities for a hairdresser?
- I Are women clients very different from men?
- I What do you do if a client doesn't like the results?
- I Have you ever had a really bad experience?
- I Is it true that hairdressers always want to cut off more hair than their clients want?
- I If you completely disagreed with what a client wanted, would you still do it?
- I Do you have any tips for having good hair?

Now tell Sts to take a few moments to think about possible answers to the interview questions, and imagine what Dino Karveli might say.

e 🔊 **8.5** Tell Sts they are going to hear the whole interview with Dino Karveli. Focus on the task and give Sts time to read sentences 1–10.

Play the audio once the whole way through for Sts to listen and mark the sentences *T* (true) or *F* (false). Remind them to correct the ones that are false.

Get Sts to compare with a partner, and then play the audio again if necessary.

Check answers, getting Sts to explain why the *F* answers are false. Ask Sts if they predicted any of Dino's answers correctly.

EXTRA SUPPORT Read through the script and decide if you need to pre-teach any new lexis before Sts listen.

> 1 F (He wasn't a barber, but Dino doesn't say what his father's job was. His aunt was a hairdresser.)
> 2 T
> 3 T
> 4 T
> 5 F (He thinks women get more stressed.)
> 6 F (It's easy.)
> 7 T
> 8 T
> 9 F (He says no to treatments.)
> 10 F (You need to use good hair products.)

🔊 **8.5**
(script in Student's Book on *p.129*)

I = interviewer, D = Dino

- I Dino, what made you choose hairdressing?
- D Er, I always liked it from when I was child. I remember being taken to the barber's by my dad when I was a child in Greece, and I really loved the atmosphere there.
- I He wasn't a barber himself, though?
- D No, but my aunt was a hairdresser.
- I What sort of training did you do?
- D When I came to London, I went to the Vidal Sassoon Academy. It was a two-year course – absolutely fantastic, very intense. I loved it!
- I What sort of things do you love or hate doing in hairdressing?
- D I love everything. There really isn't anything I don't like. And I do everything: cut, colour, highlights, straightening. Nowadays, some hairdressers specialize in maybe just colour, or just styling, but I think it's important to do everything.
- I What do you think are important qualities for a hairdresser?
- D Well, as I just said, I think being able to do everything – colour, styling, cutting – is very important. I don't believe in specializing in just one area.
- I Any other important qualities?
- D I think you need to be sociable, to be able to talk to people, calm them down if they're stressed, listen to them if they want to talk.
- I Do you enjoy that?
- D Yes, I do. The sociable side of hairdressing was one of the things that attracted me to it. Even women who want to tell me all their problems – I don't mind it at all; it doesn't distract me.
- I Are women clients very different from men?
- D Yes, definitely. They are normally the ones who want to talk, and they are much more worried – stressed – about their hair. Men are more quiet and relaxed, and they're not normally very fussy about their hair.
- I What do you do if a client doesn't like the results?
- D I try to correct it immediately. That's easy if it's the colour – less easy if it's a cut.
- I Have you ever had a really bad experience, I mean one where you couldn't correct it?
- D Only once, when I was still at college. I cut a woman's hair shorter than she was expecting it – not much, only about one centimetre shorter, but she burst into tears – and I couldn't correct that.
- I Is it true that hairdressers always want to cut off more hair than their clients want?
- D I think maybe it is. Many hairdressers want to make the hair healthier, and cut off all the parts that are, you know, damaged. Or sometimes they have a style in mind and they just want to do it. But obviously, normally I try to do what the customer wants. You have to be flexible. That's another important quality in a hairdresser.
- I So, if you completely disagreed with what a client wanted, would you still do it?
- D Well, if a client wanted a treatment that I thought was going to damage her hair – for example, if she wanted to have her hair bleached when it was already in bad condition – then I would say no. But if it was a question of style – for example, a woman who wanted to have her head shaved completely – I would try to convince her that it wasn't a good idea, but if she insisted, I would do it. It's her choice after all.
- I Do you have any tips for having good hair?
- D Yes – use good products, ones which are right for your type of hair. I notice that a lot of people take a lot of trouble choosing the right face cream – you know, for dry skin, or problem skin. For day, for night, and so on. But with shampoo, they just buy the first one they see in the supermarket.
- I Thank you very much, Dino. I won't forget this.

EXTRA SUPPORT If there's time, you could get Sts to listen again with the script on *p.129*, so they can see exactly what they understood / didn't understand. Translate / Explain any new words or phrases.

f Do the questions as a whole-class activity, or put Sts in pairs and then get some feedback. You could have a class vote for the last question.

4 SPEAKING

a Focus on the phrase *to have a bad hair day* and elicit its meaning. Ask Sts if they have the same or a similar phrase in their language.

> to have a bad hair day = have a day when everything seems to go wrong (similar to how you feel on a day when your hair doesn't look good)

Then ask Sts if they have had one recently. You could tell the class if you have.

8A

b Focus on the questions. Then give Sts time to discuss them in pairs.

Get feedback from various pairs.

EXTRA SUPPORT Sts could ask you one or two of the questions first.

5 VOCABULARY looking after yourself

a Focus on the photos on the Wellbeing Centre advert and elicit from Sts what they can see. Do the questions as a whole-class activity. Tell the class whether or not you would like to go there, and why (not).

b Tell Sts to go back to **Vocabulary Bank Looking after yourself, Parts 2** and **3** on *p.163*.

> **Vocabulary notes**
> **Keeping fit**
> If Sts aren't sure about the difference between *yoga* and *Pilates*, elicit / explain that *yoga* is a set of physical and mental exercises intended to give control over the body and mind; *Pilates* is a system of exercises, sometimes using special equipment, designed to improve physical strength, flexibility, and posture.
> You could tell Sts that *treadmill* is another word for *running machine*.

Focus on **2 Keeping fit** and get Sts to do **a** individually or in pairs.

🔊 **8.6** Now do **b**. Play the audio for Sts to listen and check.

Check answers.

🔊 **8.6**
2 Keeping fit

Equipment	Exercises
9 an exercise bike	11 do sit-ups
6 a running machine	3 do press-ups
5 weights	8 do stretches
10 a rowing machine	7 do aerobics
4 a cross-trainer	2 do spinning
12 a yoga mat	1 do Pilates

Now either use the audio to drill the pronunciation of the words and phrases, or model and drill them yourself. Give further practice of any words your Sts find difficult to pronounce.

Now do **Activation**. Focus on the items in the list and make sure Sts understand all the lexis. Put Sts in pairs and give them time to do the task. Point out that some items can go in more than one category.

Elicit answers.

> **Possible answers**
> **If you want to lose weight:** use an exercise bike / rowing machine / cross-trainer, do aerobics, do spinning, etc.
> **If you want to tone your muscles:** do / lift weights, do sit-ups, do press-ups, etc.
> **If you want to do cardio exercises:** go on a running machine, do aerobics, do spinning, etc.
> **If you have a bad back:** do stretches, do Pilates or yoga
> **If you want to improve your flexibility:** do stretches, do Pilates or yoga

EXTRA SUPPORT Get Sts to cover the words / phrases, look at the photos, and test themselves.

Focus on **3 Beauty treatments** and get Sts to do **a** individually or in pairs.

🔊 **8.7** Now do **b**. Play the audio for Sts to listen and check.

Check answers.

🔊 **8.7**
3 Beauty treatments
5 manicure
4 pedicure
6 facial
1 massage
3 waxing
2 fake tan

Now either use the audio to drill the pronunciation of the words and phrase, or model and drill them yourself. Give further practice of any words your Sts find difficult to pronounce.

Finally, do **Activation** as a whole-class activity, encouraging Sts to give as much information as possible.

EXTRA SUPPORT Get Sts to cover the words, look at the photos, and test themselves.

Tell Sts to go back to the main lesson **8A**.

EXTRA SUPPORT If you think Sts need more practice, you may want to give them the **Vocabulary** photocopiable activity at this point.

c Focus on the task and then give Sts time to read the information on the advert in **a**.

Put Sts in pairs and get them to tell each other what they would do if they had a day at the Wellbeing Centre.

Get some feedback from various pairs.

6 READING & LISTENING understanding whether people are being positive or negative

a Focus on the task and then either read the introduction and the treatments as a class, or give Sts time to read individually.

Give Sts time to answer the first question, and check the answer.

> They went to the spa to try out the treatments and write about them, and find out if men can enjoy them.

Now get Sts to speculate which of the three treatments the two journalists will like best. Check Sts understand *hydrated*.

b Focus on the task and give Sts time to read about the facial.

Check answers.

EXTRA SUPPORT Before Sts read the article the first time, check whether you need to pre-teach any vocabulary.

> Stephen thought that the treatment took too long, and he was bored.
> Joanna liked all the different processes and felt great afterwards.

Deal with any other new vocabulary. Model and drill the pronunciation of any tricky words.

c **8.8** Focus on the two remaining treatments mentioned in **a** – the banana, papaya, and strawberry body polish and the Elemis foot treatment. Tell Sts they are going to listen to four short extracts of things that Stephen and Joanna say after these next two treatments.

Give Sts time to read the four sentences / phrases and see if they can guess what the missing words might be.

Play the audio, pausing after each item to give Sts time to write. Tell Sts to use the intonation to help them decide if the comments are positive or negative.

Check answers, eliciting each time if the comment is positive or negative. Model and drill pronunciation of any words that are tricky for Sts.

1 sticky, uncomfortable – negative
2 divine – positive
3 Definitely worth – positive
4 luxury – positive

8.8
1
Stephen It was hot and sticky, and incredibly uncomfortable.
2
Joanna And the head massage was divine.
3
Stephen Definitely worth the time and money.
4
Joanna A real luxury.

d **8.9** Tell Sts they are now going to listen to Stephen and Joanna discussing first the body polish, and then the foot treatment.

Play the audio, pausing after Stephen and Joanna have discussed the body polish to give Sts time to complete the chart.

Get Sts to compare with a partner, and then play again if necessary. Repeat the process for the foot treatment. Check answers.

EXTRA SUPPORT Read through the script and decide if you need to pre-teach any new lexis before Sts listen.

		Stephen	Joanna
The body polish	Score out of 10	0	10
	Reasons	It was hot, sticky, and uncomfortable. He felt stupid.	It smelled amazing and the head massage was divine.
The foot treatment	Score out of 10	9	9
	Reasons	Now his feet look great.	It was a luxury. She loves the colour of her nails.

8.9
(script in Student's Book on *p.129*)
S = Stephen, J = Joanna
The body polish
J So? What did you think?
S It was just horrible! Horrible. First, they covered me in fruit puree, then they wrapped me in plastic film, then in blankets, and then I was left on a water bed. I mean, come on! Fruit's for eating, not for putting on your body. It was hot and sticky, and incredibly uncomfortable. And I felt so stupid. I'd never have that again. I give it zero out of ten.
J Sticky? It was fruit, for goodness' sake! I thought it was wonderful. It smelled amazing, and the head massage was divine. I mean, how could anybody not like it? That was one of my favourite spa treatments ever. Ten out of ten.

The foot treatment
S Wow!
J Don't tell me – you liked it!
S It was wonderful!
J I must say, your feet look… well, better. Clean, anyway.
S Well, I've never liked my feet much, to be honest, but now they look great. Definitely worth the time and money. Nine out of ten. What do you think?
J Yes, it was great. A real luxury. And I love the colour they painted my nails. I agree – nine out of ten. You see…

EXTRA SUPPORT If there's time, you could get Sts to listen again with the script on *p.129*, so they can see exactly what they understood / didn't understand. Translate / Explain any new words or phrases

e Do this as a whole-class activity. You could tell Sts which treatment you would enjoy most and why.

f Put Sts in pairs and get them to discuss the questions.
Get some feedback from various pairs.

7 SPEAKING

a Focus on the instructions and the three topics, making sure Sts know what they mean.

Point out the examples. Put Sts in pairs and get them to think of other examples for each category.

Elicit some more ideas of ways of looking after yourself and write them on the board, for example:

KEEPING FIT
- GOING TO THE GYM
- GOING RUNNING
- USE THE STAIRS INSTEAD OF THE LIFT
- DOING YOGA OR PILATES

BEING HEALTHY
- HAVING A HEALTHY DIET
- CUTTING OUT SOME FOOD OR DRINK (E.G. ALCOHOL, SUGAR, ETC.)
- HAVING REGULAR MEDICAL CHECK-UPS AT THE DOCTOR'S OR DENTIST'S

BOOSTING YOUR BRAINPOWER
- DOING BRAIN-TRAINING GAMES (CROSSWORDS, SUDOKU, ETC.)
- LEARNING A LANGUAGE
- LEARNING A NEW SKILL

Tell Sts they should, in pairs, agree on the three most important ones.

Get feedback from various pairs.

b Focus on the task and list of ideas. Check that Sts understand *ban*. Get Sts to discuss the question in pairs or in small groups.

If possible, Sts should then decide which one idea would work best.

Get feedback from pairs or groups.

Now ask Sts if they have any other suggestions to encourage healthy eating in schools, and write them on the board.

EXTRA CHALLENGE Get Sts to cover **b**. Tell them they need to think of ideas to encourage healthy eating in schools. Do it as a whole-class activity, or put Sts in pairs and then elicit some ideas. Then get Sts to uncover the list in **b** and see if their ideas are included.

c Focus on the instructions and make sure Sts know what a *campaign* is (= a series of planned activities that are intended to achieve a particular social, commercial, or political aim). Model and drill its pronunciation.

Put Sts in small groups of three and tell them to follow the steps given.

Monitor and help if necessary.

d Tell Sts they are going to practise presenting their campaign. They need to decide who is going to present each section.

Focus on the **Presenting a campaign** box and go through it with the class.

Give Sts time to practise. Monitor and help if necessary.

e Focus on the instructions and then get each group to present their campaign. Write the name of each group's campaign on the board.

When all the groups have finished, get Sts to look at the campaign names on the board, and then vote for the best one.

EXTRA CHALLENGE Get Sts to ask questions after each group has finished presenting their campaign.

8B Sites and sights

- **G** the passive
- **V** wars and battles, historic buildings
- **P** silent consonants

Lesson plan

Historic events and buildings are the main topic of this lesson. The lesson begins with a quiz about world history, which provides the context for revision and extension of the passive. The grammar is then practised orally with a quiz written by Sts about the history of their country. Sts then read an extract about the Battle of Hastings from the English Heritage website. After the reading, Sts talk about their own visits to historical sites. Finally, Sts take part in a role-play between a local and a tourist visiting the area.

In the second half, the vocabulary focus is on the names of some historic British buildings and various parts of these buildings, e.g. *the crypt, the dome*. This is followed by a pronunciation focus on silent consonants in these words, e.g. *aisle*. Sts then listen to a guided tour of St Paul's Cathedral in London. After that, Sts practise speaking and writing about a famous building, and the lesson ends with a documentary about the reconstructed Globe Theatre in London.

More materials
For teachers
Photocopiables
Grammar the passive *p.167*
Communicative The History Quiz *p.197* (instructions *p.176*)
Teacher's Resource Centre
Video The Globe Theatre
For students
Workbook 8B
Online Practice 8B

OPTIONAL LEAD-IN (BOOKS CLOSED)

Write the word HISTORY on the board. Elicit what the difference is between *history* and *story*.

Then ask what two adjectives you can make from the word *history* (*historic* and *historical*). Elicit / Explain the difference.

- *Historic* is used to describe sth that is so important that it is likely to be remembered, e.g. *a historic event, a historic victory, a historic occasion*.
- *Historical* describes something connected with the past or with history, e.g. *a historical novel, historical research*.

Now ask Sts to think of:

- a historic event that has happened in their lifetime
- a building of historical importance in their town / city.

Elicit Sts' ideas. Encourage them to explain why the event was important and to give a bit of information about the building.

Sts might be interested to know that some feminists have taken the word *history* to mean 'his story', in order to make a point about the lack of focus on the role of women in recorded history.

1 GRAMMAR the passive

a Books open. Focus on the lesson title, and explain the difference between the homonyms *site* (= a place where a building, town, etc. was or is located) and *sight* (= a thing of interest that you can see or visit).

Focus on the quiz and go through the questions, making sure Sts understand the following words: *defeated, battle, fleet, attacked, reunified, war, assassinated, evacuated*.

Put Sts in small groups of three or four and give them time to answer the questions.

EXTRA IDEA Get Sts to either give their team a name or simply write all their names on a piece of paper. Then get Sts to write their answers on the piece of paper, and when they have finished, they should swap with another team.

b 🔊 **8.10** Play the audio for Sts to listen and check.

Check answers. Find out how many points each group got.

1 a   2 c   3 b   4 a   5 c   6 b   7 b   8 a

🔊 **8.10**
1 Napoleon was defeated in the battle of Waterloo. Waterloo is in Belgium, just south of Brussels.
2 The American fleet was attacked in Pearl Harbor in nineteen forty-one.
3 Berlin, which had been divided by a wall for twenty-eight years, was reunified in nineteen eighty-nine.
4 The Sagrada Família in Barcelona was started in eighteen eighty-two and is still being built. It is due to be completed in twenty twenty-six.
5 According to legend, the city of Troy fought a famous war against Greece. It is thought by many to be in modern Turkey, but has never been definitively located.
6 The city of Chichen Itza was built by the Mayans between seven hundred and fifty and nine hundred AD.
7 John Fitzgerald Kennedy was assassinated while he was being driven through Dallas in nineteen sixty-three.
8 Chernobyl in the Ukraine had to be evacuated in nineteen eighty-six after a catastrophic nuclear accident.

EXTRA CHALLENGE Get Sts to write any extra information they heard when they were listening to check answers.

c Focus on the instructions and get Sts to underline the passives in the quiz in **a**, individually or in pairs, and decide what form they are.

Check answers.

1 was defeated – past simple passive
2 was attacked – past simple passive
3 had been divided – past perfect passive; was reunified – past simple passive
4 was started – past simple passive; is being built – present continuous passive
5 has never been located – present perfect passive
6 was built – past simple passive
7 was assassinated – past simple passive; was being driven – past continuous passive
8 had to be evacuated – infinitive with *to*

EXTRA SUPPORT Get Sts to just underline the passives in the questions in the quiz. Then elicit each form as a class.

d Tell Sts to go to **Grammar Bank** 8B on p.147.

Grammar notes

If Sts used *English File* Intermediate, they will have met the different forms and tenses of the passive. Although Sts should not have problems forming the basic tenses, e.g. past and present, they may still have problems with, e.g. leaving out the verb *be* or not using the participle correctly, and future and present perfect forms. Most importantly, they may still be using the active instead of the passive, e.g. *The house is going to paint next week.*

It is worth reminding Sts that we often use the passive in English (usually without *by* + person) where other languages use an impersonal form, e.g. *Olives are grown in most regions of Spain. My wallet has been stolen!*

Try to discourage Sts from using *by (somebody)* in every passive sentence. Identifying who did the action is often unnecessary.

You may also want to point out that we can use the indirect object as the new subject in a passive sentence, e.g.:

- active: *Somebody gave me this watch for my birthday.*
- passive: *This watch was given to me for my birthday.* or *I was given this watch for my birthday.*

Focus on the example sentences for **forms of the passive** and play audio 🔊 8.11 for Sts to listen and repeat. Encourage them to copy the rhythm. Then go through the rules with the class.

Focus on the **Active or passive?** box and go through it with the class.

Now focus on the exercises and get Sts to do them individually or in pairs.

Check answers, getting Sts to read the full sentences.

a
1 Many roads **were closed** to traffic for the carnival last month.
2 In recent years, many books **have been written** about the American Civil War.
3 A new shopping centre **is being built** in the town centre at the moment.
4 I think you should **be allowed** to take photos in the museum if you don't use flash.
5 The last battle on British soil **was fought** at Culloden in 1746.
6 Washington, DC **is visited** by nearly 20 million people every year.
7 I love **being shown** round a city by someone who knows it well.
8 The gallery was closed because a TV series **was being filmed** inside.
9 I**'ve been woken up** by the neighbour's noisy dog three times already this week.
10 Picasso's famous painting *Guernica* can **be seen** in the Reina Sofia museum in Madrid.

b
1 The palace **had to be closed for renovations**.
2 More information **can be found on the website**.
3 The famous 'I have a dream' speech **was given by Martin Luther King in 1963**.
4 You **must wear a seat belt at all times**.
5 Do you think you're **going to be offered the job**?

6 A fire **had destroyed the previous church**.
7 You **have to turn off your phone during take-off and landing**.
8 A new visitor centre **is going to be opened next year**.
9 The new hospital **won't be finished until July**.
10 Tea **is grown in Sri Lanka**.

EXTRA SUPPORT If you think Sts need more practice, you may want to give them the **Grammar** photocopiable activity at this point.

e Focus on the instructions and put Sts in pairs. Tell them that the questions must use a passive form, and that they can refer back to the quiz questions in **a** to help them. Remind them also that they must choose questions to which they know the answers. You could allow them to look up information on their phones if necessary.

EXTRA SUPPORT Write the passive form of any verbs Sts want to use on the board, e.g. WAS BUILT, WAS DESTROYED, etc.

Monitor and help where necessary.

When Sts have finished, get each pair to ask the class their three questions. Sts should write their answers, and then at the end they can see how many they got correct.

EXTRA SUPPORT Sts answer the questions in pairs.

EXTRA IDEA Pin all the questions around the classroom and get Sts to walk around in pairs, making a note of their answers.

2 READING & VOCABULARY understanding historical events: chronology and geography; wars and battles

a Focus on the photos and give Sts time to label the five items and decide what is happening.

Get Sts to compare with a partner, and then check answers. Model and drill pronunciation of the words. You could tell Sts that *bow* is a homograph. Here it is pronounced /bəʊ/ (as a noun). Explain / Elicit the second meaning: /baʊ/ (as a verb).

1 helmet 2 shield 3 arrow 4 bow 5 archer

Finally, elicit what is happening in the photos, but don't tell Sts if they are correct.

b Focus on the instructions and the task. You could tell Sts how to pronounce *Hastings* /ˈheɪstɪŋz/, and that it's an English town, but don't tell them where it is as they will be completing the map later.

Give Sts time to read the information and check their answer to **a**.

Check the answer. You could point out that in the first photo, there is a crowd of people watching in the background, and that of course there wouldn't be a photo of a real battle of this kind.

The photos show the historical re-enactment of a battle.

You might want to check that Sts understand the noun *armour* in paragraph 3. Model and drill its pronunciation. Then Sts use information from the website to help them label the map. This activity focuses Sts on the important places in the story and helps them visualize what happened where.

Get Sts to compare with a partner, and then check answers.

EXTRA SUPPORT Before Sts read the website the first time, check whether you need to pre-teach any vocabulary, but not the highlighted verbs.

1 Stamford Bridge 2 Norway 3 Battle 4 Hastings
5 Bayeux

c Focus on the instructions and make sure Sts know the meaning of *chronological* (= arranged in the order in which events happened). Model and drill its pronunciation /ˌkrɒnəˈlɒdʒɪkl/.

Now quickly go through the events, making sure Sts understand all the lexis, e.g. *abbey*, *tapestry*, etc. Point out that the first one (*Harold became King of England*) has been done for them.

Set a time limit for Sts to read the website again and number the events in the correct order.

Check answers.

2 The Norwegians attacked the north of England.
3 The Normans landed in Sussex.
4 The Battle of Hastings was fought between the English and the Normans.
5 King Harold was killed.
6 William became King of England.
7 Battle Abbey was built.
8 The Bayeux tapestry was finished.
9 The town of Battle was named after the battle that took place there.
10 Battle Abbey was destroyed.

You could ask Sts to look again at the photos in **a**, and, using the information in paragraphs 3 and 4 of the website, to identify which soldiers in the photos are English (*the soldiers on the left of the first photo, on foot with shields and swords*), and which are Norman (*the soldiers on horseback in the first photo, and with bows and arrows in the second photo*).

d Now tell Sts to focus on the highlighted verbs, which are all related to wars and battles. Get them to find the one irregular verb. Then, for all the verbs, they should decide what the infinitive is and work out the meaning from the context.

Get Sts to compare with a partner, and then check answers. Model and drill pronunciation.

fought is irregular. The infinitive is *fight* = to take part in a war or battle against an enemy.
defeat = to win against sb in a war, competition, game, etc.
succeed = to achieve sth that you have been trying to do / get
invade = to enter a country, town, etc. using military force in order to take control of it
kill = to make sb / sth die
crown = to put a crown on the head of a new king or queen as a sign of royal power
retreat = to move away from a place or an enemy because you are in danger or because you have been defeated
destroy = to damage sth so badly that it no longer exists, works, etc.

Deal with any other new vocabulary. Model and drill the pronunciation of any tricky words.

3 SPEAKING

a Put Sts in pairs to discuss the two questions.
Get some feedback from various pairs.

b Put Sts in pairs, **A** and **B**, and tell them to go to **Communication** *Local history*, **A** on *p.110*, **B** on *p.114*.
Go through the instructions and make sure Sts understand what they have to do. You could demonstrate by writing on the board the name of a famous person who has a connection to your town. Then get Sts to ask you questions as if they were tourists, e.g. *Who's _____? Why is he / she famous?* Answer their questions in detail.
Get Sts to take turns to role-play the questions and answers. Encourage them to ask questions (even if they know the answers), and to answer in as much detail as possible.

EXTRA IDEA You could encourage Sts to be a really difficult tourist who keeps asking questions.

Tell Sts to go back to the main lesson **8B**.

4 VOCABULARY & PRONUNCIATION
historic buildings; silent consonants

a Focus on the instructions and tell Sts to use the photos to help them complete the names of the buildings.
Get Sts to compare with a partner.

b 🔊 **8.12** Tell Sts that they will listen to the audio twice and the first time they just need to check their answers to **a**. You might also want to tell them that they are going to hear the name of the building as well as some historical facts.
Play the audio for Sts to listen and check.
Check answers.

Buckingham **Palace**
St Paul's **Cathedral**
Westminster **Abbey**
Windsor **Castle**
The **Tower** of London

🔊 **8.12**
Buckingham Palace was built in the eighteenth century for the Duke of Buckingham and became the London home of the British Royal Family in eighteen thirty-seven.
St Paul's Cathedral was rebuilt in the seventeenth century by Sir Christopher Wren.
Westminster Abbey was begun in the thirteenth century, during the reign of King Henry the Third.
Windsor Castle and the Tower of London were built in the eleventh century, during the reign of William the Conqueror.

Now focus on the question *Which are the two oldest buildings?* and play the audio again.
Check the answer.

Windsor Castle and the Tower of London are the oldest.

EXTRA IDEA Ask Sts if they know any facts about these places, e.g. *they are all in London, Windsor Castle is where the Queen lives*, etc. Then ask if any Sts have visited any of these places or seen them in films, and if so, what they thought of them.

Finally, elicit any more words for types of buildings, e.g. *mosque*, *synagogue*, etc.

c Focus on the instructions and then give Sts time to read all the definitions and work out which they can see in the photos on *pp.82–83*.

Check answers.

aisle – see where the red carpet is in the photo on *p.83*
column – see the same photo as above
crypt – see the photo on *p.82* under the title *Welcome to St Paul's Cathedral*
dome – see the photo of St Paul's Cathedral on *p.82*
gallery – see the first photo on *p.83*
tomb – see the photo on *p.82* under the title *Welcome to St Paul's Cathedral*

d Do this as a whole-class activity. Write the words on the board and elicit which consonants to cross out (the consonants to cross out are in pink in the answer key below). Tell Sts to use the phonetics in **c** to help them.

Model and drill the words.

ai**s**le   cas**t**le   colum**n**   tom**b**

e 🔊 **8.13** Focus on the instructions and tell Sts to listen and write the five sentences they hear.

Play the audio, pausing after each sentence to give Sts time to write.

Get Sts to compare with a partner, and then play the audio again if necessary.

Check answers, eliciting the sentences onto the board. Ask Sts to identify the silent consonants in each sentence (these are in pink in the answer key below).

1 You mus**t**n't ta**l**k in class w**h**en the teacher is speaking.
2 I got the **w**rong ans**w**er to ha**l**f the questions.
3 I dou**b**t if we'll have time to visit the i**s**land.
4 Lis**t**en to the sentence and copy the r**h**ythm.
5 I've wanted to learn a forei**g**n language my **w**hole life.

🔊 **8.13**
1 You mustn't talk in class when the teacher is speaking.
2 I got the wrong answer to half the questions.
3 I doubt if we'll have time to visit the island.
4 Listen to the sentence and copy the rhythm.
5 I've wanted to learn a foreign language my whole life.

5 LISTENING understanding a guided tour – note-taking

a Focus on the instructions and photos. Either read the introduction as a class, or give Sts time to do it individually.

Check the answer to the first question and elicit any other information Sts might know about the cathedral.

The wedding of Charles and Diana

b 🔊 **8.14** Focus on the instructions and tell Sts they are going to listen to a tour guide taking people around St Paul's Cathedral and talking about each section. Tell them to try and imagine they are on the tour.

Focus on the plan of the cathedral and make sure Sts are clear what the different sections are. Tell Sts they are going to listen to some extracts from the tour first, and try to understand which places in the cathedral the guide is going to take them to.

Now play the audio once, pausing after each section for Sts to listen and number the places.

Get Sts to compare with a partner, and then play the audio again if necessary.

Check answers.

EXTRA SUPPORT Read through the scripts and decide if you need to pre-teach any new lexis before Sts listen.

1 the West Door 2 the Dome 3 the South Transept
4 the South Quire Aisle 5 the Whispering Gallery
6 the Crypt

🔊 **8.14**
G = guide
G Good afternoon, everybody, everyone, and welcome to St Paul's, which, as you probably know, is one of the most famous and most historic cathedrals in Britain.
***
1
G Just behind you is the Great West Door, you can see the Great West Door. The magnificent doors are nine metres tall. And now in front of you, you see the Nave, which gives you the most wonderful view of the full length of St Paul's Cathedral.
***
2
G We're now in the centre of the cathedral. Look up above you, and you can see inside the wonderful Dome. It's one of the largest domes in the world, and I personally think the most beautiful.
***
3
G We are now in the area called the South Transept. Over there, you can see the monument to Britain's great naval hero Horatio Nelson, who died at the Battle of Trafalgar in eighteen oh five.
***
4
G We're now in the South Quire Aisle, and we're just going to stop for a moment to look at this marble statue of John Donne.
***
5
G Now, are you all feeling energetic? I hope so because we're going to go up these stairs here, to the Whispering Gallery, which goes around the inside of the great Dome, and I do need to tell you that there are two hundred and fifty-seven steps…
***
6
G We're now going to go back along the Nave, and then down into the Crypt to see some of the tombs of famous people who are buried in St Paul's.

c 🔊 **8.15** Tell Sts they are now going to listen to the whole tour, starting with the first part. This time, they will hear extra information about the history of the West Door and the nave. Give Sts time to read the gapped sentences and think about whether the missing information is a number, a name, etc.

Play the audio once the whole way through for Sts to listen and complete the gaps.

Get Sts to compare with a partner, and then play the audio again if necessary.

Check answers.

1 1066 2 Fire 3 London 4 cathedral 5 Christopher
6 nine 7 Queen 8 full length

8.15
(script in Student's Book on p.129)

Part 1

G = guide, T = tourist

G Good afternoon, everybody, everyone, and welcome to St Paul's, which, as you probably know, is one of the most famous and most historic cathedrals in Britain. The previous church on this site burned down in sixteen sixty-six, in the Great Fire of London, and the famous architect Sir Christopher Wren was asked to design a new cathedral. It took nearly forty years to build and was completed in seventeen ten.
Just behind you is the Great West Door, you can see the Great West Door. The magnificent doors are nine metres tall.
T *Ha dicho nueve metros?*
G They're normally closed, except when someone very special arrives, for example, Her Majesty the Queen.
And now in front of you, you see the Nave, which gives you the most wonderful view of the full length of St Paul's Cathedral.
T *Wie schoen.*
G Maybe some of you watched Prince Charles and Princess Diana walk down the Nave when they married here in nineteen eighty-one.
OK, now please follow me. We're going to walk down the Nave, and you'll see the North and South aisle on either side…

d 🔊 **8.16** Tell Sts they are going to listen to the rest of the tour, and this time they are going to take notes about the important places on the tour. Focus on the points in the list and make sure Sts understand all the lexis.

Play the audio, pausing after each area (indicated by *** in the script) to give Sts time to take notes.

Get Sts to compare with a partner, and then play the audio again if necessary.

Check answers.

The Dome
- **the cross:** In 1710, Christopher Wren was lifted up in a basket to watch his son place the cross on top of the Dome.
- **the height of the dome:** From the top of the Dome to the floor is exactly 365 feet, one foot for every day of the year.
- **something that was true until the 1960s:** St Paul's was the tallest building in London until the 1960s because until that time, nobody was allowed to build anything taller near St Paul's.

The South Transept
- **Horatio Nelson:** There's a monument to Horatio Nelson, who died at the Battle of Trafalgar in 1805; he's the one on top of Nelson's Column in Trafalgar Square.

The South Quire Aisle
- **the statue of John Donne:** Donne was a Dean of the Cathedral and a famous poet – he died in 1631. The statue is one of the few monuments which survived the Great Fire of London, and it has burn marks on it.

The Whispering Gallery
- **the number of steps you have to climb:** There are 257 steps.
- **the reason the gallery gets its name:** If you talk very quietly on one side, your voice can be heard very clearly on the other side.

The Crypt
- **the famous people in the tombs:** Lord Nelson, the Duke of Wellington, Sir Christopher Wren
- **the Latin words on Wren's tomb:** The words on Wren's tomb say, 'Reader, if you seek his monument, look around you.' Because the whole of St Paul's is Wren's monument.

8.16
(script in Student's Book on pp.129–130)

Part 2

G Right. Can we just stop here? Could we stop here? We're now in the centre of the cathedral. Look up above you, and you can see inside the wonderful Dome. It's one of the largest domes in the world, and I personally think the most beautiful. Now, you remember the outside of the Dome, which you saw when you arrived. Can anyone tell me what was on top of the Dome?
T A cross?
G Yeah, that's right, a cross. In seventeen ten, the year the cathedral was finally completed, Christopher Wren was eighty-one years old, and he was lifted up in a basket and was able to watch his own son place the cross on the top of the Dome. Another thing about, fascinating thing about the Dome is that from the top of the Dome to the floor, down where you're standing, is exactly three hundred and sixty-five feet, one foot for every day of the year.
T How much is that in metres?
G Approximately one-one-one, a hundred and eleven metres. In fact, St Paul's was the tallest building in London right up until the nineteen sixties because until that time, no one was allowed to build anything taller near St Paul's. We're going to move on shortly, but just spend a few minutes now looking at the magnificent paintings.
***
G We are now in the area called the South Transept. Over there, you can see the monument to Britain's great naval hero Horatio Nelson, who died at the Battle of Trafalgar in eighteen oh five.
T *C'est lui qui est sur…*
G Yes, yeah, he's the one on top of the Nelson's Column in Trafalgar Square.
***
G We're now in the South Quire Aisle, and we're just going to stop for a moment to look at this marble statue of John Donne. Donne was a Dean of the Cathedral and one of Britain's finest poets – he died in sixteen thirty-one. But this statue is also important because it's one of the few monuments that survived the Great Fire of London. And you can still see the burn marks at the bottom of the statue there…
***
G Now, are you all feeling energetic? I hope so because we're going to go up these stairs here, to the Whispering Gallery, which goes around the inside of the great Dome, and I do need to tell you that there are two hundred and fifty-seven steps…
T *Yo no voy, yo no voy…*
G …so if there are any of you who don't think you can manage it, just wait for us here.
***
G So, that wasn't too bad, was it? We're now in the Whispering Gallery. The gallery gets its name because if you whisper – talk very quietly – on one side, your voice can be heard very clearly on the other side. When there are a lot of tourists, it doesn't always work, but as there aren't so many of us today, why don't you try it…?
***
G So, did any of you try out the whispering? We're now going to go back along the Nave, and then down into the Crypt to see some of the tombs of famous people who are buried in St Paul's.
***
G Right, now the tomb over there is Lord Nelson's – you remember you saw his monument earlier – and then here we have the tomb of the Duke of Wellington, who defeated Napoleon at the Battle of Waterloo. And finally, this tomb here belongs to the great man himself, Sir Christopher Wren, the architect of St Paul's. It's just a simple stone monument, but can you see the Latin words on it? Anyone speak Latin here? No? Well, I'll translate it for you. It says, 'Reader, if you seek his monument, look around you.' Because of course, the whole of St Paul's is really Wren's monument.

EXTRA SUPPORT If there's time, you could get Sts to listen again with the two scripts on *pp.129–130*, so they can see exactly what they understood / didn't understand. Translate / Explain any new words or phrases.

8B

e Do this as a whole-class activity.

6 SPEAKING & WRITING describing a building

a Focus on the instructions and the photo, and tell Sts that the Guggenheim is a famous museum in Bilbao. Go through the questions with the class and remind Sts what an *anecdote* is (= an informal true story that's interesting or amusing).

Give Sts time to think about their famous building and plan what they are going to say. Get them to make some notes, and help them with any new vocabulary they need. Remind them that the building can be a modern one (like the Guggenheim in the photo).

Put Sts in pairs, and monitor and help as Sts describe their famous buildings.

Get some feedback.

EXTRA SUPPORT Tell Sts about a building you know well to demonstrate the activity.

b Tell Sts to go to **Writing Describing a building** on *p.121*.

Focus on **a** and give Sts time to read the description of Hagia Sofia and answer the question. Tell Sts not to worry about the highlighted relative pronouns.

Check answers.

> **a** A (a minaret) **b** B (a mosaic)

Now focus on **b**. Get Sts to read questions a–e and match them to paragraphs 1–5.

Get Sts to compare with a partner, and then check answers.

> 1 d 2 e 3 b 4 c 5 a

Focus on the **Defining and non-defining relative clauses** box in **c** and go through it with the class.

Now give Sts time to tick or cross the highlighted relative pronouns in the description. Remind them to correct the ones that are wrong.

Get Sts to compare with a partner, and then check answers.

> 1 ✓ 2 ✓ 3 ✗ where 4 ✗ which
> 5 ✓ 6 ✗ which 7 ✓ 8 ✗ which

You could do **d** as a whole-class activity, or put Sts in pairs and then check answers.

> 1 (which) could be left out.

Next, focus on **e**. Tell Sts they are going to write a description of a famous building in their town / city for a tourism website. Alternatively, they can write about a famous building somewhere else in their country.

Get Sts to use the questions in **b** (in the correct order) to help them plan their description. Encourage them to make brief notes as they answer the questions.

Now focus on the instructions in **f** and go through the **Useful language: describing a building** box with the class. Sts write their description of a building, following the plan they've made. Remind them to use the **Useful language** to help them.

You may like to get Sts to do the writing in class or you could set it as homework. If you do it in class, set a time limit for Sts to write their description, e.g. 15–20 minutes.

In **g**, Sts should check their description for mistakes before giving it in.

EXTRA IDEA Get Sts to attach a photo of the building to their description.

Tell Sts to go back to the main lesson **8B**.

7 ▶ VIDEO LISTENING

a Focus on the instructions and the photo. You could ask Sts if they have heard of or seen the Globe Theatre.

Play the video once the whole way through for Sts to watch and answer the two questions.

Check answers.

EXTRA SUPPORT Read through the script and decide if you need to pre-teach any new lexis before Sts watch the video.

> Sam Wanamaker was an American actor who loved Shakespeare. He was shocked to discover that the world-famous Globe Theatre had no memorial.

The Globe Theatre
Hello, I'm Charlie. Welcome to Shakespeare's Globe.

It's an incredible building. It's made almost entirely of wood, following authentic building practices, and it has a thatched roof. Believe it or not, this is the only thatched roof that has been allowed in London since the Great Fire of sixteen sixty-six.

In fact, it's almost exactly the same as the original theatre. The first Globe was built by Shakespeare's playing company – who were called the Lord Chamberlain's Men – in fifteen ninety-nine. It looked just like this, but it was about two hundred and thirty metres that way.

The first theatre burned down during a performance of Shakespeare's *Henry the Eighth* on the twenty-ninth of June, sixteen thirteen. The company soon had the theatre rebuilt, but sadly this second theatre was destroyed by the British government in the sixteen forties because they believed theatre was immoral.

This site was almost completely forgotten about for almost three hundred years, until an American called Sam Wanamaker tried to find it in the nineteen fifties.

Sam Wanamaker was an actor. He was from the United States, but the government banned him from working due to his political views. He decided to move to England, the home of his hero, William Shakespeare. He started performing in Shakespeare plays all over the UK, especially in Stratford-upon-Avon, Shakespeare's birthplace.

Eventually, Wanamaker followed his hero's footsteps and came to London. He wanted to see the spot where the world-famous Globe Theatre had been. He hoped to find a statue or a memorial. He was shocked when all he found was a dirty old plaque.

He came up with a plan to rebuild the famous Globe. In nineteen seventy, he launched the Shakespeare Globe Trust and put his plan into action. But it wasn't easy. First of all, he tried to find out the size of the original theatre. But the owners of the site refused to have an archaeological survey carried out.

Then he struggled to buy this riverside site from the local council. All this time, everybody was telling him that a true reconstruction of the Globe was impossible.

But Wanamaker didn't give up. He managed to buy the site, and with the help of historical advisers and extensive research, he had a theatre built that was as close as possible to Shakespeare's fifteen ninety-nine playhouse.

Sadly, Wanamaker died four years before Shakespeare's Globe opened in nineteen ninety-seven. He is remembered as the 'visionary who re-created Shakespeare's Globe', and the theatre he worked so hard to rebuild has been a huge success.

Today it's a fantastic place to see Shakespeare's famous plays. There are eight hundred and fifty-seven seats in the stalls, and seven hundred people can stand in the pit, an area with no seats which is in front of the stage.

Attached to the outdoor theatre is a modern building. The Globe Exhibition and Tour is here, housing the largest permanent exhibition on Shakespeare in the world. This explores the life of Shakespeare and re-creates the London he lived in.

Since twenty fourteen, there has also been an indoor theatre on the site, which, like the Globe, looks and feels like a theatre from Shakespeare's time. It was built using plans from the seventeenth century. The interior is made of oak wood. Above the stage there is a musician's gallery and a beautifully painted ceiling. There are no electric lights on stage – all the lighting is provided by candlelight, giving the theatre an authentic Shakespearean atmosphere.

And can you guess what it's called? It's the Sam Wanamaker playhouse, in honour of the man who made all of this possible.

b Tell Sts they are going to watch the documentary again and this time they must mark sentences 1–8 *T* (true) or *F* (false). Remind them to correct the false ones.

Give Sts time to read the sentences.

Play the video again.

Get Sts to compare with a partner, and then check answers, getting Sts to explain why the *F* answers are false.

1 T
2 F (It burned down in 1613.)
3 F (The second theatre was destroyed by the British government.)
4 T
5 F (He wanted to rebuild it in London.)
6 F (Everybody was telling him it was impossible.)
7 F (He died four years before the Globe opened.)
8 T

c Tell Sts they are going to watch four extracts from the documentary and, in pairs, they need to decide what the words in **bold** mean.

Play the video, pausing after the first extract.

Give Sts time to discuss the **bold** words, then check the answer.

Repeat the process for the other three extracts.

1 a roof covered in dried straw, reeds, etc.
2 a flat piece of stone, metal, etc., usually with a name and dates on, attached to a wall in memory of a person or an event
3 the place in a theatre just in front of the stage, with no seats
4 the light that a candle produces

EXTRA SUPPORT You could get Sts to watch the video again with subtitles, so they can see exactly what they understood / didn't understand. Translate / Explain any new words or phrases.

d Do this as a whole-class activity.

7&8 Revise and Check

For instructions on how to use these pages, see *p.39*.

More materials
For teachers
Teacher's Resource Centre
Video Can you understand these people? 7&8
Quick Test 8
File 8 Test
For students
Online Practice Check your progress

GRAMMAR

a
1 b   2 a   3 a   4 c   5 a   6 b   7 c   8 b   9 b
b
1 my photo taken   2 my hair cut   3 my flat painted
4 was built   5 should be paid   6 being told

VOCABULARY

a
1 take   2 gave   3 paid   4 living   5 be   6 back
7 away   8 after   9 off   10 up
b
1 box office   2 interval   3 plot   4 matinee   5 opponent
c
1 dyed   2 manicure   3 plaits   4 massage   5 stretches
6 Palace   7 dome   8 crypt   9 tomb   10 defeated

PRONUNCIATION

c
1 cr**ow**d /aʊ/   2 **wh**istle /w/   3 y**o**ga /əʊ/   4 ca**th**edral /θ/
5 t**o**mb /uː/
d
1 perf**o**rmance   2 **au**dience   3 ae**ro**bics   4 **pe**dicure
5 **co**lumn

CAN YOU understand this text?

b
1 the Pump Room   2 Aquae Sulis   3 the Terrace
4 the Great Bath   5 July / August   6 Bath Abbey
7 Bill Bryson   8 the King's Spring

▶ CAN YOU understand these people?

1 b   2 b   3 a   4 b   5 c

🔊 8.17

1
I = interviewer, D = Diarmuid
I Do you still go to the bank or do you do all your banking online?
D I do almost all of my banking online. The only reason I'd go into a bank is to ask for advice, so maybe for big things, like a mortgage or a loan I would go in to have a face-to-face conversation, but other than that, it's all online.
I Have you ever had a problem with online banking?
D Yes, I've had problems, um, just glitches in the system that mean you can't access it when you need to, um, I've never had a huge problem though.

2
I = interviewer, V = Victoria
I What's the best live event you've been to recently?
V Um, I would say the best live event I've been to recently is, last time I was in LA I went to a Dodgers game. Um, the Dodgers are my favourite baseball team and, um, now they're in the World Series, so it was exciting to see them play this year.
I Why did you enjoy it so much?
V I enjoyed going to the Dodger game so much this year because I live in New York now and I don't get to see them play in person that often, and they're a really good team this year, um, so getting to see them play was really exciting.

3
I = interviewer, K = Keith
I Do you ever play board games or other kinds of games with friends or family?
K Yeah, I play, um, board games with my family, with my wife and with my children.
I What's your favourite game? Why?
K Um, my favourite game. I would choose either Monopoly or Cluedo. Um, I play both of them a lot with my children, and with my family. I'd probably say Cluedo's my favourite. My children love it and I've always loved it since I was a kid as well. It's a detective game where you have to solve a crime and who's committed it, what with and where they did it, and it's a really good game.

4
I = interviewer, C = Carolina
I How often do you go to the hairdresser's?
C Um, once a month, I think.
I What do you usually have done?
C I get my hair cut. That's it.
I Have you ever had a haircut you really didn't like?
C Many times. Once I remember that it I, it turned out to be super short and I was very disappointed. I almost cried.

5
I = interviewer, E = Erin
I What's the most interesting historical site you've ever visited?
E I almost hate to say it because it sounds like a cliché, but the Colosseum in Rome. Just the, the architecture and the things that people were capable of with their brains before computers is just mind-blowing. But also the Museum of Science, the Galileo Museum in Florence is also very cool.
I Why did you go there?
E We went to Rome and the Colosseum specifically because my husband wanted to. I wasn't very interested, but I was really surprised at how it, much I enjoyed it. And we went to the Galileo Museum because someone else had recommended it and it seemed like an interesting thing to do, sort of off the beaten tourist path. And it was amazing. I think my brain melted a little bit.
I Would you recommend it to other people?
E Absolutely. If you do the Colosseum, pay extra for the guided tour. You get through the line faster.

9A Total recall

G reported speech
V word building
P word stress

Lesson plan

This lesson is about memory and provides two different angles on the topic: strategies to help you to remember, and the real-life story of a woman who is not able to forget.

The lesson begins with Sts doing a survey about how good their memory is and then discussing the results. Next, they read an extract on how to remember numbers from a book called *How to Develop a Brilliant Memory Week by Week*. The grammar section which follows uses two stories on audio to revise and extend reported speech (reported statements, questions, and imperatives).

In the second half of the lesson, Sts listen to a radio programme about a woman who can't forget anything. This leads into a vocabulary and pronunciation focus on word building and word stress related to the words in the listening. Sts then put this language into practice in a speaking activity where they tell stories and anecdotes.

More materials
For teachers
Photocopiables
Grammar reported speech *p.168*
Communicative Find the pair *p.198* (instructions *p.176*)
For students
Workbook 9A
Online Practice 9A

OPTIONAL LEAD-IN (BOOKS CLOSED)

Tell Sts that you are going to read out ten words. They must not write them, but must try to remember them.

Dictate the following words, saying each one twice (they are all from previous **Vocabulary Banks**):

toothpaste butcher's zoom rubbish thesis cartoon donkey fork hammer fringe

Then put Sts in pairs and tell them to write down as many as they can remember.

Check answers and find out which pair has the best memory.

1 SPEAKING

a Books open. Focus on the questionnaire and the task. Give Sts time to read the sentences and tick the ones that are true for them. Highlight that in 4, they can use a different social network from Facebook, or use another way of remembering, e.g. a calendar.

Now focus on the **Giving examples** box and go through it with the class.

Put Sts in pairs and get them to discuss with a partner which sentences they have ticked, and encourage them to give examples.

With a show of hands, find out how many Sts ticked each sentence.

Finally, find out if any Sts didn't tick any of the sentences. Then find out who has the fewest ticks.

b Do this as a whole-class activity, or get Sts to discuss it in pairs and then get some feedback. You could tell the class which one causes you the biggest problem and why.

2 READING understanding a theory

a Focus on the instructions and give Sts exactly 30 seconds to look at the credit card number. Make sure they don't write it down. Then tell them to close their books.

Now get Sts to write as much of the number as they can remember.

When Sts have finished, tell them to compare with a partner. Then they should open their books and see how much of the number they wrote correctly.

Find out if any Sts got all the digits in the correct order.

b Focus on the instructions and the objects. Put Sts in pairs and get them to write as many of the objects in the photo as possible.

c Tell Sts to read the extract and check their answers to **b**. Tell them not to worry about the gaps. You might want to check Sts know the meaning of *shape*.

Check answers.

EXTRA SUPPORT Before Sts read the extract the first time, check whether you need to pre-teach any vocabulary, but not the highlighted verbs.

a ball   a pencil   a swan   handcuffs   a boat   a seahorse an elephant's trunk   a boomerang   an egg timer   a balloon on a string

Now tell Sts, in their pairs, to decide if they prefer any different objects for numbers 0–9.

Elicit some feedback.

! Tell Sts not to do the task in the last paragraph of the extract, as they are going to do it later in **f**.

d Focus on phrases A–D and make sure Sts understand all the lexis.

Tell Sts to read the extract again and this time to complete gaps 1–4 with the phrases.

Check answers.

1 C   2 B   3 D   4 A

e Focus on the instructions and do this as a whole-class activity, or get Sts to do it individually.

Check answers. You could ask Sts to find two other words in the extract related to the word *memorize* (*memory* and *memorable*).

1 remind   2 recall   3 memorize

Deal with any other new vocabulary. Model and drill the pronunciation of any tricky words.

9A

f Focus on the instructions and give Sts time to memorize the 20-digit number in the last paragraph.

Then get them to memorize the credit card number in **a** again, using Dominic O'Brien's method.

Get Sts to write the numbers and then check their own answers.

Find out if any Sts managed to remember the 20 digits. If not, how many did they remember?

Then ask if any Sts remembered more digits in the credit card number, and if so, whether they think it is because of the Number-Shape System and the Link Method.

g Do this as a whole-class activity.

h Tell Sts they are now going to use pictures to help them to learn some new vocabulary. The words are all ones which are going to come up in a story they are going to read in **9B**.

The words are *bride*, *join*, *thief*, *sigh* (verb), *knock* (verb), *warning*, *upset* (adj), and *wise* (adj). If you think your Sts already know any of them, replace them with another word from **9B** or **File 10**.

Tell the class they are going to draw a picture incorporating the new words. Give a large piece of paper to each student (or they can use their own paper).

Say the first word. You may explain the word by eliciting the translation from a student or by translating it yourself, but tell Sts <u>not</u> to write it down.

Each student then draws an image for the word. The image can be a picture of, e.g. a bride, or simply an image that they associate with the meaning, or even the sound of the word. You might want to do your own drawings on the board for the first two to help Sts get the idea.

Continue with the other words. Sts must try to incorporate each image into their picture.

When Sts have drawn their eight images, they should compare with a partner, explaining what each image represents.

Now write the eight words on the board in jumbled order and ask Sts to write each word over its image.

Finally, clean the board and get Sts to turn over their picture and see if they can remember the eight words. You may now want to tell them that *join*, *sigh*, and *knock* are all regular verbs, and that the plural of *thief* is *thieves*.

3 GRAMMAR reported speech

a 🔊 **9.1** Focus on the instructions and make sure Sts know the meaning of *annoyed*.

Play the audio for Sts to listen to the first story, and then pause the audio and elicit why Sarah was annoyed.

> Because Rick, her husband, woke her up very early to help find his keys.

Now play Kim's story and elicit why she was annoyed.

> Because her sister had promised to bring a cake for their mother's birthday and had then forgotten to do it.

🔊 **9.1**
(script in Student's Book on *p.130*)
1 Sarah
My husband, Rick, always forgets where he puts things, and last night he came home very late from work and then had to leave very early again this morning, at five, while I was still in bed. I heard him crashing about downstairs getting ready, and then he shouted up the stairs, 'Sarah, have you seen my car keys?' So I shouted back, 'No', and I tried to go back to sleep, but then he came running up the stairs into the bedroom and said, 'I can't find them. I left them on the table when I went to bed last night. You've moved them.' And I said, 'I didn't move them; I was in bed when you came home. Have you looked in your coat pocket?' So he went downstairs again and shouted, 'They're not there'. So I got up, in a very bad mood, and went downstairs, and looked in his coat pocket, and – surprise, surprise – there were his car keys. I was really quite angry because by now I was completely awake. But at least he apologized.

2 Kim
It was my mum's seventieth birthday last week, and I suggested to my sister, Caro, that it would be nice to have a birthday lunch for her. I said I'd organize it because my sister isn't very good at that kind of thing. She works full time and has a very important job – so she says – but anyway, she said, 'I want to do something to help. I'll bring a birthday cake.' I said, 'Fine', even though I quite wanted to make the cake myself. Anyway, on the day, everyone arrived and Mum was really surprised and pleased, and we had lunch, and then I said to my sister, 'Where's the cake?' She went pale, and said, 'OMG, I completely forgot about it.' Mum said, 'Oh, don't make a fuss, Kim. It's no problem.' She thought it was very funny, but I was seriously annoyed.

b Focus on the instructions and give Sts time to put the initials next to the lines.

Get Sts to compare with a partner.

EXTRA SUPPORT Get Sts to work in pairs and do the activity.

Play the first story again for Sts to listen and check.

Check answers.

> **Sarah's story**
> **R** 'Have you seen my car keys?'
> **R** 'I can't find them.'
> **R** 'You've moved them.'
> **S** 'Have you looked in your coat pocket?'
> **R** 'They're not there.'

Now repeat the process for the second story.

> **Kim's story**
> **C** 'I want to do something to help.'
> **C** 'I'll bring a birthday cake.'
> **K** 'Where's the cake?'
> **C** 'I completely forgot about it.'
> **M** 'It's no problem.'

c Focus on the instructions. Look at 1 and tell Sts to also look at **Sarah's story** in **b**. Highlight that *Have you seen my car keys?* is direct speech as you are using the exact words that someone has said. In **c**, Sts need to report what the person said.

Get Sts to complete the gaps and compare with a partner. Check answers.

> **1** if **2** couldn't **3** had / 'd **4** asked **5** told **6** said
> **7** would / 'd **8** was **9** she **10** was

d Tell Sts to go to **Grammar Bank 9A** on *p.148*.

Grammar notes

In this lesson, the basics of reported speech are revised and reported imperatives are introduced. By now, Sts should have no problems with reported statements, but will need more practice with reported questions, and especially with reported imperatives and requests.

Remind Sts that *tell* is followed by a person or object pronoun, but *say* is not, e.g.
She told me her name was Anna. NOT *She told her name was Anna.*
She said she was tired. NOT *She said me she was tired.*

Remind Sts also of the past simple pronunciation *said* /sed/ and *told* /təʊld/.

Point out that the past perfect in direct speech does not change in reported speech.

Word changes in reported speech

When direct speech is reported at a different time or place from when or where it was originally spoken, word changes usually happen. However, if the time is very recent or the place is the same, these words may not need to change, e.g.

'I'll meet you this evening.'
(reported a few minutes later):
He said he'd meet us this evening.

'I'll meet you this evening.'
(reported a few days later):
He said he'd meet us that evening.

Reported questions

- **Rule 1:** Remind Sts that the auxiliaries *do*, *does*, and *did* are not used in reported questions, e.g. NOT *He asked how did I feel*.

Reported imperatives and requests

Reported imperatives and requests are difficult for many Sts because the use of the infinitive does not correspond to what they would use in their L1. As a result, they often say things like *She told us that we didn't talk* instead of *She told us not to talk*. Sts will need a lot of practice before they are able to produce this structure correctly.

Requests (but not imperatives), e.g. *Can you help me?*, can be reported in two ways, like an imperative or like a question:
He asked me to help him OR *He asked me if I could help him*.
At this level, given that the infinitive is a new structure, we recommend just focusing on this way of reporting.

In Intermediate Plus, the structure is only taught with *ask* or *tell*. Other reporting verbs used with the infinitive, e.g. *advise*, *convince*, *persuade*, etc. are introduced in *English File* Upper-intermediate.

Focus on **Revise the basics**, and use the chart to elicit the rules for reported statements, e.g. the pronoun and tense changes, and remind Sts of the difference between *say* and *tell*.

Now focus on the example sentences for **word changes in reported speech** and play audio 🔊 **9.2** for Sts to listen and repeat. Encourage them to copy the rhythm. Then go through the rules with the class.

Repeat for **reported questions** 🔊 **9.3** and **reported imperatives and requests** 🔊 **9.4**.

Focus on the exercises and get Sts to do them individually or in pairs.

Check answers, getting Sts to read the full sentences.

a
1 She said (that) **she couldn't find her purse**.
2 He said (that) **he wasn't coming to class on Friday**.
3 They said (that) **they probably wouldn't go on holiday that summer**.
4 Jane said (that) **she had / 'd finished her exams**.
5 They told us (that) **the film would be on the next day**.
6 Robert told me (that) **he hadn't been there before**.
7 She said (that) **she had to leave at 6.30**.
8 They told me (that) **they'd never forgotten their visit**.
9 He said (that) **he had / 'd seen a man hiding in the bushes**.
10 She told me (that) **she didn't really want to see me**.

b
1 She asked him **how many children he had**.
2 They asked the woman **to take a photo of them**.
3 They asked us **if / whether we would / 'd be able to come**.
4 He told me **to fill in the application form**.
5 He asked her **if / whether she had / 'd arrived on time**.
6 She told us **to bring plenty of food**.
7 She asked me **to help her with the cooking**.
8 He asked them **how long they had / 'd been waiting**.
9 He asked her **to confirm her date of birth**.
10 They told us **not to worry about anything**.

Tell Sts to go back to the main lesson **9A**.

EXTRA SUPPORT If you think Sts need more practice, you may want to give them the **Grammar** photocopiable activity at this point.

e Put Sts in pairs, **A** and **B**, and focus on the instructions and example.

Sts should each write their three questions. They should not work together on this. Encourage them to write questions to which they don't know the answers (e.g. not *What's your name?*).

First, Sts **A** ask Sts **B** their three questions, but they mustn't write the answers.

Then make sure Sts swap roles.

f Now focus on the instructions and the example. Get Sts to change partners, and tell them to report to their new partner the questions they asked their first partner and the answers. Although they may need to look at the questions in order to transform them into reported speech, they should be able to transform the answers in their head.

Make sure Sts swap roles.

Remind Sts that when they are reporting their questions and answers, they may need to change the tense, as well as other words. Monitor and help, correcting any mistakes in reported speech.

Get some feedback. With a show of hands, find out how many Sts remembered all three questions and answers.

EXTRA SUPPORT You could demonstrate the activity with a student in front of the class. First, ask the student a question, and then report the question and answer to the class (from memory).

4 LISTENING linking dates and events

a Focus on the instructions and give Sts time to think about where they were and what they did on the days listed.

Now put Sts in pairs and get them to talk about what they can remember, giving as much detail as possible.

Get some feedback from the class.

EXTRA SUPPORT You could demonstrate the activity by choosing one of the days / dates and telling the class where you were and what you were doing.

b 🔊 9.5 Focus on the task and photos, making sure Sts know what *extraordinary* /ɪkˈstrɔːdnri/ means (= unexpected, surprising, or strange). Then go through the **Glossary** with the class.

Give Sts time to read the three questions. You may want to pre-teach the pronunciation of *Manhattan*, *New Jersey*, and *Los Angeles* if you think Sts may have problems recognizing them when they listen.

Play the audio once the whole way through.

Get Sts to compare with a partner, and then check answers.

EXTRA SUPPORT Read through the script and decide if you need to pre-teach any new lexis before Sts listen.

1 Highly Superior Autobiographical Memory
2 She was 8.
3 It drives her crazy.

🔊 9.5
(script in Student's Book on *p.130*)
A = announcer, P = presenter, J = Jill
Part 1

A Can you remember exactly what you did on any day ten, twenty, or even thirty years ago? Now it's *Mind Matters*, and we're going to hear about a woman who can do just that.
P Ask Jill Price to remember any day in her life, and she can usually come up with an answer. When I met her, she asked for my date of birth, which is the twenty-fourth of January, nineteen eighty-six.
J OK, the twenty-fourth of January, nineteen eighty-six was a Friday. It was four days before the *Challenger* explosion. I was working in an ice cream shop. I hated my job. That night I went out with some friends, Tim and Candace.
P Jill could also tell me what she ate and what time she got home that evening. I tried another date. What did she do on the twenty-ninth of August, nineteen eighty?
J It was also a Friday. I went to Palm Springs with my friends Nina and Michelle and their family.
P Then I asked her, 'When was the third time you drove a car?'
J That was the tenth of January, nineteen eighty-one. A Saturday.
P Jill Price has HSAM, or 'Highly Superior Autobiographical Memory', which means she can remember exactly what happened on most days in her life. She remembers the day of the week for every date since nineteen eighty – what she was doing, who she was with, where she was. She can recall a memory of twenty years ago as easily as a memory of two days ago.
Jill was born on the thirtieth of December, nineteen sixty-five, in New York. Her first memory is when she was eighteen months old and she lived with her parents in an apartment in Manhattan. She remembers the traffic and staring out of the window down Ninth Avenue. When she was five, her family moved to New Jersey, and then when she was eight, they moved to a rented house in Los Angeles. That was the first of July, nineteen seventy-four – and on that day, she says, her 'brain snapped', and she began to be able to remember everything linking that happened to her in great detail. Her memories come without her trying to recall them.
J People have called it a gift, but for me it's a nightmare. My entire life goes through my head every day – it drives me crazy.

---

c Give Sts time to read the questions.

Play the audio again, pausing after the answer to each question is given to give Sts time to write.

Get Sts to compare with a partner, and then check answers.

1 24th January 1986 was a Friday. She was working in an ice cream shop. She went out that night with friends.
  29th August 1980 was a Friday. She went to Palm Springs with friends.
  10th January 1981 was a Saturday. It was the third time she drove a car.
2 The traffic in Manhattan and looking out of the window of her parent's apartment. She was 18 months old.
3 1st July 1974 is the day her family moved to Los Angeles and she began to remember everything.

EXTRA SUPPORT If there's time, you could get Sts to listen again with the script on *p.130*, so they can see exactly what they understood / didn't understand. Translate / Explain any new words or phrases.

d 🔊 9.6 Tell Sts they are now going to listen to the second part of the radio programme, in which the presenter talks about memory research.

Go through questions 1–10, making sure Sts understand all the lexis, and point out that the doctor's name is pronounced /məɡɒf/. Focus on the **Glossary** and go through it with the class.

Play the audio once the whole way through for Sts to listen and make notes.

Get Sts to compare with a partner, and then play the audio again.

Check answers.

EXTRA SUPPORT Read through the script and decide if you need to pre-teach any new lexis before Sts listen.

1 He asked her questions from a history book.
2 Elvis Presley and Bing Crosby died.
3 He checked with her diary and with her mother.
4 Strong emotional experiences
5 Things that she finds important
6 Facts and figures, numbers
7 Around 60
8 There's so much information in her head all the time; it's difficult to forget bad things.
9 *The Woman Who Can't Forget*
10 Because there might be things in it that he doesn't want to know.

🔊 9.6
(script in Student's Book on *p.130*)
P = presenter, D = Dr McGaugh, J = Jill
Part 2

P So what do we know about how Jill's superior memory works? Doctor James McGaugh, who is an expert in memory research, met her for the first time in June two thousand. He first tested her memory using a big history book. Jill answered the questions quickly and confidently.
D What happened on the sixteenth of August, nineteen seventy-seven?
J Elvis Presley died in his Graceland bathroom. It was a Tuesday.
D When did Bing Crosby die?
J Friday, the fourteenth of October, nineteen seventy-seven, on a golf course in Spain. I heard it on the radio while my mom was driving me to soccer practice.

P It's often difficult for scientists to confirm whether autobiographical memories are accurate, but Doctor McGaugh was able to check with Jill's detailed diary. He also checked Jill's memories with her mother.
Doctor McGaugh's research was focused on showing that strong emotional experiences are the most memorable ones, and Jill had the most vivid memories that McGaugh had ever encountered. However, her memory only stores the things that *she* finds important. When it comes to remembering things that *don't* relate to her personally or to her interests, Jill is no better than the average person.

J At school, I couldn't remember facts and figures, and I can't memorize a sequence of random numbers.

P McGaugh and other experts have now discovered around sixty people with HSAM. These people often say that there was a specific point in their lives that triggered their ability to remember in such detail. For Jill, it was her family's stressful move to Los Angeles. Most people would think that having HSAM is an advantage, but Jill says there are two big problems.

J The first is that there's so much information running through my head all the time, and the second is that I find it difficult to forget unpleasant things. For example, I can remember bad moments from my childhood as if they'd just happened, and they make me feel unhappy all over again.

P No one else in Jill's family has a memory like hers. She's published an autobiography, *The Woman Who Can't Forget*, but her brother hasn't read it. He says that there might be things in it that he doesn't want to know.

EXTRA SUPPORT If there's time, you could get Sts to listen again with the script on *p.130*, so they can see exactly what they understood / didn't understand. Translate / Explain any new words or phrases.

e Do this as a whole-class activity.

5 VOCABULARY & PRONUNCIATION
word building; word stress

a Focus on the task and the chart, and point out the examples in the chart.
Give Sts time to complete the chart, individually or in pairs.

b 🔊 **9.7** Play the audio for Sts to listen and check.
Check answers by eliciting the words onto the board.

Noun	Adjective	Adverb
1 memory	memorable	memorably
2 confidence	confident	confidently
3 emotion	emotional	emotionally
4 importance	important	importantly
5 accuracy	accurate	accurately
6 person	personal	personally

🔊 **9.7**
1 memory, memorable, memorably
2 confidence, confident, confidently
3 emotion, emotional, emotionally
4 importance, important, importantly
5 accuracy, accurate, accurately
6 person, personal, personally

EXTRA CHALLENGE Get Sts to underline the stressed syllables before they listen again. Then play the audio for them to listen and check.

Now play the audio again, pausing after each word to give Sts time to underline the stressed syllable.

Check answers by underlining the stressed syllables in the words on the board (see previous answer key).
Finally, put Sts in pairs and get them to practise saying the words.

EXTRA SUPPORT Play the audio again, pausing after each word or group of words for Sts to listen and repeat. Then put Sts in pairs to practise saying the words.

c Focus on the instructions and make sure Sts know what a *collocation* is (= a combination of words that happens very often, and more frequently than would happen by chance).
Get Sts to complete the gaps in 1–6.
Get them to compare with a partner, and then check answers. You may want to explain that *emotional intelligence* = the capacity to be aware of, control, and express one's emotions, and to handle relationships empathetically.

1 emotional 2 accurate 3 Personally 4 memorable
5 important 6 confidently

d Do this as a whole-class activity, or put Sts in pairs and then check answers. For 2, Sts might suggest *entrance* and although it is correct, it hasn't come up in this lesson.

1 atomic 2 entry 3 unlikely 4 security 5 connection
6 autobiographical 7 easily 8 ability 9 unpleasant

EXTRA SUPPORT Give Sts time to work individually or in pairs to flick through the material in this lesson and find the answers.

EXTRA CHALLENGE Get Sts to underline the stressed syllable in each word. Then check answers.

1 at<u>om</u>ic 2 <u>en</u>try 3 un<u>like</u>ly 4 se<u>cu</u>rity 5 con<u>nec</u>tion
6 autobio<u>graph</u>ical 7 <u>eas</u>ily 8 a<u>bil</u>ity 9 un<u>pleas</u>ant

6 SPEAKING

a Focus on the instructions and the topics which Sts have to talk about, making sure they understand them all.
Give Sts time to make some notes or think about what they are going to say for the two topics they choose.

EXTRA SUPPORT Demonstrate the activity by talking about one of the topics yourself.

b Put Sts in small groups of three or four. Focus on the example and tell them to discuss their topics in their groups.
Monitor and help.
Get some feedback from various groups.

EXTRA IDEA Elicit / Write on the board a few different ways of starting an anecdote, e.g.
THIS HAPPENED TO ME WHEN…
I'LL NEVER FORGET THE TIME WHEN…
WHEN I WAS AT SCHOOL, …

c Get individual Sts to tell the rest of the class about a story or anecdote they've just heard from a classmate. Remind Sts to speak from memory and not to use notes.
If there isn't enough time for everyone to speak, you could form new groups or put Sts in new pairs where they can exchange stories.

9B Here comes the bride

G third conditional and other uses of the past perfect
V weddings
P sentence stress

Lesson plan

The topic of this lesson is weddings. The lesson begins with *Mabel*, a short story by the famous British writer, William Somerset Maugham, about a wedding that was postponed for years and nearly didn't take place. The story is presented in four parts, two of which are for reading and listening, and two of which are for listening only. This is followed by the grammar focus, which looks at third conditional sentences and other uses of the past perfect. These structures are further practised in a pronunciation focus on sentence stress.

The second half of the lesson begins with a listening activity with two stories about failed proposals. The theme continues in a vocabulary focus on lexis related to weddings, including a text about the real cost of a wedding. This leads into a speaking activity where Sts read some controversial statements about weddings, decide whether or not they agree with them, and then discuss each one in small groups. Finally, Sts write a story describing a significant event.

More materials
For teachers
Photocopiables
Grammar third conditionals and other uses of the past perfect p.169
Communicative What had happened? p.199 (instructions p.177)
For students
Workbook 9B
Online Practice 9B

OPTIONAL LEAD-IN (BOOKS CLOSED)
Write the words WEDDING DISASTERS on the board.

Then put Sts in pairs and give them a few minutes to brainstorm three ideas why a wedding might be a disaster. Elicit ideas.

Now tell Sts they are going to read a short story about a wedding that almost didn't happen.

1 READING & LISTENING understanding a short story

a Books open. Focus on the instructions. You might want to tell Sts how to pronounce the author's name, William Somerset Maugham /mɔːm/.

Give Sts time to read the information. Make sure they understand the meaning of *colonies* (= countries or areas that are governed by people from another, more powerful, country).

Do the question as a whole-class activity. Encourage Sts to give reasons to justify their opinions.

EXTRA IDEA You might want to tell Sts a bit more about Maugham's life. Maugham was orphaned at the age of ten; he was brought up by an aunt and uncle. He qualified as a doctor in 1897. As well as stories, he wrote plays – in 1908, four of his plays were showing in London at the same time, which made him financially secure. During World War I, he volunteered as an ambulance driver and then worked as a secret agent. After the war, he resumed his interrupted travels and, in 1928, bought a villa in the south of France, which became his permanent home. Among his most famous novels are *Of Human Bondage*, *The Moon and Sixpence*, and *The Razor's Edge*.

b 9.8 Tell Sts they are going to read and listen to *Mabel*, a short story written by Maugham and originally published in 1930, many years after the events in the story had taken place. Point out that most of the places mentioned in the story were British colonies at that time, ruled by British colonial governments.

Focus on **Part 1** and the **Glossary** and go through it with the class. You might want to tell Sts that the country now called *Myanmar* was called *Burma* until 1989. At the same time, *Rangoon* became *Yangon*.

Give Sts time to read questions 1–5. Elicit / Explain the meaning of *dilemma* (= a situation which causes problems, often one in which you have to make a very difficult choice). Model and drill its pronunciation /dɪˈlemə/.

Now play the audio for Sts to listen and read at the same time.

In pairs, Sts answer the questions.

Check answers.

EXTRA SUPPORT Before Sts read **Part 1** of the short story, check whether you need to pre-teach any vocabulary.

1. George worked for the British colonial government in Burma, and Mabel was engaged to him (his fiancée).
2. Because there were difficulties: Mabel's father died, the war came, and then George was sent to an area which was unsuitable for a white woman.
3. He suddenly became afraid (of marrying Mabel) because he hadn't seen her for seven years and couldn't remember what she was like.
4. He didn't want to marry Mabel, but didn't want to tell her, either.
5. He decided to run away, and he got a boat to Singapore.

9.8
See text in Student's Book on p.90

Now focus on the last two questions in pink and ask them to the class. You could also get Sts to discuss them in pairs, and then get feedback.

Deal with any other new vocabulary. Model and drill the pronunciation of any tricky words.

c 🔊 **9.9** Tell Sts they are going to follow George's route on the map, so they should familiarize themselves with some of the place names. Give Sts time to find each place in the list on the map. They should also try to work out how they think the names are pronounced in English.

Play the audio for Sts to listen and check. Remind Sts that some of the cities and countries now have different names (e.g. *Saigon / Ho Chi Minh City, Burma / Myanmar*, etc.).

🔊 **9.9**
See place names in Student's Book on *p.90*

EXTRA IDEA Before Sts look at the map, get them to look at the place names in the list and see if they know in which country any of the places are.

d 🔊 **9.10** Tell Sts they are going to listen to **Part 2** of the story.

Play the audio once the whole way through for Sts to listen and mark George's route on the map.

Get Sts to compare with a partner, and then check answers, eliciting the names of the places on his route.

EXTRA SUPPORT Read through the script and decide if you need to pre-teach any new lexis before Sts listen.

(Singapore →) Bangkok → Saigon → Hong Kong → Manila → Shanghai → Yokohama → Shanghai

🔊 **9.10**
(script in Student's Book on *p.130*)
R = reader, G = George, M = Mabel
Part 2
R When George arrived at Singapore he found a telegram waiting for him.
M Quite understand. Don't worry. Love Mabel.
G My God, I believe she's following me…
R he said. He checked the passenger list of the next ship on its way to Singapore, and sure enough her name was on it. There was not a moment to lose. He jumped on the first train to Bangkok. But he was uneasy; she would have no difficulty in finding out that he had gone to Bangkok. Fortunately, there was a French boat sailing the next day for Saigon. He took it. At Saigon he would be safe. It would never occur to her that he had gone there. It was five days' journey from Bangkok to Saigon and the boat was dirty, crowded, and uncomfortable. He was glad to arrive and went straight to the hotel. A telegram was immediately handed to him. It contained only two words:
M Love Mabel.
R He started to tremble.
G When is the next boat for Hong Kong?
R he asked. He sailed to Hong Kong, but was afraid to stay there. Then he went to Manila, and from there he went on to Shanghai. Shanghai made him feel nervous; every time he went out of the hotel he expected to run straight into Mabel's arms. No, Shanghai would never do. The only thing was to go to Yokohama. At the Grand Hotel in Yokohama a telegram awaited him.
M So sorry I missed you at Manila. Love Mabel.
R Where was she now? He went back to Shanghai. This time he went straight to the club and asked if he had received any telegrams. One was handed to him.
M Arriving soon. Love Mabel.

EXTRA SUPPORT If there's time, you could get Sts to listen again with the script on *p.130*, so they can see exactly what they understood / didn't understand. Translate / Explain any new words or phrases.

e Focus on the instructions and Mabel's four telegrams.
Now play the audio for **Part 2** again, pausing as necessary to give Sts time to complete the gaps.
Get Sts to compare with a partner, and then play the audio again, pausing if necessary, for them to check.
Check answers.

1 understand, Don't worry
2 Love Mabel
3 sorry, missed, Manila
4 Arriving soon

Now focus on the two questions in pink and get the class to speculate on what George will do next. You could put Sts in pairs, and then elicit ideas.

f Focus on the instructions. Get Sts to read **Part 3** and continue marking George's journey on the map. Elicit / Explain that a *consul* /ˈkɒnsl/ is a government official who is the representative of his or her country in a foreign city.
Get Sts to compare with a partner, and then check answers, eliciting the names of the places on his route.

EXTRA SUPPORT Before Sts read **Part 3** of the short story, check whether you need to pre-teach any vocabulary.

(Shanghai along the Yangtze River →) Chungking → Cheng-tu

Next, get Sts to complete the gaps with adverbs and adverbial phrases from the list, and then compare with a partner.

g 🔊 **9.11** Play the audio for Sts to listen to **Part 3** and check their answer to **f**, pausing as necessary.
Check answers.

2 After that   3 only   4 at last   5 never   6 One morning

🔊 **9.11**
Part 3
R No, no, she wasn't going to catch him so easily. He had already made his plans. He could catch the last ship along the Yangtze river to Chungking. After that, no one could get there until the following spring. He arrived at Chungking, but he was desperate now. He was not going to take any risks. There was a place called Cheng-tu, the capital of Szechuan, and it was four hundred miles away. It could only be reached by road, and the area was full of thieves. A man would be safe there.
George set out. He sighed with relief when he saw the walls of the lonely Chinese city. He could rest at last. Mabel would never find him there. The British consul was a friend of his and he stayed with him in his luxurious house.
The weeks passed lazily one after the other. One morning George and the consul were in the courtyard when there was a loud knock at the door.

Now ask Sts what they think *He sighed with relief* means. You could demonstrate what a *sigh* /saɪ/ sounds like and point out that people make this sound for different reasons.

sigh = take and then let out a deep breath; *relief* = happiness that nothing unpleasant is happening
In this context, it means 'he felt very happy to be there, where Mabel couldn't follow'.

Deal with any other new vocabulary. Model and drill the pronunciation of any tricky words.

9B 129

h 🔊 **9.12** Ask Sts to guess how the story will end. Elicit some ideas, but <u>don't</u> tell Sts if they are correct.

Now tell Sts they are going to listen to **Part 4**, which is the end of the story. Play the audio once all the way through for Sts to listen.

Play it again if necessary.

Now ask Sts to explain, in their own words, what happened in the end (*Mabel found George and they got married*). With a show of hands, find out how many Sts were surprised. Ask individuals why or why not.

EXTRA SUPPORT Read through the script and decide if you need to pre-teach any new lexis before Sts listen.

🔊 **9.12**
R = reader, G = George, M = Mabel, C = consul
Part 4

R *One morning George and the consul were in the courtyard when there was a loud knock at the door. The doorman opened it. Mabel walked in. She was neat and cool and fresh. There was nothing in her appearance to suggest that she had just come in after two weeks on the road. George was terrified. He was as pale as death. She went up to him.*
M Hello, George, I was so afraid that I'd missed you again.
G Hello, Mabel.
R *he said.*
   He did not know what to say. He looked this way and that: she stood between him and the doorway. She looked at him with a smile in her blue eyes.
M You haven't changed at all.
R *she said.*
M I was afraid you'd got fat and bald. I've been so nervous. It would have been terrible if I hadn't been able to marry you after all.
R *She turned to George's host.*
M Are you the consul?
R *she asked.*
C I am.
M Good. I'm ready to marry him as soon as I've had a bath.
R *And she did.*

EXTRA SUPPORT If you photocopy script 9.12 from here, Sts could read and listen to the whole story. Translate / Explain any new words or phrases.

i Focus on the two questions, making sure Sts understand *sympathy* (= the feeling of being sorry for sb). Model and drill its pronunciation /ˈsɪmpəθi/.

Then put Sts in pairs and get them to answer the questions, giving as much information as possible.

Get some feedback.

You might want to tell Sts that George and Mabel were real people. The writer met George in Burma and a friend of George's told Maugham about George and Mabel's 'romance'. The story does have a happy ending. When Maugham met George, he and Mabel had been happily married for eight years – in fact, George was totally dependent on Mabel and was very unhappy that she had had to go back to England for a visit.

2 GRAMMAR third conditional and other uses of the past perfect

a Focus on the instructions and get Sts, in pairs, to match the uses of the past perfect in the story to the descriptions.
Check answers.

1 c **2** b **3** a

You may want to point out that *a* is a third conditional.

b Tell Sts to go to **Grammar Bank 9B** on *p.149*.

Grammar notes
The third conditional and other uses of the past perfect are brought together here. The most difficult structure for most Sts will be the third conditional, which is why one whole practice exercise is devoted to it.

Third conditional
This was introduced towards the end of *English File Intermediate*, but it is a difficult structure in terms of form for Sts to produce correctly and needs a lot of practice.
Typical mistakes include using *would have* instead of the past perfect in the *if*-clause of the third conditional, e.g. ~~If I would have known the band had cancelled, I wouldn't have gone to the concert.~~
Or using the past perfect instead of *would have* in the main clause of the third conditional, e.g. ~~If I had seen your text message, I had answered it immediately.~~

Other uses of the past perfect
You may want to tell Sts that in reported speech, when the tense in the direct speech is the past simple, people sometimes use the past simple again rather than the past perfect in reported speech, especially if the reporting takes place shortly after the event.
'I got up very early' > *She said she (had) got up very early.*

Focus on the example sentences for **third conditional** and play audio 🔊 **9.13** for Sts to listen and repeat. Encourage them to copy the rhythm. Then go through the rules with the class.

Focus on the **'d** box and go through it with the class.

Repeat for **other uses of the past perfect** 🔊 **9.14**.

Now focus on the exercises and get Sts to do them individually or in pairs.

Check answers, getting Sts to read the full sentences.

a
1 She **wouldn't have fallen** in love with him if he **hadn't made** her laugh so much.
2 If they**'d / had been invited** to the wedding, they**'d / would have gone**.
3 I**'d / would have forgotten** our anniversary if you **hadn't reminded** me.
4 If we**'d / had left** earlier, we **wouldn't have missed** our train.
5 If you **hadn't paid** in advance, you **wouldn't have lost** your money.
6 If they**'d / had had** enough money, they**'d / would have bought** a flat instead of renting one.
7 I **would have slept** better if I **hadn't drunk** a coffee after dinner.
8 Jane and I **wouldn't have lost** touch if she **hadn't moved** abroad.
9 If I**'d / had known** you had a problem, I**'d / would have offered** to help.
10 If he **hadn't shouted** at the policeman, he **wouldn't have been arrested**.

b
1 I **enjoyed** that play very much, even though I**'d / had seen** it three times before.
2 He **said** he**'d / had worked** for the company for six months.

3 She still **hadn't got up** at 10.00, so I **left** the house without her.
4 We **spent** an hour looking for Carol, but she **had disappeared**.
5 He **ran** across the road, but the taxi **had already been taken** by someone else.
6 I **couldn't** get on the flight because they **had overbooked** it.
7 **I'd / had only been** in Sydney for a week when I first **met** Sally.
8 She **asked** me if **I'd / had visited** China before.
9 They **told** me they**'d / had just got** engaged.
10 The shop **hadn't opened** yet, but there **were** already a lot of people waiting outside.

Tell Sts to go back to the main lesson **9B**.

EXTRA SUPPORT If you think Sts need more practice, you may want to give them the **Grammar** photocopiable activity at this point.

3 PRONUNCIATION sentence stress

a 🔊 9.15 Remind Sts that in English sentences only some words are stressed. Elicit the type of words which are usually stressed (*nouns*, *verbs*, *adjectives*, and *adverbs*).

Tell Sts they are going to hear five sentences and they must listen for the stressed words and write them in the pink rectangles in the sentences. Point out that the first one has been done for them.

Play the audio, pausing after each sentence to give Sts time to write.

Get Sts to compare with a partner, and then check answers.

2 known, weather, bad, wouldn't, come
3 soon, got, airport, remembered, hadn't, locked, windows
4 said, hadn't, seen, ages
5 bought, dress, hadn't, expensive

🔊 9.15
1 When I read your email, I understood why you'd left.
2 If I'd known the weather was going to be so bad, I wouldn't have come.
3 As soon as we got to the airport, we remembered that we hadn't locked the windows.
4 He said that he hadn't seen her for ages.
5 I would have bought the dress if it hadn't been so expensive.

b Now tell Sts to look at the words they have written and try to remember what the complete sentence is.

c Tell Sts to listen to the audio again and complete any gaps they have. Play the audio again, pausing after each sentence.

Check answers, eliciting the sentences onto the board.

See script 9.15

Play the audio again, pausing after each sentence for Sts to listen and repeat, copying the rhythm. Encourage them to pronounce the stressed words (in the pink rectangles) more strongly and not to stress the other words.

Then repeat the activity, eliciting responses from individual Sts.

EXTRA SUPPORT Put Sts in pairs and get them to practise saying the sentences.

d Focus on the instructions and give Sts time to complete the three sentences with a verb phrase in the past perfect.

Put Sts in pairs and get them to read their sentences to each other with the correct stress pattern.

Get some Sts to read out their sentences, and find out if any Sts wrote the same endings.

4 LISTENING understanding anecdotes

a Focus on the first part of the instructions and get Sts to read the introduction to the article and decide what two words complete the title.

Check the answer.

marry me

Now put Sts in pairs, and focus on the second part of the instructions, making sure Sts know the meaning of *propose* /prəˈpəʊz/ (= to ask sb to marry you). Tell Sts to look at the photos and decide who proposed, and how, for each one.

Use the photo to elicit / teach the word *beads*.

b 🔊 9.16 Tell Sts they are going to listen to Alex (from couple 1) and Emma (from couple 2), and they must check their answers to **a** and say which couple is still together.

Play the audio once the whole way through for Sts to listen.

Check answers.

EXTRA SUPPORT Read through the script and decide if you need to pre-teach any new lexis before Sts listen.

Chloe proposed to Alex. She made a necklace with letters saying *Will you marry me?*
Tom proposed to Emma. He got down on one knee.
No, only Alex and Chloe are still together.

🔊 9.16
(script in Student's Book on *pp.130–131*)
Alex
My girlfriend Chloe and I had been together for just over a year. Soon after we met, I'd told her that I didn't want to get married or have children, and she seemed fine with that. But then, Chloe began to talk about moving in together. I tried not to discuss it, and we went on like that for a couple of months. Then one afternoon – it was the twenty-ninth of February – Chloe invited me to her house. When I arrived, she was making a bracelet. I sat down and she passed me a box which contained some small beads with letters on them. When I looked into the box, I realized that the letters spelled *Will you marry me?* I was horrified. I didn't want to embarrass her, so I started putting the letters on the bracelet thread in the wrong order – I made words like 'owl' and 'yellow', but then she started crying. So we went out for a walk and she explained that the twenty-ninth of February only happens once every four years, and it's the day when, traditionally, women can propose to men. I didn't say anything and went home. I felt awful. It's probably the worst thing that's ever happened to me, and I didn't see her for three days afterwards. But we got over it, and we're still together. We're not married, but who knows? Maybe in a few years' time, I'll propose, and Chloe will say no.
Emma
When I first started going out with Tom, I was completely in love. He was ten years older than me, very good-looking, and he had been an Olympic athlete. He was also a really lovely guy. In theory, he was my perfect man, but after two years, our relationship became very difficult, so I decided to end it. Not long afterwards, Tom phoned me to say that he wanted to meet at the cathedral. I thought, 'OK, fine'.

9B 131

When I got there, Tom was waiting for me outside. He was holding a bottle of champagne and a bunch of flowers. And then before I had a chance to say anything, he got down on one knee and proposed. He gave me a necklace – not a ring, a necklace. Then a crowd of Japanese tourists rushed towards us and began taking photos – Tom was down on one knee and I was looking white and shocked. It was awful. I asked him to get up, and explained to him, in front of all the tourists, that we were not together any more, and we were definitely not going to get married. We left the cathedral, and as I was walking with him to the station, Tom said he had hoped that if he proposed to me, it would solve all our problems. But it was never going to work. We're not together now.

c 🔊 **9.17** Tell Sts they are now going to hear Alex's story again and they need to complete sentences 1–8.

Put Sts in pairs and get them to go through 1–8 and see if they can remember what Alex said.

Play the audio again for Sts to listen and complete the sentences.

Get Sts to compare with their partner, and then play the audio again if necessary.

Check answers.

1 Alex didn't want to **get married or have children**.
2 Chloe began to talk about **moving in together**.
3 On 29th February, Chloe invited Alex to **her house**.
4 Chloe gave Alex **a box with some small beads with letters on them**.
5 The letters spelled **Will you marry me?**
6 Alex started putting the letters on the bracelet in **the wrong order**.
7 Chloe got upset and explained that on 29th February, women **can propose to men**.
8 Alex didn't see her **for three days afterwards**.

🔊 **9.17**
See Alex's story in script 9.16

d 🔊 **9.18** Tell Sts they are now going to listen to Emma's story again and this time they must work out why Emma mentions items 1–8.

Now repeat the same process with Emma's story.

1 Tom was **ten years** older than Emma.
2 After **two years** their relationship became difficult and she decided to end it.
3 Tom wanted them to meet at **the cathedral**.
4 When she got there, he was holding **a bottle of champagne and a bunch of flowers**.
5 He proposed and gave her **a necklace**.
6 **A crowd of (Japanese) tourists** rushed over and started taking photos.
7 Emma was looking **white and shocked** when the tourists took their photos (because she didn't want to marry him).
8 She was **walking** with him to **the station** when he explained why he had proposed – he thought it would solve their problems.

🔊 **9.18**
See Emma's story in script 9.16

EXTRA SUPPORT If there's time, you could get Sts to listen again with the script on *pp.130–131*, so they can see exactly what they understood / didn't understand. Translate / Explain any new words or phrases.

e Do this as a whole-class activity. If you have heard of any proposals that went wrong, you could tell the class about them.

EXTRA IDEA You could ask Sts if they have the same tradition in their country regarding 29th February when women can propose to men. If not, do they think it is a good tradition?

5 VOCABULARY weddings

Vocabulary notes

Wedding traditions vary the world over. In the UK, the best man is usually a close friend or family member of the bridegroom, and it is his responsibility to be in charge of the rings and hand them to the groom at the appropriate moment. He also usually gives a speech at the wedding reception.

Very young bridesmaids are also sometimes called *flower girls*.

a Focus on the wedding photo and the list of words and phrases. Give Sts time, individually or in pairs, to match the people in the photo to the words.

Check answers, making sure Sts know what each word means. Model and drill pronunciation.

A the bride   B a pageboy   C the (bride)groom
D a bridesmaid   E the best man

EXTRA SUPPORT Let Sts use their dictionaries to help them with this activity.

b Focus on the task and make sure Sts know the meaning of all the words in the list, especially *reception* here (= a formal social occasion to welcome sb or celebrate sth).

Give Sts time to read the article and complete the gaps.

Get Sts to compare with a partner, and then check answers.

1 engaged   2 reception   3 guests   4 married
5 invitations   6 bridesmaids   7 best man   8 couples

c Focus on the task and make sure Sts know the meaning of *expenses* /ɪkˈspensɪz/ (= money spent in doing a particular job, or for a particular purpose). Now go through the list, making sure all the lexis is clear, e.g. *venue*, *veil*, *honeymoon*, etc.

Put Sts in pairs and get them to try to match the prices in the list to the cost of each item in the list. Point out that these prices are in pounds. You could tell Sts the exchange rate if you think it will help them.

d 🔊 **9.19** Play the audio for Sts to listen and check.

Check answers.

The venue for the ceremony and the reception cost £**5,500**.
The five bridesmaids' dresses cost £**350**.
The food cost £**8,500**.
The flowers cost £**1,300**.
The rings cost £**640**.
The groom's suit cost £**1,160**.
The wedding dress, veil, and shoes cost £**2,500**.
The honeymoon cost £**4,500**.

🔊 9.19

The venue for the ceremony and the reception cost five thousand five hundred pounds.
The five bridesmaids' dresses cost three hundred and fifty pounds.
The food cost eight thousand five hundred pounds.
The flowers cost one thousand three hundred pounds.
The rings cost six hundred and forty pounds.
The groom's suit cost one thousand one hundred and sixty pounds.
The wedding dress, veil, and shoes cost two thousand five hundred pounds.
The honeymoon cost four thousand five hundred pounds.

Now do the question as a whole-class activity.

e Focus on the questions and make sure Sts understand them.

Put Sts in pairs and get them to ask and answer the questions, giving as much information as possible.

Monitor and help with vocabulary.

Get some feedback from various pairs.

6 SPEAKING

a Focus on the instructions and make sure Sts understand *controversial* /ˌkɒntrəˈvɜːʃl/ (= causing a lot of angry public discussion and disagreement). Now go through statements 1–6 to make sure Sts understand them.

Give Sts time to think whether they agree or disagree with each one, and to think of reasons and examples.

b Focus on the instructions and make sure Sts understand what they have to do.

Now focus on the **Agreeing** and **Disagreeing** box and go through it with the class. Highlight that *No way!* is quite informal.

Put Sts in small groups of four and tell them to discuss each statement.

Monitor and help if necessary.

When Sts have finished, you could ask if any groups disagreed strongly about any of the statements.

EXTRA IDEA Other possible controversial statements to discuss if they are appropriate in your teaching context, could be:
'You shouldn't get married in a religious building unless you practise the religion.'
'Living together is just as valid as getting married.'

7 WRITING a story

Tell Sts to go to **Writing A story** on *p.122*.

a Focus on the instructions and give Sts time to read Matt's story about his wedding. Tell them not to worry about the gaps or mistakes in the story. Elicit / Explain that a *score* (in this context) means a written piece of music.

Get Sts to compare with a partner, and then check the answer.

> The woman who was supposed to play the violin at the wedding ceremony never arrived.

b Now focus on the **Adverbs** box and go through it with the class.

Tell Sts to read the story again and complete the gaps with the adverbs and adverbial phrases from the list. Point out that some words can go in more than one place.

Get Sts to compare with a partner, and then check answers.

1 unfortunately **2** Fortunately / Luckily **3** Luckily / Fortunately **4** in the end **5** In fact

c Tell Sts to correct the ten mistakes underlined in Matt's story.

Get Sts to compare with a partner, and then check answers.

~~wasnt~~ – wasn't (punctuation)
~~we only have~~ – we only had (grammar)
~~gests~~ – guests (spelling)
~~were hired~~ – had hired (grammar)
~~lost~~ – got lost (vocabulary)
~~stressed~~ – stressful (vocabulary)
~~good~~ – well (grammar)
~~proffessional~~ – professional (spelling)
~~corse~~ – course (spelling)
~~here~~ – hear (spelling)

EXTRA IDEA Get Sts to cover Matt's story and retell it in their own words.

d Focus on the titles in the exam question. Give Sts time to choose a title and to write down some ideas about the topic.

Sts who have chosen the same title can compare their ideas in pairs.

Get some feedback from various pairs on each of the three topics.

e Now go through the plan with the class. Encourage Sts to make brief notes on what they will write about, using 1–4 to help them plan their story.

f Focus on the **Useful language: telling a story with sentence adverbs** box. Go through it with the class.

Get Sts to write their story, following the plan and notes they made in **d** and **e**. Remind them to use the **Useful language** to help them.

If you do the writing in class, set a time limit for Sts to write their story, e.g. 15–20 minutes.

g Sts should check their story for mistakes before giving it in.

EXTRA CHALLENGE Fast finishers or Sts who want additional writing practice can choose a second title to write about.

EPISODE 5

Practical English Finding Henry

Function asking for and giving directions in a building; checking understanding

Language *Go through the door and turn right*; *Which way now?*; *Go down the stairs*, etc.

Lesson plan

In this final Practical English episode, the functional focus is on asking for and giving directions inside a building. This revises and extends Sts' previous knowledge of understanding directions, and here the focus is more on giving rather than asking for them.

In the first scene, Jenny and Luke return to Henry's house during the night and search his study for clues about 'the old man'. They find a paperweight that has 'Proteus – the old man of the sea' written on it and realize that this must be the key to the mystery. Luke does an internet search and discovers a biochemical company called Proteus in Oxford, right by St Bartholomew's Church, which is famous for its bells (another clue). They immediately contact the police and Luke directs the police in a search of the Proteus building. In the final scene, Henry is reunited with his family, and they all celebrate his return.

More materials
For teachers
Teacher's Resource Centre
Video Practical English Episode 5
Quick Test 9
File 9 Test
For students
Workbook Practical English 5
Can you remember? 1–9
Online Practice Practical English 5
Check your progress

OPTIONAL LEAD-IN (BOOKS CLOSED)

Before starting Episode 5, elicit what Sts can remember about Episode 4. Ask *What two clues have Jenny and Luke got about Henry's kidnapping? Did they go back to the police? What's their plan of action?*, etc.

Alternatively, you could play the last scene of Episode 4.

1 ▶ WHAT THE CLUE MEANS

a 🔊 **9.20** Books open. Focus on the photos and ask *Where are Jenny and Luke? What are they doing?*

Point out the object in the smaller photo and elicit / teach *paperweight*.

Now focus on the instructions and the questions. Play the video / audio once the whole way through for Sts to watch or listen and answer the questions.

Check answers.

EXTRA SUPPORT Before playing the video / audio, go through the listening scripts and decide if you need to pre-teach / check any lexis to help Sts when they listen.

Old man refers to Proteus, a Greek god who is called 'the old man of the sea'.
They think Henry is being held at a biochemical company called Proteus in Oxford.

🔊 **9.20**

N = narrator, J = Jenny, L = Luke, R = Rob, La = Laing, T = Tom

N Day four. Four a.m. Jenny and Luke have gone back to Henry's house and are in his study. They are looking for a clue about an 'old man'… but time is running out.
J Keats, *The Iliad*, poems by Byron, *The Complete Works of Shakespeare*…nothing about an old man!
L Not even a picture on the front cover.
J What about those paintings? Anything there?
L I've already checked them. Nothing. Should we look through each book?
J That could take forever and we don't have time. This is hopeless. It's OK, it's Rob. Rob.
R Jenny. Any luck?
J No. We've been here for hours and we've looked everywhere. We haven't found a single thing about an old man. Look, Rob, maybe the *old man* thing wasn't a secret message at all.
R But it sounded so odd. And why would he mention his study?
J Well, he's under a lot of pressure. He probably just…
R Wait!
J What?
R Is there anything on top of the bookcase?
L Just a load of old books. We've already been through them.
R Isn't there anything else?
L Wait a second. Yeah, there are two small paperweights.
R Do they have anything written on them?
L This one says *Apollo, god of music and poetry*.
R What about the other one?
L It says *Proteus…the old man of the sea!*
R That must be what Dad meant!
J What does it mean? Who's Proteus?
L You know, that name sounds familiar.
R I think he's a Greek god. Dad's got loads of stuff like that.
L No, no, not that. I'm sure I've seen it somewhere. I'll google it.
J Does it mean anything to you, Rob?
R No. I can't remember hearing it before. Maybe it's someone's name, or…
L Got it! Proteus is a biochemical company. It's based in Oxford and…oh, I don't believe it!
J What is it, Luke?
L It's right by St Bartholomew's Church. You know, the one with the famous bells!
J That must be where Henry is! Rob, we've got to go call the police.
N Day four. Four fifteen a.m. Inspector Laing is on night duty at the police station. She's making a cup of tea when she receives a phone call.
La Laing speaking…Yes?…Oh, Jenny Zielinski…OK, slow down… Where? Proteus?…Yes, I know it…No, Jenny, you can't go down there…It's too dangerous…and it's illegal…I know, but…OK, OK, but not on your own…We'll meet you there in ten minutes.
N Day four. Five a.m. Jenny and Luke meet Inspector Laing outside the Proteus building. They are in her car, and she's in contact with two policemen by radio. They are going to the Proteus building. Luke is looking at the plans of the building on his laptop. Jenny tells her about Henry's message.
J It was night-time and we could hear a generator in the background.
La Right, so we're looking for a room with a generator. How are you doing, Luke?
L I'm just downloading the plans for the Proteus building now. That's it. Done. OK, there's only one room with a generator. It's in the basement.
La Excellent.

134 PE5

N	*The inspector radioes the two police officers who are just outside the Proteus building.*
La	Tom, where are you?
T	We're approaching the side entrance. There's nobody around.
La	OK, Tom. I'm going to hand you over to Luke. He's going to guide you to a room in the basement. That's where we think Henry's being held.
T	Got it.
La	Be careful.
T	Don't worry. Come on.

b Now focus on 1–8 and give Sts time to read them.

Play the video / audio again for Sts to watch or listen and complete the sentences with *Jenny*, *Luke*, or *Rob*.

Get Sts to compare with a partner, and then check answers.

1 Luke 2 Jenny 3 Rob 4 Luke 5 Luke 6 Jenny
7 Luke 8 Luke

Now focus on the last question and get Sts to speculate what (or who) they will find in the building.

EXTRA SUPPORT If there's time and you are using the video, you could get Sts to watch again with subtitles, so they can see exactly what they understood / didn't understand. Translate / Explain any new words or phrases.

2 ▶ GIVING DIRECTIONS IN A BUILDING

a 🔊 **9.21** Focus on the photos and ask Sts what they think is happening, and who the people are (*the two men in the second photo are policemen*).

Now tell Sts to focus on the plan of the building. Elicit / Explain the meaning of *basement* (= the level below the ground floor of a building). Make sure Sts can see where the police are (*Start*), and where they have to continue the route from. Check that Sts understand *corridor*, *ramp*, and *double doors*.

Play the video / audio once, pausing after each set of directions for Sts to mark the route. Tell Sts to mark the police officers' route as they follow the directions.

Get Sts to compare with a partner.

Play the video / audio again to check the answer.

They end up in C

🔊 **9.21**
N = narrator, L = Luke, T = Tom, La = Laing

N	*Day four. Five ten a.m. The policemen go into the Proteus building. Luke directs them from a police car outside. He's looking at the plans of the building on his screen.*
L	OK, go to the end of the corridor, go through the door, and turn right.
T	We're in a large, open area.
L	That's right. Now, go straight ahead. You should see some stairs on your right. Go past the stairs and a coffee bar. Turn right. Carry on and you should see a set of double doors.
T	Should we go through?
L	Yes. Now, you should see some stairs on your left.
T	Yeah, I see them.
L	Right. Go down the stairs, continue straight on, and walk down the ramp.
T	We're at the end of the ramp. Which way now?
L	Turn right and carry on straight along the corridor. Go past a maintenance room and two fuse boxes, and try the next door on your right.
T	The door's locked. Is there another way?
L	Hold on. OK. Turn round and go back down the corridor.
T	Should we go back up the ramp?
L	No. Go straight to the end of the corridor and turn left.
T	We're here. There are two doors. Which one should we take?
L	Try the one on your left.
T	It's open!
L	What can you see?
T	There are three big safes and cages full of documents. Are you sure this is the right way?
L	Yes, you're in the store room. Can you hear a generator?
T	Yes! It's coming from the end of the corridor.
L	Head towards it. But watch out for guards!
T	There's a door here and a narrow corridor to the right. What should we do?
L	I don't know!
T	Wait. I can hear voices. There are people in there.
La	That must be the room.
T	OK. We're going in.

b Give Sts time to read through the conversation and to think about what the missing words might be. Then play the video / audio again for Sts to watch or listen and complete the gaps.

Get Sts to compare with a partner, and then check answers.

1 through 2 right 3 straight 4 past 5 Carry 6 left
7 down 8 way 9 Turn 10 along 11 another 12 round
13 back 14 one 15 Try 16 right 17 towards

Deal with any new vocabulary in the conversation.

EXTRA SUPPORT If there's time and you are using the video, you could get Sts to watch again with subtitles, so they can see exactly what they understood / didn't understand. Translate / Explain any new words or phrases.

c 🔊 **9.22** Tell Sts to focus on the highlighted phrases in the conversation and to listen and repeat the phrases, copying the rhythm and intonation.

Play the video / audio, pausing for Sts to listen and repeat.

🔊 **9.22**
See highlighted phrases in Student's Book on p.95

Then repeat the activity, eliciting responses from individual Sts.

d Focus on the instructions. Put Sts in pairs, **A** and **B**, and tell them to practise giving directions in a building. Sts **A** choose a place on the plan and mark it with a cross. They then give directions to Sts **B** to get there. Sts **B** mark the route on the plan, checking that they understand the directions given by Sts **A**. Make sure they both start where the arrow is, and suggest that they choose a room in the basement, which means the first part of the directions will be as in the conversation. Finally, Sts **A** should check that Sts **B** have reached the correct place.

Monitor and help Sts to give directions.

Now Sts swap roles.

When they have finished, get feedback. How many were able to find the way?

EXTRA IDEA Get Sts to give each other directions from the classroom to a destination somewhere in the building you are currently in (if appropriate). In pairs, **A** writes a place, e.g. *the coffee machines* or *the student lounge*, but doesn't show it to **B** right away. Then **A** gives directions and **B** tries to work out the destination. When **B** guesses the place, **A** shows **B** the paper. Then they swap roles.

3 ▶ A HAPPY ENDING?

a 🔊 **9.23** Focus on the photos and the instructions. Elicit ideas on what the police found. Then elicit who each character is (*Jenny, Luke, Henry, Rob, Grant, Selina, Andrew*) and ask Sts what they think happened to them.

Play the video / audio once the whole way through. Note that the video shows the arrest of Selina Lavelle – this scene is not included in the audio.

Find out how many Sts guessed correctly.

🔊 **9.23**

N = narrator, Ne = newsreader, J = Jenny, H = Henry, R = Rob, L = Luke

N *Day four. Five p.m. Henry is finally back at home with Jenny and Luke. They're talking to a relieved Rob on Skype and listening to a radio news report about the kidnapping.*

Ne Police have arrested a man and a woman following a raid on the Proteus building in Oxford early this morning. They have been named locally as Selina Lavelle and Grant McFadden. Mr McFadden has been charged with assault following the brutal attack on research scientist Andrew Page, who is still recovering in hospital. Ms Lavelle has been charged with false imprisonment, extortion, blackmail, and industrial espionage. Police believe she organized the kidnapping of university lecturer Henry Walker. Mr Walker, who was rescued in the raid, told reporters he'd been through a terrible ordeal, but hadn't been badly hurt. He wished Andrew Page a speedy recovery and said he would visit him in hospital. Mr Walker thanked the police for their hard work. He said that he was too tired to talk to reporters in detail and was just looking forward to returning home.

J Well, Henry, you're kind of a star.
H I never expected to become a celebrity – not at my age.
R Well, next time you're kidnapped, Dad, try to set us an easier clue.
H I must admit I was beginning to lose hope. It took you a long time to work it out.
R You can't blame us! Proteus – the 'old man' of the sea? How were we supposed to know that?
H You need to brush up on your classics.
L Oh, come on, Henry, I think we did really well!
H I'm joking, I'm joking. You were great. And I really have to thank you. Goodness knows what would have happened if you hadn't found me in time.
J We're just glad we did.
N *Henry puts a bottle of champagne on the table.*
H Now, I had been saving this for a special occasion, and I think this is it. Could you fetch the glasses, Luke?
L No worries.
R It's great to have you back, Dad.
J It sure is.
H I just wish you were here, Rob.
R Well, it's just stopped snowing. I could get a flight now, and maybe we could stay there for longer. What do you think, Jenny?
J Oh, I don't know. The English countryside is a little too wild for me. I can't wait to get back to the peace and quiet of New York!

---

b Focus on sentences 1–7. Go through them with Sts, making sure they understand them.

Now play the video / audio again the whole way through, and get Sts to mark the sentences *T* (true) or *F* (false). Remind them to correct the false sentences.

Get Sts to compare with a partner, and then check answers.

Point out that Jenny is being ironic when she says *the peace and quiet of New York*, a place that's often associated with excitement and plenty of noise.

1 T
2 F (They have been arrested.)
3 T
4 T
5 F (They celebrate with champagne at Henry's house, and Rob, who is still in Alaska, joins them via Skype.)
6 T
7 F (She can't wait to get back to New York.)

EXTRA SUPPORT If there's time and you are using the video, you could get Sts to watch again with subtitles, so they can see exactly what they understood / didn't understand. Translate / Explain any new words or phrases.

c Focus on the **Social English** phrases. In pairs, get Sts to see if they can remember any of the missing words.

EXTRA CHALLENGE In pairs, get Sts to complete the phrases before they listen.

d 🔊 **9.24** Play the video / audio for Sts to watch or listen and complete the phrases.

Check answers. If you know your Sts' L1, you could get them to translate the phrases.

1 admit 2 knows 3 fetch 4 great 5 wish 6 wait

🔊 **9.24**

1 I must admit I was beginning to lose hope.
2 Goodness knows what would have happened if you hadn't found me in time.
3 Could you fetch the glasses, Luke?
4 It's great to have you back, Dad.
5 I just wish you were here, Rob.
6 I can't wait to get back to the peace and quiet of New York!

Now play the video / audio again, pausing after each phrase for Sts to watch or listen and repeat.

e Focus on the instructions and make sure Sts understand what they have to do.

Get Sts to compare with a partner, and then check answers.

A 3 B 2 C 1 D 4 E 6 F 5

Now put Sts in pairs and get them to practise the conversations.

Finally, focus on the **CAN YOU…?** questions and ask Sts if they feel confident they can now do these things. If they feel that they need more practice, tell them to go to *Online Practice* to watch the episode again and practise the language.

10A The land of the free?

G *be*, *do*, and *have*: auxiliary and main verbs
V British and American English
P stress on *be*, *do*, and *have*

Lesson plan

Aspects of the USA and its relationship to other countries provide the context for Sts to revise *be*, *do*, and *have* as auxiliaries and main verbs. The lesson begins with a quiz on facts about the USA, which leads into the grammar focus. Next, a pronunciation activity focuses on when *be*, *do*, and *have* are stressed in a sentence, and this is practised with more quiz questions. Sts then listen to six people talking about life in New York. The first half ends with Sts looking at the term 'Americanization' and discussing their views on American culture, whether any aspects of their culture have been influenced by the USA, and whether any aspects of their own culture have had an influence in the world.

The second half of the lesson begins with a vocabulary focus on British and American English words and phrases. This is followed by a humorous blog where a British woman writes about things the Americans do that irritate the British, and an American woman writes about things the British do that annoy Americans.

More materials

For teachers
Photocopiables
Grammar *be*, *do*, and *have*: auxiliary and main verbs *p.170*
Communicative What's the question? *p.200*
(instructions *p.177*)

For students
Workbook 10A
Online Practice 10A

OPTIONAL LEAD-IN (BOOKS CLOSED)
Write THE USA on the board and ask Sts to write on a piece of paper the first three things that come to mind when they hear the phrase, e.g. *Hollywood*, *skyscrapers*, the name of the current president, etc.

Write their ideas on the board.

1 GRAMMAR *be*, *do*, and *have*: auxiliary and main verbs

a Books open. Focus on the instructions and the quiz, and give Sts time to read statements 1–10.

Now put Sts in pairs and get them to mark each statement *T* (true) or *F* (false).

Get some feedback, eliciting reasons from Sts, but <u>don't</u> tell them if they are correct.

b 🔊 10.1 Play the audio for Sts to listen and check, and tell them to correct the false statements.

Get Sts to compare with a partner, and play the audio again if necessary.

Check answers.

EXTRA CHALLENGE Get Sts to write any extra facts that they hear.

1 T
2 F (*Colour* is spelled without a *u* and *centre* is spelled *-ter*.)
3 F (According to a recent survey, the figure is about 40%.)
4 F (According to a recent survey, 77% of American men do no housework on any given day.)
5 F (The world's first skyscraper was in Chicago.)
6 T
7 F (There has never been an official language of the United States.)
8 T
9 F (The USA has always had the world's biggest economy.)
10 T

🔊 10.1
1 True. The USA has around six hundred billionaires. China has the second highest number, and Germany is third.
2 False. *Colour* is spelled without a *u* and *centre* is spelled *-ter*. About two hundred common words are spelled differently in British and American English.
3 False. According to a recent survey, the figure is about forty per cent.
4 False. According to a recent survey, seventy-seven per cent of American men do no housework on any given day.
5 False. The world's first skyscraper was in Chicago. It was finished in eighteen eighty-five, had ten floors, and was forty-two metres high.
6 True. Despite the rise of online dating, about fifty per cent of adult Americans are now single.
7 False. There has never been an official language of the United States. However, the most commonly spoken language is American English. Spanish is the second most common language in the USA.
8 True. Texas joined the USA in eighteen forty-five, but left again in eighteen sixty-one, during the American Civil War. It re-joined the USA when the war had ended, in eighteen sixty-five.
9 False. The USA has been the world's biggest economy since records began.
10 True. The name *soccer* was first used in the nineteenth century in British public schools, but when the sport started to be played by everyone, the name *football* took over. American football is a completely different sport.

c Focus on the instructions. Elicit that *be*, *do*, and *have* are sometimes main verbs and sometimes auxiliary verbs. Remind Sts that an auxiliary is a verb used to form a tense or questions and negatives. Unlike main verbs, auxiliaries don't have a separate meaning.

Get Sts, in pairs, to look at all the **bold** verbs in 1–10 in **a** and circle the ones that are auxiliaries.

Check answers.

2 are   3 don't   7 has   8 didn't   9 was   10 is, had, been

EXTRA SUPPORT You could do the first two sentences with the class to make sure Sts are clear about the difference between a main verb and an auxiliary verb.

d Tell Sts to go to **Grammar Bank 10A** on *p.150*.

Grammar notes

Many Sts have problems first of all in using the correct auxiliary verb, and secondly in distinguishing between when *be*, *do*, and *have* are main verbs. This difference is important, as it can affect both the form (e.g. *haven't* and *hadn't* are the negatives of *have* as an auxiliary verb; *don't have* and *didn't have* are the negatives of *have* as a main verb), and the pronunciation (main verbs are usually stressed, auxiliaries usually unstressed). Identifying and using the correct auxiliary is also vital as auxiliaries are used in so many structures, e.g. short answers, *So do I*, question tags, etc. *Have* and *be* as main verbs are also often confused by Sts who express certain concepts in their L1 with *have* where English uses *be*, e.g. age, feelings like hunger, cold, etc.

Focus on the example sentences for **be – main verb and auxiliary** and play audio 🔊 **10.2** for Sts to listen and repeat. Encourage them to copy the rhythm. Then go through the rules with the class.

Repeat for **do – main verb and auxiliary** 🔊 **10.3** and **have – main verb and auxiliary** 🔊 **10.4**.

Now focus on the exercises and get Sts to do them individually or in pairs. Encourage them to use contracted forms rather than full forms.

Check answers, getting Sts to read the full sentences.

a
1 A **Have** you ever been to the USA?
  B No, my husband **doesn't** like flying.
2 A **Did** you miss the beginning of the film?
  B No, luckily it **hadn't** started yet.
3 **Does** he know we**'re** coming, or do we need to give him a ring?
4 I'm sorry I **didn't** answer the phone when you called, but I **was** having a meeting.
5 We **don't** often travel outside Europe, but we**'ve** been to Chile twice.
6 He**'d** been working since 7.00 this morning, but now he**'s** gone home.
7 A Where**'s** Melanie going on holiday this year?
  B Rome, I think. She**'s** never been there before.
8 They're in New York, but they **don't** have much time for sightseeing – they**'re** only staying for two days.

b
1 I would have finished the exercise if I**'d had** more time.
2 She **hasn't been** to Africa before, so she's really looking forward to our trip to Namibia.
3 I **had** steak for lunch and it was delicious.
4 Nothing **is being done** at the moment to solve the problem.
5 Where **were** you at 10 o'clock this morning?
6 I **was having** a shower when the hot water stopped working!
7 I **would have been** really annoyed if you'd repeated what I told you.
8 The reception was a great success, and a good time **was had** by all.
9 I**'ll do** the washing-up as soon as I finish my homework.

Tell Sts to go back to the main lesson **10A**.

EXTRA SUPPORT If you think Sts need more practice, you may want to give them the **Grammar** photocopiable activity at this point.

2 PRONUNCIATION stress on *be*, *do*, and *have*

Pronunciation notes

This focus looks at the way the verbs *be*, *do*, and *have* are stressed or unstressed in sentences depending on whether they are main verbs or auxiliary verbs, and positive or negative. After Sts have listened to and practised the examples, they then work out the rules. One of the effects of the stress is that the vowel sound changes. Sts also practise saying these verbs with the /ə/ sound when they are unstressed.

a 🔊 **10.5** Focus on the sentences and play the audio, pausing after each one for Sts to listen and repeat, copying the rhythm. Tell them to underline the highlighted word if it is stressed.

Check answers. You could get Sts to listen again and repeat.

1 The capital of the USA is Washington, DC.
2 When are your friends arriving?
3 The world's tallest skyscraper isn't in New York.
4 Anne does Pilates twice a week.
5 Where does your sister live?
6 My brother doesn't like dogs.
7 I have a house in New Jersey.
8 How long have you known your best friend?
9 We haven't seen our cousins for ages.

🔊 **10.5**
See sentences in Student's Book on *p.96*

EXTRA SUPPORT Play the audio for Sts just to listen and read. Then play it again and get Sts to underline the highlighted words if they are stressed. Check answers. Finally, play the audio again for Sts to listen and repeat.

b Play the audio again, this time getting Sts to focus on the vowel sounds in the highlighted words that are unstressed (i.e. in sentences 2, 5, and 8). Or you could read sentences 2, 5, and 8 to the class.
Check the answer.

When *are*, *does*, and *have* are unstressed, the vowel sound is /ə/:
are = /ə/   does = /dəz/   have = /əv/

EXTRA CHALLENGE You may also want to elicit what the vowel sound is when these verbs are stressed: *are* = /ɑː/, *do* = /duː/, *does* = /dʌz/, and *have* = /hæv/.

c Give Sts time to read the rules and complete them, checking each time with 1–9 in **a**.
Check answers.

1 unstressed 2 stressed 3 stressed 4 unstressed
5 stressed

d Put Sts in pairs, **A** and **B**, and tell them to go to **Communication More facts about the USA?**, **A** on *p.110*, **B** on *p.114*.

Go through the instructions, making sure Sts understand what they have to do. You could demonstrate the activity by doing statement 1 for Sts **A** and statement 6 for Sts **B** with the whole class.

Sts take it in turns to read their statements to their partner. Remind them to give their partner the explanation of why a sentence is false.

Monitor and make sure they are using the correct rhythm and sentence stress.

Get feedback to find out who got the most correct answers in each pair.

EXTRA SUPPORT Tell Sts to look carefully at the sentences they are going to read and underline the stressed words to help them get the correct rhythm.

Tell Sts to go back to the main lesson **10A**.

3 LISTENING understanding examples – note-taking

a 🔊 10.6 Tell Sts they are going to listen to six people – four foreigners and two Americans – who live in New York, talking about life there. They must match each speaker to a topic in the list and decide which speakers are negative. First, focus on the words in the list and make sure Sts understand them all. Model and drill pronunciation, especially *bureaucracy* /bjʊəˈrɒkrəsi/, *gun culture* /ˈɡʌn kʌltʃə/, and *multiculturalism* /mʌltiˈkʌltʃərəlɪzəm/.

Tell Sts that the speakers all have different accents.

Play the audio once the whole way through for Sts to listen and complete the task.

Check answers.

EXTRA SUPPORT Read through the script and decide if you need to pre-teach any new lexis before Sts listen.

Speaker 1 multiculturalism **Speaker 2** sport
Speaker 3 bureaucracy **Speaker 4** helpfulness
Speaker 5 opportunity **Speaker 6** gun culture
Speakers 2 (Cristina) and 6 (Sarah) are negative.

🔊 10.6
(script in Student's Book on *p.131*)
1 Yannis
Um, so I've lived in New York for, uh, twelve years now, and one thing that I think I will always appreciate is the diversity of the place and the people. And every time I go away, it's so nice to come back here and…and be on the subway and see all the different faces and hear different accents. Erm, and, you know, my English is pretty good, but I have never felt judged here, you know, for having a foreign accent, and nobody is surprised, you know, if you have a strange surname, um, or if you sound different. I have never felt that. And I could say that sometimes in Europe, I did, so… This is one thing that I will always appreciate about living here.
2 Cristina
Um, one thing that, um, I don't particularly like here is the culture around American football. And maybe this has something to do with me being European and liking, uh, European football – or soccer – um, more than American football. And I did try, um, but I think, uh, the game is way too complicated – though I tried to understand the rules. And I find the atmosphere around American football, I…I just…I find it a bit too aggressive? For example, recently the Philadelphia Eagles won the Super Bowl and, um, the celebrations, so to speak, if we can call them celebrations, were more like riots.
3 Louisa
I know from having travelled a lot and having lived overseas, having an Italian husband, it's very complicated to get sort of bureaucratic tasks done in places like Italy. So I think the one thing that I like most about living in the United States is that things are pretty easy to do, and even living in a big city, it's, um, it's easy to get things done.

So it's pretty easy to, you know, change your phone company, and it's easy to renew your driver's licence.
4 Laura
Um, something that I like about America is that I find people are very keen to help, even without being asked. 'cause I lived in Germany for four years and I remember every time I flew there, at the airport, I would always really struggle to get my bag off the luggage carousel and no one would ever help me. And every time I flew back home to the US, immediately someone would come over and offer to help. And I've noticed the same thing with opening doors, with helping people carry things up the stairs in the subway.
5 Peter
Something I really like about America is the sense of opportunity here. Um, I feel like, as a new immigrant, I've been able to come into the country and get jobs that I couldn't get back home in the UK because I don't think I would have had the same opportunities there. I think that you can move here and make something of yourself very quickly, and I really like the sort of entrepreneurial spirit there is here – um, the feeling that if you have a good idea and you work hard, you can be successful. I think it really is the land of opportunity, and I really like that.
6 Sarah
I've lived in the US for three years, and something that I really dislike about American culture has to be the fascination with guns. Er, growing up in the UK – growing up in Europe – I've never seen people really want to own guns themselves. For me, it's up to the police to take care of people and to make sure everyone's safe. I can't understand why a civilian would want to own their own gun and keep it in their house. For me, that means that the country is less safe, not more safe, so that's something I don't think I'll ever be able to understand.

b Tell Sts they are going to listen again and this time they must complete the notes for each speaker. Give Sts time to read the notes.

Now play the audio again, pausing after each speaker to give Sts time to write.

Get Sts to compare with a partner, and then play again if necessary.

Check answers.

---

1 faces, accents, strange surname
2 complicated, rules, aggressive
3 phone company, driver's licence
4 bag, luggage carousel, open doors, subway
5 get jobs, spirit
6 own guns, take care, safe

EXTRA SUPPORT If there's time, you could get Sts to listen again with the script on *p.131*, so they can see exactly what they understood / didn't understand. Translate / Explain any new words or phrases.

c Do this as a whole-class activity, or put Sts in pairs and then get some feedback.

4 SPEAKING

a Focus on the book cover and either read it as a class, making sure Sts understand all the lexis, or give Sts time to read it individually.

Now focus on the questions and check the answer to the first question. Then elicit opinions to the second.

Americanization is the process of making something American in character.

---

b Focus on the photos, question, and topics. Point out the example.

Now put Sts in pairs to discuss the question.
Get some feedback from various pairs.

EXTRA SUPPORT If all your Sts are from the same country, you could do this as a whole-class activity.

c Focus on the instructions and give Sts time to think. You could demonstrate the activity by choosing one of the topics yourself and telling the class of examples in your country, and whether you prefer the American version or the one from your country. Then say whether your preference is also that of the people from your country.
Put Sts in pairs or small groups to discuss the topics.
Get some feedback from various pairs or groups.

d Do this as a whole-class activity, or put Sts in pairs and then get some feedback.

5 VOCABULARY British and American English

> **Vocabulary notes**
>
> All the American words in **a** have come up previously in *English File*, so Sts should recognize them.
>
> In **c** you may want to point out that *stingy* is also used in British English with the same meaning; however, Americans would never use *mean* as the opposite of *generous*. In US English, *mean* = likely to become angry or violent. They also sometimes use *cheap* as an alternative to *stingy*.
>
> You may also want to point out that *yard* also exists in British English, but means an area outside a building with a hard surface (not grass), e.g. *a prison yard*.

a Focus on the instructions. Put Sts in pairs or small groups and tell them to see how many British English words they know with the same meanings.

EXTRA SUPPORT You could do one or two words with the class.

b ◆)) **10.7** Play the audio for Sts to listen and check. Point out that one speaker is American, the other British.
Check answers.

| 1 mobile phone | 2 toilet | 3 cinema | 4 secondary school |
| 5 rubbish | 6 trainers | 7 lift | 8 flat | 9 postcode | 10 bill |

◆)) **10.7**
1 cell phone   mobile phone
2 restroom   toilet
3 movie theater   cinema
4 high school   secondary school
5 garbage   rubbish
6 sneakers   trainers
7 elevator   lift
8 apartment   flat
9 zip code   postcode
10 check   bill

Play the audio again, pausing after each word or phrase for Sts to listen and repeat. They will probably enjoy copying the two different accents.

c Now get Sts to match some more British English words to the American English equivalents.

d ◆)) **10.8** Play the audio for Sts to listen and check.
Check answers.

◆)) **10.8**
1 e   car park   parking lot
2 h   mean   stingy
3 d   autumn   fall
4 f   petrol   gas
5 b   queue   stand in line
6 j   garden   yard
7 a   wardrobe   closet
8 i   pavement   sidewalk
9 g   lorry   truck
10 c   tap   faucet

Then play the audio again, pausing after each word or phrase for Sts to listen and repeat.

e Focus on the instructions and make sure Sts understand what they have to do.
Give Sts time to write *Am* or *Br* next to each picture or definition. They could work individually or in pairs.
Check answers.

| 1 **a** Am **b** Br |
| 2 **a** Br **b** Am |
| 3 **a** Am **b** Br |
| 4 **a** Am **b** Br |
| 5 **a** Br **b** Am |

f ◆)) **10.9** Focus on the task and tell Sts they are going to hear five speakers saying one sentence or question. They must decide which nationality the speaker is and then 'translate' it into the other language.
Play the audio, pausing after each speaker to give Sts time to write.
Get Sts to compare with a partner, and then play the audio again if necessary.
Check answers.

1 The speaker is American.
  Excuse me, can you tell me the way to the underground?
2 The speaker is American.
  I'm so excited – we're going to Paris in the autumn.
3 The speaker is British.
  There were so many people in town today. I had to stand in line for ages at the post office.
4 The speaker is British.
  I only live on the second floor, but I always take the elevator.
5 The speaker is American.
  That brown shirt doesn't go with those blue trousers.

◆)) **10.9**
1 Excuse me, can you tell me the way to the subway?
2 I'm so excited – we're going to Paris in the fall.
3 There were so many people in town today. I had to queue for ages at the post office.
4 I only live on the first floor, but I always take the lift.
5 That brown shirt doesn't go with those blue pants.

EXTRA IDEA You could ask Sts if they know any other words that are American English. If Sts can't think of any words or phrases, you could give them some ideas, e.g. *What's 'vacation' in British English?* (holiday).

Elicit some answers and write them on the board. Try to get at least four or five.

Possible answers

American	British
drugstore / pharmacy	chemist's
store	shop
candy	sweets
cookie	biscuit
fries	chips

Finally, you could ask Sts whether they think people from their country would be more likely to recognize the American or the British word, and why.

6 READING working out vocabulary from context

a Focus on the instructions and get Sts to read the title and introduction of each blog. Elicit / Explain that *Brits* is an informal way of referring to British people.

Check answers. Ask Sts why they answered as they did.

> Ruth Margolis (writer of the first blog) is British because she's talking about what annoys her about Americans.
> Maria Roth (writer of the second blog) is American as she is talking about what annoys her about the Brits.

EXTRA SUPPORT Read the introduction to *Six things Americans do that drive Brits crazy* as a class and check that Sts understand *eccentric* /ɪkˈsentrɪk/ (= considered by other people to be strange or unusual).
Now read the introduction to *Six things Brits do that drive Americans crazy* as a class and check that Sts understand *charming* (= very pleasant or attractive) and *smart* here (= intelligent).

b Focus on the task and headings A–I, making sure Sts understand all the lexis.

Give Sts time to read the blogs and complete the gaps with the headings. Remind them that there is one extra heading.

Get Sts to compare with a partner, and then check answers.

EXTRA SUPPORT Before Sts read the blogs the first time, check whether you need to pre-teach any vocabulary, but <u>not</u> the highlighted words.

Six things Americans do that drive Brits crazy
2 G   3 I   5 F   6 C
Six things Brits do that drive Americans crazy
1 A   3 H   4 D   6 B

c Focus on the instructions and tell Sts to read the two blogs again. Each time they come across a highlighted word, they should decide if it is an adjective, noun, or verb. Then they should look at definitions 1–8 and match the highlighted word to the correct definition. Highlight that in point 5 of the second blog, *share* means 'communicate / share emotions, thoughts, and feelings'. This is a common use of *share* in American English.

Get Sts to compare with a partner.

d 🔊 **10.10** Play the audio for Sts to listen and check. Check answers.

🔊 **10.10**
1 awesome
2 creepy
3 reserved
4 weird
5 turkey
6 compliment
7 get
8 nod

Model and drill pronunciation where necessary. You could use the audio to do this.

Deal with any other new vocabulary. Model and drill the pronunciation of any tricky words.

e You could do this in pairs, small groups, or as a whole-class activity.

Get some feedback.

EXTRA IDEA You could also ask Sts if there are any other things that annoy them about Americans or the British.

10A 141

10B Please turn over your papers

G revision of verb forms
V exams
P revision of sounds

Lesson plan

The topic of this final lesson is exams, and one of its aims is to help prepare Sts for their end-of-course English exam. The lesson begins with a vocabulary focus on words and phrases connected with exams. This is followed by Pronunciation, where Sts revise several of the sounds that they have practised previously. Sts then read a short paragraph about exams in England before listening to four people talking about exams and tests, and getting further practice of multiple-choice questions. This leads into Sts talking about their own experience of exams. Finally, Sts do a writing exam task.

In the second half of the lesson, Sts read about and discuss the *gaokao*, an extremely demanding university entrance exam in China. This is followed by a grammar focus in which Sts revise all the verb forms they have learned up until now. This grammar focus only has practice exercises, not rules, as the rules have already been covered. The lesson ends with a video giving advice about taking oral exams, and Sts then do an authentic oral exam task in pairs.

More materials
For teachers
Photocopiables
Grammar revision of verb forms *p.171*
Communicative Speaking exam *p.201* (instructions *p.178*)
Teacher's Resource Centre
Video Speaking exams – top tips for success
For students
Workbook 10B
Online Practice 10B

OPTIONAL LEAD-IN (BOOKS CLOSED)
Write on the board:
EXAM

Ask Sts how they feel when they see this word. Do they know what it's short for? (*examination*) How is an exam different from a test? What kind of exams do people take in their country? What are the most important ones? What is the most important exam they've had to do in their life?
Now also write on the board:
DON'T CRAM FOR AN EXAM.
Elicit the meaning of *cram* (= to learn a lot of things in a short time, in preparation for an exam). Then ask *Have you ever done this?* Ask if they think it's good advice.

1 VOCABULARY exams

Vocabulary notes
You may want to point out in **b** that we can also say *to sit an exam* as an alternative to *do / take*.

a Books open. Focus on the instructions and the photo. You could do this as a whole-class activity, or put Sts in pairs and then get some feedback. You may want to teach Sts that a person who supervises an exam is called *an invigilator*.

Possible answers
The people in the photo are students. They look like older secondary or university students, so they are probably in their late teens or early twenties.
They are in a hall probably in a school or university building. They are taking an exam.
They are possibly nervous or they might be feeling confident if they know how to answer the questions.
There are probably some teachers in the room to check that nobody is cheating.

b Focus on the mind map and tell Sts to complete it with the words and phrases in the list.
Get Sts to compare with a partner.

c 🔊 10.11 Play the audio for Sts to listen and check.
Check answers, making sure Sts understand all the words.

🔊 **10.11**
Verbs
1 cheat
2 do
3 fail
4 pass
5 retake
6 revise
7 take
Types of exams
8 oral or speaking
9 practical
10 written
Types of questions
11 essay
12 multiple-choice
13 true or false

EXTRA SUPPORT Play the audio again to drill the pronunciation of the words, or model and drill them yourself. Give further practice of any words your Sts find difficult to pronounce.

d Put Sts in pairs, **A** and **B**. Tell them to go to **Communication Describing a photo**, **A** on *p.109* and **B** on *p.111*.

Focus on the instructions. Sts **A** should start by describing their photo. Then they swap roles.

In their pairs, Sts then decide what the photos have in common (*They both show students cheating in an exam*).

Finally, in their pairs, Sts discuss the four questions in **c**.
Get some feedback from various pairs.

Tell Sts to go back to the main lesson **10B**.

EXTRA SUPPORT Before they start, get Sts to revise language for describing a photo in **Vocabulary Bank Photography** on *p.155*.

2 PRONUNCIATION revision of sounds

> **Pronunciation notes**
> This final exercise brings together some of the common consonant and vowel sounds that have come up at this level and that frequently cause difficulties for learners from many different L1 backgrounds.

a Focus Sts' attention on the groups of words. Check that they understand all of the words, then tell them to focus on the sound picture and the pink letters in the words. Explain that in each group of three words, the pink letters in one word are pronounced differently.

Give Sts time to find the odd one out, encouraging them to say the words aloud. They could work individually and check with a partner, or work in pairs.

b ◐ 10.12 Play the audio once for Sts to listen and check. Play it again, pausing after each group of words to check the answers.

> 1 revises (-*es* = /ɪz/, the other two are /z/)
> 2 cheated (-*ed* = /ɪd/, the other two are /d/)
> 3 exam (*a* = /æ/, the other two are /ɑː/)
> 4 work (*or* = /ɜː/, the other two are /ɔː/)
> 5 professor (*o* = /ə/, the other two are /ɒ/)
> 6 essay (*e* = /e/, the other two are /iː/)
> 7 school (*oo* = /uː/, the other two are /ʊ/)
> 8 idea (*i* = /aɪ/, the other two are /ɪ/)
> 9 result (*e* = /ɪ/, the other two are /e/)

◐ 10.12
See words in Student's Book on *p.100*

c Focus attention on sentences 1–7 and the pink letters. Put Sts in pairs and tell them to decide what sound the pink letters have. Remind them that this kind of activity is easier if they say the words aloud.

Check answers.

> 1 good (*oo* = /ʊ/), school (*oo* = /uː/)
> 2 answered (*a* = /ɑː/), exam (*a* = /æ/)
> 3 report (*or* = /ɔː/), worked (*or* = /ɜː/)
> 4 practise (*i* = /ɪ/), written (*i* = /ɪ/)
> 5 cheated (-*ed* = /ɪd/), failed (-*ed* = /d/)
> 6 professor (*o* = /ə/), college (*o* = /ɒ/)
> 7 test (*e* = /e/), result (*e* = /ɪ/)

Now get Sts, in pairs, to practise saying the sentences.

EXTRA SUPPORT Model and drill each sentence before putting Sts in pairs to practise saying them.

3 LISTENING & SPEAKING exam skill – multiple-choice listening

a Focus on the instructions and the photo, and ask Sts how they think the girl is feeling and why.

Put Sts in pairs and get them to take it in turns to talk about the last time they took an exam or test.

Get some feedback from various pairs. You could tell the class about the last exam or test you took.

b Ask the class what they know about exams that Sts take at school in England.

Now tell Sts to read the text about exams in England. Deal with any new vocabulary and ask a few questions to check comprehension, e.g. *What exam do some students take when they're eleven years old? At what age do students normally take GCSEs? What were O levels? Which exams are important for admission to university?*

You may want to point out that *A levels* = Advanced levels, *O levels* = Ordinary levels, and *GCSE* = General Certificate of Secondary Education. Also point out that the system is different in Scotland, where they do exams called *Highers* instead of *A levels*.

Then find out what exams Sts do at school in their own country. If your Sts come from different countries, give them time to think, and then put them in pairs or small groups to tell each other about the exam system in their country. Then get feedback from various pairs or groups.

c ◐ 10.13 Tell Sts they are going to listen to four people talking about exams or tests they have taken. Focus on the two questions.

Play the audio once the whole way through for Sts to listen and answer the questions.

Get Sts to compare with a partner, and then check answers.

EXTRA SUPPORT Read through the script and decide if you need to pre-teach any new lexis before Sts listen.

> Speakers 1 (Mark), 2 (Sophie), and 4 (Paul) failed an exam or test.
> Speaker 2 (Sophie) used to find exams stressful.

◐ 10.13
(script in Student's Book on *p.131*)
I = interviewer, M = Mark, S = Sophie, D = Diane, P = Paul
1 Mark
I What's the hardest exam or test you've ever taken?
M My A level physics exam – I didn't understand at least half the questions.
I Have you ever done an exam where everything went wrong?
M I'm afraid so. For a history O level, there were five questions – all short essays. I'd prepared five questions from previous exam papers, but nothing else. So I was gambling that at least three of the questions would come up. But none of them did, so obviously I failed it.
I How did you usually prepare for a big exam?
M I remember it generally involved a lot of coffee and late nights!
I Did you find exams stressful?
M No, I never got that stressed about exams, but that may have had a negative effect on the results, come to think of it. I was never the world's best at exams. I usually passed, but the results were never brilliant.

2 Sophie
I What's the hardest exam or test you've ever taken?
S I think the hardest was probably my driving test – the practical part. I got so nervous each time I just couldn't drive. In fact, I failed three times before I finally passed.
I Have you ever done an exam where everything went wrong?
S Yes, in the beginning of my first driving test, I refused to stop where the examiner asked me to stop. I just didn't think it looked safe and I thought it was a trick – I mean, I thought that he was asking me to do something dangerous, to test me. Anyway, it wasn't a trick and he wasn't happy at all.
I How did you usually prepare for a big exam?
S I used to spend a lot of time writing notes; I probably spent more time making them look nice, using different coloured pens and so on, than I did actually learning the information. But I found it really helpful to stick the notes up as posters all over the house so that I could see them every day.

I Did exams use to stress you out?
S Yes. I hated exams and used to get very nervous and stressed beforehand. But once the exam had started, I usually relaxed.

3 Diane
I What's the hardest exam or test you've ever taken?
D I think it has to be the eleven plus because that was the first time I had ever felt any pressure to succeed.
I How did you do?
D I passed it.
I Have you ever done an exam where everything went wrong?
D Yes, my A level French oral exam went horribly wrong. Some friends had said, 'Whatever you do, don't say that you've been to France, otherwise they'll expect your French to be quite good'. And so what happened was I got in there and the examiner said, 'Have you ever been to France?' in French, and I said *Non*, and then I started talking about driving to Gibraltar with my parents. And then the examiner said, 'Well, how did you manage to drive from the UK to Gibraltar without driving through France?', at which point I just completely froze and couldn't say anything else at all! But I guess I'd spoken enough previously, so I passed.
I How did you usually prepare for a big exam?
D Well, for literature exams, I used to memorize loads and loads of famous passages from the books we were studying, so I could put them in my answers, and that seemed to work because I passed.
I How did you usually feel about doing exams?
D Not great, but I was usually reasonably confident, I'd say.

4 Paul
I What's the hardest exam or test you've ever taken?
P Probably the exam at the end of the first year of my geography course at university. Not because the questions were very difficult, but because I'd done so little work for it.
I Have you ever done an exam where everything went wrong?
P Oh yes. I thought I'd done quite well in my GCSE chemistry exam, but I failed it. So something must have gone very wrong.
I How did you usually prepare for a big exam?
P I used to read notes over and over again, right up till the last possible minute. Yeah, I relied heavily on short-term memory, I think.
I Did exams use to stress you out?
P Not really, though they probably would now. When I was at school and university, it was just part of life – so not particularly stressful.

d Elicit from Sts what they think the best technique is for multiple-choice listening activities. Then focus on the **TIP: Multiple-choice listening** box and go through it with the class.

Give Sts time to read the four multiple-choice questions.

Play the audio again for Sts to listen and choose the correct answers. You could pause it after each speaker to give Sts time to complete the task.

Check answers.

1 b 2 a 3 b 4 c

EXTRA SUPPORT If there's time, you could get Sts to listen again with the script on *p.131*, so they can see exactly what they understood / didn't understand. Translate / Explain any new words or phrases.

e Focus on the task and point out the two categories and the last question, which is for both options.

Put Sts in pairs and get them to ask and answer the questions from the relevant section, giving as much information as possible.

When Sts have finished interviewing each other, they should discuss the final question. Remind them to use some of the expressions for agreeing and disagreeing which they saw in Lesson **9B**.

Monitor and help with vocabulary.

Get some feedback from various pairs and elicit opinions on the last question. You could also have a class vote regarding whether exams are a good way of testing. You might want to introduce the term *continuous assessment* (= a system of giving a student a final mark / grade based on work done during a course of study rather than on one exam).

EXTRA SUPPORT Write on the board some of the expressions for agreeing and disagreeing in **9B**.

4 WRITING an exam task

Tell Sts to go to **Writing An exam task** on *p.123*.

a Focus on the instructions and give Sts time to read the essay topic and the student essay. If you didn't do it in the previous activity, elicit / explain that *continuous assessment* is a system of giving a student a final grade based on the work the student has done during the course, rather than testing what they know in one exam. Tell Sts not to worry about the gaps.

Check the answer.

The writer disagrees with the statement.

b Tell Sts to read the essay again and write each paragraph number next to the correct description.

Get Sts to compare with a partner, and then check answers.

In paragraph 1 the writer gives an introduction to the topic.
In paragraph 2 the writer gives his / her opinion and three reasons for it.
In paragraph 3 the writer gives a contrasting opinion.
In paragraph 4 the writer gives a summary of his / her opinion.

c Focus on the instructions and the connecting words or phrases in the list.

Give Sts time to read the essay again and complete the gaps.

Get Sts to compare with a partner, and then check answers.

1 because 2 when 3 so 4 instead of 5 but
6 although

d Focus on the **Useful language: essays** box and go through it with the class.

Now tell Sts they are going to write an essay for an exam using the topic *It is not a good idea to cram the evening before an exam*. If you didn't do the **Optional lead-in**, elicit / explain the meaning of *cram* (= to learn a lot of things in a short time, in preparation for an exam).

Tell Sts first to decide whether they agree or disagree with the statement and then plan their essay. They should write four paragraphs as in the model.

e It would be a good idea to get Sts to do the writing in class as practice for writing an essay in exam conditions, but if time is short, set it as homework. If you do it in class, set a time limit for Sts to write their essay which reflects the time they would have in their exam.

f Remind Sts to check their essay for mistakes before giving it in.

Tell Sts to go back to the main lesson **10B**.

5 READING exam skill – T / F reading

a Ask the questions to the whole class and elicit some opinions. If any Sts have taken university entrance exams, ask them to describe what they were like.

b Focus on the instructions, title of the article, and photo and ask Sts to say what they think is happening.
Now tell Sts to read the article.
Get some feedback from the class.

EXTRA SUPPORT Before Sts read the article the first time, check whether you need to pre-teach any vocabulary.

c Elicit how best to deal with True / False questions on reading texts. Then focus on the **TIP: True / False reading** box and go through it with the class. Highlight that using this advice will be helpful for Sts when they take exams.
Now tell Sts to read the article again and mark sentences 1–10 T (true) or F (false).
Get Sts to compare with a partner, and then check answers.

1 F 2 T 3 T 4 F 5 T 6 F 7 F 8 T 9 T 10 F

EXTRA IDEA Get Sts to say why the F sentences are false.

1 F (Driving is only prohibited on roads near schools where students are taking the *gaokao*.)
4 F (Students preparing for the exam have no time for a social life.)
6 F (Some candidates who cheat use high-tech devices which are similar to those used in James Bond films.)
7 F (Tutors get no time off. It's the students who have one day a month when they don't have to work. Teachers spend that day marking practice exams.)
10 F (The number of candidates taking the *gaokao* has fallen dramatically in recent years.)

d Do this as a whole-class activity. Encourage Sts to give reasons to justify their opinions.

6 GRAMMAR revision of verb forms

a Focus on the instructions and put Sts in pairs. Tell them to look at the highlighted verbs in the article in **5** and match them to the verb forms in the list.
Check answers.

3 present simple (*I make…*)
13 present continuous (*I'm making…*)
6 present simple passive (*It is made…*)

7 past simple (*I made…*)
5 past continuous (*I was making…*)
11 past simple passive (*It was made…*)
4 past perfect simple (*I had made…*)

1 future simple (*I will make…*)
2 future with *be going to* (*I'm going to make…*)
8 *will* passive (*It will be made…*)

9 present perfect simple (*I've made…*)
12 present perfect continuous (*I've been making…*)
10 present perfect passive (*It's been made…*)

b Tell Sts to go to **Grammar Bank 10B** on *p.151*.

This **Grammar Bank** does not include a new presentation or an audio. Instead, Sts practise all the verb forms from this level of *English File* as revision.
Focus on the exercises and get Sts to do them individually or in pairs. Encourage them to use contracted forms rather than full forms.
Check answers, getting Sts to read the full sentences.

a
1 I**'ve been working** really hard all week.
2 Is that why you **didn't come** out with us last night?
3 Yes, I **couldn't come** because…
4 I **was studying**.
5 My last exam **starts** at 9.00 tomorrow morning.
6 Really? I**'ve finished** all my exams!
7 Lucky you! What **are** you **planning** to do now they're over?
8 I**'m flying** to Australia in three days.
9 I**'ve always wanted** to go there…
10 …ever since my aunt and uncle **moved** there five years ago…
11 …, but I **haven't had** time until now.
12 Fantastic – I'm sure you**'ll love** it.
13 I **saw** Mary yesterday…
14 …and she **said**…
15 …you**'d invited** her to go to France.
16 Yes, but unfortunately she**'d already made / 's already made** other plans.
17 **Are** you **celebrating / going to celebrate**?
18 Yes, I**'m thinking** of going to that new pizzeria with some friends.
19 **Do** you **want** to come along?
20 I**'ll see** you tomorrow.

b
1 She**'s known** him for 20 years.
2 You **don't need** to bring any money.
3 If I **had** some glue, I could repair the chair.
4 I**'ve been able to swim** since I was five.
5 What **are you going** to do after you graduate?
6 He **suggests including** a covering letter.
7 The concert hall **was opened by the President** in 2019.
8 I **used to have** much longer hair when I was younger.
9 You **don't have to** pay me back until tomorrow.
10 She**'s been learning** Russian for two months.
11 He phoned the police because his car **had been stolen**.
12 My boss **let** me **leave** work early.
13 She **said she could** come to the wedding.
14 The photo would have been in focus if I **hadn't moved** the camera.
15 They **ought to be** more careful.

Tell Sts to go back to the main lesson **10B**.

EXTRA SUPPORT If you think Sts need more practice, you may want to give them the **Grammar** photocopiable activity at this point.

7 ▶ VIDEO LISTENING

a Tell Sts they are going to watch a documentary that gives tips on how to prepare for taking speaking exams.
Focus on the questions and give Sts time to think what the answers might be.
Now play the video once the whole way through for Sts to watch and answer the questions.
Get Sts to compare with a partner, and then check answers.

EXTRA CHALLENGE Put Sts in pairs and get them to brainstorm different ways to prepare for a speaking exam. Elicit ideas. Then play the video for Sts to answer the questions and see if their ideas are mentioned.

EXTRA SUPPORT Read through the script and decide if you need to pre-teach any new lexis before Sts watch the video.

> The speaking exam is the most stressful because students are face-to-face with the examiner.
> The best way to prepare is to practise talking.

Speaking exams – top tips for success

N = narrator, W = woman, E = examiner, M = Marcus, V = Valentina, S = student

- **N** Welcome to Regent Oxford, one of the oldest English language schools in the UK. For many years, Regent has helped people to improve their English, and a big part of this is preparing for English exams.
  Most of the students here are hoping to get a qualification in English. There are several different tests and certificates for them to work towards, but almost every exam tests reading, writing, listening and, of course, speaking.
  For a lot of students, the speaking exam is often the most stressful. Unlike any other exam, students are face-to-face with their examiner, so it can feel like there's less thinking time and more pressure. But don't worry, here are some tips that can help.
- **W** Tip one: Give yourself plenty of time.
- **N** The first tip may seem obvious, but it's important – get to your speaking exam in plenty of time. You should arrive at least half an hour beforehand if you can. You need to feel relaxed, and if you're late, you'll be stressed, which will make the exam much more difficult.
- **W** Tip two: Engage with the examiner.
- **N** When you first go into the exam room, greet the examiner and try to smile, even if you feel nervous. Remember, examiners want you to do well, so just be polite and friendly. Body language is really important too, so make eye contact, smile and sit up straight throughout the exam.
- **E 1** And Marcus, what do you enjoy doing at weekends?
- **M** I enjoy going to the beach and hanging out with friends, to maybe the shopping mall or some parties.
- **E 1** Valentina, where do you meet your friends?
- **V** Mostly at school, but we like hanging out at other times as well.
- **E 1** OK. And Marcus, what did you do yesterday?
- **M** Yesterday, I did a tour at Oxford city and I really enjoyed know, knowing new places, yeah and knowing new people.
- **E 1** OK, good. Excellent.
- **W** Tip three: Involve your partner.
- **N** Always look interested in what your partner is saying, respond to their suggestions and make sure you give them the opportunity to speak. Ask for their opinion and try to involve them in the conversation as much as possible.
- **E 1** Here is a picture with some ideas to help you.
- **N** Hopefully, they will do the same for you.
- **M** Would you like to start?
- **V** Oh, yeah. What do you think about the vending machine?
- **M** Oh, it will be a nice thing, but it's better to invest in something related to education. Don't you think?
- **V** Oh, yeah, I agree.
- **M** And what about the tablets?
- **V** Oh, I think they wouldn't be really helpful because we would access another side perhaps and we wouldn't focus on the lessons.
- **M** Mmm, I see your point, but maybe we can put rules in the use of it, and just put things related to the lessons and about subjects that we're going to work with them.
- **V** Oh, yeah.
- **W** Tip four: Avoid one word answers.
- **N** Another useful tip is not to just say one word when you're answering the examiner or your partner. Always answer in full sentences and add more detail wherever you can. This will not only impress the examiner, it will also make it feel much more like a natural conversation, which can help you to relax.
- **E 1** Marcus, where are you from?
- **M** Rio.
- **E 1** And Valentina, where are you from?
- **V** I live in Brazil as well, but I live in a really small town. It's called Santo Gusto, and I live there with my whole family. It's, um, it has only thirteen thousand…
- **E 1** Inhabitants.
- **V** Inhabitants, yeah.
- **W** Tip five: Don't be afraid to say that you don't understand.
- **N** It's perfectly normal to not understand a person that you're meeting for the first time. When the examiner asks you a question, don't panic if you don't understand. Just ask the examiner to repeat it.
- **E 2** What sort of accommodation would you most like to live in?
- **S** Could you repeat that, please?
- **E 2** What sort of accommodation would you most like to live in?
- **S** In apartments, of course. I don't really like living in houses.
- **W** Tip six: Don't memorize answers.
- **N** Whatever you do, don't give answers you've learned word-for-word. It's fine to memorize words and phrases that you might need, but not whole sentences or paragraphs. These are easy to spot and give a bad impression. Remember it's a test of your English, not your memory.
- **E 2** Tell me about the kind of accommodation that you live in.
- **S** I live in an apartment. I've lived there for five years. And I really love being there because it's really big and it's close to my school. Next year I will move. I don't really want to, but I have to.
- **W** Tip seven: Don't freeze if you can't find the word you need.
- **N** When it's your turn to speak, if you can't think of the word you need, don't panic and say nothing. Just try to explain it in a different way. This is also quite normal – it happens to people all the time, even in their own language.
- **E 2** …and here's your topic. I'd like you to describe an event that you attended recently. Can you start speaking now, please?
- **S** Yes. A couple of weeks ago, I went to my cousin's wedding. And we had a really… A couple of weeks ago, I went to my cousin's wedding, and we were really glad that he invited us. And we had to go to another country. Um, I was really glad that, that he got married…how can I say…it was…it was a really nice wedding, he's from another country, so I went to Paraguay. We went there and it was so nice and beautiful. In other words, so it was so emotional and touching, but my favourite part was when his mother, my, my aunt, she sang a love song to the newlyweds, and…how can I explain,…? Everyone in there cried.
- **N** There's no doubt that speaking exams are challenging, but these tips will help you to feel more confident and speak more naturally. But of course, the best preparation is practice. And the best way to practise?
  Get talking! Goodbye…and good luck!

b Tell Sts they are going to watch the documentary again and this time they have to complete the gaps in 1–7 with one to three words.

Give Sts time to read sentences 1–7 and think what the missing words might be.

EXTRA SUPPORT Get Sts to do this in pairs.

Play the video again for Sts to watch and complete the gaps.

Get Sts to compare with a partner, and then check answers.

> **1** half an hour, relaxed **2** eye, sit up straight **3** interested, opinion **4** full, detail **5** panic, repeat **6** sentences, paragraphs **7** nothing, different

EXTRA SUPPORT You could get Sts to watch the video again with subtitles, so they can see exactly what they understood / didn't understand. Translate / Explain any new words or phrases.

c This speaking activity is useful for Sts taking the Cambridge PET exam, as well as general practice of the principles mentioned in the documentary (involving your partner, turn taking, expressing your opinion) that are helpful in all speaking exams.

Focus on the instructions and make sure Sts understand the task. You might want to tell the class that this activity is based on a real oral test.

Play the video for Sts to watch the examiner giving them the task they need to complete.

I'm going to describe a situation to you.
A British couple with two children aged twelve and fourteen are going to visit your country next month. You have been asked to show them some places in your town. The parents are especially interested in history, and the children in sport and nature.
Talk to a partner about the different places they could visit, and say which they would enjoy most and why.
Here is a picture with some ideas to help you.

! If you aren't using the video in class, read the script above to Sts.

Put Sts in pairs and get them to discuss the situation for two or three minutes, using tips from the documentary and ideas from the picture. Make sure they stay within the time limit.

You could give some feedback on any tips from the documentary that Sts ignored and also tell them if they have done well.

9&10 Revise and Check

For instructions on how to use these pages, see *p.39*.

More materials
For teachers
Teacher's Resource Centre
Video Can you understand these people? 9&10
Quick Test 10
File 10 Test
Progress Test Files 6–10
End-of-course Test
For students
Online Practice   Check your progress

GRAMMAR

a
1 b 2 a 3 a 4 a 5 c
b
1 hadn't studied   2 'd / would have spent   3 'd / would have been able to   4 didn't do   5 Have…visited   6 Had…been   7 's been working   8 had finished   9 will be completed   10 had…closed   11 have sold   12 are…eating   13 was showing   14 's…been   15 was made

VOCABULARY

a
1 memorable   2 confidently   3 emotional   4 accuracy
5 personal
b
1 bride   2 honeymoon   3 best man   4 reception   5 guests
c
1 Am – cinema   2 Br – faucet   3 Am – trainers
4 Br – elevator   5 Am – rubbish   6 Br – restroom
7 Am – queue   8 Am – flat   9 Br – sidewalk   10 Br – gas
d
1 failed   2 multiple   3 essay   4 took   5 cheated

PRONUNCIATION

c
1 autobiogra**ph**y /f/   2 l**u**xurious /ʊə/   3 t**oi**let /ɔɪ/
4 r**a**ther /ɑː/   5 w**ei**rd /ɪə/
d
1 se<u>cu</u>rity   2 im<u>por</u>tant   3 pro<u>pose</u>   4 <u>brides</u>maid
5 <u>prac</u>tical

CAN YOU understand this text?

b
1 E   2 D   3 F   4 B   5 G   6 A   7 C

▶ CAN YOU understand these people?

1 c   2 b   3 b   4 b   5 b

🔊 10.14

1
I = interviewer, V = Victoria
I   Do you have a good memory?
V   Um, I have a good memory for, for things that I can picture, like details in my head. So when I meet someone, I'm really good at remembering their name because I, I just kind of plant it in my head. Um, but I'm not as good at remembering, like if you ask me what I had for dinner three days ago, I wouldn't remember that.

2
I = interviewer, J = Jan
I   When was the last time you went to a wedding?
J   It was approximately two and a half weeks ago. And it was my wedding.
I   Did you have a lovely time?
J   I did. I had a lovely wedding. And the wedding was a second time around for me. I was a widow for eight years, and I met my new husband online, which is quite avant-garde for someone my age.

3
I = interviewer, K = Keith
I   What's the best influence that the USA has had on the world?
K   Um, I think the best influence that the US has had on the world is in TV and movies. I think a lot of countries, or most countries, um, that watch a lot of US TV, US drama, US movies. I watch a lot. I've been watching *Breaking Bad* and *Ozark* recently, which are two of my favourite shows, and I just think the, the influence that they've had on TV and drama is, is a really big influence.
I   And the worst influence?
K   The worst influence, I'd probably say, is the amount of commercialism. I think, you know, the American dream was always, you know, about making money, um, and being successful, and I think that's had quite a negative impact on the world, that, um, so much now is driven by the need to be, er, er, making profits and I think all in all society's, er, not really benefitted from that.

4
I = interviewer, R = Royce
I   Are there any American fast-food places near where you live?
R   Er, yeah, there are several fast-food places near where I live.
I   Do you ever go to any of them?
R   Um, I don't, I try not to. I don't particularly like it very much and it's quite bad for you.

5
I = interviewer, D = Diana
I   How do you feel about taking exams?
D   Um, I feel all right, I like studying, so I am kind of all right at handling that situation. It's always a little bit nervous, but it's all right.
I   Have you ever had an exam disaster?
D   Um, well I remember in um, in an oral exam I went, er, blank for, like, twenty very long seconds, but then I was all right. I was just like, blank for a while.
I   Did you pass the exam?
D   Yes, I did.

Photocopiable activities

Overview

- There is a **Grammar activity** for each main (A and B) lesson of the Student's Book.
- There is a **Communicative activity** for each main (A and B) lesson of the Student's Book.
- There is a **Vocabulary activity** for each section of the Vocabulary Bank in the Student's Book.

The photocopiable material is also available on the **Teacher's Resource Centre** (TRC) and the **Classroom Presentation Tool** (CPT), allowing you to display the worksheets on an interactive whiteboard or projector. This will make it easier to set up and demonstrate the activities, and show answers.

Using extra activities in mixed ability classes

Some teachers have classes with a very wide range of levels, and where some Sts finish Student's Book activities much more quickly than others. You could give these fast finishers a photocopiable activity (Grammar, Vocabulary, or Communicative) while you help the slower Sts. Alternatively, some teachers might want to give faster Sts extra oral practice with a communicative activity while slower Sts consolidate their knowledge with an extra grammar activity.

Tips for using Grammar activities

- The grammar activities are designed to give Sts extra practice in the main grammar points from each lesson. How you use these activities depends on the needs of your Sts and the time available. They can be used in the lesson if you think all of your class would benefit from the extra practice or you could set them as homework for some or all of your Sts.
- Before using the worksheets in class, check for any vocabulary that may be either new or difficult for your Sts.
- All of the activities start with a writing stage. If you use the activities in class, get Sts to work individually or in pairs. Allow Sts to compare before checking answers.
- If Sts are having trouble with any of the activities, make sure they refer to the relevant Grammar Bank in the Student's Book.
- All of the activities have an **Activation** section. Some of them have a task that gets Sts to cover the sentences and test their memory. If you are using the activities in class, Sts can work in pairs and test their partner. If you set them for homework, encourage Sts to use this stage to test themselves. Alternatively, you could set the main activity for homework and then get Sts to do the **Activation** at the start of the next class.
- Make sure that Sts keep their worksheets and that they review any difficult areas regularly. Encourage them to go back to activities and cover and test themselves.

Tips for using Communicative activities

- Before using the worksheets in class, check for any vocabulary that may be either new or difficult for your Sts.
- We have suggested the ideal number of copies for each activity. However, you can often manage with fewer, e.g. one worksheet per pair instead of one per student.
- When Sts are working in pairs, if possible get them to sit face-to-face. This will encourage them to really talk to each other and also means they can't see each other's worksheet.
- If your class doesn't divide into pairs or groups, take part yourself, get two Sts to share one role, or get one student to monitor, help, and correct.
- If some Sts finish early, they can swap roles and do the activity again, or you could get them to write some of the sentences from the activity.

Tips for using Vocabulary activities

- These worksheets are intended to recycle and consolidate Sts' understanding of the vocabulary in the Student's Book Vocabulary Banks. As such, we suggest not using them directly after doing these exercises. Instead, get Sts to do them in a subsequent lesson.
- If Sts are having trouble with any of the activities, make sure they refer to the relevant Vocabulary Bank page.
- You could ask Sts to check their answers by referring to the relevant Student's Book Vocabulary Bank.
- All the activities are suitable for use in class. However, you may wish to set some of the tasks for homework.
- Most of the Vocabulary worksheets have an **Activation** task and this can be treated in a similar way to the Grammar ones.
- Make sure that Sts keep their and that they review any difficult areas regularly. Encourage them to go back to activities and cover and test themselves.

Customisable worksheets

There are customisable versions of some of the Grammar, Communicative, and Vocabulary activities on the **Teacher's Resource Centre**. These allow you to adapt the material to make it more applicable and/or relevant to your Sts. For instance, you could:

- change some of the names to the names of Sts in your class.
- change place names to ones that are more relevant and/or familiar to your Sts.
- change items of grammar or vocabulary to focus on the needs and interests of your Sts and/or adapt the level of challenge.
- reduce the number of items if you are short of time.

Grammar activity answers

1A pronouns
a 1 ours 2 her, She 3 their, his 4 your, mine 5 her, his
  6 your, my 7 their, him 8 yours, mine
b 2 it to me 3 them for me 4 it to me 5 it to me / us
  6 it for me 7 them for him 8 it for me

1B adjectives
a 2 worse, the worst
  3 cleverer, the cleverest
  4 more expensive, the most expensive
  5 further, the furthest
  6 lighter, the lightest
  7 luckier, the luckiest
  8 narrower, the narrowest
  9 tidier, the tidiest
  10 more tired, the most tired
b 2 much 3 most 4 one 5 the 6 less 7 ones 8 than
  9 more 10 as

2A present tenses
3 ✓ 4 ✗ I really want 5 ✓ 6 ✗ does the guidebook say
7 ✗ it depends on 8 ✗ we're waiting 9 ✓ 10 ✗ I'm going
11 ✗ Are you coming 12 ✗ I don't see 13 ✓ 14 ✓ 15 ✓
16 ✗ We're going 17 ✗ They prefer 18 ✗ we need
19 ✗ She's having 20 ✓ 21 ✓ 22 ✗ they're cleaning
23 ✗ I don't believe 24 ✓ 25 ✗ My neighbour is looking after

2B possessives
a 2 the children's
  3 ✓
  4 the centre of Glasgow
  5 my brother's
  6 florist's
  7 my grandparents'
  8 the name of the village
  9 the butcher's
  10 the men's
  11 the corner of the street
  12 Sarah and Tony's
  13 grandfather's
  14 the back of the book
  15 people's names
  16 the south of France
b 2 hers 3 our 4 theirs 5 his 6 yours 7 its 8 her
  9 their 10 mine 11 his 12 your 13 ours / mine
  14 yours 15 her 16 his

3A past simple, past continuous, or *used to*?
2 used to have 3 didn't use to wear 4 saw 5 was working
6 did she teach / did she use to teach 7 did you think
8 was / used to be 9 found 10 didn't have
11 was still writing 12 said 13 broke 14 did it happen
15 wasn't skiing 16 fell 17 were walking

3B prepositions
a 2 through, past 3 out of, towards 4 over, round
  5 on, under 6 on, at
b 2 in, at 3 about, for 4 with, about 5 with, for 6 to, on
  7 of, for 8 to, about 9 about, – 10 –, in

4A future forms: *will / shall* and *be going to*
2 Shall I turn on 3 It'll probably rain. 4 ✓ 5 I'll text
6 I'll change 7 it's coming 8 shall we go 9 I'm going to be
10 ✓ 11 I won't be 12 I was going to go

4B first and second conditionals
3 won't pass, attends
4 had, wouldn't need
5 'd enjoy, weren't
6 won't be able to pay / can't pay, don't get
7 were, 'd try
8 won't get, have
9 wouldn't be, didn't have
10 had, 'd help

5A present perfect simple
1 Well, I haven't seen the director yet!
2 Have you had breakfast?, What time did you get up?
3 How long have you known Alex?, Where did you meet?
4 I've already had three cups this morning., Have you ever thought about cutting down?
5 When did you start learning the piano?, Have you ever played in public?, No, I've never played for anyone except my teacher.
6 Have you ever been to the United States?, We've just come back from Florida.
7 Have you ever lived abroad?, Yes, I taught in Italy for a few years., How long have you been a teacher?
8 Have you tidied your room yet?, I've been out all afternoon., When did you get home?

5B present perfect continuous
2 'm trying 3 've been doing
4 Is, teaching, 's been working 5 's starting
6 Has, done, 's been playing
7 Have, been waiting, 've been standing
8 's having 9 haven't been watching
10 have, been living, 've been thinking
11 haven't been feeling 10 've been studying, 'm watching

6A obligation, necessity, prohibition, advice
2 have / need 3 mustn't 4 shouldn't 5 have / need
6 should 7 oughtn't 8 mustn't 9 have 10 needn't
11 shouldn't 12 must

6B *can, could,* and *be able to*
2 be able to 3 couldn't / wasn't able to 4 can't
5 couldn't / weren't able to 6 Can / Could 7 be able to
8 being able to 9 can't 10 be able to
11 'd be able to / could 12 be able to 13 couldn't
14 has been able to 15 can't 16 Can / Could
17 were able to 18 couldn't / wasn't able to

7A phrasal verbs

a
2 try on these trousers / try these trousers on
3 look after the children
4 look round the museum
5 take away my old cooker / take my old cooker away
6 took her best friend out / took out her best friend
7 put up the new curtains / put the new curtains up
8 looking forward to his holiday
9 lives off our parents
10 turn off your phone / turn your phone off

b 2 try them on   3 look after them   4 look round it
5 take it away   6 took her out   7 put them up
8 looking forward to it   9 lives off them   10 turn it off

7B verb patterns

a 2 to have   3 to see   4 believe   5 to let   6 wait
7 going out   8 watching   9 playing   10 be   11 to get
12 not winning

a 2 seeing   3 go   4 to rain / raining   5 getting   6 to do
7 getting   8 to take   9 to watch   10 not to be   11 losing

8A have something done

3 're having their photograph taken
4 's drying his hair
5 's painting the front door
6 's putting up some shelves
7 's having his glasses repaired
8 're having the windows replaced
9 're washing their clothes
10 's having her fringe cut

8B the passive

2 took   3 opened   4 was called   5 was renamed
6 was, being built   7 gave   8 is, known   9 was designed
10 has been awarded   11 are allowed   12 are held
13 is considered   14 became   15 holds
16 was commissioned   17 was used   18 hasn't owned
19 had   20 be visited   21 are rented   22 be missed

9A reported speech

a 2 was a beautiful morning
3 me to wake up and come outside
4 (that) I couldn't just lie there on my chair all day
5 (that) I should be catching birds
6 how I could be so lazy
7 were supposed to be fun
8 if / whether he could have a dog

b 2 (that) he'd have to take it for walks
3 (him) where it was going to sleep
4 (that) they'd have to take it on holiday with them the following month
5 not to forget about the cat
6 to let them think about it

9B third conditional and other uses of the past perfect

a 2 would have been   4 hadn't turned   5 ✓   6 ✓
7 would Sally have done   8 ✓

b 2 hadn't left   3 had gone   4 dropped   5 told
6 'd already had   7 lived   8 had, known   9 hadn't eaten
10 had stolen

10A be, do, and have: auxiliary and main verbs

2 have   3 haven't   4 had   5 do   6 's   7 Are   8 don't
9 are   10 Does   11 having   12 hasn't   13 Have   14 don't
15 be   16 are   17 're   18 has   19 did   20 was   21 do
22 doesn't   23 having   24 be

10B revision of verb forms

2 Do, forget   3 goes   4 's having   5 Were, driving
6 didn't watch   7 didn't use to like   8 loved / used to love
9 'll stop   10 'm leaving / going to leave   11 are, going to do
12 Shall, help   13 'll be   14 didn't spend   15 wouldn't go
16 wins   17 Have, ever tried   18 went   19 Did, come
20 've been   21 've been waiting   22 have, been doing
23 'm reading   24 're trying   25 's based   26 is being decorated
27 will be nominated   28 Has, been fixed   29 'd told
30 had, shut   31 didn't eat   32 Had, started

1A GRAMMAR pronouns

a Complete the conversations with the correct subject pronoun, object pronoun, possessive adjective, or possessive pronoun, e.g. *I / me / my / mine*. Write your answers in the column on the right.

1 **A** Hey! Those are ___ coffees! — *our*
  B I'm sorry, we thought they were ___. — _____
2 **A** Sara got a new phone for ___ birthday. — _____
  B Wow! ___ always gets fantastic presents. — _____
3 **A** I've met those people before, but I can't remember ___ names. — _____
  B His name is Ryan and I think ___ wife's name is Jessica. — _____
4 **A** Tom! Are these ___ keys? — _____
  B No, I've got ___ here. — _____
5 **A** Where's Sylvia? I think these are ___ glasses. — _____
  B No, they're not Sylvia's. Ask Ben, they might be ___. — _____
6 **A** Is this ___ car, sir? — _____
  B No, it isn't. That's ___ car over there. — _____
7 **A** Have Ruth and Oliver chosen a name for ___ baby yet? — _____
  B Yes, he's called Patrick. They named ___ after his grandfather. — _____
8 **A** I've left my book at home. Can I share ___? — _____
  B Sorry! I forgot to bring ___, too! — _____

b Complete the conversations with object pronouns and *for* or *to*. Write your answers in the column on the right.

1 **A** What beautiful flowers!
  B Yes, my boyfriend sent ___ ___ ___. — *them to me*
2 **A** Is that Sean's old bike?
  B Yes, he sold ___ ___ ___ for £50. — ___ ___ ___
3 **A** Where did you get those headphones?
  B My friend got ___ ___ ___ in New York. — ___ ___ ___
4 **A** Is that your tennis racquet?
  B No, it's my brother's. He lent ___ ___ ___. — ___ ___ ___
5 **A** Have you seen our new logo?
  B Yes, the Marketing Director showed ___ ___ ___ yesterday. — ___ ___ ___
6 **A** Where did you buy that hat?
  B My wife found ___ ___ ___ online. — ___ ___ ___
7 **A** I didn't think George could afford designer sunglasses.
  B He can't. His parents bought ___ ___ ___. — ___ ___ ___
8 **A** I love your sweater.
  B Thanks. My grandmother made ___ ___ ___. — ___ ___ ___

ACTIVATION

Test your memory. Cover the columns on the right. Practise the conversations in **a** and **b** with a partner.

1B GRAMMAR adjectives

a Write the comparative and superlative forms of the adjectives.

		comparative	superlative
1	addictive	more addictive	the most addictive
2	bad		
3	clever		
4	expensive		
5	far		
6	light		
7	lucky		
8	narrow		
9	tidy		
10	tired		

b Complete each sentence with one word. Write your answers in the column on the right.

1 Let's walk a ▓▓▓ further – we have time and it's a lovely day. *bit*
2 The tunnel was ▓▓▓ narrower than I thought and I accidentally damaged my car. _____
3 I really like this bike, but unfortunately, it's the ▓▓▓ expensive and I can't afford it. _____
4 My brother is definitely the lucky ▓▓▓ in our family. He's won the lottery twice. _____
5 Kim is ▓▓▓ cleverest student in our school. _____
6 I felt exhausted yesterday, but luckily, I'm ▓▓▓ tired today. _____
7 My suitcases are the two light blue ▓▓▓ over there. _____
8 My colleague's desk is tidier ▓▓▓ mine. I have papers everywhere! _____
9 Coffee is ▓▓▓ addictive than some people realize. _____
10 The exam wasn't as bad ▓▓▓ I thought it would be. _____

ACTIVATION

Test your memory. Cover the column on the right in **b** and look at the sentences. Read the sentences aloud with the correct word.

2A GRAMMAR present tenses

Tick (✓) the sentences where the **bold** phrases are right and correct the wrong ones. Write your answers in the column on the right.

1 **They usually go hiking** in Scotland in the summer. ✓

2 **I'm not knowing** where to go on holiday. *X I don't know*

3 **Their flight arrives** at Terminal 4 at 16.45. _____

4 **I'm really wanting** to try waterskiing. _____

5 Hurry up! **We only have** half an hour to get to the airport! _____

6 What **is the guidebook saying** about this museum? _____

7 We'd love to go surfing, but **it's depending on** the weather. _____

8 Our flight's delayed, so **we wait** in the departure lounge at the moment. _____

9 **Do you think** we should get a taxi or a bus to the hotel? _____

10 **I go** to the cinema with some friends this evening. _____

11 **Do you come** for a swim or not? _____

12 I'm sorry, **I'm not seeing** what you mean. _____

13 You're very quiet – what **are you thinking** about? _____

14 **£500 seems** very expensive for a flight to Madrid. _____

15 What time **does your train leave** tomorrow? _____

16 **We go** camping in the Pyrenees next summer. _____

17 **They're preferring** sunbathing to climbing mountains. _____

18 I don't think **we're needing** to take a hairdryer. _____

19 **She has** a shower at the moment – can you call back later? _____

20 **Do you remember** the name of the hotel? _____

21 **It isn't raining** any more. Shall we go to the beach? _____

22 We can't go in the pool now because **they clean** it. _____

23 **I'm not believing** it! I've won a holiday to Hawaii! _____

24 Why **are you packing** so much? It's only a weekend trip! _____

25 **My neighbour looks after** my cat when I'm away next month. _____

ACTIVATION

Test your memory. Cover the column on the right and look at the sentences. Read the sentences aloud with the correct present tense.

2B GRAMMAR possessives

a Circle the correct form. In which sentence are both forms possible?

1 She's at **the front of the queue** / **the queue's front**.
2 What are **the childrens'** / **the children's** names?
3 I needed **James's** / **James'** help.
4 I live in **the centre of Glasgow** / **Glasgow's centre**.
5 I don't get on with **my brother's** / **my brothers'** wife.
6 What time does the **florists** / **florist's** open?
7 I drove to **my grandparent's** / **my grandparents'** house. They live just outside Southampton.
8 What's **the name of the village** / **the village's name** where you were born?
9 I never buy meat at **the butcher's** / **the butchers'**. I get it at the supermarket.
10 Excuse me. Where's **the men's** / **the mens'** changing room?
11 I'll wait on **the street's corner** / **the corner of the street**.
12 We're going to **Sarah's and Tony's** / **Sarah and Tony's** wedding next weekend.
13 I went to my **grandfather's** / **grandfathers'** yesterday. It was his 90th birthday.
14 The answers are at **the book's back** / **the back of the book**.
15 I'm not very good at remembering **people's names** / **peoples' names**.
16 They go to **France's south** / **the south of France** every year.

b Complete the sentences with the correct possessive adjective or pronoun. Write your answers in the column on the right.

1 I hate living with my parents. I'd love to have a house of ▓▓ own.   _my_
2 Jane's keeping very quiet about this new boyfriend of ▓▓!   _____
3 My brother and I had ▓▓ own bedrooms when we were children.   _____
4 Both my sons smoke. It's a bad habit of ▓▓.   _____
5 My nephew never goes to the hairdresser's. He cuts ▓▓ own hair.   _____
6 Is that woman a friend of ▓▓? She's smiling at you.   _____
7 The supermarket has ▓▓ own bakery, so we can buy some bread there.   _____
8 My grandmother loves gardening. She grows all ▓▓ own vegetables.   _____
9 My cousins are thinking of opening ▓▓ own restaurant.   _____
10 A colleague of ▓▓ has just told me she's leaving.   _____
11 Tom must earn a lot of money. Have you seen that new car of ▓▓?   _____
12 I'm going out this evening, so you'll have to make ▓▓ own dinner.   _____
13 A friend of ▓▓ is going away, so we're looking after his dog.   _____
14 Are you still having problems with those noisy neighbours of ▓▓?   _____
15 My daughter loves singing and has started writing ▓▓ own songs.   _____
16 He's an amazing artist. I have a painting of ▓▓ in the living room.   _____

ACTIVATION

Test your memory. Cover the column on the right in **b** and look at the sentences. Read the sentences aloud with the correct possessive adjectives and pronouns.

3A GRAMMAR past simple, past continuous, or *used to*?

Complete the conversations with the correct form of the verbs in brackets: past simple, past continuous, or *used to*.

1

Ben Helen, do you recognize that woman over there? I think we ¹*used to go* (go) to school with her.

Helen Oh, yes. That's Clare Brown! She looks so different. She ² _____ (have) much longer hair.

Ben Yes, and she ³ _____ (not wear) glasses.

Helen I wonder what she's doing these days. The last time I ⁴ _____ (see) her, she ⁵ _____ (work) as a teacher.

Ben What subject ⁶ _____ (she / teach)?

Helen I'm not sure. Shall we go and say hello?

2

Evie What ⁷ _____ (you / think) of the exam, Oliver?

Oliver Well, I ⁸ _____ (be) good at maths when I was at primary school, but I ⁹ _____ (find) the exam today really difficult. How about you?

Evie Me too. And I ¹⁰ _____ (not have) enough time to answer all the questions.

Oliver Yeah, I ¹¹ _____ (still / write) when the teacher ¹² _____ (say) 'Stop'.

Evie Oh, well. Let's just hope we both pass.

3

Tom Welcome back, Justin. How was the skiing trip?

Justin Not so great. Unfortunately, my wife ¹³ _____ (break) her leg on the first day.

Tom Oh, that's terrible. How ¹⁴ _____ (it / happen)?

Justin Well, the funny thing is, she ¹⁵ _____ (not ski) at the time! She ¹⁶ _____ (fall) over in the hotel when we ¹⁷ _____ (walk) down the stairs to go to breakfast.

Tom Oh no! What a shame!

ACTIVATION

Test your memory. Cover the conversations and look at the pictures. In pairs, say what you can remember about the people in the pictures.

3B GRAMMAR prepositions

a Choose the correct preposition. Write your answers in the column on the right.

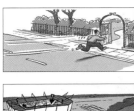
1 The man ran ▨ the road and ▨ the park.
(through / across, in / into)   *across*   *into*

2 The train went ▨ the tunnel and ▨ the stadium.
(under / through, past / along)   _____   _____

3 The woman came ▨ the bank and walked ▨ the supermarket. (out / out of, along / towards)   _____   _____

4 The cycle path goes ▨ the river and ▨ the car park.
(over / off, round / between)   _____   _____

5 They sat ▨ a bench ▨ a tree.
(in / on, under / down)   _____   _____

6 I'm still ▨ the bus, but we're nearly ▨ the bus stop.
(on / into, in / at)   _____   _____

b Complete the sentences with prepositions from the list, or write – if no preposition is needed.

about (x4)   at   for (x4)   in (x2)   of   on   to (x2)   with (x2)

1 The receptionist asked _–_ me if I was waiting _for_ a taxi.

2 I'm very interested _____ science, but I'm not very good _____ it.

3 Don't worry _____ the bill – I'll pay _____ everything.

4 My sons never agree _____ each other. They argue _____ everything.

5 Why are you still angry _____ Callum? He apologized _____ his mistake.

6 My sister is married _____ a Frenchman and they're both very keen _____ cooking.

7 I'm tired _____ applying _____ jobs – I never get an interview.

8 The boss was very rude _____ me – I don't know what he was so angry _____.

9 The professor talked _____ his research and then we discussed _____ the new project.

10 Peter told _____ me that he'd arrived _____ London on Tuesday morning.

ACTIVATION

Test your memory. Cover the sentences in **a**. Look at the pictures and try to remember the sentences.

4A GRAMMAR future forms: will / shall and be going to

● Circle the correct form. Tick (✓) if both are possible.

1 **A** Dad! I've dropped my ice cream!
   B It's OK, don't worry – **I'll get** / **I'm getting** you a new one!

2 **A** I'm freezing!
   B **Shall I turn on** / **Will I turn on** the heating?

3 **A** We're going for a walk in the country tomorrow.
   B **It'll probably rain.** / **It's probably raining.**

4 **A** Do you and David have any plans for tomorrow evening?
   B Yes, **we're meeting** / **we're going to meet** some friends for dinner.

5 **A** Don't forget to send me a message when you get there.
   B Don't worry, Mum. **I'm texting** / **I'll text** you as soon as I arrive.

6 **A** Excuse me. I ordered still water and this is sparkling.
   B I'm sorry, sir. **I'll change** / **I'm going to change** it for you.

7 **A** Have you phoned for a taxi?
   B Yes, **it comes** / **it's coming** in five minutes.

8 **A** How about going abroad for our holiday this year?
   B That sounds good! Where **shall we go** / **do we go**?

9 **A** You don't look very well. Are you OK?
   B No. I think **I'm going to be** / **I'm being** sick.

10 **A** Who do you think **will win** / **is going to win** the World Cup?
    B Italy, of course!

11 **A** The play starts at 7.30, so we need to be at the theatre by 7.15.
    B OK, **I won't be** / **I'm not being** late this time!

12 **A** Did you buy the pizza for tonight?
    B Oh sorry! **I was going to go** / **I'm going to go** to the shop earlier, but my boss called and then I forgot.

ACTIVATION

Write three short conversations, one with will, one with shall, and one with be going to.

4B GRAMMAR first and second conditionals

● Complete the second sentence so that it means the same as the first. Use contractions where possible.

1 You have to dress smartly to make a good impression at the interview.

You *won't make* a good impression at the interview if you *don't dress* smartly.

2 She can't work in France because she doesn't speak French.

If she *spoke* French, she *would be able to work / could work* in France.

3 She needs to attend all the lectures to pass the course.

She _____ the course unless she _____ all the lectures.

4 I need to get a part-time job because I don't have any money.

If I _____ more money, I _____ to get a part-time job.

5 He doesn't enjoy teaching very much because the pupils are so badly behaved.

He _____ teaching more if the pupils _____ so badly behaved.

6 I need to get a grant so I can pay the course fees.

I _____ the course fees if I _____ a grant.

7 I think you should try to get a new job.

If I _____ you, I _____ to get a new job.

8 You'll need to have a good CV to get an interview.

You _____ an interview unless you _____ a good CV.

9 You have good references, so it should be easy to get a job.

It _____ easy to get a job if you _____ good references.

10 I can't help you – I don't have time.

If I _____ time, I _____ you.

ACTIVATION

Complete the sentences so that they are true for you. Compare with a partner.

If the weather's bad this weekend,…

If I get better at English,…

I'll be really happy if…

If I had more time,…

If I lost my phone,…

I'd enjoy my job (or course) more if…

5A GRAMMAR present perfect simple

Complete the conversations with the present perfect simple or past simple.

1 **A** When / you / start working here?
   When did you start working here?
   B Only a few weeks ago.
   A you / meet everyone in the office?
   Have you met everyone in the office?
   B Well, I / not see the director yet!
   _____

2 **A** you / have breakfast?
   _____
   B Not yet.
   A What time / you / get up?
   _____
   B Only ten minutes ago.

3 **A** How long / you / know Alex?
   _____
   B For about ten years.
   A Where / you / meet?
   _____
   B At university.

4 **A** Do you want a coffee?
   B No, thanks. I / already / have three cups this morning.
   _____
   A you / ever / think about cutting down?
   _____
   B I'm trying!

5 **A** When / you / start learning the piano?
   _____
   B About three years ago.
   A you / ever / play in public?
   _____
   B No, I / never / play for anyone except my teacher.
   _____

6 **A** you / ever / be to the United States?
   _____
   B Yes, three times. What about you?
   A We / just / come back from Florida.
   _____

7 **A** you / ever / live abroad?
   _____
   B Yes, I / teach in Italy for a few years. Now I teach in London.
   _____
   A How long / be a teacher?
   _____
   B Since 2016.

8 **A** you / tidy your room yet?
   _____
   B Not yet. I / be out all afternoon.
   _____
   A When / you / get home?
   _____
   B Only about half an hour ago.

ACTIVATION

With a partner, write two short conversations using the present perfect simple and the past simple.

5B GRAMMAR present perfect continuous

Complete the conversations with the correct form of the verbs in brackets: present continuous or present perfect continuous. Use contractions where possible.

1. **A** Look, Mum. It *'s snowing*! (snow)
   B I know. It *'s been snowing* since five o'clock this morning. (snow)

2. **A** Ssh! I _____ to read. (try)
   B Sorry, Dad.

3. **A** Hi, Lisa. You look great!
   B Thanks! I _____ a lot of exercise recently. (do)

4. **A** _____ your daughter still _____ at the college, Cathy? (teach)
   B Yes, she _____ there for over three years now. (work)

5. **A** Oh no! It _____ to rain. (start)
   B I'll go and bring in the washing.

6. **A** _____ Mark _____ his homework yet? (do)
   B Of course not. He _____ games on his phone all evening. (play)

7. **A** Sorry I'm late! _____ you _____ long? (wait)
   B Yes, I _____ here for nearly 20 minutes! (stand)

8. **A** Can I speak to Mrs Johnson, please?
   B She _____ lunch at the moment. Can she call you back in half an hour? (have)

9. **A** Did you see that programme about sharks last night?
   B No, I _____ much TV lately. (not watch)

10. **A** How long _____ you _____ in Manchester? (live)
    B About two years, but recently we _____ about moving to the country. (think)

11. **A** You don't look very well, Pete. Are you OK?
    B Not really, I _____ well all week. (not feel)

12. **A** Is that the TV I can hear?
    B Yes, Dad. I _____ for my exams since lunchtime, and now I _____ the news. (study, watch)

ACTIVATION

Practise the conversations with a partner.

6A GRAMMAR obligation, necessity, prohibition, advice

● Complete the second sentence with **one** word so that it means the same as the first. Contractions (e.g. *can't*) count as one word.

1 She should buy a new house. She needs something bigger.
   She <u>ought</u> to buy a new house. She needs something bigger.

2 Is it necessary to use that teapot? Can't you just put a teabag in a mug?
   Do you _____ to use that teapot? Can't you just put a teabag in a mug?

3 It's really dangerous to drive when you're taking these tablets.
   You _____ drive when you're taking these tablets. It's really dangerous.

4 You ought to be more careful. You've made ten spelling mistakes.
   You _____ be so careless. You've made ten spelling mistakes.

5 You can borrow the car whenever you want. You needn't ask for permission.
   You can borrow the car whenever you want. You don't _____ to ask for permission.

6 It would be a good idea to book a table for Saturday night.
   You _____ book a table for Saturday night.

7 You should eat less fast food. It's not good for you.
   You _____ to eat so much fast food. It's not good for you.

8 I must remember to buy more paper napkins. We don't have any left.
   I _____ forget to buy some more paper napkins. We don't have any left.

9 We got a takeaway last night so we didn't need to cook.
   We got a takeaway last night so we didn't _____ to cook.

10 It's not necessary to send us your CV. Just fill in the form online.
   You _____ send us your CV. Just fill in the form online.

11 It's not a good idea to take a photo here without a flash.
   You _____ use flash to take a photo here.

12 You need a visa to visit India. You'll have to apply for one.
   You _____ have a visa to visit India.
   You'll have to apply for one.

ACTIVATION

Complete the sentences so that they are true for you. Compare with a partner.

I have to…
I mustn't…
I ought to…
I needn't…
I don't have to…
I shouldn't…

6B GRAMMAR can, could, and be able to

● Complete the sentences with the correct form of can, could, or be able to.

1 My cousin _can_ never find clothes that she likes.

2 Will I _____ change these batteries if they're the wrong type?

3 I _____ do my homework last night. It was too difficult.

4 Daniel _____ speak French very well – nobody understands a word he says!

5 They _____ come to the conference because there weren't any flights.

6 _____ you tell me where the nearest supermarket is, please?

7 Simon used to _____ play tennis quite well, but he's hopeless now.

8 I love _____ buy everything I need in the local shops.

9 You _____ be tired – it's only 9.00!

10 I might _____ leave work early on Friday.

11 If I got a pay rise, I _____ afford a new laptop.

12 You need to _____ swim well if you want to go surfing.

13 I spent hours looking for my wallet, but I _____ find it.

14 Laura _____ ride a horse since she was six years old.

15 The curtains _____ be too small! I measured the windows myself.

16 _____ I go to Joe's party on Saturday, please?

17 It was hard work, but we _____ assemble the furniture in the end.

18 Dad _____ fix the washing machine, so my parents bought a new one.

ACTIVATION

Complete the sentences so that they are true for you. Compare with a partner.

I can…really well.
When I was a child, I could…
The last time I went clothes shopping, I couldn't…
I'd really like to be able to…
In the next five years, I might be able to…
I hope I'll be able to…next year.

7A GRAMMAR phrasal verbs

a Look at the pictures. Complete the sentences with the correct form of a phrasal verb from box A and a noun phrase from box B.

A ~~get on with~~   live off   look after
   look forward to   look round   put up
   take away   take out   try on   turn off

B her best friend   ~~her brother~~   his holiday   my old cooker
   our parents   the children   the museum
   the new curtains   these trousers   your phone

1 She doesn't <u>get on with her brother</u> very well.

2 Can I _____ , please?

3 Her parents _____ every Saturday.

4 The schoolchildren had an hour to _____
   _____ .

5 The refuse collectors didn't _____
   _____ .

6 She _____ for dinner last night
   to celebrate her promotion.

7 We _____ last weekend.

8 He's really _____ .

9 My sister still _____ ,
   even though she's nearly 40.

10 I'm not starting the class until you _____
   _____ !

b Replace the nouns in **a** with pronouns. Change the word order if necessary.

1 <u>get on with him</u>
2 _____ _____ _____
3 _____ _____ _____
4 _____ _____ _____
5 _____ _____ _____

6 _____ _____ _____
7 _____ _____ _____
8 _____ _____ _____ _____
9 _____ _____ _____
10 _____ _____ _____

ACTIVATION

Use the phrasal verbs below to write sentences that are true for you. Compare with a partner.

get on with (somebody)   look forward to
grow up   throw (something) away
look after (somebody / something)

7B GRAMMAR verb patterns

a Complete the texts with the correct form of the verbs in brackets.

My wife and I both love ¹ *going* (go) to the theatre. Last month, for our anniversary, our son booked tickets for us to see the musical *Wicked*. It was a matinee, so we decided ² _____ (have) lunch in a restaurant before the show. When we arrived at the theatre after lunch, we were surprised ³ _____ (see) how quiet it was, so we checked our tickets and suddenly realized why. The start time was 2.00 p.m. and it was already 2.15 p.m. We were sure it started at 2.30 p.m. We couldn't ⁴ _____ (believe) we'd been so stupid! The attendant refused ⁵ _____ (let) us in, so we had to ⁶ _____ (wait) until the interval and missed the whole of the first half.

My boyfriend Sam and I usually look forward to ⁷ _____ (go out) with friends on Saturday evenings. Last Saturday, however, we were both really tired, so we stayed in. We didn't feel like ⁸ _____ (watch) TV, so Sam suggested a game of Scrabble. Generally, I'm not very keen on ⁹ _____ (play) board games, but I enjoy Scrabble. That might ¹⁰ _____ (be) because I usually win. With this game, however, Sam managed ¹¹ _____ (get) high scores for most of his words, while my scores were really low. In the end, I lost the game by over 100 points! I really hate ¹² _____ (not win), so I spent the rest of the evening in a bad mood!

b Complete the texts with the correct form of the verbs in the lists.

get   go   ~~miss~~   rain   see

I'm a huge fan of Adele, so when she came to Auckland a few years ago, I really didn't want to ¹ *miss* ² _____ her perform. I was still at school at the time and it finished quite late, but luckily my dad let me ³ _____ with a friend. The concert was at Mount Smart Stadium, which is open-air, and on the night of the performance, the weather was awful. It started ⁴ _____ really heavily, but I didn't mind ⁵ _____ wet as it was just such an amazing experience.

do   get   lose   not be   take   watch

I'll always remember the 2018 Football World Cup. People didn't expect England ⁶ _____ very well, but the team amazed everyone by ⁷ _____ through to the semi-final. The match was against Croatia and kick-off was at 7.00 p.m. My friends persuaded me ⁸ _____ the evening off work and we went to the local pub together ⁹ _____ the game. We told ourselves ¹⁰ _____ too disappointed if England didn't win, but when they ended up ¹¹ _____ 2–1, we were still absolutely heartbroken.

ACTIVATION

Write a paragraph about a memorable night out (or in) with friends.

8A GRAMMAR *have something done*

● Look at the pictures. Are the people *doing something* or *having something done*? Write sentences.

1		clean / the windows	She*'s cleaning the windows*.
2		service / his car	He*'s having his car serviced*.
3		take / their photograph	They _____.
4		dry / his hair	He _____.
5		paint / the front door	He _____.
6		put up / some shelves	She _____.
7		repair / his glasses	He _____.
8		replace / the windows	They _____.
9		wash / their clothes	They _____.
10		cut / her fringe	She _____.

ACTIVATION

Test your memory. Cover the sentences. Look at the pictures and try to remember the sentences.

8B GRAMMAR the passive

● Complete the texts with the correct form of the verb in brackets, active or passive.

The Gherkin ¹ *is situated* (situate) in the City of London's financial district. It ² _____ (take) two years to construct and first ³ _____ (open) its doors in April 2004. Originally, it ⁴ _____ (call) the Swiss Re Building, but it ⁵ _____ (rename) later to its street address – 30 St Mary Axe. While it ⁶ _____ still _____ (build), however, Londoners ⁷ _____ (give) the tower the nickname 'The Gherkin', because of its distinctive cucumber-like shape. It ⁸ _____ still commonly _____ (know) by that name today. The building ⁹ _____ (design) by the famous British architect Sir Norman Foster and since its completion, it ¹⁰ _____ (award) a number of prizes for architecture. The Gherkin contains private offices and a few restaurants and cafés, which are the only areas that members of the public ¹¹ _____ (allow) to visit. However, each year, several special events ¹² _____ (hold), giving more lucky visitors the chance to step inside this iconic landmark.

The Chrysler Building ¹³ _____ (consider) by many contemporary architects to be one of New York City's finest structures. When it first opened in 1930, it ¹⁴ _____ (become) the world's tallest building. Today, it still ¹⁵ _____ (hold) the title of the tallest brick building in the world. The skyscraper ¹⁶ _____ (commission) by Walter Chrysler, founder of the Chrysler Corporation, and ¹⁷ _____ (use) as the car company's headquarters until the 1950s. Although the building still has the Chrysler name, the family in fact ¹⁸ _____ (not own) it since 1953. Originally, the tower ¹⁹ _____ (have) a public observation deck on the 71st floor. Nowadays, however, only the lobby can ²⁰ _____ (visit), as the other floors ²¹ _____ (rent) to private businesses. For visitors to New York, the Chrysler Building is one attraction that really shouldn't ²² _____ (miss).

ACTIVATION

Test your memory. Cover the texts. In pairs, say what you can remember about each building.

9A GRAMMAR reported speech

a Read the cartoon. Complete the paragraph below.

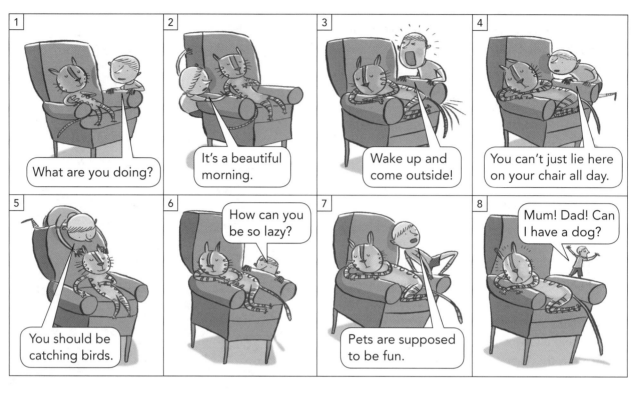

Tim asked me ¹ *what I was doing*.

He said it ² _____,

and told ³ _____.

He said ⁴ _____.

He told me ⁵ _____,

and asked ⁶ _____.

Then he said that pets ⁷ _____,

and asked his parents ⁸ _____!

b Write the things Tim's parents said in reported speech.

1 'Do you really want a dog?' They asked him *if he really wanted a dog*.

2 'You'll have to take it for walks.' They said _____.

3 'Where's it going to sleep?' They asked _____.

4 'We'll have to take it on holiday with us next month.' They said _____.

5 'Don't forget about the cat!' They told him _____.

6 'Let us think about it.' They told him _____.

ACTIVATION

Think of a short conversation you've had with a friend or a member of your family. Write it in reported speech. Compare with a partner.

9B GRAMMAR third conditional and other uses of the past perfect

Third conditional

a Tick (✓) the sentences which are right and correct the wrong ones. Write your answers in the column on the right.

1 We would have been late for the wedding if we didn't take a taxi.   *✗ hadn't taken*
2 Would you have taken me on holiday if you'd won the competition?   *✓*
3 If we'd bought our tickets online, they would be cheaper.   _____
4 I would have gone home if you didn't turn up.   _____
5 If John had met his wife earlier, they would have had more children.   _____
6 If you'd asked me, I would have helped you.   _____
7 What did Sally do if Rob had taken the job in Dubai?   _____
8 If I hadn't studied languages, I wouldn't have moved to Italy.   _____

Other uses of the past perfect

b Complete the sentences with the correct form of the verbs in brackets: past simple or past perfect. Write your answers in the column on the right.

1 Marianne told me her parents ▨▨▨ married for forty years. (be)   *had been*
2 I thought we were going to miss the train, but luckily it ▨▨▨ yet. (not leave)   _____
3 Nobody answered the phone because everyone in the office ▨▨▨ home. (go)   _____
4 I ▨▨▨ my phone yesterday, but I think it's OK. (drop)   _____
5 Where's Matt? He ▨▨▨ me he'd be here at 9.00. (tell)   _____
6 Fabio said he wasn't hungry because he ▨▨▨ lunch. (already have)   _____
7 We saw our friends every weekend when we ▨▨▨ in Bristol. (live)   _____
8 How long ▨▨▨ you ▨▨▨ Tom when he proposed to you? (know)   _____
9 Lucy said she ▨▨▨ meat since she was ten years old. (not eat)   _____
10 When I came out of the café, I realized that someone ▨▨▨ my bike. (steal)   _____

ACTIVATION

Test your memory. Cover the columns on the right and look at the sentences. Read the sentences aloud with the correct verb forms.

10A GRAMMAR *be*, *do*, and *have*: auxiliary and main verbs

Complete the conversation with the correct form of *be*, *do*, or *have*. Use contractions where possible.

Mum Kate, darling! It [1] **'s** great to hear from you. How [2] _____ you been?

Kate Good, thanks Mum. Sorry I [3] _____ phoned for ages. I've [4] _____ to [5] _____ a lot of work on my dissertation this term.

Mum Sounds like hard work. How [6] _____ the course going? [7] _____ you still enjoying it?

Kate Yes, mostly. I [8] _____ like going to some of the lectures, but the seminars and tutorials [9] _____ really interesting.

Mum That's good, then. And what about that flatmate of yours? [10] _____ she still leave her dirty dishes all over the place?

Kate No, I told her I hated [11] _____ to live in an untidy flat, so she [12] _____ been as messy recently.

Mum Great. And what about romance, darling? [13] _____ you met anyone special?

Kate Not yet, Mum. But [14] _____ worry, you'll [15] _____ the first to know when I do. Anyway, how [16] _____ you and Dad?

Mum Oh, we [17] _____ OK, thanks, although your father [18] _____ hurt his back again.

Kate Not again! How [19] _____ it happen this time?

Mum He [20] _____ on the treadmill at the gym and he fell off.

Kate Oh, poor Dad!

Mum Well, I keep telling him not to [21] _____ too much at the gym, but of course he [22] _____ listen to me! Anyway, Kate, I'm [23] _____ my hair cut at half past three, so I'd better go.

Kate OK, Mum. I'll [24] _____ in touch again soon. Bye!

ACTIVATION

Practise the conversation with a partner.

10B GRAMMAR revision of verb forms

● Complete the sentences with the correct form of the verb in brackets.

present simple / present continuous (2A)

1. We'*re thinking* about buying a new car. (think)
2. _____ you often _____ your keys? (forget)
3. Sarah _____ for a run every evening. (go)
4. He can't come to the phone – he _____ a shower. (have)

past simple / past continuous / used to (3A)

5. _____ you _____ when I called you? (drive)
6. We _____ any TV last night. (not watch)
7. Hannah _____ swimming but now she goes every day. (not like)
8. I _____ watching baseball when I lived in New York. (love)

will / shall / be going to / present continuous (4A)

9. Look, we're nearly out of petrol. I _____ at the next petrol station. (stop)
10. I _____ at 7.30 tomorrow morning. (leave)
11. What _____ you _____ when you finish university? (do)
12. _____ I _____ you take the rubbish out? (help)

first and second conditionals (4B)

13. I _____ late for work if I don't leave now. (be)
14. If you _____ so much on clothes, you wouldn't have to borrow from your parents. (not spend)
15. Young people _____ abroad if there were enough jobs at home. (not go)
16. If she _____ the next game, she'll be Wimbledon champion. (win)

present perfect simple / past simple (5A)

17. _____ you _____ windsurfing? (ever try)
18. She _____ to Turkey three times last year. (go)
19. _____ you _____ to work by bike yesterday? (come)
20. I _____ here all day and I want to go home. (be)

present perfect continuous / present continuous (5B)

21. We _____ for you since 7.00! (wait)
22. Hi John! What _____ you _____ lately? (do)
23. I _____ a really good book at the moment. (read)
24. Ssh! We _____ to listen to the news. (try)

the passive (8B)

25. It's a very interesting film – it _____ on a true story. (base)
26. Our house _____ at the moment. (decorate)
27. Do you think the film _____ for an Oscar? (nominate)
28. _____ the air conditioning _____ yet? (fix)

third conditional / past perfect / past simple (9B)

29. If he _____ me the truth, I'd have forgiven him. (tell)
30. I didn't hear you because I already _____ the door (shut).
31. We were in a hurry, so we _____ breakfast. (not eat)
32. _____ the meeting already _____ when you got there? (start)

25–32 Excellent. You can use different verb forms very well.

16–24 Quite good, but check the Grammar Banks for any forms that you got wrong.

0–15 This is still a bit difficult for you. Read the rules in the Grammar Banks again. Then ask your teacher for another photocopy and do the exercise again at home.

Communicative activity instruction

1A Talk for a minute
A group board game

Sts move around the board and revise pronouns. Copy one worksheet per group of three or four Sts. You also need one dice per group and one counter per student.

> **LANGUAGE**
> Pronouns and possessive adjectives (*I / my / mine, he / his / him*, etc.)
> *My favourite TV series is 'The Walking Dead'. I usually watch it with my sister.*
> *One of my best friends is Linda. I met her at school.*

- Put Sts in groups of three or four. Give each group the worksheet, a dice, and enough counters.

! If you don't have a dice, give each group a coin. Sts toss the coin for their go and move 1 for heads and 2 for tails.

- Each player puts a counter on **START**.
- Explain the rules of the game. Sts take turns to throw the dice and move their counter. When they land on a circle, they must talk for one minute about the topic. They must try and use correct pronouns wherever possible. Focus on the example on the worksheet (*The best cook I know is my mum…*) to show how Sts should use the correct pronouns as they speak. If the other Sts hear the speaker use a pronoun incorrectly, they should try to correct it. Be the final judge in case of dispute.
- If a pronoun is wrong, Sts move back a circle. If it is correct, they stay on the circle.
- Sts play the game in their groups. Monitor and correct any mistakes. The first student to reach **FINISH** wins.
- Get feedback on some of the more interesting answers.

1B Good, better, the best
A pairwork questionnaire

Sts revise comparative and superlative adjectives by completing a questionnaire and then asking and answering the questions. Copy one worksheet per pair and cut into **A** and **B**.

> **LANGUAGE**
> Comparative and superlative adjectives
> *When you feel stressed, what do you do to feel calmer?*
> *The most delicious meal I've had recently was beef with vegetables in the new Chinese restaurant in the town centre.*

- Put Sts in pairs, **A** and **B**, and give out the worksheets.
- Focus on **a**. Tell Sts to complete each question with the comparative or superlative form of the adjective / adverb in brackets. Tell them that they may also need to add *than* or *the* if necessary.
- Check answers by eliciting only the comparative or superlative, not the whole question.

> A 2 the most delicious 3 busier 4 the oldest
>   5 more creative 6 the best 7 the laziest 8 calmer
>   9 the furthest 10 fitter than
> B 2 better 3 cheaper than 4 the closest 5 the latest
>   6 more active 7 the greatest 8 the most useful
>   9 the safest 10 healthier than

- Now focus on **b**. Put Sts face to face if possible to ask and answer their questions. They can either ask alternate questions, or Sts **A** can interview Sts **B** and they then swap roles. Encourage Sts to ask for more information. If there's time, they could also return the questions, asking *What about you?*
- Get some feedback from various pairs.

2A Ask me a question
A pairwork speaking activity

Sts revise the present simple and present continuous. Copy one worksheet per student.

> **LANGUAGE**
> Present simple for habits / states / timetables
> Present continuous for present / future
> *What does your best friend look like?*
> *Why exactly are you learning English?*

- Put Sts in pairs, **A** and **B**, and give out the worksheets.
- Focus on **a**. Tell Sts they have ten minutes to complete the questions individually, using either the present simple or the present continuous form of the verbs in brackets.
- Check answers.

> 2 do, think 3 are, learning 4 Does, speak 5 Are, going
> 6 Is, looking 7 Are, thinking 8 Do, prefer 9 does, look
> 10 are, reading 11 are, doing 12 do, belong
> 13 do, start 14 do, use 15 Do, know, is getting

- Focus on **b**. Tell Sts to choose eight questions each from the worksheet to ask their partner.
- Put Sts face to face if possible and tell them to take turns to ask each other their questions. If they don't understand a question, they should ask their partner to repeat it slowly. Encourage Sts to give and ask for as much information as possible. The student who answers should try and reply with *What about you?* Monitor and help where necessary.

EXTRA IDEA Fast finishers could ask more questions from the sheet.

- Get feedback from various pairs.

2B Describe and draw

A pairwork describing activity

Sts describe their pictures to each other and draw them. Copy one pair of worksheets (**A** and **B**) per pair.

> **LANGUAGE**
> Possessives / present continuous revision
> *The man is holding an umbrella in his left hand.*
> *His dog is next to him. The dog's ears are big and long.*

- Put Sts in pairs, **A** and **B**, ideally face to face, and give out the worksheets. Make sure Sts can't see each other's worksheet. Get Sts to fold their worksheet along the fold line.
- Explain that they both have different pictures, and that one of them will describe their picture and the other must draw it in the empty space under **Draw**. Describe some Sts in the class as an example, emphasizing the use of the present continuous and possessives, e.g. *'Steve is sitting on a chair. His hair is short and black and his T-shirt is blue. Steve's pen is in his left hand.'*
- Focus on **a**. Give Sts a minute to look at their pictures.
- Sts **A** begin by describing their picture, and Sts **B** listen and draw. **B** should ask their partner questions if necessary. **B** then compares their drawing to **A**'s picture. Ask them to find any differences. Then Sts swap roles. Monitor and help where necessary.

3A When you were younger

A pairwork speaking activity

Sts choose some topics and then talk about their past using the past simple / continuous / *used to*. Copy one worksheet per student.

> **LANGUAGE**
> Past simple, past continuous, *used to*
> *The first trip I went on without my family was a school trip to Wales.*
> *One day, my friend and I were cheating in a maths exam and the teacher saw us.*
> *I used to love eating crisps.*

- Give out the worksheets.
- Focus on **a**. Go through the phrases in the circles and make sure Sts understand what they have to do. Demonstrate by choosing a couple of circles and write your notes on the board, e.g. a kind of food you used to love eating – *crisps*, and a group or singer you used to like but don't any more – *Coldplay*.
- Give Sts time to work individually and think of something for at least three circles in each group. Monitor and help.
- Now focus on **b** and the example. Put Sts in pairs. Tell them to use their notes in the circles and take turns to tell their partner about their past. Again, demonstrate the activity and give more information.
- Remind Sts to use *used to* to express habits, and the past simple / continuous to talk about events.
- Give Sts time to talk about their past. Remind them to always ask for more information.
- When Sts have finished, get some feedback.

3B What's the preposition?

A pairwork activity

Sts revise prepositions by asking and answering questions. Copy one worksheet per student.

> **LANGUAGE**
> Dependent prepositions (*afraid of*, *rely on*, etc.), prepositions of place (*in*, *on*, etc.)

- Put Sts in pairs and give out the worksheets.
- Focus on **a**. Sts look at the boxes and the questions. Tell them that the preposition is missing from each question. The missing preposition is the same for all the questions in that box. In their pairs, Sts write the missing preposition in the space provided at the top of each box. Tell Sts not to complete each individual question with the preposition.
- Check answers.

  2 on 3 at 4 to 5 in 6 about 7 with 8 for

- Now focus on **b**. Tell Sts to take turns to choose a box and ask their partner all the questions in it. Remind them to ask for more information. The student answering the questions could ask *What about you?* Then they swap roles, and the other student chooses a different box and repeats the process. Alternatively, this part of the activity could be done in small groups, allowing Sts to ask more follow-up questions.
- Monitor and correct any mistakes with prepositions.
- Get feedback on some of the more interesting answers.

4A The Green Quiz

A pairwork quiz

Sts read some questions related to green issues and choose an answer. Copy one worksheet per pair and cut into **A** and **B**.

> **LANGUAGE**
> Environmental issues, rubbish and recycling, future forms
> *Which of these things can't be recycled?*
> *How long will it take most plastics to decompose?*

- Tell Sts that they are going to answer some questions about the environment.
- Put Sts in pairs, **A** and **B**, ideally face to face, and give out the worksheets. Give Sts time to read the questions. Before Sts start, check whether you need to pre-teach any vocabulary, e.g. *decompose*, *fuel*, etc. Tell Sts that the correct answers are in **bold**.
- Sts **A** read their questions to Sts **B** with the three options. Sts **B** choose an option and Sts **A** circle their answer. Then Sts swap roles.
- When Sts have finished, get them to add up their partner's score. Each correct answer is worth one point.
- Sts swap worksheets so that they can see their score and what questions they got wrong. The student with more points wins.
- Get some quick feedback from pairs to find out which facts were surprising / new to them. Find out if any Sts got all the answers correct.

4B What if…?

A group board game

Sts move around the board and complete sentences about study and work. Copy one worksheet per group of three or four Sts. You also need one dice per group and one counter per student.

> **LANGUAGE**
> Study and work, first and second conditionals
> *I wouldn't do an internship unless I wanted to change careers.*

- Put Sts in groups of three or four. Give each group the worksheet, a dice, and enough counters.

❗ If you don't have a dice, give each group a coin. Sts toss the coin for their go and move 1 for heads and 2 for tails.

- Each player puts a counter on **START**.
- Explain the rules of the game. Sts take turns to throw the dice and move their counter. When they land on a circle, they must complete the sentence using the first or second conditional. Focus on the example on the worksheet (*If I went to university again, I would study history.*) to show how Sts should use the conditionals correctly. Tell Sts not to worry about making the sentences true for themselves – they simply have to make grammatically correct sentences.
- The rest of the group has to decide if the sentence is correct and makes sense. Be the final judge in case of dispute. If the sentence is wrong, Sts move back a circle. If it is correct, they stay on the circle.
- If a student lands on a circle that another player is on, they must make a different sentence.
- Sts play the game in their groups. Monitor and correct any mistakes. The first student to reach **FINISH** wins.
- Get feedback on some of the more interesting answers.

5A Soap opera

A group activity

Sts work in groups to plan the plot for a pilot episode of a soap opera. Copy one worksheet per student.

> **LANGUAGE**
> Television, dramatic present for describing a plot, suggesting, agreeing and disagreeing, expressing enthusiasm
> *Why don't we…?*
> *I agree / don't agree.*
> *That's a good idea!*

- Put Sts in small groups of four and give out one worksheet to each student.
- Tell Sts they are going to plan the plot for a pilot episode of a soap opera. Make sure Sts know what a pilot is here (= a single TV programme made to find out if people will like it and want to watch further episodes).

- Focus on **a** and the characters. Give Sts a few minutes to look at the photos and read the information. Put Sts in each group in two pairs and tell them that they are going to check they understand the relationships between the characters by drawing a family tree. Point out that Simon isn't related to anyone, so he isn't on the family tree.
- When Sts have finished, they can compare their tree with the other pair in their group. Check answers by eliciting the family tree onto the board to ensure that Sts have the correct model.

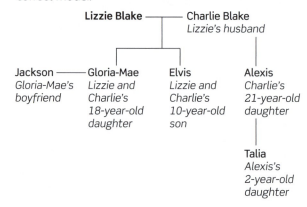

- Focus on **b**. Make sure Sts understand that they have to develop a plot outline for a one-hour pilot episode. Their ideas should be general – they don't have to write any dialogue or give too much detailed information. Tell Sts to use the present simple to describe the plot. Give some examples, e.g. *'Lizzie is very happy about the party, but everyone else is angry about it. Five minutes after the party starts, the doorbell rings and…'*
- Sts work in their groups and discuss their ideas. Get each group to appoint a secretary to make notes of the plot outline. Monitor and help.
- Now focus on **c**. Sts plan their presentation and make notes on what each student is going to say.
- Finally, focus on **d**. Each group presents their proposed pilot episode to the class.
- Get feedback on some of the more interesting plots and decide as a class which is the best plot.

EXTRA IDEA If you see that your Sts are enjoying the task, you could let them continue developing more plots for some more episodes.

5B Why did you write…?

A pairwork activity

Sts write information about themselves. They then swap with a partner and try to guess what their partner's information is about. Copy and cut up one pair of worksheets (**A** and **B**) per pair.

> **LANGUAGE**
> Present perfect continuous
> **A** *I think you wrote 'tired' because it's how you've been feeling today.*
> **B** *Almost! It's because it's how I've been feeling this week.*

- Put Sts in pairs, **A** and **B**, and give each student their instructions and a 'shapes' chart.

- Give Sts five minutes to write answers in the appropriate places in the chart. When they have finished, take back the instructions sheet or tell Sts to turn it over.
- Now get Sts to swap 'shapes' charts. Demonstrate the activity by taking a chart from a student and saying *OK, Circle 1. I think you wrote 'tennis' because…* Get the student to tell you if you guessed correctly or not. Ask follow-up questions to continue the conversation.
- Make it clear to Sts that they were given different instructions, and stress that they can guess the information in any order. Sts now do the activity in their pairs. Monitor and help where necessary. Stop the activity when most Sts have guessed all their partner's information.

EXTRA IDEA While Sts are doing the activity, monitor and make notes on any errors they are making with the use of the present perfect continuous. Use these for a whole-class error correction activity by writing some of the errors on the board and asking Sts to correct them in pairs.

6A What's the problem?
A pairwork role-play activity

Sts revise the topic of the lesson by taking the parts of waiter or waitress / customer and cashier / customer. Copy one pair of worksheets (**A** and **B**) per pair.

LANGUAGE
At a restaurant
Do you have a reservation?
I'd like to eat in, please.

- Put Sts in pairs, **A** and **B**, ideally face to face, and give out the worksheets. Make sure Sts can't see each other's worksheets. If you have odd numbers of Sts, make one pair a three and have two **A**s (or take part in the role-play yourself).
- Tell Sts they are going to role-play two situations. Tell them to read Role-play 1 and prepare the information they will need. Encourage the waiters / waitresses and customers to be as imaginative and inventive as possible in their questions and answers.

EXTRA SUPPORT Give Sts time to make a few notes about what they want to say.

- When Sts are ready, tell Sts **A** to begin the conversation. Give Sts time to act out the role-play. Monitor and note down anything you might want to draw their attention to afterwards.
- Repeat the process for Role-play 2. Tell Sts **B** to begin the conversation.
- Get feedback from some pairs on what the outcomes of the conversations were and if the customers think they got good service.

6B What can I do?
A group speaking activity

Sts ask questions and answer using *can*, *could*, and *be able to*. Copy and cut up one worksheet per group of three to five Sts.

LANGUAGE
can, *could*, and *be able to*, DIY and repairs
You could ask a friend to help you with the instructions to put the furniture together.

- Put Sts in groups of three to five and give each group a set of cards face down. Demonstrate the activity by getting a student to pick a card and read the problem. Offer solutions using *can* or *could*, e.g. *'You could try cleaning it with bicarbonate of soda…'*, etc. Get other Sts to offer solutions and get the student who read the card to choose his/her favourite solution.
- Sts take turns to pick up the top card and read the problem. The person who offers the best solution keeps the card. The person with the most cards at the end of the game is the winner. Monitor and help if necessary.
- Get feedback about the most inventive solutions to the problems.

EXTRA IDEA Sts can do this as a mingle activity instead. Copy and cut up one worksheet per 20 Sts and give each one a card. Sts mingle and ask their question and answer others. At the end, ask them about their favourite answers.

7A Talking of money…
A pairwork speaking activity

Sts complete questions with particles and then ask each other some of the questions. Copy one worksheet per pair and cut into **A** and **B**.

LANGUAGE
Phrasal verbs
I don't think children over 18 should live off their parents.
I wouldn't give away any money because…

- Put Sts in pairs, **A** and **B**, and give out the worksheets. Explain that they have different questions and tell Sts they have five minutes to complete the questions individually with the correct particle (a preposition or an adverb).
- Check answers by eliciting only the particles, not the whole question.

A	2 down	3 off, back	4 back	5 away	6 out	7 for
	8 off					
B	2 out	3 for	4 back	5 up	6 away	7 after	8 back

- Now tell Sts to choose five questions each from their worksheet that they would like to ask their partner.
- Put Sts face to face if possible and tell them to take turns to ask each other their questions. If they don't understand a question, they should ask their partner to repeat it slowly. Encourage Sts to react to what their partner says and to ask for more information when they can. Monitor and correct any mistakes with particles.

EXTRA IDEA Fast finishers could ask more questions from the worksheet.

- Get feedback on some of the more interesting answers.

7B Talk for 30 seconds
A group board game

Sts move around the board and talk about a topic using different verb patterns. Copy one worksheet per group of three or four Sts. You also need one dice per group and one counter per student.

> **LANGUAGE**
> Verb patterns
> *A person I know who's very good at telling jokes is my brother. He's really funny.*
> *Something I do to relax is watch series on Netflix.*

- Put Sts in groups of three or four. Give each group the worksheet, a dice, and enough counters.

❗ If you don't have a dice, give each group a coin. Sts toss the coin for their go and move 1 for heads and 2 for tails.

- Each player puts a counter on **START**.
- Explain the rules of the game. Sts take turns to throw the dice and move their counter. When they land on a circle, they must talk about that topic, completing it with a gerund, infinitive with *to*, or infinitive without *to*. Focus on the example on the worksheet (*A time I did something that someone told me not to do, was when my friend Sarah told me not to tell another friend…*) to show how Sts should use the correct verb pattern as they speak. If the other Sts hear the speaker use an incorrect verb pattern, they should try to correct it. Be the final judge in case of dispute.
- If the sentence is wrong, Sts move back a circle. If it is correct, they stay on the circle.
- Sts play the game in their groups. Monitor and correct any mistakes. The first student to reach **FINISH** wins.
- Get feedback on some of the more interesting answers.

8A Do it yourself or have it done?
A pairwork speaking activity

Sts talk about things they do or have done for them. Copy one worksheet per pair.

> **LANGUAGE**
> *have something done*
> *I prefer having things repaired. I hate repairing things in my house.*

- Put Sts in pairs and give out the worksheets.
- Explain to Sts that they are going to discuss some topics in pairs, saying whether they do the things themselves, or have them done for them.
- Allow a minute for Sts to read through the list of topics with the two options. Then focus on the example. Role-play this conversation with a student as a demonstration of the activity.
- Remind Sts that they will need to give reasons for their answers and that their partners should ask for more information. People answering a question can use *What about you?*

- In their pairs, Sts take turns to choose a topic from the list and ask questions about which option their partner prefers or normally does and why. Monitor and correct any mistakes.
- Get feedback on some of the more interesting answers.

8B The History Quiz
A pairwork quiz

Sts revise active / passive verb forms by completing questions in a quiz. Copy one worksheet per pair and cut into **A** and **B**.

> **LANGUAGE**
> Passive and active in question forms
> *Why did the British royal family change its name in 1917?*
> *The sale of what was banned in the USA in January 1920?*

- Put Sts in pairs, **A** and **B**, and give out the worksheets.
- Focus on **a**. Tell Sts to complete the questions using the verb in brackets in the correct form (past simple active or passive). Tell them not to discuss the answers at this stage.
- Check answers by eliciting only the missing verbs, NOT the whole question.

> **A** 1 did, take 2 were, killed 3 was given
> 4 was assassinated 5 were, used 6 did, change
> 7 was destroyed 8 wrote
> **B** 1 was banned 2 were, allowed 3 attacked
> 4 was, made 5 invented 6 was, built
> 7 was, introduced 8 appeared

- Now focus on **b** and tell Sts that the correct answers are in **bold**. Sts **A** read their questions to Sts **B** with the three options. Sts **B** choose an option and Sts **A** circle their answer. Then Sts swap roles.
- When Sts have finished, get them to add up their partner's score. Each correct answer is worth one point.
- Sts swap worksheets so that they can see their score and what questions they got wrong. The student with more points wins.
- Get some quick feedback from pairs to find out which facts were surprising / new to them. Find out if any Sts got all the answers correct.

9A Find the pair
A group card game

Sts revise reported speech by playing a card game in small groups. Copy one worksheet per group of four Sts and cut up into cards.

> **LANGUAGE**
> Direct speech / reported speech
> *'Do you like your present?' she asked.*
> *She asked me if I liked my present.*

- Put Sts in groups of four and give each group one set of cards divided into the 12 large and 12 small rectangles.

❗ This activity can also be played in pairs.

- Show Sts how to play the game by pointing out that there are two types of card (two different sizes). Shuffle the cards and arrange them one by one, face down on your table in the two groups: the sentences in direct speech (small rectangles) on the left and the sentences in reported speech (large rectangles) on the right. Ask a student to turn over a direct speech card and read out what it says (e.g. *'Do you like your present?' she asked.*). Then elicit from the student the sentence in reported speech (e.g. *She asked me if I liked my present.*). Now ask the student to try to find this sentence in the reported speech group by turning over <u>one</u> card. If he / she finds the corresponding sentence, he / she keeps both cards and has another turn. If not, he / she must put the cards back in the place where they were, and another student has a turn.
- Highlight that:
  – Sts have to say what they think the reported speech card will say before they try to find it.
  – Sts must always put the cards back in the same place, unless they get a pair, in which case they keep both cards.
  – this is a memory game, so Sts must watch the cards other Sts turn over and try to remember where the cards are so they can try and find the matching pair.
- Monitor and ensure that Sts are doing the activity correctly. Stop after a group has no cards remaining, or after time is up, e.g. after ten minutes.
- Get feedback from each group (or pair) to find out who has won / got the most pairs.

NON-CUT ALTERNATIVE Copy one worksheet per pair and fold into two sections down the centre line. Put Sts in pairs. Sts take turns to read the direct speech and to try to say / write the reported speech. When Sts have finished, ask them to check answers on the reported speech side of the sheet. Get feedback from each pair to find out who got most answers correct.

9B What had happened?
A group writing activity

Sts revise the third conditional and the past perfect by writing group stories. Copy one worksheet per group of eight Sts and cut up into cards.

> **LANGUAGE**
>
> Third conditional, other uses of the past perfect
> *Jamie would never have married Nicola if he had known her terrible secret.*
> *When Sheila opened the door, she saw that someone had cleaned her house.*

- Put Sts in pairs. Then put four pairs together in a group. Give each group a set of cards, face down.
- Explain that Sts are going to write some short stories in their groups, each pair of Sts contributing a sentence to each story. Tell each pair to take a card. Set a time limit, e.g. two minutes, for Sts to complete the first sentence on their card. When the time is up, say 'Stop', and tell Sts to pass their card to the pair on their left. Now tell Sts, in their pairs, to read the first sentence of the new story passed to them and add a second sentence. Monitor and check Sts are using tenses correctly.

- Repeat the process for the third sentence. When time is up and Sts have passed on their story, tell Sts that now they have to finish the story with their fourth sentence.
- Get Sts to read out their stories in their groups and decide which one they like best.
- If there's time, get Sts to repeat the process with the remaining cards.
- Finally get each group to read out their best story to the class. You could have a class vote on the best stories.

10A What's the question?
A group card game

Sts revise asking questions with forms of *be*, *do*, and *have* as auxiliary and main verbs by playing a card game in small groups. Copy one worksheet per group of four Sts and cut up into cards.

> **LANGUAGE**
>
> *be*, *do*, and *have*: auxiliary and main verbs
> *Where are you going on your next holiday?*
> *What have you bought online recently?*

- Put Sts in groups of four and give each group a set of cards.
- Explain the rules of the game. Sts take turns to pick up a card, complete the questions with a form of *be*, *do*, or *have*, and then answer the questions. Demonstrate the activity by picking up a card. Write the prompts on the board and elicit the complete questions from students. Answer the questions yourself and provide as much information as you can.
- Sts must try and ask the questions correctly. If the other students hear the speaker use an incorrect verb or verb form, they should try to correct it.
- Encourage Sts to ask for more information. Sts who are answering can ask *What about you?*
- Sts play the game in their groups. Monitor and correct any mistakes.

> What is your favourite name? What do you like about it?
> What colour do you almost never wear, or use in your house? Why do you think you dislike it?
> Where are you going on your next holiday? Why have you chosen that place?
> What have you bought online recently? Why did you buy it?
> What were you like ten years ago? How have you changed since then?
> What is your favourite photo of yourself? What do you like about it?
> What are some things that people could do to help reduce waste? How do you think they would help?
> What would your ideal job be? Why?
> Do you prefer watching films at home or at the cinema? Why?
> Have you ever thought of living in the countryside? Why (not)?
> Do you like eating out? What is the best restaurant you have ever been to?
> What things in your house have you mended? Do you think you are good at DIY? Why (not)?
> What would you do if you had one million pounds? Would you leave your job or stop your studies? Why (not)?
> Did you go out or stay in last New Year's Eve? What did you do?
> When did you last have your hair cut? Do you like it? Why (not)?
> How many different historical sites in your local area have you been to? Which is your favourite? Why?

> Do you usually forget to take things with you when you leave home (keys, phone)? What do you do to help you remember?
> What is the best wedding you have ever been to? What was special about it?
> What do you think is the best thing about the USA? And the worst?
> Have you ever taken any official English exams? Was it a good experience? Why (not)?

- The activity ends when the group runs out of cards.
- Get feedback on some of the more interesting answers.

EXTRA CHALLENGE Encourage the student who is answering the questions to give extra information and the other Sts in the group to ask follow-up questions as appropriate.

10B Speaking exam

A pairwork speaking activity

Sts practise common speaking exam tasks. Copy one worksheet per pair and cut into **A** and **B**.

> **LANGUAGE**
>
> Answering personal questions, describing photos, a discussion, general revision and exam practice
> *My full name is Maria Gonzalez.*
> *In my photo there's a…*
> *I like visiting museums. How about you?*

- Put Sts in pairs, **A** and **B**, face to face if possible, and give out the worksheets. You could explain that the activity they are going to do is similar to the Cambridge Preliminary exam.
- Focus on **1**. Sts **A** ask Sts **B** their five questions. Remind Sts **B** to give as much information as they can. Set a time limit, e.g. three minutes. Then Sts swap roles.
- Focus on **2**. Sts **A** describe their photo. Sts **B** listen. Set a time limit, e.g. two minutes. Then Sts swap roles. At the end, they compare the two photos.
- Finally, focus on **3**. Sts interact by discussing the topics. Set a time limit, e.g. five minutes. Remind them to ask questions for more information.

EXTRA IDEA Monitor for any grammar or vocabulary errors during the activity. Use them at the end of the lesson to do a whole-class error correction activity.

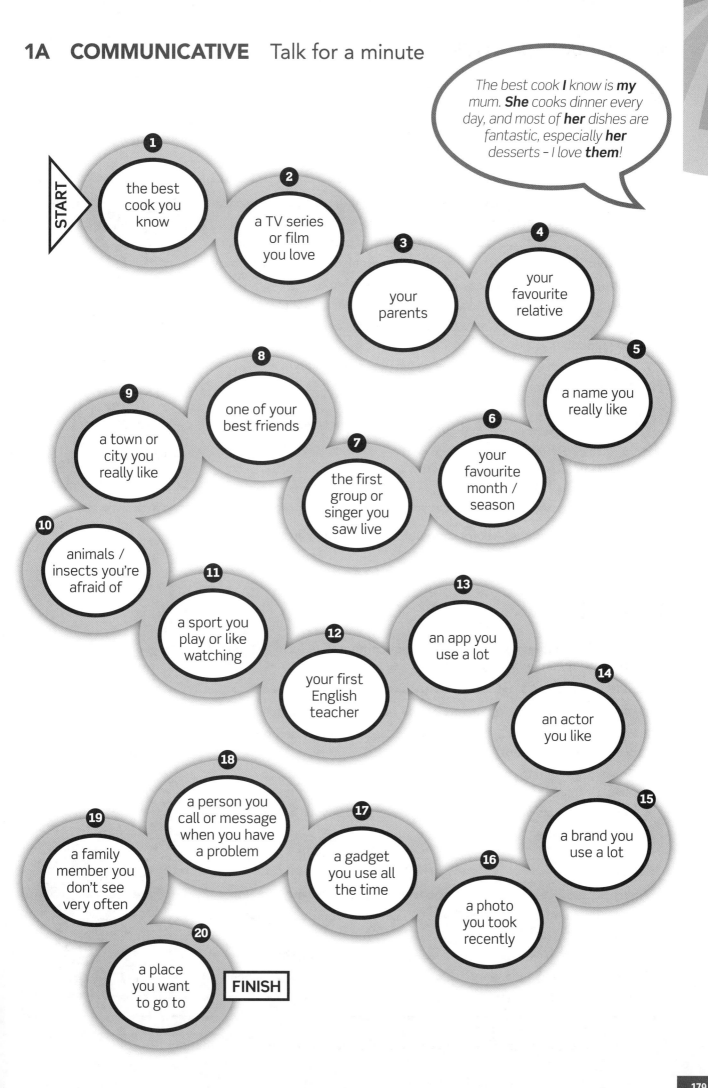

1B COMMUNICATIVE Good, better, the best

Student A

a Complete the questions with the correct comparative form (+ *than* if necessary) or *the* + superlative form. Use the adjective in brackets.

1 Do you think that a holiday with your friends is <u>more enjoyable than</u> one with your family? (enjoyable)
2 What's _____ meal you've had recently? (delicious)
3 Are you _____ during the week or at weekends? (busy)
4 Who's _____ person you know? (old)
5 Are you _____ in the mornings or at night? (creative)
6 What's _____ brand and model of phone you've ever had? (good)
7 Who's _____ person in your family? (lazy)
8 When you feel stressed, what do you do to feel _____? (calm)
9 What's _____ you've ever travelled? (far)
10 If you wanted to get _____ you are now, what should you do? (fit)

b Ask **B** your questions. Ask for more information. Then answer **B**'s questions.

- -

Student B

a Complete the questions with the correct comparative form (+ *than* if necessary) or *the* + superlative form. Use the adjective in brackets.

1 What's <u>the most beautiful</u> country you've ever visited? (beautiful)
2 Which do you think is _____ – a yellow bedroom or a black bedroom? (good)
3 Do you think buying something online is always _____ buying it from a shop? (cheap)
4 Which person are you _____ to in your family? (close)
5 How important is it to you to have _____ gadgets? (late)
6 Are you _____ in the mornings or in the evenings? (active)
7 Who's _____ sportsperson in your country? (great)
8 Apart from English, what would be _____ language for you to learn? (useful)
9 What do you think is _____ form of transport? (safe)
10 Do you think vegetarians are _____ people who eat meat? (healthy)

b Answer **A**'s questions. Then ask **A** your questions. Ask for more information.

2A COMMUNICATIVE Ask me a question

a Complete the questions with the present simple or continuous form of the verbs in brackets.

1 How often <u>do</u> you <u>go</u> to the hairdresser's? And to the dentist's? (go)

2 Are you happy with your lifestyle or _____ you _____ it could be healthier? (think)

3 Why exactly _____ you _____ English? (learn)

4 _____ anybody in your family _____ a foreign language really well? (speak)

5 _____ you _____ away this weekend? (go)

6 _____ anyone you know _____ for a job at the moment? (look)

7 _____ you _____ of doing any official English exams in the near future? (think)

8 _____ you usually _____ seeing films which are dubbed, or films which are subtitled? (prefer)

9 What _____ your best friend _____ like? (look)

10 What book _____ you _____ at the moment? (read)

11 What _____ you _____ tomorrow night? (do)

12 What clubs, organizations, or charities _____ you _____ to? (belong)

13 What time _____ you usually _____ work or school in the morning? (start)

14 What kind of things _____ you _____ your phone for? (use)

15 _____ you _____ anybody who _____ _____ married soon? (know, get)

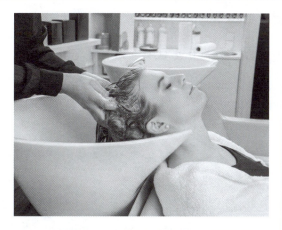

b Choose eight questions to ask your partner.

2B COMMUNICATIVE Describe and draw

Student A

a Look at your picture.

b Describe it to **B**. Answer **B**'s questions.

Describe

---

c Listen to **B**'s description of a picture and draw it. Ask questions if you need to.

Draw

d Now compare your drawing to **B**'s picture. Are there any differences?

English File fourth edition Teacher's Guide Intermediate Plus   Photocopiable © Oxford University Press 2020

2B COMMUNICATIVE Describe and draw

Student B

a Look at your picture.

b Listen to A's description of a picture and draw it. Ask questions if you need to.

Draw

c Now compare your drawing to A's picture. Are there any differences?

d Describe your picture to A. Answer A's questions.

Describe

3A COMMUNICATIVE When you were younger

a Tick three topics in each group that you can talk about. Write notes for each topic you've ticked.

b Compare with a partner. Look at the topics you've ticked. Take turns to tell each other about them.

I'm going to tell you about some food I used to love eating…

Past habits

- a kind of food you used to love eating
- a place you used to love going to
- a group or singer you used to like, but don't any more
- a TV programme you used to love watching
- something naughty you used to do
- what you used to want to be when you were little
- a game you used to play a lot

Past events

- the first trip you went on without your family
- a memorable celebration you once had
- an embarrassing situation you once had
- a childhood holiday you will always remember
- the first film you saw in a cinema
- a time when you lost something important
- a really nice present you once received

3B COMMUNICATIVE What's the preposition?

a Look at the questions. Write the missing preposition for each box.

b Take turns to choose one of the boxes and ask your partner all the questions in it.

1 of
- If you had to speak in front ___ a large audience, how would you feel?
- Do you know anyone who has a phobia, or is really afraid ___ something?
- When was the last time you felt proud ___ something you had done?
- Are there any things in your home that you're really tired ___?

2
- Who can you rely ___ when you have a problem? Can they rely ___ you, too?
- What do you always have ___ your desk at home?
- Would you prefer to live ___ the ground floor or ___ the top floor of a flat?
- What kind of entertainment do you spend most money ___?

3
- What sport or activity would you like to be really good ___?
- Why do you think some people are bad ___ learning languages?
- What's the first thing you do when you arrive ___ a nice hotel?
- Do you like telling jokes? Do people laugh ___ the jokes you tell?

4
- What sports clubs or organizations do / did you belong ___?
- Is there anyone who you talk ___ every day, in person or on the phone? Who is it?
- What are you most looking forward ___ this year?
- What are the advantages of being married ___ someone from another country?

5
- What period of history are you most interested ___?
- Do you believe ___ love at first sight? Why (not)?
- When you arrive ___ a new city or country, what's the first thing you usually try to find out?
- What things do you normally carry ___ your bag or wallet?

6
- What are some of the typical things couples argue ___?
- What would you tell visitors ___ before they visit your city or country?
- Is there anything you always worry ___ before or during a trip? What?
- When you were little, did you get excited ___ your birthday? How did you use to celebrate it?

7
- Can people still be friends if they don't agree ___ each other about politics?
- Do you feel pleased ___ your progress in English this term?
- What kind of photos do you share ___ friends on social media?
- Have you ever been given a present that you were really disappointed ___?

8
- How do you feel about waiting ___ people when they're late?
- Should a man pay ___ a woman's meal on a first date?
- Are you (or is anyone you know) applying ___ a job or course at the moment?
- Who's usually responsible ___ cooking dinner in your house?

4A COMMUNICATIVE The Green Quiz

Student A

1 The average person in the UK throws away their body weight in rubbish every…
   a 5–6 weeks.
   b 7–8 weeks.
   c 9–10 weeks.

2 Scientists predict that by the year 2100, temperatures will be…
   a the same as today.
   b between 1.5 and 3.2°C higher.
   c between 3.2 and 5.9°C higher.

3 How many tonnes of plastic end up in the ocean every year?
   a 4 million
   b 12 million
   c 20 million

4 It's predicted that between 2030 and 2050, 250,000 people will die each year because of…
   a air pollution.
   b climate change.
   c landfill sites.

5 If you're going out for the night, it's less wasteful to…
   a turn the lights off.
   b leave the lights on.
   c do nothing. It makes no difference.

6 How long will it take most plastics to decompose?
   a 200 years.
   b 300 years.
   c More than 400 years.

7 On the motorway, you'll use less fuel if you…
   a drive at the speed limit.
   b drive at an average speed of 55–60 miles per hour.
   c drive really slowly.

8 Which of these things can't be recycled?
   a computers
   b paint
   c used pizza boxes

9 What percentage of all plastics ever produced have been recycled?
   a 9%
   b 17%
   c 22%

10 Which country recycles the most?
   a the USA
   b Germany
   c Sweden

Student B

1 In which of these products can you find plastic?
   a a teabag
   b a wine bottle
   c a bar of soap

2 If you throw a pair of shoes away, how long will it take for them to decompose?
   a 30 years
   b 40 years
   c 50 years

3 Scientists think that by the year 2100, sea levels will rise by…
   a 25 cm.
   b 45 cm.
   c 65 cm.

4 By what year do experts think there will be more kilos of plastic than fish in the ocean?
   a 2030
   b 2050
   c 2070

5 Scientists predict that by the year 2070, winter rainfall in parts of the UK will increase by…
   a up to 20%.
   b up to 35%.
   c up to 50%.

6 What percentage of plastic bottles in the UK gets recycled?
   a around 50%
   b around 60%
   c around 70%

7 The UK government hopes that all new cars will be electric by the year…
   a 2040.
   b 2045.
   c 2050.

8 How many single-use plastic bottles are used in the UK every day?
   a 21.5 million
   b 38.5 million
   c 50.5 million

9 How many tonnes of food waste does the UK send to landfill sites every year?
   a about 5.3 million tonnes
   b about 6.3 million tonnes
   c about 7.3 million tonnes

10 How much domestic waste in the UK is recycled?
   a about 35%
   b about 45%
   c about 55%

English File fourth edition Teacher's Guide Intermediate Plus   Photocopiable © Oxford University Press 2020

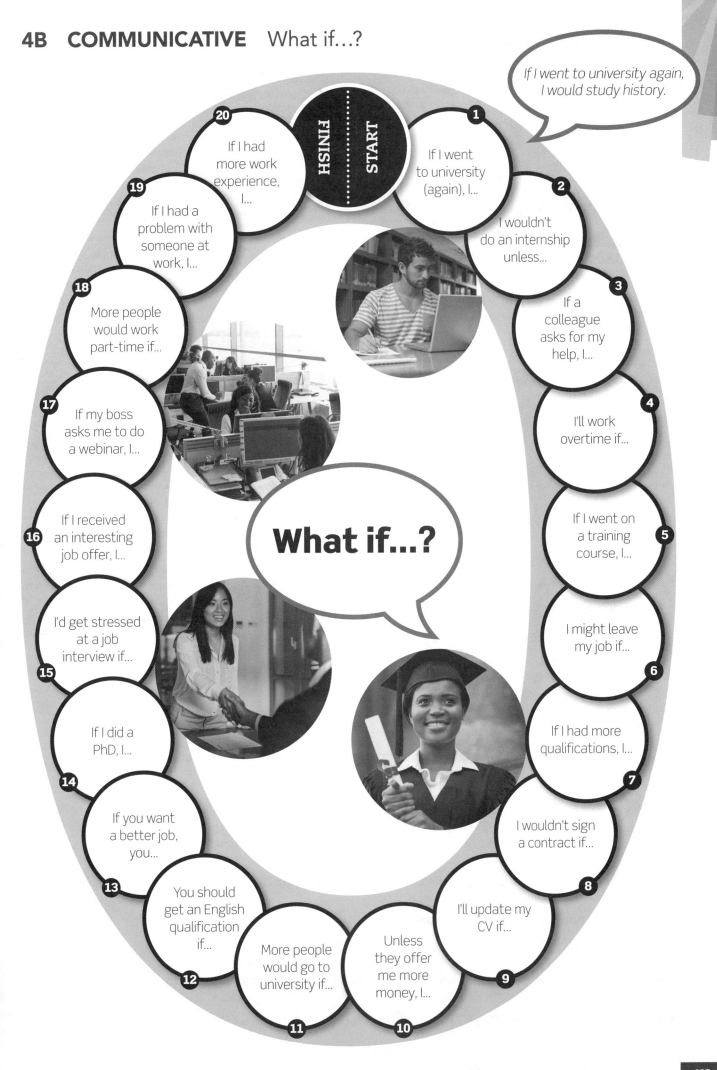

5A COMMUNICATIVE Soap opera

Lizzie
Lizzie Blake is the 44-year-old 'head' of the family. She has several properties she rents out and so she doesn't have to work. She will protect her family at all costs.

Charlie
Charlie Blake is Lizzie's 45-year-old husband. He's being investigated for fraud at the moment. He's only interested in himself and making 'fast' money. He has never worked and was married before.

Alexis
Alexis is Charlie's 21-year-old daughter from a previous marriage. She had a baby at the age of 19 and has always refused to say who her daughter's father is. She has always had a bad relationship with Lizzie. She and Talia live with Lizzie and Charlie. She works as a PA to a fashion designer.

Talia
Talia is Alexis's two-year-old daughter.

Gloria-Mae
Gloria-Mae is Lizzie and Charlie's 18-year-old daughter. She doesn't get on with Alexis. She's studying computing at college. She's engaged to Jackson and is desperate to get married and leave home as soon as possible.

Jackson
Jackson is Gloria-Mae's boyfriend. He lives with her and the rest of her family. He's unemployed, so he volunteered to look after Talia while Alexis is at work. He's engaged to Gloria-Mae, but he's not in love with her. He's attracted to Alexis!

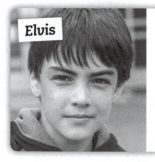
Elvis
Elvis is Lizzie and Charlie's 10-year-old son. He's jealous of Talia because he thinks she gets all the attention. He hates Jackson and would like him to leave the house forever.

Simon
Simon works for Lizzie. He repairs anything that is broken in her properties. He went to the same school as Alexis and Gloria-Mae. He's very good friends with Gloria-Mae, but he never speaks to Alexis.

a Read the information about the characters. In groups, draw a family tree showing the relationship between the people.

b An independent television company is planning to make a one-hour pilot for a soap opera. If it's successful, a series will be made. The television company wants your group to present a plot outline for the pilot, based on the descriptions of the people you've just read about.

The soap opera will begin on Lizzie's 45th birthday. She has organized a big dinner and she wants everyone to be there. In your group, discuss:
- the relationship between the people.
- incidents that might happen before, during, and after the dinner.

c Now plan your presentation. Make notes about what each person in your group is going to say.

d Now, with your group, explain your plot for the pilot to the class, and listen to other groups' plans. Which pilot do you think is the best?

5B COMMUNICATIVE Why did you write…?

Student A instructions

a Read your instructions and write your answers in shapes 1–10 in the chart.

In circle 1, write the name of a sport / activity you've been doing a lot recently.
In triangle 2, write an adjective which describes how you've been feeling this week.
In square 3, write the name of a person who you've been talking to a lot recently.
In circle 4, write how long you've been living in your present house or flat.
In triangle 5, write the name of a TV series you've been watching since it started.
In square 6, write the name of a social media website or app you've been using for a long time, e.g. Facebook.
In circle 7, write the name of some food you've been eating a lot recently.
In triangle 8, write the time you've been going to bed this week.
In square 9, write something you've been doing to improve your English recently.
In circle 10, write the name of a book you've been reading, but haven't finished yet.

b Swap charts with **B**. Try to guess what **B**'s answers are about. Ask for more information.

OK, circle 1. I think you wrote 'Coke' because it's something you drink a lot.

No. It's a drink I've been trying to cut down on.

How long have you been trying to cut down?

c Now listen to **B**'s guesses about your answers. Tell **B** if they're right or wrong and answer his / her questions.

Student A chart

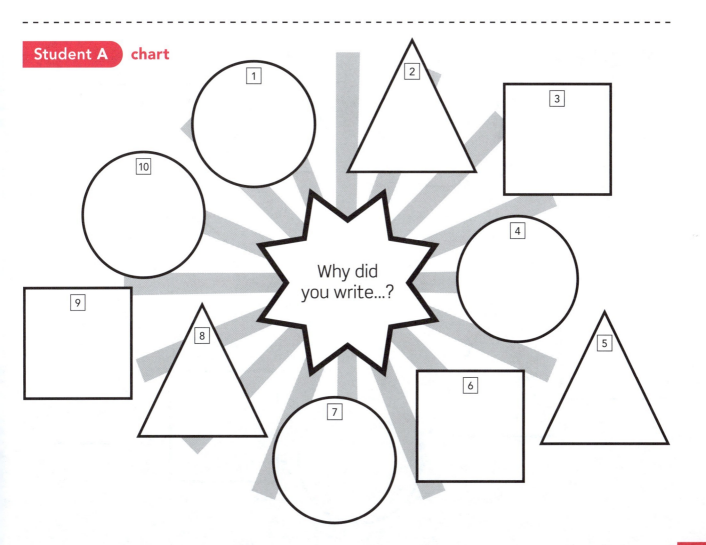

5B COMMUNICATIVE Why did you write…?

Student B instructions

a Read your instructions and write your answers in shapes 1–10 in the chart.

In circle 1, write the name of a food / drink you've been trying to cut down on.
In triangle 2, write the name of someone who's been helping you a lot this year.
In square 3, write an activity you've been thinking of trying for a long time.
In circle 4, write the name of a song that you've been listening to a lot recently.
In triangle 5, write the name of a sports team you've been following since you were young.
In square 6, write the number of years you've been studying English.
In circle 7, write the name of something you've been thinking of buying.
In triangle 8, write the name of a TV programme you've been watching a lot recently.
In square 9, write a holiday you've been hoping / planning to go on for a long time.
In circle 10, write the name of a restaurant or bar you've been going to for a long time.

b Swap charts with **A**. Listen to **A**'s guesses about your answers. Tell **A** if they're right or wrong and answer his / her questions.

c Now try to guess what **A**'s answers are about. Ask for more information.

OK, circle 1. I think you wrote 'tennis' because it's a sport you've been doing for a long time.

Close! It's a sport I've been doing a lot recently.

How long have you been playing?

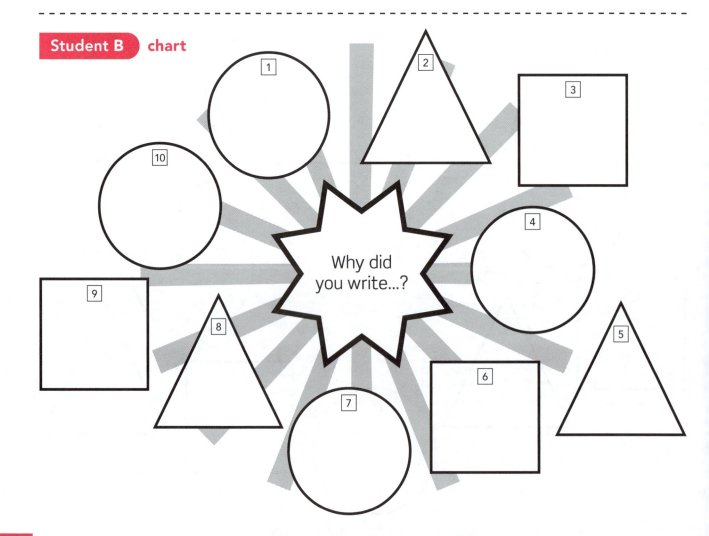

6A COMMUNICATIVE What's the problem?

Student A

● **Role-play 1** You're a waiter / waitress in a restaurant. **B** is a customer.

It's Saturday night and you think that you're going to be very busy. This is good because the restaurant hasn't been very full recently. If the restaurant closes, you'll lose your job and so you always do everything you can to keep your customers happy and get good tips. You smile a lot, listen, and remember that the customer is always right! It's 8.20 in the evening and **B** walks into the restaurant with his / her partner.

- Greet **B**. Ask for his / her name, if he / she has a reservation, and at what time.
- The only table that you have left is one at the back of the restaurant in a corner next to the kitchen. Offer it to **B**. Try to make it sound nice (it's intimate, dark, quiet, perfect for a romantic evening).
- A short time later **B** calls you back to the table. He / She has several problems. Try to deal with them politely. You don't want **B** to leave. However, bear in mind the following:
  - There are no other free tables, though there should be one in 30 minutes.
  - The kitchen is very busy because one of the chefs is ill, and **B** arrived at the same time as a lot of other customers.

Begin the role-play. You start the conversation: *Good evening. How can I help you?*

● **Role-play 2** You're a customer. **B** works in a fast food restaurant.

You're having a terrible day. Your boss shouted at you at work, you have a really important project that you need to finish today, and you left your lunch at home. You only have 20 minutes for lunch, so you rush to the fast food restaurant right next to your office. When you get there, there's a long queue. By the time you are served, you only have 10 minutes for lunch!

- You're a vegetarian, so you order the vegetarian burger. Make sure it isn't cooked with the meat burgers. You want to eat in because you want a break from the office.
- When **B** asks you if you want anything else, ask for a Diet Coke (you don't like any other soft drinks) and some chips. Tell **B** to make sure he / she is charging you for a meal deal and not the separate items.
- Tell **B** you'll never come to the restaurant again if you don't get what you ordered quickly. You really need to be back at work in 10 minutes, so you'll take the food away if you have to.

Begin the role-play. **B** will start the conversation.

6A COMMUNICATIVE What's the problem?

Student B

● **Role-play 1** You're a customer in a restaurant. **A** is a waiter / waitress.

You're excited because you're on a first date and you've organized the perfect evening, so nothing could go wrong... or could it? You arrive at the restaurant at 8.20.

- Ask for your table. Your booking was for 8 p.m. for a table near the window and you know that you're only 20 minutes late.
- You are given another table. After a few minutes, you decide you're not happy because:
  – the table you've got is next to the kitchen, which means it's noisy and hot.
  – you need to get your food quickly, because you're going to a nearby cinema after dinner. The film starts at 9.30. The waiter hasn't even taken your order yet!
- Call **A** and ask him / her to deal with your problems. You don't really want to leave, because it's Saturday night and you probably wouldn't find anywhere else, but you want a good explanation and solution.

Begin the role-play. **A** will start the conversation.

● **Role-play 2** You work in a fast food restaurant. **A** is a customer.

It's your first day in this job. You've been training with the manager all morning and he's just left you on your own for the first time. You don't really know all the burger options yet. You really want to do well in this job because you need the money. **A** comes to your till.

- Greet **A**. Ask him / her what he / she wants to eat and if it is to eat in or take away.
- You don't think the vegetarian burger is cooked with the meat, but you're not sure.
- Ask politely if he / she wants anything else. The till automatically charges customers ordering a burger, chips, and a soft drink for a meal deal.
- You don't have any Diet Coke at the moment. Try to convince **A** to have a different soft drink (make suggestions). If he / she doesn't have a drink, you will have to charge for the burger and chips separately and it will be more expensive.
- The kitchen is very busy and **A** is getting impatient. Try to find a solution. You don't want to lose a customer!

Begin the role-play. You start the conversation: *Hello. How can I help you today?*

6B COMMUNICATIVE What can I do?

I've spilt some coffee on my friend's new carpet and I can't get it out. I know she's going to be really angry with me. What can I do?	I bought a new table. It comes already assembled, but now I can't get it up the stairs to my flat! What can I do?	I bought some flat-pack furniture, but I don't understand the instructions and can't put it together. What can I do?	I have a red spot on my nose and I have a really important meeting today. What can I do?
There's a hole in my favourite work trousers. They're grey and they're very delicate. What can I do?	I need to change a lightbulb in my bathroom, but it's quite high up and I don't have a ladder. What can I do?	When I was opening the door to my flat, the key broke inside the lock. I can't get it out. What can I do?	It's really cold and my car won't start. What can I do?
I dropped my earring into the sink and it's gone down the plughole. What can I do?	My brother kicked the door and now there's a hole in it. Our parents aren't home. What can we do?	My watch has stopped working. What can I do?	I borrowed a very old, valuable book from a friend and then I pulled one of the pages out. What can I do?
My neighbours can see into my garden. I really want to be able to spend time outside, but I don't want my neighbours to see everything I do. What can I do?	My room always looks untidy because I have a lot of clothes and books and I only have one shelf and a small wardrobe. What can I do?	I put up a painting on my wall, but it keeps falling down. I'm afraid it will break. What can I do?	I have a lot of charging cables in my drawer and they're always in a mess – I can never find the one I want. What can I do?
I hit my partner's car when I parked next to it. He / She will be upset when he / she sees it! What can I do?	One of the legs on my bed broke. I tried to fix it, but it broke again. It's late and all the shops are closed. What can I do?	I took apart my bookshelf and I painted it. Now I'm putting it together again, but I've lost one of the screws! What can I do?	I want to make something for my sister for her birthday. I have some wood, screws, a drill, nails, and a hammer. What can I do?

7A COMMUNICATIVE Talking of money...

Student A

a   Complete the questions with the correct particle.

1 When you go shopping, do you just buy the things on your list, or do you like to look *round* for other things you might want to buy?
2 Are any kinds of businesses closing _____ in the area where you live?
3 Would you prefer to get a loan that you have to pay _____ quickly, or one that you'll have for many years? Why?
4 If you were given too much change in a shop or restaurant, would you give it _____ or keep it?
5 If you won a lot of money, would you give any _____? Who to?
6 Do you prefer taking money _____ of a cash machine in the street or inside the bank? Why?
7 If you asked _____ the bill in a bar or restaurant and found you didn't have enough money, what would you do?
8 Do you think it's OK for children over 18 to live _____ their parents, or do you think they should get a job? Why?

b   Choose five questions to ask your partner.

Student B

a   Complete the questions with the correct particle.

1 Do you think that the minimum wage in your country is enough to live *on*?
2 When you take someone _____ for dinner, do you usually pay for them or do you pay separately?
3 When you go shopping, do you look _____ special offers in shops and supermarkets?
4 Has anyone ever stolen your purse or wallet? Did you get it _____?
5 Are there any activities you'd like to take _____ but can't afford?
6 If you saw someone being robbed, would you try to help, or run _____?
7 When it comes to managing your money, do you take _____ someone in your family?
8 What do you do if you lend money to someone and they don't pay you _____?

b   Choose five questions to ask your partner.

8A COMMUNICATIVE *Do it yourself or have it done?*

Which do you prefer, taking photos or having your photo taken?

I prefer taking photos. I hate having my photo taken! Which do you normally do?

I normally take photos on my phone, of my friends and me. But I never take selfies.

taking photos	OR	having your photo taken
cutting your hair yourself	OR	having your hair cut
repairing things in your house or flat	OR	having things repaired
cooking a meal for someone else	OR	having a meal cooked for you
washing and ironing your own clothes	OR	having your clothes washed and ironed
taking your shopping home yourself	OR	having your shopping delivered
cleaning your house or flat	OR	having your house or flat cleaned
doing your nails yourself	OR	having your nails done
decorating your house or flat	OR	having your house or flat decorated
washing your car	OR	having your car washed
going out to a restaurant	OR	having a takeaway delivered
organizing a holiday	OR	having a holiday organized for you
tidying your room	OR	having your room tidied

8B COMMUNICATIVE The History Quiz

Student A

a Complete the questions with the correct form of the verbs in brackets: active or passive.

1 In which city _____ the second Olympic Games of the modern era _____ place in 1900? (take)
   a Athens   **b Paris**   c Rome
2 In what year _____ Tsar Nicholas II and his family _____ by the Bolsheviks? (kill)
   a 1916   b 1917   **c 1918**
3 In 1922, a 14-year-old boy _____ the first human experimental dose of what? (give)
   a penicillin   **b insulin**   c paracetamol
4 Which famous American _____ on 4th April 1968? (assassinate)
   a Martin Luther King   b Bobby Kennedy   c Malcolm X
5 When _____ bar codes first _____? (use)
   a the 1960s   **b the 1970s**   c the 1980s
6 Why _____ the British royal family _____ its name from 'Saxe-Coburg and Gotha' to 'Windsor' in 1917? (change)
   a because it sounded too German   b because it was too long
   c because it was too difficult to pronounce
7 Which Italian city _____ when a volcano erupted in 79 AD? (destroy)
   a Rome   b Naples   **c Pompeii**
8 Who _____ his thoughts in a 'Little Red Book'? (write)
   a Lenin   **b Mao Zedong**   c Gandhi

b Ask your partner the questions.

Student B

a Complete the questions with the correct form of the verbs in brackets: active or passive.

1 The sale of what _____ in the USA in January 1920? (ban)
   a cigarettes   b tobacco   **c alcohol**
2 What _____ Swiss women finally _____ to do in 1971? (allow)
   a get a divorce   **b vote in national elections**   c open a bank account
3 Who _____ the ancient city of Troy, according to Homer? (attack)
   a the Greeks   b the Egyptians   c the Persians
4 When _____ the first Hollywood film _____? (make)
   a 1910   b 1920   c 1930
5 Who _____ champagne in 1697? (invent)
   a Monsieur Moët   b Señor Freixenet   **c Dom Perignon**
6 Who was the American president when the Berlin Wall _____ first _____ in 1961? (build)
   a Bill Clinton   b Richard Nixon   **c John F Kennedy**
7 When _____ the electric washing machine _____? (introduce)
   a 1908   b 1918   c 1928
8 Which first _____ in 2006? (appear)
   a tablets   **b blu-ray discs**   c smartphones

b Ask your partner the questions.

9A COMMUNICATIVE Find the pair

'Do you like your present?' she asked.	She asked me if I liked my present.
'Don't start!' the teacher told them.	The teacher told them not to start.
'Please help me!' the old woman said.	The old woman asked me to help her.
'What time are we meeting?' I asked her.	I asked her what time we were meeting.
'We're leaving tomorrow,' they said.	They said they were leaving the next day.
'I won't tell anybody,' he told me.	He told me he wouldn't tell anybody.
'I can't remember your name,' she said.	She said she couldn't remember my name.
'I bought my trousers in the sales,' she told me.	She told me she'd bought her trousers in the sales.
'Who invited you to the party?' Mike asked.	Mike asked who had invited me to the party.
'What were you doing in New York?' she asked.	She asked me what I'd been doing in New York.
'I haven't spoken to Susan since Christmas,' Mary said.	Mary said she hadn't spoken to Susan since Christmas.
'You must turn off the alarm first!' he told me.	He told me I had to turn the alarm off first.

9B COMMUNICATIVE   What had happened?

Story 1
1. Jamie would never have married Nicola if he had… _____
2. _____
3. _____
4. _____

Story 2
1. I would never have found out about Richard's new job if I hadn't… _____
2. _____
3. _____
4. _____

Story 3
1. Harriet wouldn't have met Ben if she hadn't… _____
2. _____
3. _____
4. _____

Story 4
1. The moment I bought the painting I knew I had… _____
2. _____
3. _____
4. _____

Story 5
1. I didn't recognize Jonathan when I saw him because he had… _____
2. _____
3. _____
4. _____

Story 6
1. When I picked up the phone, a voice told me that I had… _____
2. _____
3. _____
4. _____

Story 7
1. When Sheila opened the door, she saw that someone had… _____
2. _____
3. _____
4. _____

Story 8
1. Jenny was absolutely furious with her sister because she had… _____
2. _____
3. _____
4. _____

10A COMMUNICATIVE What's the question?

What / your favourite name? What / you like about it?	What colour / you almost never wear, or use in your house? Why / you think you dislike it?	Where / you going on your next holiday? Why / you chosen that place?	What / you bought online recently? Why / you buy it?
What / you like ten years ago? How / you changed since then?	What / your favourite photo of yourself? What / you like about it?	What / some things that people could / to help reduce waste? How / you think they would help?	What would your ideal job / ? Why?
/ you prefer watching films at home or at the cinema? Why?	/ you ever thought of living in the countryside? Why (not)?	/ you like eating out? What / the best restaurant you / ever / to?	What things in your house / you mended? / you think you / good at DIY? Why (not)?
What would you / if you / one million pounds? Would you leave your job or stop your studies? Why (not)?	/ you go out or stay in last New Year's Eve? What / you /?	When / you last / your hair cut? / you like it? Why (not)?	How many different historical sites in your local area / you / to? Which / your favourite? Why?
/ you usually forget to take things with you when you leave home (keys, phone)? What / you / to help you remember?	What / the best wedding you / ever / to? What / special about it?	What / you think / the best thing about the USA? And the worst?	/ you ever taken any official English exams? / it a good experience? Why (not)?

10B COMMUNICATIVE Speaking exam

Student A

1

a Ask **B** your questions.
1. What's your full name?
2. How do you spell your surname?
3. Where do you live?
4. Can you tell me what you enjoy doing in your free time?
5. Why are you learning English?

b Answer **B**'s questions. Give as much information as you can.

2

a Describe your photo to **B**.

b Listen to **B** describing his / her photo. What do the two photos have in common? How are they different?

3 Now talk to each other about:
- the kind of places you like visiting when you're on holiday.
- places you wouldn't go to on holiday.
- your favourite holiday.
- one of your favourite cities.

Student B

1

a Answer **A**'s questions. Give as much information as you can.

b Ask **A** your questions.
1. What's your full name?
2. How do you spell your surname?
3. What do you do?
4. Can you tell me about a typical day in your life?
5. How do you think you'll use English in the future?

2

a Listen to **A** describing his / her photo.

b Describe your photo to **A**. What do the two photos have in common? How are they different?

3 Now talk to each other about:
- the kind of places you like visiting when you're on holiday.
- places you wouldn't go to on holiday.
- your favourite holiday.
- one of your favourite cities.

Vocabulary activity instructions

1B Adjective suffixes

A pairwork activity

Sts read definitions and write the adjectives. Then they complete sentences with the correct adjective form. Copy one worksheet per student.

> **LANGUAGE**
> Adjectives describing people, places, and things, suffixes -*ful* and -*less*

- Put Sts in pairs and give out the worksheets.
- Tell Sts that they have to read the definitions in **a** and write the correct adjectives, using the words in the list with a suffix. After that, they have to complete the sentences in **b** with the correct adjective form of the words in **bold**. Remind Sts to write their answers in the column on the right.
- Check answers.

> **a** 2 creative 3 reliable 4 assertive 5 envious
>   6 affectionate 7 helpful 8 powerful 9 impulsive
>   10 glamorous 11 sociable 12 rebellious
> **b** 2 restful 3 noisy 4 profitable 5 careless 6 risky
>   7 spacious 8 hopeful 9 impressive 10 suitable
>   11 useful 12 stressful

- Now focus on **Activation**. Get Sts to cover the columns on the right and read the definitions in **a** and say the adjectives. Then have Sts read the sentences in **b** with the missing words. They can test each other or themselves.

2A Packing

A card game

Sts define words for other Sts to guess. Copy and cut up one set of cards per pair or small group.

> **LANGUAGE**
> Things to take on holiday, documents, and packing verbs

- Put Sts in pairs or small groups. Give each pair / group a set of cards face down or in an envelope.
- Demonstrate the activity. Choose another word (not one of the ones on the cards) from **Vocabulary Bank** Packing p.153. Describe it, e.g. *It's a noun. It's a liquid or cream which you put on your body when it's very hot*, until a student guesses the word (*sunscreen*). Highlight that Sts are not allowed to use the word(s) on the card in their definition.
- Sts play the game, taking turns to pick up a card and describe the word. Sts describing mustn't let their partners see what's on the card. Tell Sts to wait until their partner has finished his / her description before trying to guess the word.

EXTRA IDEA If Sts are playing in groups, they could play this as a competitive game. Sts who correctly guess the word first keep the card. The student with the most cards at the end of the game wins.

NON-CUT ALTERNATIVE Copy one sheet per pair and fold it down the middle. Put Sts in pairs. Sts look at one half each, and take turns to describe the words on their half of the sheet to their partners until they guess the correct answer.

2B Shops and services

A pairwork vocabulary race

Sts read a series of clues and write the words. Copy one worksheet per pair.

> **LANGUAGE**
> Places, phrasal verbs related to shops and shopping

- Put Sts in pairs and give out the worksheets. Set a time limit. Tell Sts that they have to write as many words as they can within the time limit. Each word begins with a different letter of the alphabet. Letters K, X, and Y don't have clues and can be ignored.
- Check answers. The first pair to complete all the words correctly wins, or the pair with the most correct answers at the end of the time limit wins.

EXTRA SUPPORT Give Sts a few minutes to revise the vocabulary in **Vocabulary Bank** Shops and services p.154 before they start.

> **b**utcher's **c**hain **d**ry-cleaner's **e**state agent's **f**lorist's
> **g**reengrocer's **h**airdresser's **i**n stock **j**eweller's
> **l**aunderette **m**arket stall **n**ewsagent's **o**n **p**ound shop
> **q**ueue **r**ound **s**tationer's **t**ravel agent's **u**pstairs
> **v**itamins **w**ood **Z**ara

EXTRA CHALLENGE Ask Sts to turn over or cover their worksheets. Sts go through the alphabet in pairs and try to remember the words they wrote (remind them of the letters K, X, and Y which don't have words). If they can, they should think of some more examples for some of the letters.

3B Photography

A pairwork photo description

Sts describe photos to each other and ask questions. Copy one worksheet per pair and cut into **A** and **B**.

> **LANGUAGE**
> Describing a photo, taking photos

- Put Sts in pairs, **A** and **B**, ideally face to face, and give out the worksheets.
- Focus on **a** and get Sts **A** to describe their photo to Sts **B**. You could set a time limit if you wish.
- Focus on **b**. Sts swap roles and Sts **B** describe their photo to Sts **A**. Again, set a time limit if you wish.
- Focus on **c**. Give Sts time to discuss the questions. Remind them to ask for more information if possible.

EXTRA IDEA Monitor for any errors during the activity. At the end of the lesson do a whole-class error correction activity.

4A Rubbish and recycling
A pairwork vocabulary race
Sts identify the missing words and complete sentences. Copy one worksheet per pair.

LANGUAGE
Rubbish nouns and phrasal verbs, packaging, the prefix *re-*

- Put Sts in pairs and give out the worksheets. Set a time limit. Tell Sts that they have to complete as many words as they can within the time limit.
- Check answers. The first pair to complete all the sentences correctly wins, or the pair with the most correct answers at the end of the time limit wins.

2 lid   3 can   4 packet   5 plastic bags   6 carton
7 tin   8 sell-by date   9 bin bag   10 refuse collectors
11 waste-paper basket   12 tub   13 wrapper
14 give away   15 pot   16 take out   17 throw away
18 Recycle   19 rethink   20 reuse

4B Study and work
An information gap activity
Sts define words to help their partner complete a crossword. Copy one worksheet per pair and cut into **A** and **B**.

LANGUAGE
Higher education, applying for a job or course

- Put Sts in pairs, **A** and **B**, ideally face to face, and give out the crosswords. Make sure that Sts can't see each other's worksheet. Explain that **A** and **B** have the same crossword but with different words missing. They have to define words to each other to complete their crosswords.
- Give Sts a minute to read their instructions. If Sts don't know what a word means, they can look it up in **Vocabulary Bank** Study and work p.157. Remind them that they can't use any part of the word in their definition.
- Sts take turns to ask each other for the definitions of their missing words (e.g. *What's 3 across?*). Their partner must define / describe the word until the other student is able to write it in his / her crossword. Sts should help each other using clues if necessary.
- When Sts have finished, they should compare their crosswords to make sure they have the same words and have spelled them correctly.

5A Television
A pairwork vocabulary race
Sts read a series of clues and write the words. Copy one worksheet per pair.

LANGUAGE
Types of programme, TV phrasal verbs

- Put Sts in pairs and give out the worksheets. Set a time limit. Tell Sts that they have to write as many words in **a** and **b** as they can in the time limit.
- Check answers. The first pair to write all the words correctly wins, or the pair with the most correct answers at the end of the time limit wins.

a 2 advert   3 chat show   4 cookery programme
   5 documentary   6 current affairs programme
   7 quiz show   8 reality show   9 weather forecast
   10 soap   11 live sport   12 period drama
b 2 season   3 streaming services   4 series   5 turn over
   6 turn down   7 Turn up   8 Turn off   9 Turn on
   10 is on

5B The country
A pairwork labelling activity
Sts look at a picture and write the words for the items in it. Copy one worksheet per pair.

LANGUAGE
Nature, on a farm

- Put Sts in pairs and give out the worksheets. Focus on **a**. Set a time limit. Tell Sts that they have to write as many words as they can in the time limit. The first pair to write all the words correctly wins, or the pair with the most correct answers at the end of the time limit wins.

2 tractor   3 hens   4 sheep   5 leaves   6 stream   7 bush
8 farmhouse   9 donkey   10 field   11 hedge   12 path
13 rocks   14 cow   15 hill

- Focus on **b**. Tell Sts to write the words from **a** in the correct category in the mind map.
- Check answers.

Buildings: barn, farmhouse
Animals: hens, sheep, cow, donkey
Equipment: tractor
Nature: leaves, stream, bush, field, hedge, path, rocks, hill

EXTRA IDEA Give Sts time to add other words to the different categories to complete the mind map. Remind Sts that they can refer to **Vocabulary Bank** The country p.159 for ideas.

6A At a restaurant
An error correction activity

Sts correct vocabulary mistakes. Copy one worksheet per pair.

> **LANGUAGE**
> Things on the table, things people do in restaurants

- Put Sts in pairs. Give out the worksheets, and focus on the instructions. Focus on sentence 1 and elicit that it is correct. Then focus on sentence 2 and elicit that it is wrong, as the **bold** word should be *spoon*.
- Sts continue in pairs.
- Check answers.

EXTRA SUPPORT Give Sts a few minutes to revise the restaurant vocabulary in **Vocabulary Bank** At a restaurant p.160 before they start.

> 3 courses 4 ✓ 5 knife 6 ✓ 7 ✓ 8 ✓ 9 glass
> 10 meal 11 clear 12 ✓ 13 cups / mugs 14 ✓
> 15 ✓ 16 send it back 17 ✓ 18 leave a tip 19 ✓
> 20 ask for the bill 21 ✓ 22 lay the table

6B DIY and repairs
A card game

Sts define words / phrases for other Sts to guess. Copy and cut up one set of cards per pair or small group.

> **LANGUAGE**
> Things in a shed, things in a drawer, verb phrases

- Put Sts in pairs or small groups. Give each pair / group a set of cards face down or in an envelope.
- Demonstrate the activity. Choose another word (not one of the ones on the cards) from **Vocabulary Bank** DIY and repairs p.161. Describe it, e.g. *It's a noun. It's the thing you use to stick together something that's broken*, until a student guesses the word (*glue*). Highlight that Sts are not allowed to use the word(s) on the card in their definition.
- Sts play the game, taking turns to pick up a card and describe the word / phrase. Sts describing mustn't let their partners see what's on the card. Tell Sts to wait until their partner has finished his / her description before trying to guess the word / phrase.

EXTRA IDEA If Sts are playing in groups, they could play this as a competitive game. Sts who correctly guess the word first keep the card. The student with the most cards at the end of the game wins.

NON-CUT ALTERNATIVE Copy one worksheet per pair and fold it down the middle. Put Sts in pairs. Sts look at one half each, and take turns to describe the words / phrases on their half of the sheet to their partners until they guess the correct answer.

7A Phrasal verbs
A gapfill revision race

Sts read the sentences and complete the phrasal verbs. Copy one worksheet per student.

> **LANGUAGE**
> Revision of phrasal verbs, phrasal verbs to do with money, phrasal verbs with *away*, *back*, and *take*

- Give out the worksheets. Tell Sts that they have to read the sentences and write as many of the particles (prepositions or adverbs) as they can in five minutes. Remind Sts to write their answers in the column on the right.
- Check answers. The first student to write all the particles correctly wins, or the student with the most correct answers at the end of the time limit wins.

> 2 over 3 on 4 out 5 away 6 apart 7 back
> 8 round / in 9 away 10 on 11 back 12 after
> 13 away 14 on 15 away 16 out 17 away 18 back
> 19 back 20 back

- Focus on **Activation**. Get Sts to cover the column on the right and read the sentences with the missing words. They can test each other or themselves.

8A Looking after yourself
A team game

Sts explain the difference between two words / phrases. Copy and cut up one set of cards.

> **LANGUAGE**
> At the hairdresser's / barber's, keeping fit, beauty treatments

- Put Sts in two teams (or more if you have a lot of Sts) and explain the activity.
- Give a card to each team and give Sts a minute to decide what the difference is between the two words / phrases.
- Write the two words / phrases on each team's card on the board.
- A spokesperson from the team takes turns to explain the difference to the rest of the class. If the explanation is correct, the team gets a point. If it isn't correct, the other team can try to win an extra point by explaining the difference correctly, before having their own turn.
- Then give each team another card.
- Write up the teams' points on the board. The team with the most points wins.

NON-CUT ALTERNATIVE Put Sts in pairs. Copy one sheet per pair. Set a time limit, e.g. ten minutes, and Sts take turns to ask each other *What's the difference between…?*, choosing words at random. Sts decide if their partner's explanation is correct. Finally, check answers with the whole class.

Possible answers

A facial is a beauty treatment for the face.

A massage is a treatment for the body involving rubbing and pressing muscles and joints.

Yoga is an activity which involves doing physical and breathing exercises, and simple meditation.

Pilates is a type of exercise which develops the abdomen muscles in order to control your body movement.

Lift weights is to exercise by lifting heavy objects.

Do cardio exercises is to do exercises which raise your heart rate.

Stretch your muscles is doing exercises which deliberately flex or stretch specific muscles in your body, releasing pain and tension.

Tone your muscles is doing exercises which aim to change the shape and definition of your muscles.

A manicure is a beauty treatment for your hands and nails.

A pedicure is a beauty treatment for your feet and toenails.

A fringe is short hair that hangs down over your forehead.

A parting is the line of head showing when sections of hair are brushed or combed in opposite directions.

Have your hair dyed is to have the colour of your hair changed.

Have highlights is to have parts of your hair made lighter than the rest.

Have a shave is to cut the hair off the face.

Have a buzz cut is to have a very short haircut where the hair is shaved close to the head.

A cross-trainer is an exercise machine with parts that you stand on and parts that you hold. You can then move your arms and legs backwards and forwards.

A rowing machine is an exercise machine with a moving handle and a sliding seat. You pull the handle towards you, as if you are rowing a boat.

A running machine is an exercise machine with a flat moving surface that you walk or run on.

An exercise bike is a bicycle that stays in one place and is used for exercise.

Do sit-ups is to do a physical exercise where you sit up from lying down without using your arms or lifting your feet.

Do press-ups is to do a physical exercise where you lie down facing the floor and lift your body up on your hands whilst keeping your back straight.

Do aerobics is to do very active physical exercises while listening to music.

Do spinning is to do aerobic exercises on an exercise bike while listening to music.

A ponytail is a hairstyle where hair is tied at the back of the head and hangs down.

Plaits are a hairstyle where each plait is formed by twisting three separate lengths of hair over each other.

Have your hair curled is to have your hair styled in curls, usually using curling tongs.

Have your hair straightened is to have your hair styled straight, usually using a hairdryer and/or straightening irons.

Have a treatment is to have hair and beauty products used on your hair, skin, etc. to improve quality and look.

Have a trim is to have your hair cut so that it looks tidy.

Have a blow dry is to have your wet hair dried by the warm air from a hairdryer.

Have your hair put up is to have your hair styled and pinned up off your neck, shoulders, and back.

1B VOCABULARY Adjective suffixes

Definitions

a Read the definitions. Choose the correct word from the list and make an adjective using a suffix. Write your answers in the column on the right.

affection   assert   create   envy   glamour   help   impulse   power   rebel   rely   ~~sense~~   social

1 He's easily hurt, especially if you criticize him. — *sensitive*
2 She has an amazing imagination and she's very original. _____
3 He can be trusted to do something well. _____
4 She can express her opinions clearly and confidently. _____
5 He always wants what other people have. _____
6 He shows caring feelings towards everyone he knows. _____
7 She likes to offer solutions if you have a problem. _____
8 She has lots of control and influence over people and events. _____
9 He does things suddenly, without thinking about what might happen. _____
10 She's beautiful, exciting, and different from ordinary people. _____
11 He really enjoys going out with his friends and meeting new people. _____
12 She doesn't like rules, or doing what other people tell her to do. _____

b Complete the sentences with the correct form of the words in **bold**. Write your answers in the column on the right.

1 My living room was white, but now it's really ▆▆. **colour** — *colourful*
2 My idea of a ▆▆ holiday is to stay at a nice hotel and do absolutely nothing. **rest** _____
3 Marie's class is very ▆▆. I can hear them from the next floor! **noise** _____
4 The café is a successful business and it's very ▆▆. **profit** _____
5 Ruth's very ▆▆ – she never checks what she's written. **care** _____
6 Travelling alone can be ▆▆, so I prefer doing it with other people. **risk** _____
7 The flat is really ▆▆ – the living room is enormous! **space** _____
8 The government is ▆▆ that unemployment will go down this year. **hope** _____
9 The architect's buildings are really ▆▆ – they've won lots of awards. **impress** _____
10 It's a violent film, so it isn't ▆▆ for children under 15. **suit** _____
11 This app is really ▆▆ for learning new vocabulary. **use** _____
12 I don't like crowded places, like shops during the sales. I find them really ▆▆! **stress** _____

ACTIVATION

Test your memory. Cover the columns on the right. Read the definitions in **a** and say the adjectives. Then read the sentences in **b** aloud with the correct form of the words in **bold**.

2A VOCABULARY Packing

 a driving licence	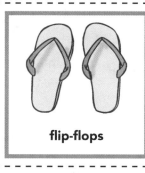 flip-flops	 a first-aid kit	 a hairdryer
 (to) pack	 a phone charger	 headphones	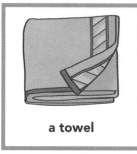 a towel
 a guidebook	 insect repellent	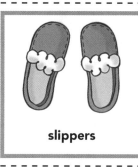 slippers	 swimming trunks
 (to) wrap	 a washbag	 a comb	 an adaptor
 a bathrobe	 a razor	 (to) fold	 nail scissors
 make-up	 a rain jacket	 a passport	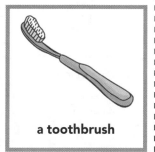 a toothbrush

2B VOCABULARY Shops and services

A Off-licences sell _alcohol_, but only to people over 18.

B Vegetarians don't usually buy anything in this shop! _____

C The Body Shop and H&M are examples of _____ stores.

D The place you take some types of clothes to be cleaned. _____-_____

E You can buy or rent a house here. _____ _____

F This shop is very popular on Valentine's Day! _____

G It's the name of the shop where they sell fruit and vegetables. _____

H You go here to get your hair cut. _____

I If a shop is out of something, it means they don't have it _____ _____.

J People might get their wedding rings here. _____

L You can wash and dry your own clothes in this place. _____

M A table or a small shop with an open front. It often sells fruit and vegetables. _____

N Newspapers, magazines, and sweets are sold here. _____

O If you want to make sure that clothes fit, you should try them _____ before buying them.

P This shop sells a variety of goods, all at one cheap price! _____ _____

Q Sometimes you have to wait in one when you want to pay for something. _____

R We had a look _____ the shop, but we didn't buy anything.

S Students might buy pens and exercise books from this shop. _____

T An exciting city break, or a restful stay at a beach resort? Book your next holiday here! _____ _____

U We're on the first floor. Women's clothing is _____, on the second floor.

V You can buy multi-_____ from a health food store. Take one a day to keep you healthy.

W If you want to make a shelf, you can buy a tool to cut the _____ in a DIY store.

Z _____ is a very popular chain store that sells clothes.

3B VOCABULARY Photography

Student A

a) Describe your photo to **B**. Say what you can see in the foreground, in the background, and in the distance. Add any more details about where things are.

b) Listen to **B** describing his / her photo.

c) Now discuss the questions together.

1. What do you think are the advantages and disadvantages of being:
   a. a celebrity photographer?
   b. a wildlife photographer?
   c. a war photographer?
   d. a portrait photographer?

2. If you were a professional photographer, what kind of photos would you like to take? Why?

Student B

a) Listen to **A** describing his / her photo.

b) Describe your photo to **A**. Say what you can see in the foreground, in the background, and in the distance. Add any more details about where things are.

c) Now discuss the questions together.

1. What do you think are the advantages and disadvantages of being:
   a. a celebrity photographer?
   b. a wildlife photographer?
   c. a war photographer?
   d. a portrait photographer?

2. If you were a professional photographer, what kind of photos would you like to take? Why?

4A VOCABULARY Rubbish and recycling

What's the word?

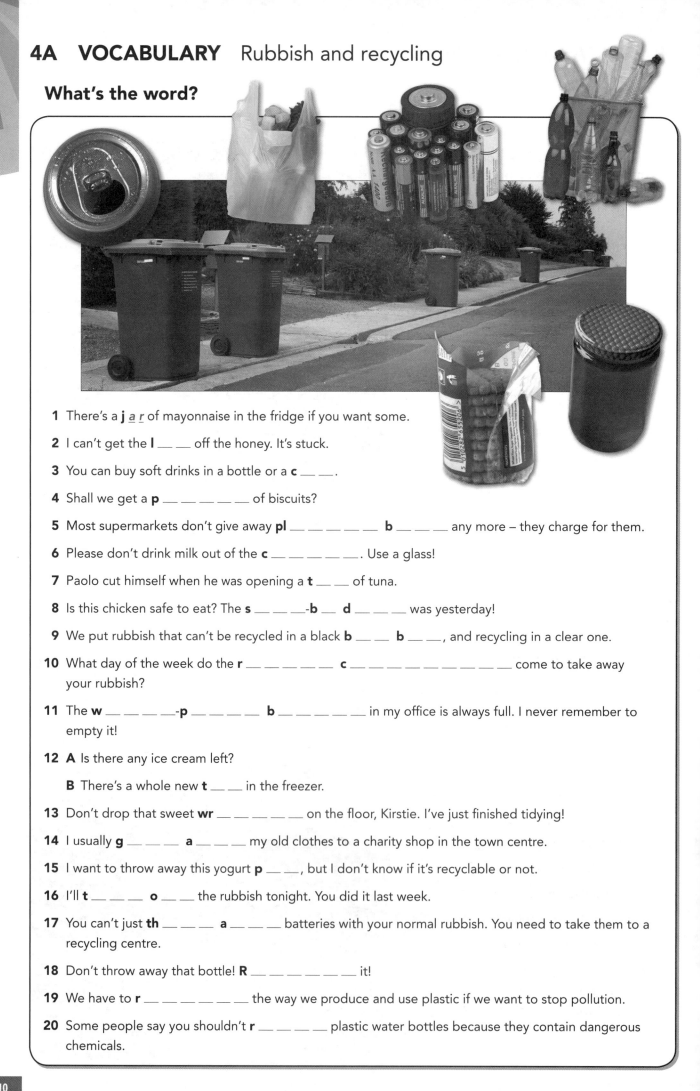

1 There's a **j a r** of mayonnaise in the fridge if you want some.
2 I can't get the **l _ _** off the honey. It's stuck.
3 You can buy soft drinks in a bottle or a **c _ _**.
4 Shall we get a **p _ _ _ _ _** of biscuits?
5 Most supermarkets don't give away **pl _ _ _ _ _ b _ _ _** any more – they charge for them.
6 Please don't drink milk out of the **c _ _ _ _ _**. Use a glass!
7 Paolo cut himself when he was opening a **t _ _** of tuna.
8 Is this chicken safe to eat? The **s _ _ _-b _ d _ _ _** was yesterday!
9 We put rubbish that can't be recycled in a black **b _ _ b _ _**, and recycling in a clear one.
10 What day of the week do the **r _ _ _ _ _ _ c _ _ _ _ _ _ _ _ _ _** come to take away your rubbish?
11 The **w _ _ _ _-p _ _ _ _ b _ _ _ _ _** in my office is always full. I never remember to empty it!
12 **A** Is there any ice cream left?
   B There's a whole new **t _ _** in the freezer.
13 Don't drop that sweet **wr _ _ _ _ _** on the floor, Kirstie. I've just finished tidying!
14 I usually **g _ _ _ a _ _ _ _** my old clothes to a charity shop in the town centre.
15 I want to throw away this yogurt **p _ _**, but I don't know if it's recyclable or not.
16 I'll **t _ _ _ o _ _** the rubbish tonight. You did it last week.
17 You can't just **th _ _ _ a _ _ _** batteries with your normal rubbish. You need to take them to a recycling centre.
18 Don't throw away that bottle! **R _ _ _ _ _** it!
19 We have to **r _ _ _ _ _** the way we produce and use plastic if we want to stop pollution.
20 Some people say you shouldn't **r _ _ _** plastic water bottles because they contain dangerous chemicals.

4B VOCABULARY Study and work

Student A

a. Look at your crossword and make sure you know the meaning of all the words you have.

b. Ask **B** to define one of your missing words for you. Ask, for example, *What's 8 down?* Listen to **B**'s definition and write the word in your grid.

c. Now **B** will ask you to define a word.

Student B

a. Look at your crossword and make sure you know the meaning of all the words you have.

b. Ask **A** to define one of your missing words for you. Ask, for example, *What's 8 across?* Listen to **A**'s definition and write the word in your grid.

c. Now **A** will ask you to define a word.

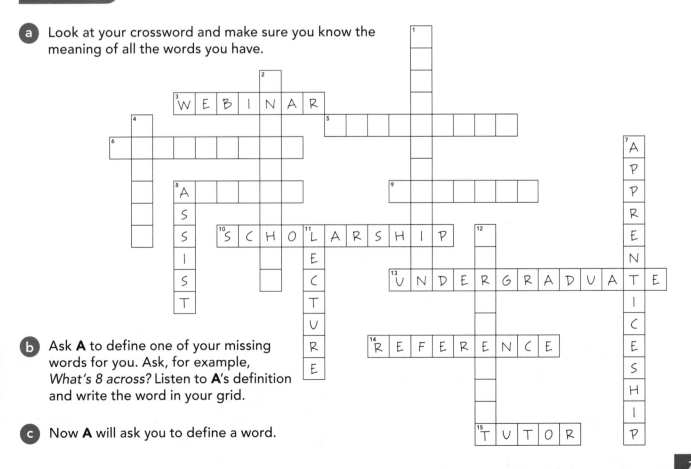

English File fourth edition Teacher's Guide Intermediate Plus   Photocopiable © Oxford University Press 2020

5A VOCABULARY Television

a Read the speech bubbles. Write the type of programme.

1. Hey Marge, what time does Bart get home tonight? — C A R T O O N
2. Buy two, get one free. — ☐☐☐☐☐☐
3. With me in the studio is Drake, who'll be talking about his new album. — ☐☐☐☐☐ ☐☐☐☐☐
4. For this recipe, you'll need 250 g flour, two eggs, and some sugar. — ☐☐☐☐☐☐☐☐☐ ☐☐☐☐☐☐☐☐☐☐
5. Elephants live in groups and are very sociable animals. — ☐☐☐☐☐☐☐☐☐☐☐☐
6. In tonight's show, we're investigating education in UK schools. — ☐☐☐☐☐☐☐ ☐☐☐☐☐☐☐☐
7. And now, for €500, what's the capital of Australia? — ☐☐☐☐☐ ☐☐☐☐
8. What a surprise! Kylie's nominated Barry to leave the house. — ☐☐☐☐☐☐☐☐ ☐☐☐☐
9. Tomorrow, it'll be sunny and dry. — ☐☐☐☐☐☐☐ ☐☐☐☐☐☐☐☐
10. But if Leo's not the father, who is? — ☐☐☐☐☐
11. And it's a penalty for Chelsea! — ☐☐☐☐ ☐☐☐☐☐
12. My Lady, the carriage is at the door and His Majesty awaits us at noon. — ☐☐☐☐☐☐ ☐☐☐☐☐

b Complete the second sentence so that it means the same as the first.

1. 'I can't wait to see what happens next week!' — 'I can't wait to see next week's **e**_episode_.'
2. 'I'm sad this series is finished for now, but there will be more.' — 'There will be another **s**_____.'
3. 'I don't watch TV anymore, I just use Netflix and Amazon Prime.' — 'I just use **s**_____ **s**_____.'
4. 'Which one is my favourite? Game of Thrones, I think.' — 'Game of Thrones is my favourite **s**_____.'
5. 'Oh, I hate this programme! Please change the channel!' — 'Please **t**_____ **o**_____.'
6. 'Please make the TV quieter!' — 'Please **t**_____ the TV **d**_____.'
7. 'I can't hear the TV. Make it louder, please!' — '**T**_____ the TV **u**_____, please.'
8. 'Don't leave the TV on when you go to bed.' — '**T**_____ the TV **o**_____ when you go to bed.'
9. 'Why is the TV off? It's time for the news.' — '**T**_____ the TV **o**_____. It's time for the news.'
10. 'Channel 4 is showing my favourite film right now!' — 'My favourite film **i**_____ **o**_____ Channel 4 right now.'

5B VOCABULARY The country

a Write the words.

1 _barn_	4 _____	7 _____	10 _____	13 _____
2 _____	5 _____	8 _____	11 _____	14 _____
3 _____	6 _____	9 _____	12 _____	15 _____

b Now put the words from **a** in the correct category in the mind map.

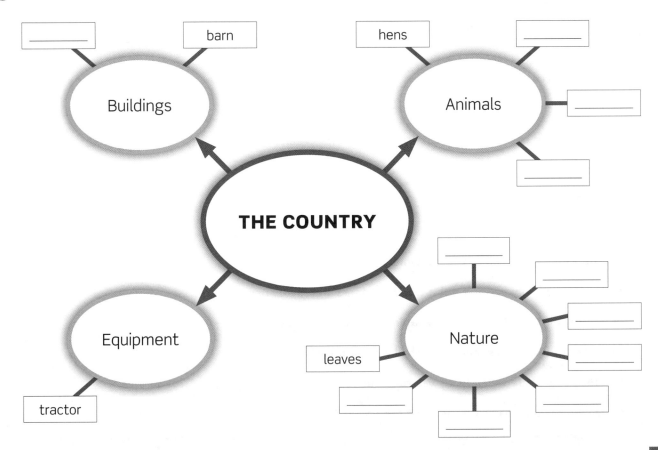

English File fourth edition Teacher's Guide Intermediate Plus   Photocopiable © Oxford University Press 2020

6A VOCABULARY At a restaurant

Right or wrong?

Look at the word / phrase in **bold**. Right (✓) or wrong (✗)?
If you think it's wrong, write the correct word / phrase in the column on the right.

1 We use paper **napkins** at home. It saves on the washing!	✓	
2 You usually eat soup with a **teaspoon**.	✗	_spoon_
3 We had three **plates** every night on holiday – a starter, a main course, and a dessert.		
4 Screw-top wine bottles aren't opened with a **corkscrew**.		
5 This **fork** doesn't cut very well. Could you change it, please?		
6 That new waitress is really nervous. There's more coffee in the **saucer** than in the cup.		
7 Would you like me to bring you some **oil and vinegar** for your salad?		
8 Most people make tea in a mug, but my grandmother always uses a **teapot**.		
9 Would you like a **cup** of champagne before dinner?		
10 What's your favourite **dish**: breakfast, lunch, or dinner?		
11 Excuse me, could you **clean** the table? These glasses are from the previous customers.		
12 Can you get one more soup **bowl** from the cupboard, please?		
13 My husband has cereal and two **jugs** of coffee for breakfast.		
14 Would you like a **tray** to carry those drinks?		
15 I don't like it when people serve hot food on cold **plates**.		
16 This fish isn't cooked. Call the waiter, I'm going to **take it back**.		
17 The waiter asked me to **try the wine**.		
18 In New York, if you don't **put a tip**, the waiters aren't very happy.		
19 For my birthday, I've **booked a table** at my favourite restaurant.		
20 Look at the time! It's really late. Shall we **ask the bill**?		
21 I'm starving. Are we all ready to **order our food**?		
22 Dinner's nearly ready. Can you **put the table**?		

6B VOCABULARY DIY and repairs

7A VOCABULARY Phrasal verbs

What's the particle?

● Read the sentences. Write the missing particle(s) in the column on the right.

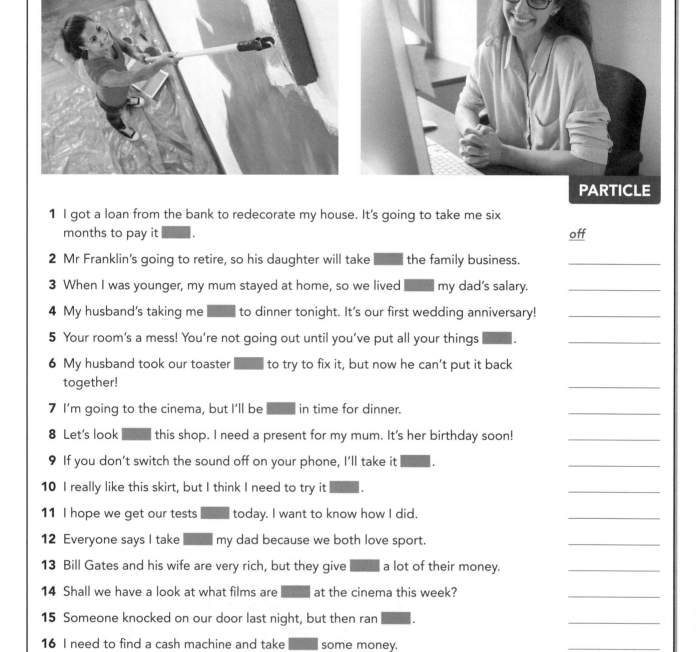

PARTICLE

1 I got a loan from the bank to redecorate my house. It's going to take me six months to pay it ▓▓▓. _off_

2 Mr Franklin's going to retire, so his daughter will take ▓▓▓ the family business. _____

3 When I was younger, my mum stayed at home, so we lived ▓▓▓ my dad's salary. _____

4 My husband's taking me ▓▓▓ to dinner tonight. It's our first wedding anniversary! _____

5 Your room's a mess! You're not going out until you've put all your things ▓▓▓. _____

6 My husband took our toaster ▓▓▓ to try to fix it, but now he can't put it back together! _____

7 I'm going to the cinema, but I'll be ▓▓▓ in time for dinner. _____

8 Let's look ▓▓▓ this shop. I need a present for my mum. It's her birthday soon! _____

9 If you don't switch the sound off on your phone, I'll take it ▓▓▓. _____

10 I really like this skirt, but I think I need to try it ▓▓▓. _____

11 I hope we get our tests ▓▓▓ today. I want to know how I did. _____

12 Everyone says I take ▓▓▓ my dad because we both love sport. _____

13 Bill Gates and his wife are very rich, but they give ▓▓▓ a lot of their money. _____

14 Shall we have a look at what films are ▓▓▓ at the cinema this week? _____

15 Someone knocked on our door last night, but then ran ▓▓▓. _____

16 I need to find a cash machine and take ▓▓▓ some money. _____

17 We're going to be ▓▓▓ for a week. We're going to Paris! _____

18 When do you think you'll be able to pay ▓▓▓ the money I lent you? _____

19 Give me ▓▓▓ my shoes right now! Don't borrow my things without asking me first. _____

20 I have a missed call from Monica. I'd better call her ▓▓▓. _____

ACTIVATION

Test your memory. Cover the column on the right. Read the sentences aloud with the correct particles.

8A VOCABULARY Looking after yourself

a facial a massage	a cross-trainer a rowing machine
yoga Pilates	a running machine an exercise bike
lift weights do cardio exercises	do sit-ups do press-ups
stretch your muscles tone your muscles	do aerobics do spinning
a manicure a pedicure	a ponytail plaits
a fringe a parting	have your hair curled have your hair straightened
have your hair dyed have highlights	have a treatment have a trim
have a shave have a buzz cut	have a blow dry have your hair put up